MILLROSE
A CENTURY OF FAMILY, FARM AND FOOD

MILLROSE
A CENTURY OF FAMILY, FARM AND FOOD

Jim Weishaar

Copyright © 2020 Jim Weishaar

All rights reserved.

ISBN-13:

DEDICATION

To Mother, who encouraged me to work my way through the garden and the kitchen.

To Aunt Mill who was not only an aunt, but also a second mother, excellent cook and saint. She taught me so much about gardening, cooking, baking and preserving, and most importantly how delicious food should be.

To a dear, long-time friend and former co-worker, Rose, who shared with me a number of recipes and always seemed to enjoy what I prepared for "Food Day" at the office.

TABLE OF CONTENTS

TABLE OF CONTENTS vii
FORWARD 1
ACKNOWLEDGMENTS 3
1 THE BASICS 5
    In the Pantry 7
    Recipe Preparation 15
    Food Preservation 19
    Homemade Dairy Products 23
    Formulas and Foundations 27
    Everyday Recipes 37
    Dips and Dressings, Sauces, Seasonings and Spreads, and Drinks 45
2 PLAN OVERS 59
3 SPRING 65
    Lenten Meals 67
    Breakfast 73
    Easter Dinner 79
    Spring Fruits and Vegetables 83
4 SUMMER 97
    Summer Fruits and Vegetables 99
    Salads 147
    Canning and Preserving 157
    Ice Creams and Sherbets 175
5 FALL 179
    Fruitcakes 181
    Thanksgiving Dinner 187
    Fall Fruits and Vegetables 193

6 WINTER 205

    Christmas Dinner 207

    Yeast Breads and Rolls 211

    Quick Breads 223

    Muffins 233

    Cookies 241

    Candies 257

    Butchering 261

    Desserts 271

    Cakes, Cupcakes, Coffee Cakes 275

    Pies 299

    Main and Side Dishes 307

    Meat, Fish, Poultry and Game 313

7 AN ODE TO MEXICO 335

8 THE SLOW COOKER 347

9 FOR THE BOYS 351

AFTERWORD 355

INDEX 357

FORWARD

I began writing this book in 2007. It was a year after Aunt Mill died. I asked for one thing from her estate: a little red book of handwritten recipes and her recipe box. My memories of her baking, cooking and gardening are among my most cherished. I was richly rewarded because I received her entire collection of recipes. Going through them brought back so many happy memories, many of which became family traditions. I reference some of those throughout this book. I encourage you to make your own memories and to establish your own traditions.

The title of this book, MillRose, is named after Aunt Mill and Rose, and is the same name of a service accommodation business I operated for several years in the 1990s. My initial goal to publish was 2015, the 100th anniversary of the family farm. However, life happens. I then targeted 2020, which is the anniversary of Aunt Mill's 100th birthday.

MillRose, A Century of Family, Farm and Food, is organized by season. Farm life revolved around the seasons. There were always certain activities and happenings specific to each season. Patterns, preferences and traditions evolved from those activities and happenings. It is my account of those who worked hard, loved the land and were rewarded by the fruits of their labors at a time and in a place I cherish. They were, as Aunt Mill often said, "Heavenly days."

This book is a culmination of more than 40 years of learning, experiencing, experimenting and doing. I encourage you to do the same. You'll find several master or base recipes, "Variations on a Theme," and "Master Mixing Methods," as well as tips, anecdotes, and other hopefully useful information in this book. So, why a cookbook of "old recipes and old memories?" Because I find homemade food means more to both those who make it and those who eat it. My parents, aunts, uncles, cousins and co-workers taught me through their examples, attitudes, behaviors, faith and work ethic that all you can take out of life is what you give away.

ACKNOWLEDGMENTS

I could never have written this book if I didn't work my way through the family garden and kitchen. Nor could I have experienced the sheer joy and pleasure of simple, good food without my family, friends and co-workers. And finally, I could never have honed my culinary skills and expanded my repertoire without the support and encouragement of my good friend, Juan, whose rating of something he really enjoyed should not be printed in a family book.

1 THE BASICS

This chapter includes basic information to cook your way through this book:
In the Pantry – notes about ingredients used in the recipes in this book.
Recipe Preparation – information to assist preparing the recipes in this book.
Food Preservation – tips to preserve food and ingredients for future use.
Homemade Dairy Products – a collection of recipes for frequently used dairy products you can make yourself.
Formulas and Foundations – recipes and techniques to prepare certain ingredients to improve your cooking and baking which you can use every day.
Everyday Recipes – these recipes are the ones I use most frequently, so much so I have memorized them. These are good foundation recipes which can be used in many different ways and modified to reflect your individual tastes and preferences.

In the Pantry

A properly stocked pantry, including the refrigerator and the freezer, will ensure you are always equipped to prepare something delicious and nutritious at a moment's notice. The following is a list of common ingredients and types, unless otherwise indicated in specific recipes, for each used in this book.

Milk is whole.
Eggs are large and should always be at room temperature before using.
Fat, if generally listed, refers to lard, butter, oil or shortening (in order of preference).
Butter is unsalted.
Olive oil is light; vegetable, corn or peanut oil is preferred for deep-fat frying.
Salt is regular table salt; but I prefer to use natural sea salt when cooking savory dishes and to salt cooking water for vegetables, meats and pasta.
Pepper is black, freshly ground from whole peppercorns; however, ground pepper from the can is perfectly acceptable.
Flour is unbleached, all-purpose, unless otherwise called for in individual recipes. You may use other flours, but the results will be different.
Sugar is regular white, granulated.
Brown sugar is light.
Cocoa is regular-strength, unsweetened.
Cream cheese, Sour Cream and cottage cheese are full fat.
Molasses is dark, unsulphured.
Honey is light, raw.
Mustard is prepared, yellow.
Rice is white, long-grain.
Herbs are fresh whenever possible; consult dried herb packaging for substitutions.
Yeast is active dry.
Vanilla is pure extract.

Brands – the following brands have provided consistent, reliable results for me over the years.

Campbell's condensed soups
Cool Whip frozen non-dairy whipped topping
Fleischman's active dry yeast
Grandma's unsulphured molasses
Hershey's cocoas
Jell-O gelatin
Jif Peanut Butter

Lyle's Golden Syrup (cane syrup)
Medaglia d'Oro instant espresso coffee powder
McCormick's and Spice Islands dried herbs, spices and seeds
Molina vanilla
Philadelphia cream cheese
Pillsbury and King Arthur flours
Ritz butter crackers

The Herbs
I debated heavily where to include this information and finally ended on In the Pantry because well-endowed is the cook who has a treasury of herbs, fresh and dried, to add flavor and variety to dishes sweet and savory.
Herbs are easy to grow from seeds or started plants. Perennial herbs, except for mint which does best in fertile soil, prefer poor soil. Herbs can also be grown indoors provided you have an adequate light source and turn the plants one-quarter way around each week for even growth.

Basil – several types of basil, including scented basils such as cinnamon and lemon, are commonly available. I always grow Lettuce Leaf, Neapolitan and Genovese. Lettuce Leaf basil generates very large leaves which can be used for miniature wraps. Basil is a favorite flavoring for tomato sauces and the key ingredient for pesto. It is reputed to repel mosquitos and flies.

Pesto
I like my pesto very simply prepared. You can go wild with different herbs, spices, nuts and oils. This is a basic recipe from which to launch all sorts of different sauces.
Combine in a food processor:
> **2 c fresh basil leaves, washed and firmly packed into the cup**
> **3 garlic cloves, peeled**
> **4 T pine nuts or toasted English walnuts**
> **½ c olive oil**
> **½ t salt**

Process until mixture is pasty. Add:
> **½ c grated Parmesan cheese**

Process until well blended. Add additional oil, 1 t at a time, if too stiff.
Taste and adjust salt, if needed.
Variation on a Theme: use young carrot leaves in place of the basil and replace the pine nuts with pistachios, if desired.

Bay – best grown potted in cold climates. Leaves repel leas, lice, moths and the bugs found in flour or cereal. Use to flavor fish or meat stocks, soups and sauces.

Caraway – all parts of the caraway plant are edible. The seeds can be used in cakes, cookies, breads, cheese, cabbage, sauerkraut and potatoes. The leaves can be cooked as spinach or beet greens. The white mature root resembles a carrot, is highly nutritious and may be eaten raw, boiled or baked.

Caraway Cheese Bread

Preheat oven to 350 degrees. Have ready two greased and floured 9x5x3-inch loaf pans.
Combine in large bowl of electric mixer:
- 4 c flour
- ½ c sugar
- 2 T baking powder
- 2 t salt

Combine in another bowl:
- 2 eggs
- 2 c milk
- ½ c oil (preferably olive oil)

Add liquid mixture to dry. Beat at low speed until moistened, then at medium speed 30 seconds. Scrape sides and bottom of bowl to combine batter.
Stir in:
- 2 c grated Cheddar cheese
- 2/3 c cooked, crumbled bacon
- 2 t caraway seeds

Divide batter into prepared pans.
Bake 45-50 minutes. Cool in pans 10 minutes before removing to wire rack to cool. Wrap in plastic wrap and then aluminum foil. Let sit several hours or overnight before slicing and serving.

Chervil – often referred to as "the gourmet cook's parsley." It has leaves which resemble parsley and can be used in place of parsley as both a garnish and ingredient.

Chives – these onion cousins grow in clumps and may be raised in the house with equal success. Chives complement cheese, soups, salads, egg dishes, dips, spreads and just about any food in which you would use onions.

Coriander – the seeds can be used in pickling, marinades and brines. The ground seeds are good in stir-fry and Mexican dishes.

Dill – both the leaves (referred to as dillweed) and seeds are a boon to cooking. Most often associated with pickles, dill can be used in breads, with most fish dishes, and in dips, spreads and salad dressings. It is prolific and will self-seed, if allowed. I planted dill once when I returned to Kansas and have had a steady supply ever since.

Epazote – this pungently flavored herb is usually used cooked; however, I like to use if fresh in avocado and salsa recipes. It is excellent in bean dishes, especially black bean and pinto, and in a wide variety of sauces, especially Mexican sauces.

Garlic – another onion cousin, garlic comes in two main forms: artichoke and hard-necked. The former is best used shortly after harvest; the latter stores well for many months. Garlic cloves should always be peeled before using (an exception is Roasted Garlic) and can be left whole, sliced, chopped, minced or smashed. A garlic press is an invaluable tool to have in your arsenal to finely mince garlic for salad dressings, etc.

Marjoram – pairs well with meats, salads, eggs, soups, sauces, vinegars, vegetables, teas and jellies. The flavor is pervasive, so use with discretion.

Mint – all mints are spreading. It is best, if you grow several different mints, to grow them separately. I grow mine in a large tub rather than in the ground because it can be invasive, and cross-pollination and inter-rooting will weaken the flavor. Mint is useful for flavoring drinks, candies, vegetables and lamb. Mint also comes in scented or flavored varieties including apple, orange and pineapple in addition to the more well-known peppermint and spearmint. Kentucky Colonel is my preferred variety.

Oregano – similar in taste and fragrance to marjoram, but stronger and less sweet. Greek and Hot Mexican oreganos are two good varieties for the home herb garden. It is especially good in beef dishes, and Mexican dishes and sauces.

Parsley – this common herb comes in two varieties: French or curly and flat-leafed Italian. Both are nutritious, but the flat-leafed variety seems to have more flavor. Its uses range from appetizers to main dishes and side dishes.

Rosemary – a shrubbery type herb best grown in pots where it will do well indoors. It is best to start you own plants in late-Winter or early-Spring each year because the plants will quickly become root-bound if kept longer than one growing season. Use in tomato sauces and in chicken, duck, goose, lamb, venison and other game dishes as well as breads and cookies.

Rosemary Cake
Add 1 T minced fresh rosemary to any Angel Food, Pound or White Cake batter. Add 1 T minced fresh rosemary to Whipped Cream served with the cake.

Sage – reported to delay the aging process and prevent wrinkles. I still remember Sister Verona, who taught seventh and eighth grades, having a quart jar of sage tea which she kept warm on the radiators in the school. Use to season pork dishes, sausage, poultry dishes and cheese.

Savory – both Summer and Winter savories are grown as a food seasoning. Some use the "peppery" tasting herb as a salt-substitute. Savory adds zest to all bean dishes and when used to flavor vinegar makes a fine marinade for beef.

Tarragon – the French variety is used in cooking. It has a flavor similar to licorice which pairs well with poultry. I use only fresh tarragon as it has a better flavor than dried (which is difficult to find if you don't grow and dry your own). Tarragon vinegar is great to have on hand to flavor salad dressings and marinades.

Tarragon Chicken Loaf
Best made in late Spring through Fall when the fresh herbs are readily available. Preheat oven to 350 degrees. Have ready a greased 8x4x2-inch loaf pan. Combine in large mixing bowl:
- 2 c soft breadcrumbs
- 1 T minced fresh parsley
- 1 T minced fresh tarragon
- ½ t salt
- ½ t pepper
- 2 c chopped, cooked chicken

Mix together in a separate bowl:
- ½ c Sour Cream
- 3 eggs
- 1 T lemon juice
- 4 T butter, melted and cooled
- 3 T grated onion

Stir into chicken mixture. Spoon into prepared pan.
Bake about 35 minutes or until knife inserted in the center comes out clean.

Thyme – the upright, woody-stemmed English, Broadleaf and French Narrowleaf varieties of thyme are preferred for culinary use. There are more than 400 varieties of thyme, but most are better suited to rock gardens or pathways where it will release its wonderful fragrance when trod upon. Thyme pairs well with mushrooms and lamb.

Storing Herbs
Store herbs in a glass of water in the refrigerator covered loosely with a plastic bag; or store rolled in a slightly dampened paper or cloth towel in a plastic bag in the refrigerator.

Drying Herbs
Herbs are easy to dry. Harvest early in the day as soon as the dew has dried and before the heat of the sun evaporates the essential oils which provide much of the flavor. Wash in cool water to remove any dust and dirt. Spread in a single layer on clean dish towels to air dry.
Tie herbs into small bunches and hang upside down in warm, well ventilated area away from light to dry, or remove leaves and place on wire racks or mesh screens to dry. When dry and crisp, store leaves in tightly covered glass containers in a cool, dark, dry place.

Freezing Herbs
Freezing herbs preserves the fresh-picked flavor and texture. However, it does take room in the freezer. I prefer to freeze parsley to drying, but any herb can be frozen. Prepare as for Drying Herbs. You can freeze whole or minced leaves:
1. Freeze the leaves on baking sheets and then store in plastic bags or freezer containers.
2. Mince the herbs, place in ice cube trays, fill with water and freeze. Remove cubes to plastic bags or freezer containers to store.

Herb Vinegars
Herb vinegars enable you to preserve the harvest to use in sauces, marinades, salad dressings, stews and beverages.
Have ready a clean, sterilized 1-quart class canning jar and lid.
Wash gently in cool water, being careful not to bruise the leaves which will release the essential oils needed to flavor the vinegar:
1 c (minimum amount, more preferred) fresh, firmly packed herbs
Allow to air dry thoroughly or spin dry in a salad spinner.
Using a wooden spoon, pack herbs in prepared jar.
Add:
3 – 3 ½ c vinegar (white, apple cider, white wine, red wine or white balsamic)
Fill jar to within 1 inch from the top.
With the wooden spoon, push the leaves down into the vinegar, bruising the leaves as you do so.
Cover jar first with plastic wrap and then the lid.
Store in a cool, dark place for 4-6 weeks, shaking the jar every few days.
When you are satisfied with the flavor, strain through a fine-mesh strainer to remove leaves and stems. Then, strain through paper coffee filters until the

paper is clean and the vinegar is clear (note: moisten the filters first to prevent the filters from absorbing too much of the precious, flavored vinegar). Pour into clean, sterilized bottles or canning jars. Add a sprig of the fresh herb(s) used to flavor the vinegar. Store in a cool, dark, dry place.
Variations on a Theme: some of my favorite herb blends:
    Dill, chive and peppercorn
    Basil, garlic
    Basil, chive
    Sage, caraway (for pork)
    Mint, rosemary (for lamb)
    Basil, savory (for beef)
    Sage, thyme (for poultry)
    Dill, bay (for fish)
    1 part parsley to ½ part each thyme, base and rosemary
    1 part each basil and marjoram to ½ part each rosemary, thyme and savory

Herb Teas

You can use just about any herb to make a cup of tea by simply pouring a cup of boiling water over 1 or 2 herb leaves in a covered, non-metallic cup or pot and steeping for 10 minutes. The mints make excellent teas to serve hot or cold. Other herbs which make fine teas are sage, thyme, marjoram and basil. I like the following combinations:
    Equal amounts of rosemary, thyme and lavender flowers
    Sage, thyme, marjoram and chamomile flowers

Herb Blends

If you grow and dry your own herbs, it is very economical to make your own herb blends. Here are two of my most-used blends.
Salad Seasoning Blend – combine 1/3 c toasted sesame seeds with 4 ½ T onion powder, 2 T poppy seeds, 1 ½ T garlic powder, 1 ½ T paprika, ¾ t celery seed and ¼ t pepper. To make a liquid dressing, combine 1 T of this mixture with ¾ c oil and ¼ c vinegar or lemon juice.
No-salt Herb Blend – Combine 4 T each oregano leaves and onion powder, 4 t each marjoram, basil, savory, garlic powder, thyme and rosemary, and 1 t each sage and pepper. Grind, in batches, in a spice grinder to a fine powder. Spoon into a saltshaker.

Sources

    Buffalo Gal – buffalogal.com, buffalo/bison, elk, Swabian Hall pork, beef
    Dartagnan.com - fresh and frozen beef, pork, chicken, turkey, duck, etc.
    King Arthur Flour Baker's Catalogue - www.kingarthurflour.com, flours and other ingredients
    Lehman's Hardware store – lehmans.com, an excellent source for many

things
- nuts.com - dried and candied fruit, and nuts
- Wilton – wilton.com, bakeware, baking supplies

Recipe Preparation

It is well to read through the recipe before beginning. This enables you to check you have all ingredients and equipment available as well as it familiarizes you with the preparation method.

It is also important to note pan sizes over the years have changed. I find it almost impossible to find a standard jelly roll pan which should be 10x15x1-inch. The pans today are not made, for the most part, in that size. There are sheet pans, half-sheet pans, and pans in practically every dimension except for a standard 10x15x1-inch measure. I search estate and garage sales, antique stores and online if I need a baking pan, dish, etc. The recipes in this book are for standard- (perhaps vintage-) sized vessels and have not been adjusted to accommodate contemporary sizes.

Take note also of weights and measures. Again, the recipes in this book are constructed of weights and measures that have not remained consistent over time. For example: chocolate chips were sold in 12-oz packages. Good luck finding that size today—some have been reduced down to 10 oz or less along with a higher price. Canned, boxed and frozen items have also changed sizes. Where possible, I provide measurements (e.g., 2 cups) rather than a package weight or size.

You can, of course, use what equipment and ingredients are available, but your results will differ—sometimes slightly, sometimes greatly.

Capitalized recipes (e.g., Sauerkraut, Apricot Filling, Everyday Bread, etc.) are recipes in this book.

Recipe Action Verbs - Another important thing to know is the placement of the cooking action verb (chopped, minced, sifted, etc.) in the ingredients list. If the action verb comes before the ingredient, complete that action before measuring. For example: 1 c chopped nuts means you should chop the nuts then measure; 1 c nuts, chopped, means you should measure the nuts (either whole, halves or pieces) then chop. The same for sifted: 1 c sifted flour means you should sift the flour into the cup and then level; 1 c flour, sifted means you should measure the flour and then sift.

Measures/Measuring – how you measure and what you use to measure ingredients is important to achieving good results.

Use a glass measuring cup to measure liquids. I find the Pyrex brand most accurate. Use dry measuring cups to measure dry ingredients. I find the Tupperware brand most accurate.

Measuring spoons are used to measure both liquid and dry ingredients. Again, I find the Tupperware brand the most accurate.

Flour can be measured one of three ways, as directed in individual recipes (Note: always stir the flour in the canister with a wire whisk before measuring):
1. By lightly spooning into the measuring cup and then leveling.
2. By sifting directly into the measuring cup or spoon and then leveling.
3. By dipping the cup or spoon into the flour and then leveling (dip-and-sweep).

Brown sugar is always tightly packed into the measuring cup or spoon and then leveled.

The following abbreviations are used in this book:
- c – cup
- ga. - gallon
- lb – pound/pounds
- oz – ounce/ounces
- pkg. – package
- qt. - quart
- t – teaspoon
- T – tablespoon

Substitutions – don't. Just don't.

Chopped, Coarsely Chopped, Diced, Finely Diced – these terms refer to how to cut various foods for further cooking.
1. Chopped pieces are about ½ inch.
2. Coarsely chopped pieces are larger than ½ inch.
3. Diced pieces are about 3/8 inch.
4. Finely diced is ¼ inch (for fruits, vegetables, nuts, etc.) or 1/8 inch for herbs.

Equipment – good, solid baking and cooking equipment is the best investment you can make. I have amassed a collection over the years that has lasted for decades. It is worth the time and effort to search out equipment made in the USA and that is vintage. You can buy unused, boxed (quaintly referred to as new old-store stock) equipment online, at the thrift store or at yard sales or auctions. Equipment today, even if made in the USA, is not of the same gauge and quality as vintage—the metal is thinner, the plastic is more brittle, the gears are usually cheap plastic or aluminum. These are the brands I have in my arsenal:
- Wear-Ever
- Nordic Ware
- Chicago Metallic
- Cuisinart
- EKCO

Robeson Shur-edge
Lodge
Wilton
Tupperware
Pyrex
Fire-King
Farberware
KitchenAid

Food Preservation

In addition to the recipes for freezing and canning various foods, it is well to know how to preserve and store food for future use. In this way, you can accumulate foodstuffs a little at a time, as available, until you have enough for a single or multiple recipes. The following is designed to help you achieve this:

Eggs – whole eggs, in the shell, should not be frozen. However, separated egg yolks and egg whites freeze very well and are especially useful for making Noodles and Angel Food Cake, or other meringue based items with yolks and whites, respectively. To freeze egg yolks, place the yolks in an airtight, freezer-safe container and cover with a thin film of oil. The oil provides further protection from freezer burn. To use, thaw the yolks in the refrigerator and mix together. If they are somewhat stiff, stir in a couple tablespoons of warm water before proceeding with the recipe for Noodles. I don't use frozen yolks for other recipes such as breads or cakes because the additional oil and water, if used, throws off the recipe balance.

To freeze egg whites, place the whites in an airtight glass container. Avoid using plastic containers (unless brand-new, never used and reserved specifically for this purpose) because just a speck of fat will cause the egg whites to not beat properly. You can continue adding egg whites to the same container as you have them until the container is filled to 1 inch from the top (to allow for expansion). To use, thaw the whites in the refrigerator. You can use them straight from the container for omelets, etc. To use for meringue-based recipes, including Angel Food Cake, add one fresh egg white in addition to the amount called for in the recipe.

Sliced, Breaded Vegetables - green tomatoes, zucchini, and eggplant slices that have been breaded freeze well, too. Follow the directions in Bound Breading to bread the vegetable slices. Place on a metal baking sheet lined with parchment or waxed paper. Freeze until solid and then package the individual slices in either freezer proof storage bags or in an airtight container, separating layers with waxed or freezer paper. Remove the quantity needed and cook according to the recipe for Potato Patties. Do not allow to thaw because the breaded coating will not crisp and the vegetables will be very watery.

Soups – prepare as for immediate use. Chill rapidly over ice water. Store in any container suitable for liquids, leaving ½ inch headspace for pints and 1 inch for quarts. Concentrated meat or fish stock, simmered until reduced to one-half or one-third original quantity may be frozen in ice cube trays for additions to gravy and sauces, then put frozen cubes in plastic freezer bags and seal. If a soup calls for potato, it is preferable to add freshly cooked potato to the thawed soup. If you do freeze the potato, undercook it. To serve, bring to a boil in a saucepan, unless the soup is thick or cream-based, in which case it is best to use a double boiler.

Casseroles – line a casserole pan with foil, add the cooled casserole mixture and freeze. When frozen solid, remove the foil-wrapped food, seal tightly and freeze. When ready to serve, remove the food from the foil, place in casserole dish and heat the dish in the oven.

Unbaked Pastry, Cookies and Doughs – all of these freeze well. Having these at hand lessens the need for processed, store-bought items, streamlines everyday meal preparation and provides an arsenal of treats for unexpected guests. Cake doughs and batters are not recommended for freezing; however, the baked products, either whole or in individual servings, do freeze well.

Unbaked yeast doughs should be made up as usual, kneaded and allowed to rise once before shaping and freezing. Thaw, covered with a damp towel and let rise until doubled (this may take 3-4 hours, depending on size). Bake according to recipe directions.

The bread doughs in this book respond well to the "brown-and-serve" method. Mix, knead, let rise, shape and let formed loaves or rolls rise according to recipe directions. Bake at recommended temperature until the surface of the dough is set and barely starting to color. Remove from oven, let cool in pan on a rack until thoroughly cooled. Wrap tightly in baking pan. Freeze. To serve: remove from freeze and bake according to recipe directions until done. There is no need to thaw before baking.

Unbaked Biscuits may be frozen on trays and then packaged before freezing. Thaw the number needed, wrapped, at room temperature 1 hour and bake per recipe directions.

Pie and pastry dough freeze well. Prepare as usual and divide into separate portions to make preparing top and bottom pie crusts, tart crusts, etc. Wrap tightly in plastic wrap, then in foil, before placing in plastic freezer bags. Thaw, wrapped, in the refrigerator before proceeding with your recipe.

Cookie doughs should be rolled into logs, if baking sliced; spread in pans for bar cookies; or shaped into balls and frozen on sheet pans. Wrap logs in plastic, then in foil, before placing in plastic freezer bags. Wrap bar cookies tightly in pan in plastic, then in foil. Place frozen cookie balls in plastic freezer bags. Thaw logs before slicing and baking according to recipe directions. Thaw pans of bar cookies before baking according to recipe directions. There is no need to thaw cookie balls, but these do benefit from a modified baking method: Bake frozen on a cookie sheet lined with parchment paper or a silicone baking mat, at 400 degrees about 8 minutes; rotate pan from front to back; bake at 375 degrees about another 8 minutes or until edges are crispy and golden and cookies are done. Remove from oven. Let cookies sit on pan 1-2 minutes before removing to a wire rack to cool.

Baked Pastry, Cakes, Cookies and Breads – freeze these either whole or cut into individual servings. Place in airtight containers, or wrap in plastic, then in foil, before placing in plastic freezer bags. Thaw pastry, cookies and breads, wrapped, in the refrigerator. Thaw breads, wrapped, at room temperature. Thaw cakes, unwrapped, in a covered cake dish at room temperature.

Unbaked Pies – form and fill pies in a foil-lined pie pan, unless you are fortunate to have enough stock to freeze directly in the pan in which the frozen pie will be baked. Freeze until solid. Wrap well in plastic, then in foil, and freeze. Bake frozen pies at 400 degrees 15-20 minutes, then at 375 degrees until juices are thickly bubbling at the center. Cover edges with foil if browning too quickly. Cream and custard pies, and meringue do not freeze well.

Baked Pies – wrap baked pies in plastic, then in foil, and freeze. Thaw, uncovered, at room temperature. Cream and custard pies, and meringue do not freeze well.

Dried Fruits and Nuts – for long-term storage, freezing is ideal for dried fruits and nuts. Freeze whole, chopped or ground in convenient quantities. Freeze in airtight containers or plastic freezer bags.

Homemade Dairy Products

You can make Buttermilk, Crème Fraiche, Cottage Cheese and Sour Cream at home without any special equipment. These are easy to make and well worth the effort if you have your own milk cow or access to fresh (raw, unpasteurized) milk and cream. You can also make these products with milk and cream from the grocer.

Buttermilk

This, of course, is not the milk that results from actually making butter—true buttermilk—but does produce the same product as commercial buttermilk available at the grocer. Use this buttermilk in the recipes that follow.
Combine:
>   **2 c milk**
>   **2 T commercial buttermilk**

Mix well.
Let stand, covered with plastic wrap, in a warm place for 16-24 hours or till thickened. Refrigerate in a covered container up to 2 weeks.
Shake well before using. Reserve 2 T for your next batch of Buttermilk.

Crème Fraiche

True crème fraiche is a French specialty made from raw cream allowed to mature naturally, but not to sour. There are many concerns and restrictions regarding raw milk and cream that makes this a good way to obtain very acceptable results from commercial milk. It is a good substitute for Sour Cream in cooking and also good served chilled over sliced fruit.
Mix in a medium-sized bowl:
>   **1 c whipping cream**
>   **1/3 c commercial buttermilk, or your own**

Let stand, uncovered, at room temperature for 6-7 hours or overnight until mixture has thickened. Do not stir.
Store in covered container in the refrigerator up to 1 week. Reserve 2 T for your next batch.

Cottage Cheese

My grandparents sold milk and cream when Father and his siblings were growing up. I remember Father telling how they would milk the cows twice a day and sell gallons of milk and cream each week to the grocer in town. In fact, we still have the electric cream separator they used to separate the cream from the milk. Father also told how Grandmother would make cottage cheese and set it on a hedge pole to ripen. This recipe takes rennet. You can find rennet tablets in the baking section of most grocers.

Crush:
> ¼ **tablet rennet**

Dissolve in:
> ½ **c water**

In large stainless steel kettle or Dutch oven heat to 70 degrees:
> **1 ga milk**

Remove from heat and stir in:
> ¼ **c Buttermilk**
> **Rennet water**

Cover with towel and let sit at room temperature 12 - 20 hours or till a firm curd forms.

With a knife, cut curd into ½-inch pieces.

Transfer curd and whey to a large stainless steel bowl or saucepan that fits securely over a Dutch oven filled with 1-2 inches of water.

Heat curd slowly over hot water to 120-130 degrees (do not overheat). Hold curd at this temperature for 20-30 minutes. Stir gently every 5 minutes to heat the curd uniformly.

Pour mixture into fine cheesecloth-lined colander and allow whey to drain. Occasionally shift curd on cloth by lifting corners of the cloth. After the whey has drained (8-10 minutes), lift the curd in cheesecloth and immerse in a pan of cold water for 2 minutes. Then immerse in ice water 2 minutes. Return curd in cloth to colander; drain the curd until it is free from moisture. This could take several hours.

Put cheese in a bowl and gently stir in:
> ½ **c light cream**
> ½ **t salt**

Cover and chill. Use within 3 weeks.

Sour Cream

You can easily make Sour Cream with either Buttermilk or commercial sour cream. The version made with commercial Sour Cream will be thicker and more tangy than that made with Buttermilk. Also, it will thicken sufficiently in 20-24 hours.

Combine in a hot, clean glass 1-quart jar:
> **2 c cream**
> **2 T commercial buttermilk (or your own) or commercial sour cream**

Cover tightly and shake well.

Let stand in a warm place till thickened (24-48 hours if made with Buttermilk; 20-24 hours if made with commercial Sour Cream).

Store, covered, in the refrigerator. Stir before serving. Use within 3 weeks. Reserve 2 T for your next batch.

Butter
Butter making like many other culinary art forms (as I call them) has been abandoned except for a few communities and artisanal efforts. Unless you have an abundance of fresh cream, this recipe will most likely be a novelty for readers. I have an antique crock butter churn as well as glass churns and the one and only electric churn Aunt Mill had from the former Montgomery Ward department store. You can use a blender or a quart jar to make butter in a small quantity if you'd like to for a classroom experiment or a rainy-day activity.

Butter is only as good as the cream from which it is made. Father would milk the cow in the morning and bring it to house in a galvanized bucket. He would use an old, clean white tee shirt to strain the milk into a large white and red enamel bowl. Mother would cover the bowl with a large plastic lid and set it in a sink of cold water to cool before refrigerating. We allowed the cream to separate by gravity. As the milk cooled and sat in the refrigerator, the cream would separate and rise to the top. We skimmed the cream into a separate container to store.

Cream should be cooled to 50 degrees or less before making butter and then kept at 55 – 60 degrees during the butter-making process. A higher temperature will result in a greasy consistency; a lower temperature, a brittle, tallow texture. A gallon of cream will yield about 3 pounds of butter.

Fill a sterile churn one-third to one-half full of cream. Depending on quantity, the butter should make within 15-40 minutes. The cream will be foamy during the first half of churning, then form lumps about the size of cornmeal and then the size of corn kernels. Stop churning at this point.

Drain off and measure the buttermilk (authentic buttermilk). Reserve buttermilk for a refreshing drink or to use in other recipes.

Wash the butter at least twice with as much 50 – 70-degree fresh, pure water as you have Buttermilk. If you have city or rural water, it is best to use bottled water that does not contain chlorine or fluoride. Wash by using a large wooden spoon or paddle to fold and smash the butter into the water. The butter should eventually form a solid mass and the liquid in the final wash should be clear.

Pack the butter into a mold, butter dish or other airtight container. Store in the refrigerator or in the freezer wrapped in plastic then foil and in a plastic freezer bag for extended storage.

Blender method: Chill the blender. Blend 1 c whipping cream at high speed about 15 seconds or until the cream coasts the blades. Add ½ c ice water. Continue to blend at high speed until the butter rises to the surface. Strain out the butter, press out any additional moisture, mold and chill. The remaining liquid is not rich enough to substitute for buttermilk but is good to use in soups.

Formulas and Foundations

Through the years, I've learned to rely on basic formulas for much of my cooking. The only exception is baking in which a recipe is a must for consistent, reliable results. Once you master a recipe or a technique, then you'll not need to rely on a recipe for the most basic of dishes. The following provides several examples of how one basic formula, with slight variations, leads to many delicious outcomes.

Variations on a Theme – you will find several of these following individual recipes. Several of the recipes or components of recipes in this book are interchangeable. For example: the shortbread crust featured in "Coconut Bars" can be baked plain, or topped with any number of different toppings. Likewise, the coconut and nuts can be replaced with any combination of nuts, dried fruit, chocolate pieces, etc. to make your own bars.

The directions for Bound Breading works well for many vegetables (green and ripe tomatoes, zucchini, eggplant) and sliced meats. You can vary the final coating by using bread crumbs, butter cracker crumbs or just flour. Pork, veal and steak cutlets, as well as fish fillets, sliced or pounded chicken and turkey breasts, and even ground meat patties all do well breaded. The recipe for Everyday Biscuits can be changed by increasing the sugar, exchanging an egg for part of the milk, and pressing the dough into a glass pie dish to make Shortcake. You can also use the Biscuit dough as a pizza crust.

Master Recipes and Methods – you will also find several foundation or master recipes which can be used in various ways and provide variety to your menus and food options. These are recipes and methods I have worked out over the years to both simplify preparation and to increase variety without sacrificing flavor or satisfaction. Mastering these recipes will equip you with countless variations. In addition, I have also included several Master Mixing Methods which I have developed over the years. Mastering these will equip you with skills and methods to work with just a list of ingredients and achieve excellent results. I sincerely hope this will inspire you to explore even more.

White Sauce

All sorts of delicious sauces, binders and extenders can be made using this simple recipe. The recipe easily multiplies. Ingredients are listed for thin (medium) [thick] sauces.

Melt in a saucepan:
> **1 (2) [3] T butter**

Add and cook until tender, but not browning:
> **1 T grated onion**

Add and cook, stirring constantly, 1-2 minutes:
> **1 (2) [3] T flour**

Add slowly:
   1 c warm milk (or a combination of milk, cream or stock)
   ½ t salt
Bring slowly to a boil and cook 2-3 minutes until there is no raw flour taste. Adjust salt and add ground black pepper to taste.
Depending on its use, you may add for additional flavoring:
   A dash or two of nutmeg, or
   1 T prepared mustard
Variations on a Theme:
Cream Soups: use the Thin recipe and add ½ - 1 c pureed vegetables to each cup of sauce. Heat without boiling.
Scalloped Vegetables: use the Medium recipe and make half as much sauce as vegetables to be scalloped. Butter a 2-quart baking dish. Combine sauce and cooked vegetables (potatoes, cauliflower, cabbage, broccoli, turnips, beets, carrots, parsnips, etc. or a combination) along with 1/3 c grated cheese (Gruyere, aged Cheddar or Parmesan are good choices), if desired. Sprinkle evenly over all ½ c breadcrumbs and 1/3 c grated cheese. Bake at 350 degrees until bubbly and browned on top, about 25 minutes. Serve sprinkled with paprika.

Gravy
An essential menu item any time of year. We made gravy two ways. The first is pan gravy made after frying meat; the second is gravy made from the stock of a roast or other braised meat or fowl. The formula is similar to the one for a medium White Sauce (e.g., 2 T fat and 2 T flour for each cup of liquid). I usually allow ½ cup gravy per person plus extra for second helpings and Plan Overs.
Pan Gravy - after frying meat, drain off all but enough fat for the quantity of gravy needed. Add in the required amount of flour. Cook 1 minute. Add in the quantity of liquid needed. We usually used the water in which we cooked potatoes for the meal, but the liquid can be milk and/or cream (especially for serving with fried chicken), stock, water from cooking vegetables to be served with the meal, or a combination. Bring to boiling, stirring constantly and cook for 2-3 minutes. Season to taste with salt and pepper.
Stock Gravy - made by thickening the liquid with a slurry of stock and flour. Measure out the total amount of stock needed (allowing about ½ c of gravy per person). Pour 2/3 of the liquid into a saucepan. To the remaining 1/3 of the cooled liquid, add 2 T flour for each cup of liquid. Mix until thoroughly smooth. Bring liquid to a boil, add flour slurry, return to boil and cook for 2-3 minutes. Season to taste with salt and pepper. Keep warm until serving.
If storing gravy in the refrigerator to use for Plan Overs, or to freeze, I use a combination of flour and cornstarch as the thickening ingredients. Two tablespoons of flour equal 1 T of cornstarch. Adjust recipes accordingly.

Hard-boiled Eggs
A foundation ingredient which has many uses as a snack, salad ingredient, garnish, etc. A perfectly cooked egg has a tender white, a moist yolk, no greenish-black line between the yolk and white, and it peels easily. The first three depend on the heat. Despite the name, eggs should never be boiled. The last depends mostly on the age of the egg. The older the egg, the larger the air sac and the easier to peel. I have used the following method, from the Georgia Egg Board, throughout my decades of cooking. It requires a bit of gymnastics, but releasing the air, shrinking the egg from the shell, and expanding the shell from the egg does produce the perfect egg.

There is a bubble of air at the large end of the egg which expands when the egg is heated and can cause the shell to crack. Prick the end of the egg with an egg-pricker or a push pin, going in at least ¼ inch, to let the air escape.

Heat water to cover the eggs by at least 1 inch in a pan large enough to hold the eggs in one layer. Recommended:
- For 1 – 4 eggs, 1 quart
- For 5 – 8 eggs, 2 quarts
- For 9 – 12 eggs, 4 quarts
- For 13 – 16 eggs, 5 quarts
- For 17 – 20 eggs, 6 quarts
- For 21 – 24 eggs, 8 quarts

Set the pan with eggs and water over high heat and bring just to boiling.
Remove pan from heat. Cover pan and let eggs sit exactly 17 minutes.
Transfer eggs to a large bowl of ice and water. Chill for 2 minutes while bringing cooking water to the boil again.
Transfer eggs (6 at a time, maximum) to the boiling water, bring water back to boiling and boil for 10 seconds.
Return eggs to ice water, cracking the shells gently in several places.
Chill 15-20 minutes before peeling to prevent the dark line from forming.
To peel: gently crack the shell all over. Then, starting at the wide end, and either under a thin stream of cold water or in the bowl of ice water, start peeling. Return peeled egg immediately to the ice water to continue cooling.
To store: place peeled eggs in an uncovered bowl of water in the refrigerator, 2-3 days.

Roasted Garlic
Useful in a number of dishes.
Cut off the top one-third of a head of garlic (you should see the tops of the cloves). Wrap tightly in aluminum foil and bake at 350 degrees 30-40 minutes or until very tender. Unwrap, let cool a few minutes and then squeeze out the baked cloves into a small bowl.

Roasted Peppers
Both hot and sweet peppers are a boon when roasted.
Grill, broil or rotate over a gas flame peppers until the skins are blistered and dark in spots all over. Place in a brown paper bag. Close bag and let sit until cool enough to handle. Discard seeds and stems and peel off skins.

Toasted Coconut
Preheat oven to 350 degrees. Spread coconut on a cookie sheet. Bake 5-10 minutes until evenly toasted, depending on quantity, stirring often and watching carefully so coconut does not burn. Remove immediately to another cold cookie sheet to stop cooking. Let cool completely before using or storing in an airtight container.

Toasted Nuts
Toasting nuts enhances their flavor, provides a bit of crunch and prevents them from turning soft or soggy. Preheat oven to 350 degrees. Spread nut halves or coarsely chopped nuts on a cookie sheet. Bake 7-10 minutes or until fragrant and evenly toasted. Remove immediately to another cold cookie sheet to stop cooking. Let cool completely before using or storing in an airtight container.

Glazed Nuts
Glazed nuts can be used as a topping for savory or sweet dishes, a crunchy sweet addition to salads, and as a garnish for cakes, cupcakes, pies and other desserts.
Have ready a large, rimmed sheet pan lined with aluminum foil, waxed paper, parchment paper or a silicone baking mat.
Bring to a boil in a deep, wide skillet or pan:
> ½ c water
> ½ c brown sugar

Add:
> **1 c walnut or pecan halves, or whole almonds, pistachios or peanuts**

Stir constantly and cook until syrup is thickened and nuts are evenly coated, 5-10 minutes.
Remove, using a slotted spoon and allowing excess glaze to drain, to prepared sheet. Carefully separate nuts and cool thoroughly. Store tightly covered in a cool, dark place (not the refrigerator).

To Peel Tomatoes, Peaches, Nectarines, etc
Fruits and vegetables with thin or fuzzy skins tightly enclosing the flesh can be easily peeled with this method. The exceptions are plums and apricots which do not need to be peeled.
Bring a large quantity of water to the boil.
Immerse one fruit or vegetable into the boiling water for 20 seconds to start. Check if peel will easily remove. If not, return to water in 5 second increments until you can easily remove the peel. Place in a large bowl of ice and water.

Repeat with remaining fruits and vegetables.
When cool enough to handle, peel, core and remove seeds/pits.

Lemon Curd
This is a delightful item which is equally delicious as a spread on Biscuits, Waffles and Pancakes, used as a filling for tarts or cakes, or as a topping for Cheesecake. It stores well for several weeks tightly covered and refrigerated. I have found using bottled lemon juice (especially an organic, volcanic version imported from Italy) produces as good results as freshly squeezed lemon juice.
Strain through a sieve into a heavy saucepan:
> **6 egg yolks**

Add:
> **1 c sugar**
> **½ c lemon juice**
> **½ c butter, cut into small pieces**

Stir to combine.
Cook over low heat, stirring constantly, 10-12 minutes, until the mixture thickens and coats the back of a wooden spoon. A finger drawn through the curd on the spoon should leave a definite path. Remove from heat. Cover with plastic wrap, pressing onto top surface to prevent a crust from forming and let cool completely before refrigerating.

Variations on a Theme:
Lime Curd – substitute lime juice for the lemon juice.
Orange Curd – substitute orange juice for the lemon juice; decrease sugar to 2/3 c.

Apricot Filling
An intensely flavored filling for tarts, jelly rolls, cakes (including Cheesecake) and which can also be served like jam in sandwiches, on Biscuits or French Toast, etc.
Place in a small saucepan:
> **1 ¾ lb dried apricots**
> **1 qt. water**

Allow to stand, covered, for 2 hours.
Simmer 20 minutes over very low heat, tightly covered, or until the apricots are soft.
Puree, along with any liquid in the pan, in a food processor or blender.
Press through a food mill or sieve, if desired.
You should have 3-4 c puree.
Add:
> **3 ½ T lemon juice**
> **1 c sugar**

Stir to combine. Taste and add more sugar, if desired. Store covered in the refrigerator or freeze.

Raspberry or Strawberry Puree

Frozen raspberries and strawberries have much better flavor than fresh berries at the grocer, unless you grow your own. These purees are good to have on hand to serve with ice cream, over cake (especially Angel Food) or to dress up a last-minute store-bought dessert. You can adjust the amount of sugar to your preference.

Place in a colander suspended over a bowl:
- **2 12-oz bags frozen raspberries or**
- **1 20-oz bag frozen strawberries**

Let thaw completely.

Press on the berries to remove all the juice, but not so hard you press the pulp through the colander. You should have 1 c of raspberry juice or 1 ¼ c strawberry juice.

For both: in a small saucepan, boil the juice until reduced to ¼ c.

For raspberries: press berries through a fine sieve to remove all seeds. You should have 1 c puree. Add reduced juice to puree.

Add:
- **2 t lemon juice**
- **Up to 2/3 c sugar**

For strawberries: process berries in a food processor. You should have 1 c puree. Add reduced juice to puree.

Add:
- **2 t lemon juice**
- **Up to ¼ c sugar**

Whipped Cream

Perfectly Whipped Cream is a bit of heaven on earth. Of course, the best Whipped Cream is make with fresh cream, but you can get satisfactory results from commercial heavy (whipping) cream. Cream roughly doubles in volume when whipped to stiff peaks; slightly less if softly whipped (the cream will mound softly when dropped from a spoon). The following master recipe and its variations are for a base amount. You can double the recipe in most standard mixers. You'll need a very large mixing bowl if making a greater quantity. Whipped Cream will hold (that is, it will not weep out liquid) for up to one hour. To hold longer, replace the sugar with 1 ½ T powdered sugar. Turn Whipped Cream into a fine-mesh sieve suspended over a bowl. The slight amount of cornstarch in the powdered sugar prevents the liquid from weeping out of the cream. The variations are good to fill and frost cakes and cupcakes.

Place in a large mixing bowl:
- **1 c heavy cream**
- **1 T sugar**
- **½ t vanilla**

Chill this mixture and the beaters in the refrigerator at least 15 minutes.

Beat on high speed until stiff peaks form when the beaters are lifted (see note, above, for softly Whipped Cream).

Variations on a Theme:

Mocha Whipped Cream – Increase sugar to 2 T and add 1 T cocoa and 1 t instant espresso powder; refrigerate for 1 hour to dissolve cocoa and espresso powder.

Chocolate Whipped Cream – Increase sugar to 2 ½ T and add 2 T cocoa; refrigerate for at least 1 hour to dissolve cocoa before whipping.

Fruit Curd Whipped Cream – beat cream just until beater marks begin to show; add ½ c Lemon, Lime or Orange Curd and beat just until stiff peaks form when the beaters are raised.

Fruit Whipped Cream – use ½ Strawberry Puree, Raspberry Puree or Apricot Filling for each base recipe. Dissolve 1 ¼ t gelatin in 2 T puree in a small bowl placed in a pan of simmering water. Stir the gelatin mixture into the rest of the puree. Whip cream softly then add puree and beat until stiff peaks form when the beaters are lifted. Taste and add more sugar, if desired.

Chocolate Ganache

The one-stop recipe for chocolate frosting and filling (for cakes, tarts, etc.).
Grate or chop fine:
>**12 oz semisweet chocolate**
>**1 oz unsweetened chocolate**

Place in a heat-proof bowl.
Heat to boiling:
>**1 2/3 c whipping cream**

Pour over chocolate and stir until chocolate is melted and mixture is smooth. Chill, stirring often until thick enough to spread.

Variation on a Theme:

Truffles - reduce cream to 1 c. Chill in a shallow pan until solid. Use a small ice cream scoop to form balls. Roll in cocoa, coconut or chopped nuts. Store, tightly covered, in the refrigerator.

Jams and Jellies

It is always well to have a variety of jams and jellies on hand for a variety of uses. There are several recipes in this book. The variety is practically endless when you combine different fruits and/or herbs, spices and other flavorings. I particularly like the following: red raspberry-rhubarb; gooseberry-red raspberry; gooseberry-blueberry; pear-pineapple; sour cherry-cranberry; and tomato. The best way to explore making your own jams and jellies is to follow the directions on a package of pectin. You'll be able to create your own signature products once you master the technique.

I like to make 6 half-pint jars of jam at one time because I prefer to buy bulk pectin, the measurements required are even and larger batches may not jell. For this you need:
> **4 c prepared fruit (crush berries; finely chop other fruits)**
> **4 ½ T pectin**
> **2 T lemon juice**
> **5 c sugar**

Combine the fruit, pectin and lemon juice in a large (8-quart) saucepan or kettle. Gradually stir in the pectin. Bring mixture to a full rolling boil that cannot be stirred down, over highest heat, stirring constantly. Add the entire measure of sugar, stirring constantly to dissolve. Return mixture to full rolling boil. Boil hard 1 minute, stirring constantly. Remove from heat. Skim foam if necessary. Pour into prepared jars. Wipe rims, cover and seal. Let cool. Store in cool, dark, dry place.

Mayonnaise

Mastering making Mayonnaise—which is actually quite easy—will make you feel peerless. After all, how many people do you know who make their own these days? This is a perfect example of how delicious simple can be. Try it with hard-boiled eggs, roast chicken and tomato, cold lobster or crab, chicken or potato salad or cole slaw. Use the best quality oil available. I prefer regular or light olive oil. You may want to use a combination of olive oil and salad oil the first time you make it, graduating to all olive oil. You can make this with an electric mixer or with a wire whisk.

Beat for several minutes or until pale, thick and the yolks leave a slowly dissolving ribbon when the beater or whisk is raised:
> **3 egg yolks**

Add:
> **¼ t dry mustard**
> **½ t salt**
> **2 t lemon juice**

Beat another minute.
Add, by half-teaspoon dribbles:
> **2 c oil, olive oil or salad oil or a combination**

Do not stop beating until ½ c oil has been added and you have a thick Mayonnaise. You may take a break now if beating by hand.

Add the remaining oil in tablespoon additions, beating several seconds after each addition until yolks absorb the oil.

When the sauce becomes too thick to beat, thin out with drops of lemon juice and continue to add the rest of the oil.

Taste and add more salt, lemon juice and black pepper as needed.

Transfer to small bowl or jar and cover tightly. Refrigerate if not using immediately. It will keep 5-6 days in the refrigerator, but bring to room temperature before using because stirring chilled Mayonnaise may cause the yolks to release the oil.

Rice Master Recipe
As simple and versatile as plain cooked rice is, it is sometimes the bane of the cook. The unappetizing gumminess often results from overcooking or not rinsing off the flour that coats each grain upon cooking. The following boil-steam-and rinse method produces perfectly cooked rice which can be used in hot or cold dishes, or served straight as a side dish to any number of main dishes. Always use a fork to stir and fluff cooked rice to avoid breaking the grains.
Have ready a large saucepan or kettle with a tight-fitting lid, and a sieve or colander large enough hold the cooked rice, but that fits inside the saucepan or kettle.
Measure the amount of rice you need to cook. Raw rice will roughly double in amount when cooked. I usually allow about ½ c raw rice per person.
Measure three times the amount of water as rice into the saucepan or kettle
Add salt in the ration of 1 t per quart of water.
Cover and bring to the boil.
Slowly trickle in the rice so as to not stop the boiling.
Boil uncovered to 10-12 minutes or until several grains tested still have a slight crunch. Begin testing at 10 minutes.
Pour the rice into the colander and immediately place the colander into the pan. The excess water will drain into the pan.
Cover rice with a piece of foil or parchment or waxed paper and the lid.
Let sit to steam in the residual heat for 20 minutes.
If serving cold: rinse rice under cold running water, fluffing with a fork.
If serving hot: rinse rice under hot running water, fluffing with a fork.

Bound Breading
Into one each of three shallow containers, place (for every four slices):
    ½ c flour
    1 egg mixed well with 2 T milk
    1 c fine, fresh or dry bread crumbs
Dip sliced vegetables, meat, chicken, fish, etc. into flour, then egg, then crumbs, pressing on crumbs to make them adhere and to evenly coat each slice. You can fry immediately, or the coated foods may rest on a wire rack for at least an hour before frying.

Everyday Recipes

This collection of recipes includes some I use most often. It is not exhaustive by any means, but these will provide numerous options with the many *Variations on a Theme* as well as your own takeoffs.

Everyday Biscuits
Preheat oven to 400 degrees. Have ready an ungreased baking sheet.
Combine in a large mixing bowl:
- 2 c flour
- 4 t baking powder
- ½ t cream of tartar
- ¾ t salt
- 1 T sugar (optional)

Cut in, until the mixture resembles cornmeal:
- ½ c fat (lard, butter or shortening)

Stir in all at once:
- 2/3 c cold milk

Stir only until all flour mixture is moistened
Scrape onto floured surface. Knead gently 8-10 times until dough is smooth. Roll to ½-inch thick and cut with floured cutter, or use a sharp knife to cut into squares. Place on baking sheet 1 inch apart.
Bake 12-15 minutes or until biscuits are golden brown and done (test by using fork to split one in half; biscuits should not be doughy).

Variations on a Theme:

Cheddar Biscuits
Especially good to top a Pot Pie of any variety.
Add ¾ c grated Cheddar cheese, 2 t minced garlic (optional), and ½ t cracked black peppercorns to the flour mixture. Knead, roll, cut and bake as directed.

Drop Biscuits
These eliminate the need to knead, roll and cut the dough and result in biscuits with a moist center and a crispy, crunchy crust.
Increase milk to 1 c. Dough should be moist and sticky, but not smooth, and should hold its shape when dropped from a spoon. Use an ice cream scoop or large spoon to drop 12 biscuits onto baking sheet, lightly greased or lined with a silicone baking mat. Bake until deep golden brown.

Pizza Crust
Roll the kneaded the dough to fit a 10x15x1-inch pan (for thin crust) or 9x13-inch pan for a thicker crust. Prebake the crust in a 400-degree oven for 10 minutes. Complete the pizza by layering on your choice of sauce and toppings. Bake at 350 degrees about 20 minutes until the dough is baked and toppings are heated through.

Top with shredded cheese and bake an additional 5 minutes to melt the cheese.

Everyday Bread
A delicious bread with a most distinct texture. This makes the most luxurious toast for breakfast to slather with butter and preserves, or as a base for poached or sunny-side-up eggs. Toasted slices are also delicious served topped with vine-ripe tomatoes, chopped and marinated in coarse salt, olive oil and fresh basil. The texture of crispy toasted bread that has soaked up the tomato juices is wonderful.
This is the only bread I use for fresh bread crumbs, bread pudding and French Toast. This dough is mixed and kneaded very little compared to other doughs—just enough to make it cohesive. Be careful to not overbake the bread. Begin checking for doneness when you can smell the bread; the bread should sound hollow when tapped with a finger.
Have ready one greased 9x5x3-inch loaf pan (if making a single loaf), or one 8x4x2-inch loaf pan and one 8-inch round or square pan (if making a loaf and six rolls), or two 8-inch pans or a 9x13x2-inch pan (if making 12 rolls).
Heat, in a small saucepan just until the fat begins to melt:
> **1 c milk**
> **¼ c butter, lard or shortening**

Set aside and let residual heat completely melt the fat.
Combine in a small bowl and set aside:
> **1 t salt**
> **1 T sugar**

Stir together in a large bowl of electric mixer:
> **1/3 c lukewarm water**
> **1 pkg. yeast**

Sprinkle the top evenly with a thin layer of flour. Cover and let sit until yeast is foamy and breaks through the flour.
The milk mixture should now be lukewarm.
Mix in:
> **1 small egg**

Add to the proofed yeast:
> **1 ½ c flour**
> **The salt-sugar mixture**
> **The milk mixture**

Mix on low speed if using an electric mixer, or with a spoon if mixing by hand, until dry ingredients are moistened. If mixing by hand, beat about 400 strokes. If using an electric mixer, mix on low speed 2 minutes.
Scrape down bowl and beat in only until combined:
> **1 ½ c flour**

Continue to beat by hand or on low speed just until dough leaves the sides of the bowl, adding up to ½ c additional flour. Scrape dough into a ball.
Cover bowl. Let rise until doubled.

Preheat oven to 350 degrees.

Turn out dough onto lightly floured surface. Gently knead dough until it is smooth. Shape into a ball. Invert mixing bowl over dough and let rest 10 minutes. Cut dough in half, roll and form into loaves and/or rolls.

Let rise until about ½-inch above rim of loaf pan, or until rolls are doubled in size and fill the pan. Bake: large loaf 40-45 minutes; small loaf 30-35 minutes; rolls 20-25 minutes.

Remove from pans to a wire rack to cool.

Variations on a Theme:

Raisin Bread - knead into dough 1 cup of raisins that have been plumped and well drained. To plump raisins, cover with boiling water and let sit, covered for about 15 minutes. Follow master recipe for shaping, rising and baking.

Cinnamon Bread - divide dough in half; roll each half into 8-inch square. In small pan, slowly heat 2 T corn syrup and 2 T butter until butter just begins to melt. Remove from heat and stir until butter is fully incorporated into syrup. Brush mixture over dough. Sprinkle with 2 T sugar and then with 2 t ground cinnamon. Roll up tightly, and place seam side down in two greased 8x4x2-inch loaf pans. Follow master recipe for rising and baking.

Cinnamon Rolls - follow directions for Cinnamon Bread. Cut each roll of dough into six pieces. Place in greased muffin tins or two cake pans. Let rise until doubled in size. Follow master recipe for rising and baking.

White-Chocolate Cinnamon Rolls – follow directions for Cinnamon Rolls adding ¼ c finely grated white chocolate with the cinnamon to each roll of dough; omit sugar.

Pecan Rolls – in small saucepan, melt ½ c butter. Add 1 c brown sugar. Cook and stir until sugar is dissolved and mixture is smooth. Pour into two greased cake pans. Sprinkle ½ c chopped pecan into each pan. Proceed with recipe for Cinnamon Rolls.

Almond-Poppy Seed Rolls – follow directions for Cinnamon Rolls, using this filling: combine ½ c butter, melted, ½ c finely chopped almonds, 3 T poppy seeds, 3 T golden brown sugar, 2 T sugar, ½ t cinnamon.

Garlic Bread – use olive oil for the fat. Peel and mince five large garlic cloves. Poach the minced garlic in the olive oil over very low heat until fragrant. Cool completely. Proceed with recipe. Excellent shaped into hotdog or hamburger buns and served accordingly. Can also be used to wrap 12 hot dogs to make "pigs in the blanket."

Everyday Chocolate Cake

This is my absolute favorite chocolate cake (and cupcake) recipe. I based it on an old-fashioned Mayonnaise layer cake. I wanted a similar cake that was easy to mix and had an intense chocolate flavor. I replaced the Mayonnaise with oil. You can vary the chocolate intensity by using different varieties of cocoa. I use light olive oil because it provides a subtle richness and depth of flavor other oils do not. The following is a half recipe that makes 12 cupcakes or one nine-inch cake layer. You can double the ingredients for 24 cupcakes, two nine-inch cake layers or one 9/x13x2-inch cake.

Preheat oven to 350 degrees. Have ready a greased and floured 9-inch cake pan, or a 12-cup muffin tin lined with paper cups.
Sift into a large mixing bowl:
> 1 c flour
> ½ c sugar
> ¼ c + 2 T cocoa
> 1 t soda
> ½ t salt

Combine thoroughly in a separate bowl:
> 1 T vinegar
> 1 T vanilla
> 1 c boiling water
> ¼ c + 2 T oil

Quickly, gently and thoroughly add liquid ingredients to dry. Spoon into prepared pan. Bake 18-20 minutes for cupcakes, 22-25 minutes for layer cake or until tester inserted in center comes out clean. Let cool in pans five minutes before removing to a wire rack or serving plate.

Variation on a Theme: walnuts and chocolate have a natural affinity. Replace 2 T oil with 2 T walnut oil.

Everyday Meat Loaf

Meatloaf is one of those dishes which is perfect for making into your own signature recipe. There are no hard-and-fast rules other than: mix gently to avoid the baked loaf being tough and dry, and season well to taste equally good hot, warm or cold.
Preheat oven to 350 degrees. Have ready a greased 9x5x3-inch loaf pan or a shallow baking pan lined with foil (grease the foil).
Combine in large mixing bowl:
> 2 eggs, well beaten
> 4 slices white bread, cut into small cubes, or
>> 1 tube saltine crackers crushed into crumbs
>
> 1 onion, grated
> 1 t each salt and pepper

Mix well.
Add enough to completely moisten the bread:
> **Milk or cream**

The amount you need will depend on the how large the eggs and how thick the bread slices, if using.
Let sit until all liquid is absorbed. The mixture should be light and moist, but not at all runny—like cooked oatmeal. The crumbs should be blended into the other ingredients.
Mix in gently:
> **2 lb ground beef**

Shape into loaf and place into prepared pan. Bake for 1 hour.

Pour over the top:
> ½ - 1 c Everyday All-purpose Sauce

Bake about 10 minutes longer or until topping is bubbly and glazed. Let sit 5 minutes before cutting and serving.

Variations on a Theme: Use one of the following mixtures to replace the ground beef. Two meats is a good combination; three make a very robust meatloaf.
Equal portions of ground beef, sausage (or ground pork) and venison.
Equal portions of ground turkey or chicken and ground pork.
Equal portions of ground beef and ground pork (or sausage), and bison or lamb.

Everyday Baked Potatoes

This method works equally well for both white and sweet potatoes. Timing depends on your equipment and the number of potatoes.
Scrub well:
> **Potatoes, white or sweet**

Place in a spoke, not touching, on a flat microwave safe plate or pan.
Microwave on high until potatoes yield when gently squeezed, rotating top to bottom halfway through cooking. Start with 6 minutes for one potato; 9 for two.
Remove potatoes from oven and wrap in a clean, thick kitchen towel (preferably terry cloth) and let finish cooking from residual heat 5-8 minutes.
Serve immediately, or let cool, uncovered, to use in Potato Salad or other recipes.

Everyday All-purpose Sauce

This is my go-to sauce for barbeque, meat toppings, baked beans, etc. You can vary it greatly by changing the herbs/spices used, and the heat level (add hot peppers, curry seasoning, etc.). The base recipe uses 1 c Ketchup. You can make various quantities by multiplying the ingredients for each cup of Ketchup used.
Combine:
> **1 c Ketchup**
> **¼ c mustard**

Add:
> **¼ c vinegar**
> **½ c brown sugar**
> **1 T Worcestershire Sauce**
> **1 t paprika or smoked paprika**
> **½ t coarsely ground black pepper**

Everyday Salad Dressing

We used this dressing most often to dress coleslaw. Also, delicious with sliced cucumbers and onions, or as a quick dip with vegetables. This is very good made with half Mayonnaise (or salad dressing) and half Sour Cream.
Combine in a mixing bowl:
> **1 c Mayonnaise or salad dressing**

    1 T vinegar, optional
    1 T sugar
    ¼ t salt and pepper
    2 T milk or cream

Mix well. You want a fairly stiff mixture for slaw and cucumbers. If using to dress a salad of greens, add additional milk or cream, by teaspoonful, if needed to thin dressing to consistency of heavy cream. You can flavor with the same variations as in the *Variations* to Basic Salad Dressing I.

Everyday Quiche

Aunt Mill introduced us to quiche, which she pronounced, "kish." I was immediately hooked and started cooking quiches on a regular basis, especially for breakfast. A traditional quiche is made with only bacon, no cheese. However, you can customize your quiche in infinite ways by varying the addition of meat, vegetables and/or cheese. This is the basic formula. *Note:* use 1 ½ times the filling for a 10-inch quiche. Preheat oven to 375 degrees. Have ready an 8- or 9-inch partially pre-baked Pie Crust Fry until crisp:

    ½ lb bacon

Drain bacon and then crumble coarsely into the crust.
Beat until uniform in color:

    3 eggs

Add:

    1 ½ - 2 c whipping cream or half-and-half
    ½ t salt
    ¼ t pepper
    Dash of nutmeg

Mix well. Pour into pastry shell.
Dot the top with:

    1-2 T butter

Bake 25-30 minutes or until well puffed, and a knife inserted into the center comes out clean.

Variations on a Theme: Use 1 – 1 ½ c total of cooked chopped meat, shredded cheese and cooked diced vegetables to make various quiches. Some of my go-to combinations are: ham, broccoli and white Cheddar cheese; bacon, tomato and mozzarella cheese; chorizo, potato and Monterrey Jack cheese; asparagus, caramelized onions and parmesan cheese; bacon, spinach (cook, chop and squeeze out moisture in a clean towel) and Gruyere cheese.

Everyday Chicken Burgers

These chicken burgers are tender, juicy and flavorful. Mix with a gentle hand and let rest before frying. Especially good fried in rendered chicken fat.
Grate into a large mixing bowl:

    1 medium onion

Add:
>1 egg
>2 T cream or milk
>1 T fresh minced parsley or 1 t dried
>2 t Worcestershire sauce
>½ t paprika
>½ t salt
>½ t pepper
>¼ t minced dried garlic

Mix well.
Add:
>2 slices white sandwich bread made into crumbs
>1 lb ground chicken

Mix gently, but thoroughly.
Let sit 30 minutes.
Heat until hot in a large heavy skillet, preferably cast iron:
>¼ c fat

Using a ½-cup measuring cup, scoop mixture into hot fat in skillet. Flatten to ½ inch with a spatula. Lower heat and gently fry until evenly browned, rotating several times, about 10 minutes. Turn and fry until evenly browned and cooked through, rotating several times, about 10 minutes. Remove fried burgers to a plate, tent with foil and keep warm in a 200-degree oven while frying the remaining burgers.

Everyday Meat Salads or Sandwich Fillings

Any number of salads and sandwich fillings can be made with a few simple, everyday ingredients. These basic recipes can be jazzed up with many imaginative additions: fresh or dried fruits, nuts, chopped vegetables, etc. I use a formula for making these which I apply to the available ingredients on hand. These also lend themselves well to hot dishes. Use to stuff sweet pepper halves (precook in boiling water about 5 minutes, then drain before filling), hallowed tomatoes, or pasta shells. Top these with cracker or potato chip crumbs before baking at 350 degrees about 35 minutes.
The meat:
>1 ½ c meat (canned tuna, crab, shrimp or lobster, or chopped cooked chicken, ham, pork or beef roast, corned beef, tongue, or diced hard-boiled eggs)

The vegetables:
>½ c chopped celery
>¼ c finely diced onion
>2 T finely diced pimiento, optional
>2 T finely chopped Sweet or Dill Pickle (or one of the relishes, drained, in the Canning chapter)

The herbs:
- **1 - 2 T finely chopped fresh herbs or ½ - 1 t dried, or to taste**
  - **Parsley for any of the selected meats**
  - **Dill with tuna, crab, shrimp or lobster**
  - **Tarragon with chicken**
  - **Thyme with ham**
  - **Sage with pork**
  - **Marjoram with beef or tongue**

Corned beef and eggs are best left to their own devices

The binding:
- **¾ c Mayonnaise or Sour Cream or a combination; or**
- **½ c Thousand Island dressing (especially with corned beef)**

Lightly and gently mix all ingredients until well combined.

For salads: Use as a filling for hallowed out tomatoes, avocado halves, lettuce cups, Chinese Cabbage, radicchio or endive leaves, sweet pepper rings, or on a bed of shredded lettuce or salad greens.

For sandwiches: Spread about ½ c on your favorite bread.

For appetizers: Spread about 1 T on your favorite crackers or thin slices of Zucchini Bread, Carrot Bread, Pumpkin Bread, Apple Cheese Bread or Poppy Seed Bread, or use as a filling for Stuffed Mushrooms.

Dips and Dressings, Sauces, Seasonings and Spreads, and Drinks

A selection of various dips, dressings, sauces and seasonings equips the cook to assemble an endless variety of main and side dishes, salads and appetizers.

Chocolate Cheese Ball

I received this recipe from Ava, a former co-worker at Fort Leavenworth. It is a surprising alternative to the usual cheese balls. It goes well with gingersnaps, poppy seed crackers and even jicama. I prefer it made without the cinnamon.

Cream together:
- 1 ½ lb cream cheese, at room temperature
- 1 c sifted powdered sugar
- 1 scant T cinnamon, optional

Stir in until well combined:
- 2 c miniature chocolate chips (preferably semi-sweet)

Roll into a ball and wrap in waxed paper. Chill at least 5 hours or until set. When set, mold into desired shape (e.g., log, egg, round, etc.).

Roll in:
- 1 c finely chopped pecans

With a vegetable peeler, shave onto the top:
- 1 7-oz milk chocolate candy bar

Bring to room temperature before serving.

Boursin

Another wonderful appetizer from Ava. I prefer this version to the ones available in stores.

Cream:
- 8-oz cream cheese, room temperature
- ¼ c butter, room temperature

Mix in:
- ½ t Beau Monde
- 1 medium clove garlic, mashed
- ½ t Herbes de Provence
- 1 t minced parsley
- 1 t red wine vinegar
- 1 t Worcestershire sauce

Chill several hours or overnight to allow flavors to meld. Bring to room temperature before serving

The Cream Cheese Bar

An 8-oz bar of cream cheese, softened, can serve as the base for countless spreads. Serve with toasted French or Italian bread slices, crackers, pita chips or tortilla chips.
Place on a serving platter:
- **1 8-oz bar of cream cheese**

Top with one of the following:
1. Jalapeno pepper jelly
2. Salsa
3. Cocktail Sauce
4. 1 12-oz jar apricot preserves, 1 T Horseradish, 2 T coarse mustard, black pepper to taste

Chili-Rub

This rub is excellent on all cuts of meat. My favorite is to coat chicken breasts and bake at 350 degrees for 45 minutes or until done.
Combine and store in an airtight container:
- **2 T chili powder**
- **1 ½ T ground cumin**
- **2 T paprika**
- **Salt and freshly ground black pepper**

Use as a rub for meats to be grilled, broiled or pan-fried.

BBQ or Barbeque Sauces

— just one example of how varied and personal recipes can be. These sauces range from sweet to spicy hot to vinegary and everything in between. These sauces are very much regional and reflect traditions and tastes of those who make them. I prefer a tomato-based, slightly sweet sauce for most uses.

Barbeque Sauce I

I received this recipe from Aunt Mill.
Combine:
- **1 c catsup**
- **3 T vinegar**
- **1 T Worcestershire Sauce**
- **3 T brown sugar**
- **3 T grated onion**
- **6 T water**
- **Salt and pepper to taste**

Nice to use to dress cooked, pulled meats (beef, chicken, pork) or sausages.

Barbeque Sauce II

Combine equal amounts of Ketchup, mustard and brown sugar. For each cup of Ketchup add:
- **1 T paprika (sweet or smoked)**

1 T Worcestershire Sauce
1 t freshly ground black pepper
2 T vinegar (white, cider or flavored)

Barbeque Sauce III
I like this version, with lemon juice, with chicken and fish; the optional juniper berries are very good with venison.
Mix all together.
>   1 c catsup
>   3 T chopped onion
>   3 T brown sugar
>   6 T lemon juice
>   3 T vinegar
>   1 T Worcestershire Sauce
>   1 t juniper berries, crushed, optional
>   Salt and pepper to taste

Basic Salad Dressings
Salad dressings coming up took one of the three forms provided in this book (see also Everyday Salad Dressing). Which one to use? Your choice.

Basic Salad Dressing I
This is an oil-and-vinegar-based dressing. Also known as a vinaigrette—the traditional does not contain sugar and uses olive oil. See the Notes for variations. Combine in a glass jar with a tight-fitting lid and shake vigorously until smooth and emulsified.
>   ½ c vinegar (white, apple cider, red wine or balsamic)
>   2 T sugar
>   Salt and pepper to taste (start with ¼ t each)
>   1 c oil

Taste and adjust seasonings. Use at once, or cover and let sit (best if using dried herbs for additional flavor) for several hours for flavors to meld. Refrigerate leftovers.

Variations on a Theme:: these are my most-often used variations. Experiment until you find your own favorite or a signature version.

For a creamy dressing: add up to 2 T Mayonnaise or Sour Cream or 1 T prepared mustard.

If you like garlic, mash into a paste one or more peeled garlic cloves and 2-3 pinches of salt.

Add 2 T chopped fresh herbs or 1 t dried herbs according to what you are dressing.

Add 1-2 t seeds (poppy, caraway, celery, mustard, or dill, etc. or a combination) according to what you are dressing.

Add 1 T cracked dried peppercorns (black, white, green or pink)—a great marinade

or sauce for meat.
For an Oriental variety: substitute the vinegar for half rice wine vinegar and half soy sauce; omit salt and pepper; add ½ t hot pepper flakes; substitute 2 T oil with 2 T sesame oil.

Basic Salad Dressing II
This dressing does not contain oil. We used this dressing on leaf lettuce in the Spring and cucumbers in the Summer. Add this dressing to hot fat (bacon drippings or fat from frying meat); heat to boiling and pour over lettuce, spinach or cabbage for a wilted salad.
Combine in a jar with a tight-fitting lid:
- **1 c vinegar**
- **1 c sugar**
- **½ t salt and pepper**

Shake vigorously until the sugar and salt are dissolved. Taste and adjust sugar, salt and/or pepper to taste.

Creamy Oriental Dressing
This is delicious served over a Pasta Salad or a salad of cooked chicken and traditional stir-fry vegetables such as onions, peppers, baby corn, broccoli, snap peas, bamboo and water chestnuts.
Place into a large glass jar with a tight-fitting lid:
- **6 T soy sauce**
- **¼ c olive oil**
- **2 T Mayonnaise**
- **1 T minced garlic**
- **1 T minced, peeled ginger or ½ t ground ginger powder**
- **1 T vinegar**
- **1 T sugar**
- **1 T sesame oil**
- **¾ t hot red pepper flakes**
- **½ t Chinese Five-Spice**
- **1 t sesame seeds**

Cover jar and shake well until emulsified.

French Dressing
This is a delicious salad dressing. Growing up, Father would fry hamburgers and then sauce them with this dressing. He poured it over the hamburgers in the skillet, after draining off the fat, and would cook them until the dressing glazed the hamburgers. Cooked this way, Father elevated hamburgers to something divine. It also makes a good dip for fresh vegetables. I like to use it in Fiesta Salad in place of bottled Catalina dressing.
Mix well in a mixing bowl with a wire whisk, or place in a one-quart jar with a tight-

fitting lid and shake well:
>   1 can condensed tomato soup, undiluted
>   2/3 c sugar
>   2/3 c vinegar
>   1 t salt
>   1 t pepper
>   1 t mustard
>   1 t Worcestershire sauce
>   1 t paprika
>   1 ½ c oil
>   1 T grated onion

Ranch Dressing

A good alternative to the bottled varieties some of which I find have an off taste. I prefer to use Roasted Garlic because the raw garlic taste can sometimes be overwhelming. The same is true for lemon juice. I prefer lime juice in this dressing to provide a subtle acidity. Best made with fresh herbs. Omit the Sour Cream if you want to use as a marinade for meat.

Mash into a paste in a small bowl:
>   1 clove garlic, peeled, or 1 or more Roasted Garlic cloves
>   2-3 pinches salt

Transfer to a jar with a tight-fitting lid and add:
>   ¾ c Buttermilk
>   1/3 c Sour Cream, optional (the dressing will be runny if you don't use)
>   2 T lime juice
>   1 T minced fresh parsley or cilantro
>   1 T snipped fresh chives (or the green part of green onions)
>   Salt and pepper to taste

Shake vigorously until well mixed and emulsified. Use at once, or cover and refrigerate.

Variation on a Theme: a simpler version can be made with 1 large clove garlic, minced, ½ c each Sour Cream, Mayonnaise and Buttermilk, 2 T lime juice, salt and freshly ground pepper.

Rose's Dip

Working at the Finance and Accounting Office at Fort Leavenworth expanded my culinary experience. We never ate many chips and other snacks growing up, and certainly never with a dip of any kind. I got this recipe from my close friend and co-worker, Rose. Beau Monde is a seasoning made from celery seed, onion and salt. A jar will very quickly go rancid or clump if not used soon after opening. I make my own by grinding to a fine powder equal amounts of celery seed, dried onion flakes and sea salt in a spice or coffee grinder.

Mix well in a mixing bowl:
- **1 c Mayonnaise (not salad dressing)**
- **2 c Sour Cream**
- **2 t Beau Monde**
- **2 t dried celery flakes**
- **2 t dried onion flakes**
- **1 t caraway seed**
- **1 ½ t dill weed**

Cover and refrigerate overnight (or make very early in morning) before serving.

Shrimp Dip

I received the best compliment ever for this recipe. Someone told me it was so good she "could bathe in it." I prefer it with crackers or celery sticks.

Have ready a 6-cup mold sprayed with non-stick cooking spray.

Drain, reserving the liquid:
- **2 small cans tiny shrimp**

Soften:
- **1 ½ envelopes unflavored gelatin**

In:
- **¼ c reserved shrimp liquid**

Set aside.

Heat to boiling:
- **1 c condensed tomato soup, undiluted**

Add:
- **8 oz cream cheese, cubed**

Stir until cheese is melted.
Let cool until lukewarm.

Add:
- **Gelatin mixture**
- **1 c Mayonnaise**
- **¾ c each finely diced celery and green onion**

Fold in:
- **Drained shrimp**

Pour into mold. Chill overnight to allow flavors to meld.

Crab Dip

My own recipe perfect for a Summer buffet or any occasion which calls for a sophisticated starter. I created this recipe for a wedding rehearsal dinner when I operated MillRose.

Have ready a 6-cup mold sprayed with non-stick cooking spray.

Grate:
- **1 medium cucumber**

Place in sieve and let drain while proceeding with recipe.

Drain, reserving liquid from:
>   **1 large can crab meat**

Flake crab if it's in large chunks. Set aside.
Soften:
>   **2 envelopes unflavored gelatin**

In:
>   **¼ c + 1 T reserved liquid**

Heat to boiling:
>   **1 c heavy cream**

Add, stirring until melted:
>   **1 lb cream cheese, cubed**

Add:
>   **1 c Mayonnaise**
>   **Cucumber**
>   **Crab meat**
>   **½ c finely diced or grated celery**
>   **1 t caraway seed**
>   **1 t dill weed**
>   **1 t Beau Monde**

Mix well. Pour into mold. Chill overnight to allow flavors to meld.

Reuben Dip

I like to serve this dip with roasted Brussels sprouts, baby carrots, green onions and boiled new potatoes—an appetizer version of a St. Patrick's Day buffet.
Combine in a 1 ½ quart slow cooker:
>   **8 oz deli corned beef, finely diced**
>   **8 oz cream cheese, cubed**
>   **8 oz Sauerkraut, rinsed and drained**
>   **1 c Sour Cream**
>   **1 c shredded Swiss cheese**

Cover and cook on low heat 2 hours or until cheese is melted.

Peanut Butter

I raised peanuts one year while living in Indiana. Peanuts are surprisingly easy to grow, but require special handling after harvesting. Most importantly, they must thoroughly dry before being used because they contain a mild toxin when freshly dug. I have been making my own Peanut Butter for nigh-on 20 years. It is easy to make with a food processor, stores well in the refrigerator and does not separate.
Place in a food processor fitted with a metal blade:
>   **16 oz roasted, unsalted peanuts**

Add:
>   **2 T olive oil, preferably extra virgin**
>   **1 T honey, preferably raw**

¼ t kosher salt

Process at high speed until completely smooth, scraping down the sides of the processor bowl, as needed. This process will take 7-9 minutes depending on the power of the food processor.

Transfer to a glass storage container. Place in the refrigerator, uncovered, until completely cold. Store tightly covered.

Spicy Peanut Sauce

This sauce is a perfect addition to stir-fried vegetables (with or without meat), pasta or sautéed meat (beef, pork, chicken, shrimp).

Combine in blender and whir until thoroughly mixed and homogenous:

- 2 T Peanut Butter
- 2 T soy sauce
- 2 T lemon juice
- 1 clove garlic, minced
- 1 t red pepper flakes
- 1 ½ c hot water (or stock to complement the meat used)

Mole Sauce

A traditional Mexican recipe. This is a delicious alternative to barbeque sauce for chicken, beef, pork, and fish. I sometimes use up to 2 oz of bittersweet chocolate in the recipe. The result is very flavorful.

Blend together in a large saucepan:

- 1 14.5-oz can diced tomatoes
- 1 4-oz can chopped mild green chilies
- ½ c whole blanched almonds, finely ground
- ½ small onion, grated
- 1 clove garlic, minced
- 1 T chili powder (you can vary the heat and flavor depending on what type of chili powder you use: ancho, pasilla, New Mexico, etc.)
- 1 t cumin
- 1 t ground coriander
- 1 t salt
- ¾ t cinnamon
- ½ t sugar
- ½ oz grated unsweetened chocolate

Simmer about 30 minutes to allow flavors to meld.

Thousand Island Dressing

This homemade version is leagues better than anything store-bought. Wonderful served over lettuce wedges, corned beef sandwiches, tomato slices, etc.

Mix in a medium bowl or large glass measuring cup:

- 1 c Mayonnaise

    ¼ c chili sauce, Larry's Taco Sauce or Ketchup
    ¼ minced pimento-stuffed green olives
    1 T minced green bell pepper
    1 T minced onion, regular or green
    1 T capers, drained
    1 T finely chopped Sweet Pickles
    1 hard-boiled egg, peeled and finely chopped, optional

Transfer to a storage container, preferably glass, cover and chill several hours.
Variations on a Theme: add ½ c Sour Cream and use as a dip with fresh vegetables, chips or bread cubes.

Pimento Cheese

I embarked on making my own Pimento Cheese after having several pre-packaged spreads that were disappointing—most often tasting chemical.
Coarsely shred, using the large holes on a box grater:
    1 lb sharp Cheddar cheese
Transfer to large bowl of electric mixer or food processor bowl.
Add:
    3 T grated onion
    1 4-oz jar diced pimentos, drained well
    ½ c Mayonnaise or salad dressing
    1 ½ t prepared mustard
    4 t milk or light cream
    ½ t black pepper, preferably freshly ground
    ¼ t hot pepper sauce, optional

Mix at moderate speed of electric mixer or pulse quickly in food processor just enough to combine the mixture. If it seems too stiff to spread easily, add a little extra milk or cream. Transfer mixture to a storage dish, preferably glass, cover and refrigerate overnight to allow flavors to meld.
Variations on a Theme: this makes a nice dip if you use finely shredded cheese and thin to dunking consistency with additional milk or cream. You can also make a hot dip by baking in a bread bowl.
I first had a grilled Pimento Cheese sandwich in South Carolina. Just substitute Pimento Cheese for other cheese in your favorite grilled cheese sandwich recipe.

Tartar Sauce

I like this made with half Mayonnaise and half Sour Cream. A well-known accompaniment to fish, this is also quite good with sliced tongue for sandwiches.
Combine in a glass storage container:
    1 c Mayonnaise or salad dressing
    ¼ c relish (any one of those in the Canning section), drained, or finely chopped Sweet Pickles
    1 T minced fresh parsley (or 1 t dried)

      1 t minced fresh dill weed (¼ t dried)
      ¼ t black pepper, preferably freshly ground
      ¼ t salt
Cover and refrigerate overnight.

Cocktail Sauce
A zippy sauce to serve with shrimp.
Combine in a glass storage container:
      1 c Ketchup (preferably from the Canning Section)
      1 T prepared Horseradish
      ½ t coarsely ground black pepper
      A dash of lemon juice
Cover and refrigerate overnight.

Hot Barbequed Meatballs
A coworker, Lynne, brought these to the office for one of our Food Days. I was immediately hooked, even though hers were beyond hot. I asked for the recipe, and she gave it to me written in pencil on a yellow sticky note. I still have her original recipe. She listed only ingredients, no measurements or quantities. I present it here just as she provided. The sauce is enough for two pounds of meatballs (the frozen variety, thawed, works just fine).
Mballs
      Hamburger
      Oregano
      Egg
      Cracker crumbs
      Dried diced garlic
      Dried diced green onion flakes
      Diced jalapeno pepper
Mix and shape into balls. Fry or bake until done. Remove to a slow cooker.
Sauce
      Barbeque sauce
      Worcestershire sauce
      Oregano
      Cumin
      Chopped peppers (based on the brand name Lynne provided, I worked out these are crushed red pepper flakes)
      Hot taco seasoning
      Chopped jalapeno peppers
      Jalapeno pepper puree
      Dried diced garlic
      Dried diced onions
Combine all ingredients. Pour over mballs. Cover and cook on low 3-4 hours or until

heated through and sauce is bubbling.

Elderberry Blossom Wine

In addition to his kindness and generosity, Grandfather was known for his wine. Father often told how Grandfather would make barrels of grape wine and leave them to ferment in the barn. Father and his brothers would sample the wine with a clean piece of straw. Grandfather stored the wine in the "cave," i.e., the root cellar. Elderberry bushes grow wild in abundant numbers along roads, creeks, waterways and pastures. In late-Spring, the bushes are covered in masses of large, creamy blooms which have a lovely fragrance. The blooms bear clusters of small, dark, tart berries which are good cooked into jams and juice. The blooms are delicious dipped into a Fritter batter and deep-fried. I got this recipe from Aunt Frieda in the early 1980s. This wine uses the blossoms and is a sweet, delicate wine best used as a cordial.

In large, non-reactive container, place:
1 qt. fresh elderberry blossoms, pulled from stems
Pour over the blossoms:
1 ga. boiling water, preferably fresh well water or bottled spring water
Let stand 1 hour. Strain into a large pot and let stand 1 hour.
Add:
3 pounds sugar; use less for a dry (less sweet) wine
Bring to rolling boil. Skim scum from surface. Remove from heat and let stand until morning.
Add:
Juice of 3 lemons, the lemon pulp and rinds
1 t yeast
Let stand 24 hours. Strain into gallon glass jug. Cover with a piece of cheesecloth. Let sit in cool dark place 3 months before testing. Siphon off wine into clean, sterilized jars (leaving sediment in bottom of gallon container). Seal tightly before storing. Let sit 4 months before serving.

Eggnog

Beat until thick and foamy:
1/3 c sugar
2 egg yolks
Add:
¼ t salt
Stir in:
4 c milk
Cook over medium heat, stirring constantly, until mixture coats the back of a spoon. Cool.
Beat until foamy:
2 egg whites

Gradually add, beating to soft peaks:
> **3 T sugar**

Fold whites into custard along with:
> **1 t vanilla**

Chill 3-4 hours. Pour into punch bowl or cups.
Add, to taste:
> **Brandy or rum (or flavoring)**

Top with:
> **½ c heavy cream, whipped**
> **Ground nutmeg**

Sherbet Punch
Aunts Mill, Marcelline and Geraldine hosted wedding showers for their nieces through the years. They served this punch with other refreshments. The note to this recipe stated, "May use raspberry, too."
Combine in large container:
> **2 pkgs. orange drink mix**
> **1 ga. cold water**
> **1 can unsweetened pineapple juice**
> **1 c sugar, or to taste**

Chill until cold. When ready to serve, add:
> **1 bottle ginger ale, chilled**

Dip into punch or place directly in serving cups and then pour punch over:
> **1 small carton orange sherbet**

Cheese
It's amazing how four simple ingredients—milk (usually from cows, goats or sheep), salt, culture and enzymes—can yield so many fascinatingly distinct cheeses. Cheeses fall into six basic types. As with all other ingredients and foods, it pays to experience a variety of cheeses to find your favorites. Many grocers and department stores feature a wide variety of cheeses and some even have helpful information to guide you through selection, tasting and pairing with other foods and drinks.

Fresh Cheeses – these are soft, have no rinds and are made to be used soon after making. Fresh cheeses include chevre, cream cheese, feta, fresh mozzarella, mascarpone, Neufchâtel, and queso fresco. These cheeses are best served a little cooler than room temperature.

Soft-ripened Cheeses – these fresh and creamy cheeses have soft rinds which may be fuzzy or wrinkly if a natural mold has been added during the cheese-making process. These are best served at room temperature and include Brie, Camembert and soft-ripened goat cheese. Included in this group are also the washed-rind cheeses. As the cheese ages, its rind is washed with a solution of salt-and-water, beer, wine or brandy.

Semisoft and Semihard Cheeses – these have a smooth interior and high moisture content. Whether a cheese is semisoft or semihard depends on aging—the longer a cheese ages, the harder it gets as it loses moisture. Included in this group are American process cheese, Asiago, Bel Paese, brick, Cheddar, Cheshire, Colby, Edam, Gjetost, Gouda, Gruyere, Comte, Havarti, Jarlsberg, Monterey Jack, mozzarella, Muenster, Port du Salut, provolone and Swiss.

Hard Cheeses – these cheeses have low moisture content which causes a firm texture and pungent taste. These are best for grating. Included in this group are Manchego, Parmigiano-Reggiano and Pecorino Romano.

Blue Cheeses – these cheeses have distinctive blue veins created by the addition of mold during the cheese-making process. The flavor ranges from mild to pungent while the texture ranges from soft to creamy to crumbly. These cheeses are also best served at room temperature. Included in this group are gorgonzola, Maytag Blue, Roquefort and Stilton.

2 PLAN OVERS

It seems people have either a love-it or hate-it relationship with leftovers. I know some who cannot abide having leftovers and others who cannot abide throwing away even the smallest amount of food. I am with the latter.

I now use the term "plan overs." A quaint phrase I found in a vintage stove manual. The thought at the time was to plan ahead when cooking to have extra servings available for other meals. I have found plan overs can be used in a number of delicious dishes immediately, or smaller quantities can be frozen to use at a later date. You can purchase many different types and sizes of containers perfect for making your own frozen meals for serving at another time.

It is also well to invest in a counter-top pressure cooker. These latest kitchen wonders are perfect for small batch canning. You do not need to heat a large amount of water and occupy your stovetop for these canners. They hold a few quart or pint jars, and are pretty much hands-off—just fill with jars, attach the cover, set the timer and pressure, and off you can! This makes canning leftover soups, stocks, etc. easy to do. You'll save time and money doing so. It will also provide an excellent way to practice canning to give you confidence to graduate to a full-size pressure cooker to preserve your harvests (or farmers market purchases).

This chapter provides my favorite recipes for using plan overs. These recipes are perfect examples of why it is good practice to plan ahead.

Hash

Most are familiar with Corned Beef Hash. This easy-to-prepare dish can be made with any variety and number of ingredients. Hash takes on the personality of the cook and what's available. We often made hash the day following a supper of pot roast, using the leftover beef roast, potatoes, carrots, onions and gravy.

Cut the meat from a chicken or turkey carcass or from a beef roast; combine it with leftover gravy, vegetables, etc. and reheat it briefly. Never allow to boil or overcook once the meat is added. There should be about half as much gravy as other ingredients. Heat the gravy to boiling, add in the other ingredients and immediately lower heat and let warm thoroughly.

Another way to make hash is what we called a "dry hash." Using this method, heat your choice of fat in a large, heavy skillet until hot—almost smoking hot. Add in chopped meat and vegetables. Flatten evenly to cover bottom of pan. Stir up, flatten and allow bottom to brown again. Repeat several times. Serve hot, passing gravy separately if desired.

Pot Pie

Similar to Hash, Pot Pie is perfectly suitable to plan overs—cooked meats and vegetables in a richly flavored sauce and topped with Everyday Biscuits (especially the Cheddar variation) or Pie Crust. This is a good example of using a basic formula and whatever ingredients you have on-hand or suits your mood. I like to make the sauce

with the stock of whatever meat I am using in the filling.
Preheat oven to 400 degrees. Have ready a lightly greased 2-quart casserole.
Combine in a large mixing bowl:
- **2 c cooked, chopped meat**
- **2 c cooked, chopped vegetables**
- **2 – 3 c Medium White Sauce made with milk, cream, or stock or a combination**

Taste and adjust seasonings, adding fresh or dried herbs, if desired
Turn mixture into the prepared casserole.
Cover tightly and bake about 30 minutes or until filling is bubbling.
Top with:
- **Cheddar Biscuits**
- **Pie Crust, or**
- **Fresh breadcrumbs**

Bake until topping is cooked through and deep golden brown, about 25 minutes.

Potato Plan Overs

Cooking or baking extra potatoes for plan overs isn't too much additional work and requires little, if any, additional time. I've included Potato Salad in this section because you can use extra boiled, baked or Mashed Potatoes to make into a salad. I like this salad on the "dry" side—just enough dressing to bind the ingredients. I've had some salads with so much dressing the result is practically a soup. If fresh herbs are not available, use one-third the amount of dried.

Potato Salad I

Place in a large mixing bowl:
- **4 c warm cooked (boiled or baked) potatoes, peeled or not to your preference and cut in ½-inch cubes or ¼-inch slices**

Sprinkle over and toss lightly with:
- **¼ c white vinegar**

Let potatoes cool to absorb the vinegar.
Add:
- **½ c each chopped onion, celery and sweet pickles**
- **4 hard-boiled eggs, peeled and chopped**

Toss lightly to combine.
In a separate bowl, combine:
- **1 c Mayonnaise or salad dressing (or use half Mayonnaise and half Sour Cream)**
- **2 T prepared mustard, optional (use more or less to your taste)**
- **1 T sugar**
- **2 T chopped parsley**
- **1 T chopped dill weed**
- **½ t caraway seed (optional)**

Pour dressing over potato mixture and fold together. Season to taste with:
>   **Salt and pepper**

Transfer to storage container. Cover and refrigerate several hours or overnight.

Potato Salad II
This and the following recipe are good uses for extra Mashed Potatoes.
Follow the recipe for Salad I, using Mashed Potatoes and omitting the vinegar. This is especially good made using all Sour Cream in the dressing.

Potato Patties
This is an excellent use for extra Mashed Potatoes. Form cooled (room temperature) Mashed Potatoes (either regular or sweet) into patties about 3 inches in diameter and three-quarters-inch thick. Refrigerate, uncovered, overnight (to allow excess moisture to evaporate).

Follow the directions for Bound Breading to coat the patties. Let the patties rest on a wire rack for one hour before frying. Alternately, coat with only flour just before frying.

In heavy skillet, heat just enough fat to cover the bottom over medium heat until hot. Place each patty, in turn, into hot fat in skillet. Fry on each side until deep golden brown and heated through.

Remove to a wire rack set over a shallow pan to drain. Keep warm in a 200-degree oven until all are fried.

Potato Casserole I
Preheat oven to 350 degrees.
Make two layers of the following (in order provided) in a 9x13x2-inch pan:
>   **1 ½ lb baked potatoes, cut into 1-inch cubes**
>   **Salt and pepper**
>   **1 c crumbled, crisp cooked bacon (about 8 slices)**
>   **1 c sliced green onions (white and green parts)**
>   **3 c Sour Cream**
>   **3 c Cheddar cheese, shredded**

Bake 30-35 minutes until heated through and cheese is melted.

Potato Casserole II
A large casserole for a crowd. You can use either leftover boiled or baked potatoes for this casserole.
Preheat oven to 350 degrees. Have ready a greased, shallow 4-quart casserole.
Combine in a large bowl:
>   **8 oz American process cheese, cubed**
>   **1 large onion, finely chopped**
>   **1 large green pepper, chopped**
>   **1 2-oz jar diced pimientos, drained**

>   1 slice bread made into crumbs
>   2 T fresh minced parsley
>   ½ t salt

Set aside.
In prepared pan, layer:
>   12 large potatoes, peeled, cubed and cooked
>   Cheese mixture

Make three layers of each.
Pour over all:
>   ½ c milk
>   ½ c butter, melted

Cover casserole with:
>   1 ½ c crushed cornflakes, butter cracker crumbs or bread crumbs

Cover and bake 45 minutes. Uncover and bake 10-15 minutes or until bubbly and top is browned.
Sprinkle with:
>   1 T minced fresh parsley.

Pasta Plan Overs

Pasta also makes for good plan overs, especially in the form of a salad with endless variations.

Spaghetti Pie

This is an adaptation of the recipe my sister, Ann, received during her Home Economics class.
Preheat oven to 350 degrees. Have ready a 9x13x2-inch pan.
Bring to room temperature:
>   16-oz spaghetti, cooked and drained

In large skillet, cook until done:
>   1 lb ground beef
>   1 medium onion, chopped

Stir in:
>   2 c Spaghetti Sauce

In large bowl, whisk together:
>   2 large eggs
>   ½ c grated Parmesan cheese, preferably fresh
>   5 T butter, melted

Add spaghetti and toss to coat.
Place half of spaghetti in prepared pan.
Make two layers with:
>   Meat mixture
>   2 c 4% Cottage Cheese, preferably small curd, or Ricotta cheese
>   4 c shredded mozzarella cheese

Remaining spaghetti

Cover and bake 40 minutes. Uncover and bake 20-25 minutes longer until cheese has browned.

Pasta Salad

I use Pasta Salad as a main course during the Summer or as a side dish during the other seasons. You really can make this one of your signature dishes based on the ingredients you use and the dressing you choose. I encourage you to explore various meat, vegetable and dressing combinations. You really can't go wrong. The most important steps to complete are: 1) do not rinse the pasta after draining; and 2) let pasta cool completely in a single layer in a sheet pan before making the salad. These steps ensure the pasta does not absorb the dressing and become mushy.

Because this is a "personal" salad, I provide the proportions which work well for me after years of working to develop the perfect Pasta Salad.

Cook according to package directions:

1 lb pasta

Drain and transfer to a baking sheet large enough to hold the pasta in a single layer. Let completely cool before assembling the salad. Can be prepared a few days in advance. Store covered in the refrigerator until ready to use.

A good proportion to make a substantial salad is to add 2 pounds total of the following components:

Raw and cooked vegetables
Meat, poultry or seafood
Mild or strong cheeses
Canned beans (navy, pinto, garbanzo, etc.)
Olives, capers
Nuts
Herbs, fresh or dried
Onion, red, white, yellow or green
Dressing of your choice. One of recipes in the Dips, etc. chapter, or one of the dips thinned to pouring consistency.

Rice Plan Overs

Extra rice, white, brown and wild, can be used in many ways—hot or cold.

Rice Croustades

Combine in a mixing bowl:

2 ½ - 3 c cooked Rice
¾ c thick White Sauce
1 egg yolk
A pinch of nutmeg
Salt and pepper to taste

Pour into buttered 9-inch square pan. Cover with buttered wax paper. Weight by placing another 9-inch square pan on top of wax paper and filling that pan with canned goods. Refrigerate until thoroughly chilled.

Turn out onto board covered with finely crushed cracker crumbs. Cut into rounds. Dip in additional crumbs to coat evenly. Dip into egg/milk mixture (see Bound Breading) and into crumbs again. Place on wire rack and let sit for 30 minutes.

Heat 3 inches of oil or melted shortening in large, deep pan. Heat to 375 degrees. Fry until golden brown and heated through. Delicious served with your favorite fish, and fresh steamed broccoli and mushrooms.

Wild Rice Salad
Combine leftover wild rice with chopped celery and apples, or chopped mixed dried fruits (apricots, cranberries, raisins, cherries, etc.) and toasted walnuts or pecans. Season with freshly ground black pepper and fresh herbs, if desired (parsley, chives, dill, tarragon, thyme and marjoram are all good choices). Dress lightly, just enough to moisten the salad, with Salad Dressing I. Add crumbled blue, feta or queso cheese, if desired. Serve in lettuce cups or hallowed out oranges.

Rice Casserole
This casserole makes good use of rice and cooked meat. You can use this formula to make any number of variations using different meat, cheese and vegetable combinations.

Preheat oven to 350 degrees. Have ready a lightly greased 2-quart casserole. Combine in a large mixing bowl:
    2 c cooked Rice
    2 c shredded cheese
    1 ½ c chopped cooked meat
    1 12-oz can evaporated milk or 1 ½ c half-and-half
    ½ c finely chopped onion
    2 large eggs, lightly beaten
    ¼ c finely chopped cilantro or parsley
    2 T butter, melted
    1 T diced jalapeno peppers, seeds and ribs removed (optional)

Mix well. Pour into prepared casserole. Bake 45-50 minutes or until a sharp knife inserted into center comes out clean. Let sit 5 minutes before cutting and serving.

Variations on a Theme:
Chicken – use chicken and Monterrey Jack cheese.
Cheeseburger – use hamburger, Cheddar cheese, 1 T prepared mustard
Rueben – use corned beef, Swiss cheese, replace cilantro or parsley and jalapenos with ¾ c Sauerkraut, drained and chopped.
Chorizo – use chorizo, queso fresco and ½ t ground cumin.

3 SPRING

Spring was a time of rebirth and growth. Although we would have sunny, warm days well before the Vernal Equinox, for us the beginning of Spring was always marked by planting potatoes and peas (both were always planted on or as close to St. Patrick's Day--March 17-- as possible). We followed these with the first plantings of cool-weather crops that could withstand a light frost such as radishes, lettuces and spinach. Usually before the end of March, or early April at the latest, we would set out the onion plants. A few weeks later, usually in mid-April, we would set out the cabbage and broccoli.

The Spring garden and fields were lovely. The garden provided a feast for the eyes and the nose. Spring flowers, including tulips, daffodils, and peonies would be in bloom for several weeks. The fruit trees and berry bushes would quickly bloom and then set fruit—provided we didn't experience a late freeze! The wheat and oats provided a veritable live carpet of many shades of green. The fields resembled large rambling beings as wave upon wave undulated in the breeze.

Always in Spring, and most often the week after school let out in May, we would clean the entire house from top to bottom. This usually took the entire week by the time we removed all the furniture from the rooms, washed and polished it, washed the windows, doors, moldings and floors. We always applied a fresh coat of wax to the floors and buffed them with a vintage floor polisher Aunt Mill gave to me. Our windows were wood on the inside with triple-paned aluminum windows on the outside. We would remove the screens and storm windows to wash them and always used newspaper to dry the windows, which left them sparkling clean and lint free.

We also got new baby chicks in the Spring. These we coddled by providing plenty of straw, fresh water and warmth from a heat lamp. Later in the Spring or early Summer, we would cull out the males and butcher them. Our favorite chickens were Plymouth Red Rock which provided good meat and plenty of eggs. Father always preferred the brown-shelled eggs. White- or brown-shelled, the eggs were divine—the whites were thickly set, and the yolks were a rich gold-orange color (brought on by the free-range grazing in which we allowed the chickens to engage), and the flavor was exceptional!!

The harvests from our garden began quite early in the season. We usually chose simple preparations that showcased the freshness of the produce and let the flavors of the particular fruit or vegetable take center stage:

Radishes were eaten raw or used in simple sandwiches of white bread, butter and salt. Lettuce (always a loose-leaf variety like Black Seeded Simpson's) was served very simply—usually just a sprinkling of sugar to balance sometimes bitter leaves, or a simple vinegar and sugar mixture (oil was seldom used), or wilted with a hot dressing made with fat from frying the meat served with the meal. We served spinach wilted, too.

Rhubarb—a tart, refreshing vegetable—was made into pies, crisps and cobblers, or baked simply with a bit of sugar, dotted over with butter and then sauced with heavy cream. I also made Gingered Rhubarb Jam spiced with crystalized ginger. The jam was delicious served on toast or hot Biscuits, and as an accompaniment to pork or poultry dishes.

Strawberries were sweet and delicious in Spring. We ate them fresh, and lightly crushed and sweetened on the best Shortcake ever made. We also preserved many quarts by freezing: some we left whole, and others we crushed and sweetened lightly with sugar. We also made Strawberry Preserves.

We got fresh fish—bass, crappie, and catfish—from our own ponds and creek, or we fished the neighbors'. Several times throughout Spring and Summer Father would take us kids and our cousins on great fishing trips, and then we would clean and fry the fish, dividing the bounty among everyone.

Lent, which always started in mid- to late-Winter and culminated in Spring, was a time of fasting and prayer. We didn't eat meat on Fridays, but we didn't miss it for the food served then was every bit as filling and delicious. Most popular were Salmon Patties served with Creamed Peas (except for Father, who did not like peas) and Mashed Potatoes. Occasionally, we would have a Salmon Loaf or salmon Quiche, or even sardines served with saltine crackers and cottage cheese.

Two times a year, my father's family would gather for a potluck dinner—Easter and Christmas. All of Father's brothers and sisters and their children gathered together and shared in the dinner. In the early years, we would gather at either Aunt Mill's, or the house Aunts Marcelline and Geraldine shared. As the family grew, we moved the dinner to the church hall or grade school cafeteria. The grade school was a favorite for years because we had access to the gym and the kids could play basketball, hide-and-seek, or just run around. A few times, we had the family dinner at the local café because Aunt Mill worked there. Fried Chicken with Mashed Potatoes and Cream Gravy took center stage at Easter (Baked Chicken with Dressing at Christmas) and were accompanied by homemade Egg Noodles, a large selection of vegetables, salads and desserts. The most popular dessert of all was Cheryl's Chocolate Dessert.

While the recipes in this section are most appropriate to Spring, you will find each is delicious throughout the year and provide great variety with other seasonal offerings. You will never have a dull menu!

Lenten Meals

Lent always begins mid- or late-Winter and ends in Spring, because Easter is a moveable feast which occurs each year on the "first Sunday after the first full moon of Spring." Meals during Lent, especially on Fridays, were meatless, but always satisfying. Aunt Mill was famous for the Friday luncheons she served at the café in Nortonville. She proposed serving Salmon Patties with Creamed Peas and Mashed Potatoes. That meal was a best seller all the years she worked there.

One Pan Tuna and Noodles
In a three-quart saucepan, cook until tender:
>   ½ c chopped onion

In:
>   **2 T butter**

Add, and bring to a boil:
>   **1 can cream of mushroom soup**
>   **1 soup can milk**
>   **2 soup cans water**
>   **¼ t pepper**
>   **Dash of curry powder, optional**

Add, and cook gently until tender, stirring often:
>   **4 c uncooked wide Egg Noodles**

Add:
>   **1 7-oz can tuna, well drained and flaked**
>   **½ c cubed American cheese**

Stir until cheese is melted. Turn off heat and let stand on burner 10 minutes before serving.

The same can be made in a slow cooker, by sautéing the onions as above. Combine ingredients in slow cooker and cook on the low setting 3 ½ - 4 hours or until noodles are tender. Test beginning after 2 ½ hours of cooking as slow cookers vary. Turn off and let stand 10 minutes, covered.

Salmon Patties
Depending on the size, you can serve these as appetizers (use 2 T per patty), a light luncheon or salad topping (use 1/3 c per patty) or a main course (use ½ c per patty). Drain, reserving liquid in a mixing bowl, from:
>   **1 14.75 – 16-oz can salmon**

Flake salmon in a separate bowl, removing bones.
Add to reserved liquid::
>   **1 small onion, grated**
>   **1 egg**

Mix well.
Stir in:
> ½ tube saltine crackers, finely crushed
> 1 T minced parsley

Add, a tablespoon at a time, if needed, to moisten cracker crumbs:
> **Milk**

Season with:
> **Salt and pepper**

Let sit so crackers can absorb the liquid. The mixture should be soft, but not at all loose or runny.

Add flaked salmon. Mixture should be light and hold its shape when molded into balls.

Heat just enough fat to coat the bottom of a large, heavy skillet until hot. Use a one-half cup measure to spoon salmon mixture into pan, flattening into patties about 1/2-inch thick and three inches in diameter. Fry until golden brown. Turn patties and fry until golden brown. Remove to towel-lined rack to drain. Keep warm in 200-degree oven while frying remaining patties. Makes 4-5 patties. Recipe can easily be doubled or tripled.

Variations on a Theme: you can make these patties with different meats like chopped, cooked beef, corned beef, pork, chicken, turkey, etc. Use two cups of finely chopped meat in place of salmon. You can also make these with fresh salmon by removing the skin from one pound of salmon filets. Cut filets into one-inch pieces and freeze for 15-20 minutes until firm. Pulse the chunks in a food processor until coarsely chopped like sausage. You should have about two cups of chopped salmon. Use in place of the canned salmon.

Salmon Bake

Preheat oven to 350 degrees. Have ready a 2-quart, greased baking dish.
Melt in large saucepan:
> **¼ cup butter**

Add:
> **¼ c flour**

Cook 1 minute.
Add:
> **2 c milk**

Cook until thickened.
Add:
> **1 14.75 – 16-oz can salmon, boned and drained**
> **2 T grated onion**
> **2 oz chopped pimentos, drained**
> **2 c peas, cooked (if using frozen peas, thaw before adding to salmon mixture)**

Place in prepared baking dish. Top with Everyday Biscuits. Bake about 25 minutes.

Salmon Loaf I
Preheat oven to 350 degrees. Have ready a greased 9x5x3-inch loaf pan.
Drain, reserving liquid in a mixing bowl:
> **2 14.75 – 16 oz cans salmon**

Remove skin and bones from salmon and flake into a bowl.
Add to the liquid in the mixing bowl:
> **4 slices bread, shredded or cut into cubes**
> **4 eggs**
> **½ medium onion, grated**
> **1 T minced fresh parsley or 1 t parsley flakes**

Let sit for several minutes, stirring occasionally until bread is thoroughly moistened and mixture is evenly mixed.
Add, if necessary to moisten bread:
> **Milk or cream**

Mix in the salmon and season to taste with:
> **Salt and pepper**

Turn mixture into loaf pan. Bake until a knife inserted in the center comes out clean; about 45 minutes. Let sit in pan 5 minutes before cutting into slices to serve.

Salmon Loaf II
Use the recipe for Salmon Patties, adding ¼ c cream to the egg-crumb mixture which should be about the consistency of cooked oatmeal. Spoon into a well-greased 8x4x3-inch loaf pan. Bake at 350 degrees about 45 minutes or until a knife inserted in center comes out clean. Let rest in pan 5 minutes. Slice and serve.
Ideas for Plan Overs: 1) dredge in flour and fry in hot fat until golden on both sides; or 2) serve at room temperature on shredded lettuce, masked with Mayonnaise or Thousand Island Dressing.

Salmon and Noodle Casserole
Born of necessity. Use Amish egg noodles, if available. These are thicker than other egg noodles and work well in this recipe. Alternately, make your own. To make a complete meal in one casserole, add 2 cups frozen cut green beans or peas, thawed. No need to cook the beans or peas before adding as they will cook in the oven.
Preheat oven to 350 degrees. Have ready a buttered 2-quart casserole.
Cook in boiling, salted water until noodles are done:
> **½ lb wide egg noodles**
> **1 c thinly sliced celery**
> **1 T dried, minced onion**
> **1 T dried parsley**

Drain well.
Drain, reserving liquid in a 2-cup glass measuring cup:
> **1 14.75 – 16-oz can salmon**

Break salmon into large junks, removing skin and bones. Add to noodle mixture in

large bowl.
Add water or milk to the salmon liquid to make 2 cups
Melt in a saucepan:
>	¼ c butter

Add and cook one minute:
>	¼ c flour

Add salmon liquid mixture. Bring to boil. Cook 2 minutes.
Add:
>	**1 can cream of potato soup**

Mix well. Taste and season with salt, if needed, and pepper. Pour over salmon and noodles. Mix well. Turn into casserole. Bake 25-30 minutes or until bubbling and top is lightly browned.

Sardines

We occasionally had sardines during Lent. Father especially liked them. We didn't do anything fancy with them in terms of cooking or preparing. Most often we ate them out of the can with saltine crackers and Cottage Cheese and lots of black pepper. Something I still enjoy today. Few other fish are as healthful, sustainable and affordable as sardines. Simple arrangements are best to enjoy this flavorful fish:
Make an open-faced sandwich with bread, Mayonnaise, sardines, sliced cucumber, shredded carrot and cilantro.
Top with a relish of pine nuts, capers and golden raisins.
Layer with pasta, sautéed onions and breadcrumbs.
Spread sardines canned in tomato sauce on thick slices of toasted bread and top with shredded lettuce.
Mix with eggs, breadcrumbs and parsley; fry to make sardine fritters (similar to Salmon Patties).

Corned Beef Dinner

St. Patrick's Day, March 17, invariably occurs during Lent and, even though technically it is still Winter, I have included recipes here with Corned Beef. It was quite some time after leaving the farm that I explored Corned Beef, and now I like to serve it more often than just on St. Patrick's Day. It was not long ago I tackled how to cook a complete Corned Beef Dinner using one pot and cooking everything at the same time. The solution: the slow cooker and the following layering technique. Select a head of cabbage with its outer leaves attached and evenly sized vegetables to ensure all cook in the same time. The following is designed to serve four and uses a 6-quart slow cooker. Use the leftover Corned Beef to make Hash or Reuben Casserole. Note: if your slow cooker is not large enough to hold all the ingredients, use a tightly covered kettle. Bring the water to the boil while assembling the pot and then bake, tightly covered, at 250 degrees about 6 hours or until done.
Place in a slow cooker:
>	**3 lb Corned Beef brisket**

If using the seasoning packet provided, tie the contents in a square of cheesecloth. Add to cover by one-half inch:
> **Water**

Cover and turn on to the "low" setting while preparing the vegetables.
Remove the large outer leaves from:
> **1 head green cabbage**

Wash the leaves and set aside. Quarter the cabbage, leaving the core intact.
Peel and cut in half, leaving the root end intact (just trim any remaining roots):
> **2 large onions**

Peel and cut crosswise in half:
> **2 large carrots**

Wash and dry:
> **4 medium size potatoes**

Place the large cabbage leaves on top of the brisket with the curved side down forming "bowls" in which to place the vegetables. Place into the leaves the prepared vegetables. Cover the slow cooker and cook on low about 6 hours or until the brisket is fork-tender and the vegetables are cooked through.

Divide the vegetables among four serving plates. Slice and plate the brisket.

Cool the leftover brisket in the broth in the slow cooker before removing to a separate bowl and refrigerating.

Rueben Casserole

This casserole is perfect for those who like Rueben sandwiches, but are watching their carbohydrates. I found this recipe in Aunts Marcelline's and Geraldine's recipe box on a slip of paper labeled "Kitchen Scribbles." It's worth buying and preparing an entire brisket. However, I find a pound of deli corned beef, sliced thick, works very well.

Preheat oven to 350 degrees. Have ready a 2 ½-quart casserole.
Layer in the casserole in the following order:
> **1 pint Sauerkraut, drained**
> **1 lb Corned Beef, chopped**
> **2 c grated Swiss cheese**

Combine and pour evenly over the layers in the casserole:
> **¼ c Thousand Island dressing**
> **½ c Mayonnaise**

Top, in a single layer, with:
> **2 tomatoes, cut into thick slices (about ½-inch)**

Cut slices, if needed, to fit in the casserole.
Spread over all:
> **1 ½ c fresh bread crumbs**

Bake about 40-45 minutes or until heated through and bread crumbs are deeply browned. Remove from oven. Let sit 5 minutes before cutting and serving.

Breakfast

It seems only appropriate to include Breakfast recipes in the Spring section because breakfast begins the day as Spring begins the year—not according to the calendar, but according to the cycle of life on the farm.

Growing up, weekday breakfasts consisted of cold cereal with milk and juice in Spring and Summer, and oatmeal or Cream of Wheat in the Fall and Winter. Occasionally, we had toast, too. Sunday breakfasts, though, were feasts with bacon (or sausage) and eggs, some type of bread—toast, French Toast, Pancakes, or Waffles, Fried Potatoes and occasionally fruit of some variety. We most often scrambled our eggs, but sometimes Father would fix them omelet style with cheese, or fry them.

Eggs

This is a delicious breakfast casserole. Delores, one of my first supervisors, gave the recipe to me titled simply "Eggs." I still have her hand-written recipe. This recipe uses O'Brien potatoes (diced potatoes with onions and peppers). *Note*: if the potatoes are frozen into a solid mass (or multiple large masses), drop the package from on high several times onto a table or countertop to break into individual pieces. Alternately, you can thaw the potatoes. If you do, reduce temperate to 325 degrees.
Preheat oven to 350 degrees.
Melt in a large glass baking dish (I use a 9x13x2-inch pan) while preparing eggs:
- **¼ lb butter**

Mix well in a large mixing bowl:
- **18 eggs**

Add:
- **1 12-oz can evaporated milk**
- **1 t salt**
- **1 t pepper**
- **1 pkg. frozen O'Brien potatoes**

Pour into pan after butter melts completely.
Sprinkle evenly over the top:
- **1 c mixed grated cheese (Cheddar and mozzarella)**

Bake, stirring several times during baking until eggs are set, but not dry, throughout.

Scrambled Eggs

Farm fresh eggs are utterly delicious, and not like the insipid ovals sold in stores today. Both white- and brown-shelled eggs are delicious, although my family always preferred brown-shelled eggs. To scramble eggs that are light and fluffy, I heat a cast-iron pan in a 350-degree oven (often while cooking the bacon or ham) until it is thoroughly heated and very hot (contrary to years of advice that eggs should be

cooked gently over low heat). Transfer the pan to a burner set on medium-high heat. Use roughly 1 ¼ teaspoon fat for each egg. To prevent cooked eggs from "watering," combine the following mixture and let sit for at least 15 minutes. For a luxurious treat, substitute heavy cream for the milk.
To serve two:
Beat well:
> **4 eggs**

Add for each egg:
> **½ T milk (or 1 T heavy cream)**
> **A big pinch of salt and several grinds of black pepper**

When thoroughly mixed and fat is hot, swirl skillet to evenly distribute the hot fat. Pour in the eggs and let cook undisturbed for a few seconds until the edges are set. Shuffle the outer edges into the center of the pan, folding all the while. Cook quickly and briefly before turning out onto hot plates.

Variation on a Theme: Cut two slices bread (preferably Everyday Bread) into ½-inch cubes. Toast cubes on baking sheet in 350-degree oven until lightly toasted. Fold into beaten egg mixture just before pouring into hot skillet. The combination of toasted bread with the scrambled eggs is delightful!

Soft Fried Eggs

These eggs are somewhere between a fried egg—they start out that way—and a poached egg.
In a large skillet with a tight fitting cover, heat until hot:
> **4 T oil**

Add:
> **2 T butter**

When butter has melted and quits foaming, break into the skillet, spacing evenly:
> **4 eggs**

After the last egg has been added, pour **¼ cup hot water** around the outside edge of the pan. Cover tightly, increase heat and cook over medium-high heat to desired doneness (about 2 minutes for very soft, liquid centers). Remove with slotted spatula to heated plates.

You can increase this to include as many eggs as will fit into the pan in one layer.

Breakfast Bars

Preheat oven to 350 degrees. Grease and flour a 10x15x1-inch jelly roll pan.
Beat together with an electric mixer:
> **1 c butter, softened**
> **1 ½ c sugar**

Beat until light and fluffy.
Beat in, one at a time:
> **4 eggs**

And then:
> **1 t vanilla**
> **1 t almond extract**

Sift together:
> **3 c flour**
> **1 ½ t baking powder**

Stir flour mixture into butter mixture.
Spread three-fourths of the batter into prepared pan.
Spoon evenly over the top:
> **1 can of your favorite pie filling**

Spoon, by teaspoon, the remaining batter over the filling.
Bake about 25 minutes until golden brown.

Oven Baked Meats

This is the only way I cook bacon and ham for breakfast now because it is so easy. Also, bacon doesn't curl with this method, no matter how thinly sliced it is. On the farm, we always had fresh, uncured (often called "green") bacon. If you have fresh bacon, liberally season with salt and pepper before baking.

Line a heavy-gauge, large, rimmed baking sheet with aluminum foil. Add in slices of bacon or ham (or a combination) in a single layer. Bake at 350 degrees 15-25 minutes, turning once, or until desired doneness is reached (longer cooking will result in crispier meat). Drain on a layer of paper towels that has been laid on top of several sheets of newspaper. Strain, cool, cover and refrigerate drippings to use in other recipes.

Sausage Potato Casserole

Preheat oven to 350 degrees. Have ready an 11x7x2-inch pan.
In skillet, cook until no longer pink:
> **1 lb bulk sausage**

Drain.
Combine:
> **1 can cream of mushroom soup**
> **¾ c milk**
> **½ t salt**
> **¼ t pepper**

Make two layers of the following in the pan:
> **3 c thinly sliced potatoes**
> **Sausage**
> **Soup mixture**

Cover and bake for 1 ½ hours. Uncover and sprinkle with:
> **1 c shredded Cheddar cheese**

Return to oven and bake until cheese is melted.

Let cool in pan 5 minutes before cutting and serving.

Fried Cornmeal Mush

This is an easy, comforting and filling breakfast dish that is equally good either served right from the pot, or poured into a pan, chilled, sliced and then browned in hot fat (the same as Scrapple).
Bring to boil in a large saucepan:
>3 c water

Combine:
>1 c yellow cornmeal
>1 c cold water
>1 t salt
>1 t sugar

Gradually add to boiling water, stirring constantly. Cook until thick, stirring frequently. Continue to cook over low heat about 10 minutes. Remove from heat. Serve spooned onto plates or into bowls. Serve with butter and syrup, or topped with poached eggs, crumbled bacon and shredded cheese.

Alternately, scrape cooked meal into greased 8x4x2-inch loaf pan. Chill overnight. Turn out of pan. Slice 1/2" thick. Coat slices in flour, shaking off excess. Fry slowly in hot fat, turning once. Serve with butter and syrup.

Waffles

A good all-purpose recipe. You can omit the sugar if serving as a savory main dish, but I find the waffles will not brown as nicely. A fond memory is having waffles with sausages for Saturday night supper. I recall watching "Wild Kingdom" and "Hee-Haw" while Mother and Father prepared supper. Many waffle recipes call for egg whites to be beaten stiff and folded into the batter. I have found this is an extra step with no value added. You will obtain perfectly acceptable results blending the whole eggs into the batter as in this recipe.
Heat a waffle iron according to manufacturer's directions.
Sift together in a large mixing bowl:
>1 ¾ c sifted flour
>3 t baking powder
>1 T sugar, optional
>½ t salt

Combine in a separate bowl:
>2 eggs, beaten
>1 ¾ c milk
>½ c oil

Quickly and gently stir liquid ingredients into dry only until moistened, making sure to scrape the bottom of the bowl. Do not worry if there are lumps. Overbeating the batter will result in poor waffles. The batter will seem to be thin, but this is as it should be. Bake in hot waffle iron according to manufacturer's directions, using a

1/3-cup measure to ladle the batter into the iron. Be sure each section has at least a thin layer of batter, which will spread when the iron is shut, to ensure completely formed waffles. Place cooked waffles on a wire rack set over a baking sheet and keep warm in a 200-degree oven while cooking the remaining batter.

Make ahead: waffles freeze very well in airtight plastic freezer bags. Reheat in a 350-degree oven on a rack set in a baking sheet or in a toaster, on lowest setting, until heated through.

Pancakes

Pancakes, like Waffles, require a light hand when mixing. You can vary these by topping with a tablespoon of: miniature chocolate chips; finely chopped nuts, dried fruits, apples or pears; blueberries, raspberries, or blackberries; or, for a savory presentation, finely chopped onions sautéed in butter, or fried, crumbled bacon. Measure all ingredients. Heat a cast iron pan or griddle over medium heat while mixing the batter.

Sift together into a large mixing bowl:
- **1 ¼ c sifted flour**
- **3 t baking powder**
- **1 T sugar**
- **½ t salt**

Combine in a separate bowl or glass measure:
- **1 egg, beaten**
- **1 c milk**
- **2 T oil**

Quickly and gently stir liquid ingredients into dry, stirring only until dry ingredients are moistened, making sure to scrape the bottom of the bowl. Test heat the skillet or griddle by sprinkling on a drop of water which should sizzle and dance on the pan. Continue to heat until it does. Brush with oil, shortening or lard to grease evenly. Pour 1/3 c batter onto pan. Fry until bubbles break the surface. Sprinkle evenly with additions, if using. Turn and continue to cook for about 3 minutes or until done. Remove to a rack set over a metal baking pan. Place in 200-degree oven to keep warm while cooking remaining pancakes.

French Toast

All of the breads in this book make wonderful French Toast. The Whole Wheat Bread is especially hearty and makes for a good breakfast in advance of a lot of work or other physical activity. Do try Everyday Bread made with golden raisins in this recipe. Whichever the bread, I lightly toast the bread slices and pierce multiple times with a fork before dipping into the egg mixture so that the bread soaks up the egg mixture. The following is sufficient for 6 slices of bread cut 1/2-inch thick. Heat a large skillet, preferably cast iron, over medium heat while making the batter.

Lightly toast:
- **6 slices of bread**

Combine until well mixed and emulsified:
- **3 large eggs, well beaten before adding the other ingredients**
- **¼ c cream**
- **2 T milk**
- **1 T sugar**
- **¼ t salt**
- **½ t vanilla**

Add fat (I like to use a combination of lard and butter) to skillet to evenly coat the bottom.

Dip bread into egg mixture, pricking in several places with a fork, turn to coat second side. Let excess egg mixture drip from each slice. Add to skillet, being sure not to crowd the slices. Fry slowly until evenly browned on both sides. Remove to a wire rack set over a baking sheet and keep warm in a 200-degree oven until all slices have been fried. Replenish fat in skillet, as needed. Serve hot with butter, syrup, jelly, sugar (granulated or powdered), etc.

Easter Dinner

Father's family gathered for years for Easter and Christmas dinner (see the introduction to "Spring.") Featured here are recipes for my favorite additions to the buffet.

Potato Refrigerator Rolls

These small, cinnamon-flavored rolls (always crowned with a perfect, plump pecan half) were a staple at the family Christmas and Easter potluck dinners. These rolls are best when made small—flatten the dough wide enough to roll no more than three times after filling with cinnamon and sugar. Also, slice the rolls about ½-inch wide. The slow initial rising in the refrigerator develops their unique flavor and texture. Aunt Marcelline made these rolls in cupcake pans, with a pecan half in the bottom, and with just a dusting of sugar and cinnamon as the filling.

Peel, slice and cook in boiling water until very tender:
- **2 large potatoes**

Drain, reserving cooking water, mash, measure out and cool to lukewarm:
- **1 c Mashed Potatoes**

Measure into a large mixing bowl:
- **1 ½ c reserved potato cooking water (add water if needed to make 1 ½ c)**

Stir in until dissolved:
- **2 pkgs. active dry yeast**

Add and mix well:
- **2/3 c sugar**
- **1 ½ t salt**
- **2 eggs, room temperature**
- **2/3 c lard or butter, melted or cooled**
- **1 c lukewarm Mashed Potatoes**

Add by hand until dough is easy to handle:
- **7 – 7 ½ c flour**

Turn out onto lightly floured board and knead until smooth and elastic. Place in greased bowl. Lightly oil top of dough and cover with a damp cloth. Place in refrigerator to rise about 2 hours before baking.

Preheat oven to 350 degrees.

Shape dough into rolls, coffee cake, etc. Cover with damp towel and let rise until double. Bake 20-25 minutes or until done. Turn out onto wire rack to cool thoroughly before storing in an airtight container.

Cheryl's Chocolate Dessert
This dessert was one of the staples—and most popular—at the Weishaar family Christmas and Easter dinners. Cheryl was a hairdresser in town before she married cousin Larry who was the town barber into 2020. For years I enjoyed and admired the dessert before working up the nerve to ask her for the recipe. One year we exchanged recipes. I received this one in exchange for my recipe for Broccoli and Rice Casserole.
Note: Cheryl's recipe called for a 9x13x2-inch pan. However, that makes an extremely thin dessert. I prefer a 9x9x2-inch pan.
Preheat oven to 350 degrees. Grease baking pan.
Combine:
>   **1 c flour**
>   **2 T sugar**
>   **½ c butter, softened**

Press mixture into greased pan.
Sprinkle top with:
>   **½ c finely chopped nuts (walnuts or pecans)**

Bake for 12 minutes or just until set (crust should not begin to brown, but should be firm throughout). Remove from oven and let cool.
Cream:
>   **8 oz cream cheese, softened and at room temperature**
>   **2/3 c powdered sugar, sifted**

Spread on cooled crust.
Prepare according to package directions:
>   **1 large box instant chocolate pudding**

Spread on top of cream cheese layer. Spread over pudding:
>   **1 8 – 9-oz container frozen, non-dairy whipped topping, thawed**

Sprinkle chocolate chips over. (Cousin Cheryl precisely placed single chips atop the dessert to designate 20 individual servings in a 9x13-inch pan—use nine if using a 9-inch pan). Chill thoroughly before cutting and serving.

Broccoli and Rice Casserole
This casserole has been a staple at holiday dinners for years. It is easy to make and serves a crowd. It is equally delicious made with fresh or frozen broccoli.
Preheat oven to 350 degrees. Have ready a lightly buttered 2 ½-quart casserole dish.
Cook according to the master recipe:
>   **1 c Rice**

Cut florets from:
>   **1 large head broccoli** (or use two 10-oz packages frozen broccoli, thawed).

Peel and coarsely chop stems.
Blanch in boiling, salted water 5 minutes or until tender. Drain.

In large bowl, combine:
- **2 cans cream of mushroom soup**
- **1 soup can milk**
- **Freshly ground black pepper**
- **Pinch of nutmeg**

Add in rice and broccoli. Mix to blend. Fold in:
- **8 oz Cheddar cheese, cut into ½" cubes**

Turn mixture into prepared casserole dish.
Melt in skillet over medium heat:
- **¼ c butter**

When foaming ceases, add in:
- **1 c butter cracker crumbs or dry bread crumbs**

Stir and cook until lightly toasted, about 5 minutes. Spread crumbs atop casserole. Bake about 30 minutes or until casserole is bubbling and crumbs are golden brown.

Variation on a Theme: I have also made this casserole with the newly popular **Cauliflower Rice**. It is easiest prepared using a food processor. Take one head of washed cauliflower, cut into 1-inch pieces. Pulse in batches in the food processor with the metal blade until evenly cut to the size of rice. You should have about 4 cups. Melt 2 T butter or heat 2 T olive oil in a large skillet. When hot, add in the riced cauliflower. Cook about 10 minutes until heated through, stirring several times. Remove from heat and let cool. Proceed with the recipe, substituting this cauliflower "rice" for the Rice and adding 2 t cornstarch with the milk.. Alternately, you can use commercially prepared fresh or frozen cauliflower rice. If using the frozen variety, thaw and drain before assembling the casserole.

Spring Fruits and Vegetables

The following fruits and vegetables are typically planted and harvested in the Spring (and early Summer, if you're lucky). This section, as well as the sections in the Summer and Fall chapters, includes those we grew on the family farm as well as those I have grown or use regularly. There are tips for selecting (if you don't grow your own), storing and preparing along with some recipes which prominently feature, or showcase, particular selections.

Asparagus – one of the first vegetables ready for picking in Spring. If not picked, the young shoots grown into tall ferny branches with bright red berries. Asparagus is easy to grow, and an established bed will be productive for 20 years or more. Control the weeds, fertilize freely and mulch heavily. Asparagus should be picked when the shoots are eight inches high and the buds at the tip of the stems are still tightly compressed. The picking season is over when stems no longer grow larger than ½-inch in diameter. To pick asparagus, bend the stems until they snap; the portion that is too tough to snap is also too tough to eat.

If purchasing asparagus from the grocer or farmers market, select crisp, tightly closed stalks whose cut ends are not dry.

To store: place in a container of water to cover the ends and store in the refrigerator.

To prepare: wash stalks. Hold each spear with one hand at the base of the stalk and the other hand an inch or two farther toward the tip. Bend the spear. It will break at the point where the tender stalk starts to toughen. I peel large, thick stalks and leave the peel on thin stalks (about the size of a pencil and thinner).

Asparagus responds best to simple preparations—steamed, boiled, sautéed, or stir-fried.

To boil: Use a deep skillet large enough to hold the spears in one layer. Bring 5 cups water and 1 T salt to the boil. Lay in the spears. Bring rapidly back to the boil and cook until the point of a sharp knife easily pierces the stalk. Time will range from 4-10 minutes depending on the thickness of the spears. Drain and serve with lots of melted butter.

Roasted Asparagus

An easy preparation with infinite variations possible by varying the fat, herbs and other seasonings used to flavor the asparagus.

Preheat oven to 400 degrees. Have ready a large baking sheet lined with aluminum foil, parchment paper or a silicone baking mat.

Snap off bottoms and peel:
> **1 lb asparagus**

Arrange prepared spears in a single layer in pan and drizzle over very lightly:
> **Olive oil**

Toss spears to coat lightly. Roast until tender, but still slightly firm, 8-10 minutes. Sprinkle with:
> **Salt and freshly ground black pepper**

Variations on a Theme: after initial roast, sprinkle lightly with lemon juice and freshly grated Parmesan cheese. Return to oven, reduced to 350 degrees, and bake 3-5 minutes or until cheese is melted.

Use up to 2 tablespoons of fresh minced herbs such as parsley, tarragon and/or chives, depending on what you are serving; minced orange rind, a splash of fresh orange juice and toasted hazelnuts; a blend of poppy and sesame seeds; minced fresh ginger, garlic and sesame oil; or walnut oil, crumbled goat cheese and toasted walnuts.

Cactus – the large, flat, fleshy, oval green pods of the nopal cactus have the texture of green pepper or green beans when cooked, but are viscous like okra. The flavor is something between green pepper and asparagus—unique and delicious. Nopals are available all year-round, especially in Mexican markets. The boiled, grilled or roasted nopals make a fine addition to the menu, especially in Winter when fresh vegetables, in season, are desired. They are good in salads, tacos, omelets and casseroles.

If purchasing cactus paddles from the grocer or farmers market, select nopales that do not have any soft or wrinkled or dark spots and those with as few thorns as possible. Most will have had their thorns removed or be a so-called spineless variety. Paddles should be brightly colored and stiff. Flacid paddles usually do not refresh even when placed in water. I have found size does not affect flavor or tenderness, and larger ones are easier to prepare.

To store: place in plastic bags in the refrigerator crisper.

To prepare: use a scissors to trim the outside edges. Cut off the thick base. Use a knife or a vegetable peeler to remove the little dark bumps that held the thorns. I have found after years of preparing fresh nopals a tweezer works perfectly to pop out the bumps. Cut into slices ¼-inch thick or squares up to ¾-inch.

To boil: cook in a large quantity of salted, boiling water until tender, but not soft, 10-15 minutes. Start testing before the minimum time. Drain well and, if not using immediately or if using in a cold salad, plunge into a large quantity of ice water to stop the cooking. Drain before using or serving.

To roast: toss the prepared nopals in 1 T oil. Place on a foil-lined baking sheet and roast at 375 degrees about 20 minutes or until tender and all exuded liquid has evaporated.

To grill: rub whole prepared paddles with oil and grill slowly until tender. Excellent in tacos.

Nopales Salad

A quick salad that is excellent for a Southwestern or Mexican buffet.
Combine in any proportion:
> **Sliced, cooked nopales**
> **Diced tomatoes**

    Diced onions
    Diced jalapeno peppers (seeds and ribs removed for less heat)
Toss well.
Season to taste with:
    Lime juice
    Chopped fresh cilantro
    Salt
Serve chilled or at room temperature.

Nopales Pie

Similar to a crust-less quiche. It comes together quickly, and the Variations are all worth a try. Perfect for Lenten meals.
Preheat oven to 350 degrees. Have ready a lightly buttered 10-inch pie pan.
Cook over medium heat until soft, but not browned:
    3 medium onions, thinly sliced
In:
    2 T oil
Add:
    2 c prepared, diced nopales
Cook until beginning to brown.
In a large bowl, beat to blend:
    6 eggs
    ½ c cream
Add:
    1 c soft bread crumbs
    ½ c grated Parmesan cheese
    ¼ c minced cilantro
    2 T minced parsley
Add onion-nopales mixture.
Mix well.
Turn into prepared pie pan. Bake about 25-30 minutes or until knife inserted in center comes out clean.

Variations on a Theme:
Onion Pie – use 6-8 medium onions, cook until soft, but not browned; omit nopales and cilantro; increase parsley to ½ c.
Potato Pie – use 2 c diced, boiled potatoes in place of nopales; omit cilantro; increase parsley to ½ c and add 1 ½ t minced fresh thyme, sage or marjoram leaves.

Dandelions - One of the things I remember when we visited Aunt Mill and Grandma was the immaculate lawn and garden she kept. She loathed dandelions and used an old long-bladed butcher knife to remove the plants from the lawn. I never knew her to use any type of pesticide or herbicide on her lawn or in her garden. I have come to appreciate dandelions. They dot the landscape in early Spring with

brightly colored blossoms.
The young leaves provide a pleasantly bitter addition to salads. The blossoms also make a fine wine—actually more like a liqueur similar to Drambuie.

Dandelion Wine
I have been making this wine for several years. I made this one year with honey (use half as much honey as sugar) and the result was delicious! I now make this with ½ cup of honey because it has naturally occurring antibacterial and preservative qualities.
Pick early in the day when the blossoms first open:
   1 ga. dandelion blossoms
Be sure to remove any stems.
Place the blossoms in a large crock, or glass or other non-reactive container.
Add:
   1 orange, scrubbed and sliced, optional
Pour over:
   5 qts. boiling noncarbonated spring, well or bottled water
Cover with a clean cloth and let sit in a warm place 3 days.
Strain through a thin, clean and odor-free cloth into a clean container.
Stir in:
   3 lb sugar
   ½ c raw, natural honey
Pour into a clean glass jar. Cover with a clean cloth and leave in a warm draft-free place 3 weeks. Check daily. The wine should bubble and have a slight alcohol aroma. Strain into clean, dry jars (like glass canning jars). If you want a bubbly wine, cover tightly and store in a dry, dark place about 4 months before using.
Alternately, cover the jars with a clean cloth and let sit in the same place about 4 weeks, or until the wine is no longer effervescent. Strain into clean, dry jars and seal.
Variations on a Theme: you can add ½ t yeast to the wine after straining the blossoms to increase the alcohol content.

Lettuce – salads are the best use for lettuces of all type. Nothing beats iceberg lettuce for crispness. A simple salad, great any time of year is a wedge of iceberg lettuce served with your favorite dressing, chopped hard-boiled egg, crisp bacon and a sprinkling of freshly grated Parmesan cheese.
A recent en vogue use of lettuce is to replace bread, rolls, tortillas, etc. for sandwiches or wraps. You can also use leaves to wrap whole fish or fillets for steaming. See also Peas with Lettuce.

Peas – fresh peas are a feast from Spring through early Summer. Peas are easy to grow beginning in early Spring as soon as the soil can be worked. It is best to grow on a trellis so the vines remain upright and the pea pods fully develop. Peas are delicious simply boiled or steamed and served as is.

If purchasing peas from the grocer or farmers market, select medium-sized pods that are bright green, moist, firm and filled end-to-end with fat peas.

To prepare: wash the peas, then shell them into a bowl. Snap off the stem end and pull it down the side—a string will come with it opening the pod.

To boil: bring 8 c of water and 1 t salt to a boil. Add the shelled peas, bring water to boiling again, and cook, uncovered, just until tender, 4-10 minutes, depending on size. Drain and serve hot.

To steam: place peas in a steamer basket over 1-2 inches boiling water and cook, covered, until tender, 5-10 minutes, stirring once or twice during cooking.

Creamed Peas

Empty into a medium saucepan:
- **1 can green peas**

Add to turn liquid in the pan white and to barely cover the peas:
- **Milk**

You should have slightly more than 1 cup liquid.

Add and begin to heat:
- **2 T butter**

Combine in a small bowl, whisking until well blended:
- **3 T sugar**
- **2 T flour**
- **Salt and Pepper**

Stir into peas. Cook, stirring constantly until mixture comes to a boil. Stirring constantly, boil for 1 minute. Taste and adjust seasonings, if needed.

You can make this dish with cooked fresh peas, or with a 10-ounce package of frozen peas, thawed. Use all milk for the liquid (about 1 c) to barely cover the peas. Simmer about 10 minutes until peas are tender and then continue with the recipe.

Peas in Cream

Another option is to use extra cream. In which case, cover fresh peas in heavy cream, omitting the butter, sugar and flour and cook slowly until peas are tender and cream has reduced and thickened. Season with salt and pepper to taste only after the cream has reduced; otherwise, the peas may be too salty.

A very useful item, which is in little use today, was the wood cook stove. It provided a steady source of heat with which foods could cook slowly or remain warm for serving for an extended period. Absent that, a slow cooker set to "low" and left uncovered will also work. Timing depends on the size and wattage of your slow cooker. Peas can be kept warm over hot water until ready to serve.

Peas and Lettuce

There are two ways to cook peas with lettuce, which is a good way to cook more mature peas.

Peas and Lettuce I

Place in a large, heavy-bottomed saucepan:
- **2 lb fresh peas (about 3 c, shelled)**
- **1 medium head Boston or Iceberg lettuce, washed and shredded**
- **½ t salt**
- **1-2 T sugar**
- **4 T minced green onions**
- **4 T butter, softened**

Squeeze roughly with hands to bruise the peas. Add cold water so peas are barely covered. Set over medium-high heat, cover and boil until tender, testing peas for tenderness after 15 minutes. Uncover and continue boiling until peas are tender and liquid is evaporated. Season with additional salt, if needed and serve.

Peas and Lettuce II

Remove core and flesh, leaving a ½-inch thick wall, from:
- **1 large head Iceberg lettuce**

Shred inner flesh and reserve.
Place lettuce, open end up, in a pot just large enough to hold the lettuce.
Place in a mixing bowl:
- **Fresh shelled peas, or frozen peas, thawed**

Depending on the size of the head of lettuce, you'll need about 2 c.
Season with:
- **Salt**
- **Pepper**
- **Sugar**
- **Butter, softened**

Transfer peas to lettuce "bowl."
Cover top with reserved shredded lettuce.
Add water to the pot, outside the lettuce "bowl" to the depth of 2 inches.
Cover pot tightly and bring to boil. Reduce heat and simmer until peas have steamed until tender, 30-40 minutes.
Remove peas to serving bowl. Discard lettuce or reserve to serve at another time.
Variation on a Theme: Drain the cooked lettuce. Coarsely chop and place on a clean kitchen towel. Wring tightly to remove excess moisture. Combine with leftover peas. Heat in a skillet with 2 T butter. Moisten with heavy cream and season with salt, pepper and parsley.

Peas and Carrots
A classic duet.
Combine in any proportion:
- **Hot cooked carrots**
- **Hot cooked peas**

Drain well and dress with melted butter, chopped fresh parsley, salt and freshly ground black pepper.

Purslane – Considered a weed in many parts of the country, purslane has been eaten for centuries in other parts of the world. Juan introduced me to purslane; something his mother called "caletes" (ironically, Spanish for "weed").
Collect purslane from late Spring into mid-Summer while the leaves are tender. Purslane has purplish colored, succulent stems and small oval jade-green leaves. Also, it is important to note when the stem is broken, the sap is clear. Avoid a similar looking plant that has a milky sap. You are not likely to find purslane at the grocer or farmers market. If you don't have it growing wild in your yard or garden, you can purchase seeds to get started. Purslane is prolific and will self-seed year-to-year if given full sun and a weed-free patch. Excess can be fed to the chickens or hogs.
To store: place in plastic bags in the refrigerator crisper.
To prepare: Wash to remove dust and grit.
Use purslane leaves in salads or cook as you would spinach, including creaming. I especially like purslane creamed in a medium White Sauce with diced, cooked chicken or ham as a luncheon course or light Summer supper. Purslane is also delicious sautéed in bacon drippings. Serve as-is, or garnish with crisp crumbled bacon.

Purslane Salad I
Prepare and dice:
- **2 tomatoes, cored and seeds removed**
- **1 cucumber, peeled**

Place in salad bowl and add:
- **6 oz purslane leaves**
- **4 oz feta cheese, crumbled**

Combine in a covered jar:
- **2 T lemon juice**
- **2 T olive oil**
- **1 T minced onion**
- **Salt and pepper to taste**

Shake well.
Pour dressing over salad. Let sit at least 30 minutes to allow flavors to meld.

Purslane Salad II
Combine in a large salad bowl:
> 2 c cherry and/or pear tomatoes
> 8 oz fresh mozzarella pearls
> 2 c purslane leaves
> ¼ c chopped fresh basil

Pour over all:
> ¼ c olive oil

Mix well.
Season to taste with:
> **Kosher salt**
> **Pepper**

Let sit at room temperature before serving to allow flavors to meld and for tomatoes to release some of their juices. Toss well before serving.

Radishes – another easy-to-grow vegetable that does well both in the ground, and in pots or planters. Sow early and every two weeks to ensure a successive harvest. Provide plenty of water to prevent bitterness or excessive heat. Harvest by pulling, retaining stems and roots. Wash well soon after harvesting. Small, tender leaves may be added raw to salads; mature, but not bitter, leaves can be cooked like turnip or Beet Greens.

If purchasing radishes from the grocer or farmers market, select crisp, solid radishes with no blemishes, cuts or soft spots, preferably with leaves and roots still attached. To store: place in plastic bags in the refrigerator crisper. Crisp, or slightly wilted, radishes can be revived by soaking in ice water. You can also store the radishes in a bowl of water in the refrigerator.

To prepare: wash and trim off leaves and root end.

Serve raw with dips, or sliced or diced in salads, or with softened sweet butter, sea salt and freshly ground black pepper (an excellent accompaniment to ice-cold beer). Slice thinly and sandwich on cocktail bread spread with Mayonnaise or butter and serve with tea, cocktails or as appetizers.

Radishes are also delicious served cooked. Cut large radishes into halves or quarters; otherwise cook whole, or slice for a quick stir-fry. Cook gently over medium heat in 1 T butter and ½ c chicken stock, covered, until tender, 3-4 minutes. Uncover, increase heat to medium-high, and boil rapidly to reduce pan juices while shaking pan a few times.

Roast as for asparagus, seasoning with olive oil, salt and pepper. Adjust cooking time depending on size.

Rhubarb – One of the most versatile products of the garden in Spring, rhubarb is technically a vegetable, but is often prepared like a fruit—in pies, cobblers, jams, relishes, etc. Available principally in April, May and June (an old adage is to stop harvesting rhubarb on July 4 so the plants can develop and save energy through

Summer for the next year). A rhubarb plant can be productive for many years if properly planted and cared for.

If purchasing rhubarb at the grocer or farmers market, choose crisp, firm stalks, ideally no more than one-inch wide, and deep red in color. If leaves are attached, they should be crisp.

To store: wrap in plastic or place in plastic bags and store in the refrigerator crisper.

To prepare: wash well in cool water. Remove leaves and immediately discard; the leaves are mildly toxic.

Rhubarb is quite simply delicious. Some think rhubarb is too tart to eat raw, but I like it finely diced in salsa. You can easily prepare it by chopping, mixing with a bit of sugar to taste and then baking, adding a bit of heavy cream toward the end. You can also poach it in a saucepan in a similar manner. I find people most often err by making rhubarb too sweet. The tart flavor is refreshing, especially with rich game or meat dishes. In addition to pies and cobblers, rhubarb makes a great addition to muffins, cakes and breads. It freezes well—simply wash, chop into ½" pieces and freeze on cookies sheets until solid. Place frozen rhubarb in large freezer containers and simply remove the amount needed.

Nutty Rhubarb Muffins

Dawn, a former co-worker gave this recipe to me, along with a recipe for Rhubarb Bread. She returned home to Iowa every year to get rhubarb from her mother. I think she probably enjoys rhubarb more than I.

Preheat oven to 350 degrees. Line 12 muffin cups with paper cupcake liners.
Combine in a small mixing bowl and set aside while preparing the batter:
- **¼ c brown sugar**
- **¼ c chopped nuts**
- **½ t cinnamon**

Mix well in large mixing bowl:
- **¾ c brown sugar**
- **½ c Buttermilk**
- **1/3 c oil**
- **1 egg**
- **1 t vanilla**

Combine in another mixing bowl:
- **2 c flour**
- **½ t baking soda**
- **½ t salt**
- **1 c finely diced rhubarb**
- **½ c chopped nuts**

Add dry ingredients to Buttermilk mixture. Stir only until combined. Fill paper-lined baking cups 2/3 full. Top with sugar-nut mixture. Bake about 20 minutes or until knife inserted into center comes out clean. Let sit in pan 5 minutes after removing from oven. Remove from pan to wire rack to cool.

Gingered Rhubarb Jam
This is the very first jam I made on my own. It is easy to make and a good spread for toast, a filling for tarts, or a condiment with pork, goose, or game.
Combine in a large saucepan and let stand about 15 minutes or until sugar is moistened by juice:
- 4 c thinly sliced fresh rhubarb
- 3 c sugar
- ¼ c finely snipped candied ginger
- 2 T lemon juice

Cook over medium-high heat, stirring frequently till thick and clear, 12-15 minutes. Skim off foam. Ladle into hot, sterilized ½-pint jars. Seal and process 10 minutes in a boiling-water bath (see the Canning and Preserving chapter).

Rhubarb Bars
From Aunt Mill's recipe box. Equally good made with frozen rhubarb, thawed, in the Winter.
Preheat oven to 375 degrees. Have ready a lightly greased 9x13x2-inch pan.
Cook until thick:
- 3 c chopped rhubarb
- 2 T cornstarch
- 1 ½ c sugar
- ¼ c water

Stir in:
- 1 t vanilla

Cool mixture.
Mix until crumbly in a medium mixing bowl:
- 1 ½ c oatmeal
- 1 ½ c flour
- 1 t baking soda
- 1 c brown sugar
- 1 c butter, softened
- ½ c chopped nuts

Press three-quarters of mixture into prepared pan. Pour cooled rhubarb mixture over crust; spread evenly. Top evenly with remaining crumb mixture. Bake about 30 minutes or until golden brown.

Rhubarb Sauce
This sauce is especially good with pheasant, duck, goose, venison and bison. It pairs well with chicken, turkey and pork, too. You can use any type of vinegar in this recipe; however, balsamic provides an exceptional depth of flavor.
Bring to a boil, uncovered, in a large saucepan, in water to cover:
- 5 c sliced fresh or frozen rhubarb

Cook until just tender, 8-10 minutes.
Drain well; return to pan; mash until blended.
In a large kettle or Dutch oven, heat:
> **3 T fat**

Add:
> **1 medium onion, chopped**
> **4 cloves garlic, minced**

Cook until tender, about five minutes.
Stir in:
> **Mashed rhubarb**
> **1 c packed brown sugar**
> **¾ c Ketchup**
> **½ c vinegar**
> **¼ soy sauce**
> **¼ c honey or molasses**
> **2 T Worcestershire sauce**
> **1 t crushed red pepper flakes, optional**
> **1 t coarsely ground pepper**

Cook over low heat, stirring often, until slightly thickened, about 30 minutes.
Cool, then stir in:
> **½ c bourbon**

Rhubarb Upside-Down Cake

Preheat oven to 350 degrees. Have ready two lightly greased 8x8x2-inch cake pans.
Divide evenly and place in the bottom of each pan:
> **4 ½ c diced rhubarb**
> **15 large Marshmallows, halved**
> **1 c + 2 T sugar**

In large mixing bowl, cream:
> **¾ c butter, softened**
> **1 ½ c sugar**

Beat in:
> **3 eggs**

Mix until light and fluffy.
Sift together:
> **2 ½ c + 2 T flour**
> **4 ½ t baking powder**
> **¼ t salt**

Add dry ingredients to creamed mixture alternately with:
> **¾ c milk**

Divide evenly between pans.
Bake about 25-30 minutes or until tester inserted in the center comes out clean.
Cool in pan on wire rack 5 minutes.

Loosen edge of cake from pan with a knife.
Remove from pan to a serving platter. Serve warm with Whipped Cream.

Spinach – this bright green vegetable, rich in iron and vitamins, is at its peak in the cool of Spring and Fall. Spinach is easy to grow and well worth having a short row or large planter of it in Spring and Fall. Spinach can stand a light frost.
If purchasing spinach from the grocer or farmers market, try to select individual leaves that are bright and crisp.
To store: place in plastic bags in the refrigerator crisper.
To prepare: wash thoroughly just before cooking. Cut off stems. If using for salads, it is well to run through a salad spinner to remove excess water, or lay on a clean kitchen towel, roll up and refrigerate until needed. Either cook the leaves whole or stack leaves and cut crosswise into thin ribbons.
The easiest way to cook spinach is to heat a pan large enough to hold the raw spinach leaves. Add the spinach, with water still clinging to it. Cover the pan and cook until the spinach is tender, stirring several times during cooking. Remove the cover and cook a few additional minutes to evaporate any remaining moisture. Serve as is, or with butter, salt and pepper.

Creamed Spinach
Creamed Spinach is a nice dish to serve with a variety of main dishes. It is easy to prepare, and you can season it as much or as little as you like. It is a good use for frozen and canned spinach, too. Thaw frozen spinach before creaming. Chop both frozen and canned varieties and wring out in a clean, odor-free towel to remove excess moisture. Two versions are provided: one uses a basic White Sauce; one uses heavy cream.

Creamed Spinach I
Cook spinach as above and press out as much moisture as possible. Bring to a boil in a large skillet:
> ½ **c heavy cream.**

Add the cooked spinach, and season to taste with:
> **Salt**
> **Freshly grated nutmeg**
> **Ground black pepper**

Cook over medium heat until cream is reduced, about 3 minutes.

Creamed Spinach II
Cook and press spinach as above. Combine with one-third as much medium White Sauce seasoned with a dash of nutmeg. Thin, if needed, with cream.

Strawberries – most plentiful between late-Spring and mid-Summer, strawberries are best if obtained locally or self-grown. The berries sold in grocery stores are harvested before ripe and never achieve their glorious nature if not vine-ripened. There are available now many ingenious tools to grow strawberries in even the smallest spaces. These include strawberry pots, tiered raised beds and others. Consult a good horticulture book for instructions to grow. You won't be disappointed!

If purchasing strawberries from the grocer or farmers market, try to select individual berries with the hull (leaves and stems still on – removing the hull exposes the berries to spoilage). Do not wash until ready to use.

To store: place in a shallow container, preferably in a single layer, cover lightly and store on the refrigerator shelf.

To prepare: wash only if commercially grown, or if from your garden to remove mud. A light toss in a clean kitchen towel will remove any dust. Remove the hull and halve, slice, or dice before serving.

Strawberry Preserves

Place in large glass, enamel or stainless steel saucepan:
- **1 qt. strawberries**
- **2 T vinegar**

Cook gently until berries make juice. Boil 3 minutes.
Add:
- **4 c sugar**

Boil 6 minutes. Let cool, shaking pan gently to help berries absorb liquid. Fill jars, seal and process 10 minutes in a boiling-water bath (see the Canning and Preserving chapter).

Shortcake

If ever there was a dessert that screams "Spring!" this is the one. Hot from the oven, sliced into wedges and topped with fresh-picked strawberries, lightly crushed and macerated with sugar, and topped with Whipped Cream combines to make a thoroughly enjoyable event. This is also equally delicious with frozen strawberries. We would freeze perfectly ripe strawberries, lightly crushed and mixed with sugar for serving throughout Winter. We also froze whole berries that were delicious with oatmeal for breakfast, or mixed with other frozen fruit (rhubarb, gooseberries) to make pies. If you find yourself with leftover shortcake (a rarity!), serve it reheated for breakfast spread with soft butter and liberally sprinkled with cinnamon and sugar.

Preheat oven to 350 degrees. Lightly grease a 9-inch glass pie pan.
Sift together:
- **2 c flour**
- **4 t baking powder**
- **½ t cream of tartar**
- **½ t salt**
- **2 T sugar**

Cut in until mixture resembles cornmeal:
- **½ c fat (butter, lard or shortening)**

Beat well in a glass measuring cup:
>**1 egg**

Fill cup to 2/3 mark with:
>**Milk**

Add to dry ingredients. Mix quickly and gently just until dry ingredients are evenly moistened.

Press lightly into prepared pan, forming 1-inch-wide ridge around edge. Sprinkle top with granulated sugar. Bake about 30 minutes or until done and top is golden brown. Serve hot cut into wedges and topped with sugared strawberries and Whipped Cream.

Variation on a Theme: During Summer, you can substitute for the strawberries sliced and sugared peaches, nectarines, apricots, raspberries or blackberries, or a combination.

Fresh Strawberry Pie

All of Aunt Mill's and Mother's pies were delicious, but this pie was especially welcome in Spring with the first fresh fruit of the season after having pies throughout Winter made from frozen or canned fruit.

Have ready:
>**1 fully baked 9-inch Pie Crust**

In a small saucepan, crush:
>**1 c fresh strawberries**
>**1 c water**

Bring to boiling; then simmer 2 minutes. Sieve berry mixture into a bowl, pressing on solids to extract all the berry juice. Discard remaining solids or feed to the chickens.

Combine in a medium saucepan:
>**¾ c sugar**
>**3 T cornstarch**

Stir in sieved berry mixture. Cook over medium heat stirring constantly, till strawberry glaze is thickened and clear. Spread about ¼ c glaze into bottom of pie crust.

Arrange, stem end down, in pastry shell:
>**3 c fresh whole strawberries**

Carefully spoon half of glaze over berries, making sure all are covered.

Add another layer, filling in all gaps, using:
>**3 c fresh whole strawberries**
>**The remaining glaze**

Chill at least 3-4 hours before serving with Whipped Cream.

4 SUMMER

Summer was the height of activity on the farm. We planted the crops, baled the hay and the garden was full of bounty. We canned many jars of green beans, tomatoes, Sauerkraut and pickles to carry us through the Winter. We ate the fresh vegetables daily, too. Summer also was the time to enjoy what the garden and field provided, including:
Cantaloupe with plenty of salt and pepper (either each one singly or together).
Fried fish we caught ourselves from our own ponds and creek. We used fishing poles, trout lines and seines. One Summer we caught a large crappie that was a pure gold color. We thought it was a giant goldfish and kept it for a while in a water tank. Fishing on Sunday afternoons was always an adventure. Father would take the family and several of our cousins fishing at the neighbors'. We would pile into Old Blue (a Chevy pickup which at the time was relatively new and had a blue cab). Sometimes we would journey to a pond that could only be accessed by driving past an ancient cemetery that was reported to be haunted. It seemed forever away, but was actually closer than we'd ever want it to be. Bass were plentiful in that pond, and after an afternoon of fishing my brother and Father would clean the fish and then Father would fry it for all. We served it with French-fried potatoes or Hush Puppies and coleslaw. Mother made a very simple yet pleasantly refreshing coleslaw by shredding cabbage on the fine holes of a grater and then dressing it with an equal amount of vinegar and sugar.
We picked mulberries during the Summer. These juicy, purple, and occasionally white, berries grew on very large trees along the creek and the road. We had a particularly productive tree just down the hill from our house. It produced large, juicy black-purple berries. We also had a most interesting tree that grew at the edge of a windbreak of cedar trees along the west side of the house. That tree was interesting because it produced white mulberries. We would use clean fruit cans, made into berry buckets by punching holes into opposite sides and using baling wire to form the handles, to carry the berries. Birds love mulberries and will take to them over any other fruit. It pays to have a mulberry tree in your orchard—if only for the birds—to save other fruit that ripens around the same time such as cherries, raspberries, strawberries and apricots. A mulberry pie is a treat! Make it just like a raspberry or blackberry pie, but use much less sugar as it is easy to over-sweeten the fruit. In fact, a splash of lemon juice provides a bright counterpoint to temper the sweetness. You may also use a good-quality cider or raspberry vinegar in place of the lemon juice.
We didn't use a lot of chemicals in the fields when we were growing up. Father and we four kids would spend late Spring and early Summer mornings picking up rocks in the fields and using a hoe to cut out weeds. A person hasn't worked if he or she hasn't picked up rocks or cut weeds out of 20 acres of soybeans or corn. One year, my brother, oldest sister and I cut thistles out of the neighbor's pasture which was just across the road from our fields. There were probably four hundred thirty-seven thousand five hundred twenty-three thistles in that pasture which we dug out with

dirt shovels and then chopped off the blossoms so those would not open and scatter seeds into our fields and three surrounding counties. It was hard work, and it was rewarding. As Aunt Mill, often said, "Work is a blessing," and "You can rest when you're dead."

Speaking of rest, it was easy to sleep, despite not having central air conditioning, after working like that all day. We didn't have central air conditioning growing up. In fact, the family home didn't have it until 2007 when I restored the house. I was actually fortunate in that regard because the dorms I lived in at university also did not have air conditioning—and that was in the late 1980s and early 1990s.

For years the social event of the year was the annual Church Picnic. This was a community affair. The parishioners donated all the food, and auction and bingo prizes. Father and the menfolk would construct the various game stands, a hamburger/hot dog stand, and a large area for the auction and bingo—all set in the street between our church and the parish school (which Grandfather and relatives built in 1951). We had a potluck dinner which people from miles around would attend. I recall Mother and Father frying chicken, making Waldorf Salad and pies for the dinner. It took most of the day, and then we'd all pack into the car and drive to the school for an evening of good food and entertainment. There was usually a dance in the school gym, too. The menfolk also gathered the next day to take down the stands and store the materials in the church basement for the next year. The only game of bingo I've won in my life was at one of the church picnics. It was a $10 prize—which I had to share with Aunt Mill because she bought my bingo card!

Summer Fruits and Vegetables

This section includes recipes that feature Summer fruits and vegetables as the main ingredient to showcase the best of each. Recipes which contain Summer fruits and vegetables are included in the appropriate section, e.g., Breads, Canning and Preserving, etc.

Apricots – the three most delicious experiences in the world are fresh tomatoes, strawberries and apricots. Nothing in the world, in my opinion, tops the vine- or tree-ripened taste and flavor of this triad. You can ripen the fruit by placing in a brown paper bag and leaving at room temperature for a few days (check daily) until softened, ripe and fragrant.
If purchasing from the grocer or farmers market, select fruits that are free of spots, bruises or shriveled skins.
To store: place in perforated plastic bags in the refrigerator. Do not wash before storing.
To prepare: wash, cut in half and remove the seed. There is no need to peel apricots.

Avocados – most are familiar with the green avocados: Hass, a purplish-black, pebbly skinned avocado of the Guatemalan type which can weigh as much as 8 ounces and has twice as much fat as the Mexican type of avocado with smooth green skin. These are available year-round. There is also a yellow-skinned West Indian avocado.
If purchasing from the grocer or farmers market, choose unblemished fruit that is heavy for its size, ideally one that gives slightly when gently pressed between your hands.
To store: not all avocados may be ripe when you buy them. Place them in a paper bag on the countertop and they will ripen in about 3 days. Refrigerate ripe avocados for a few days. Overripe fruit can be used for mashing, but are not attractive for slicing.
To prepare: cut in half, remove the pit by whacking with a sharp knife, gently twisting and pulling free and release the flesh from the skin with a spoon. Insert the spoon at a side-ways angle starting at the top and sliding the spoon down the side, around the bottom and up the other side to release the fruit in a whole piece. You can make dicing extremely easy and efficient by slicing through the flesh while still in the skin from top-to-bottom and side-to-side the length and width of the avocado, but don't cut through the skin, in whatever size you desire. Remove as for a whole half.

Guacamole

I like my guacamole very simple. However, you can vary it by adding diced jalapeno peppers and/or tomatoes, cumin and/or chili powder and/or oregano leaves, or just about anything that strikes your fancy. Epazote is an herb native to Mexico, and easy to grow, that has a fresh grassy flavor. It adds a delicious piquancy to guacamole. These proportions are for 1 avocado. I like to allow 1 per person, but I always find there is never any left.

Peel, remove the pit, and coarsely mash:
> 1 avocado

Add:
> 2 T grated onion
> 1 T minced fresh cilantro leaves
> 1 T minced fresh epazote leaves, optional
> 1 T fresh lime juice
> ¼ t salt

Mix well. Mash again if you prefer a smooth sauce.
Cover with plastic wrap placed directly on the surface and let stand for a few minutes to let the flavors meld before serving.

Avocado Filling
A good base recipe with many possibilities that make fine additions to a Mexican or southwestern style supper.

Peel and remove pits from:
> 3 avocados

Place in the bowl of a food processor along with:
> 8 oz cream cheese, at room temperature
> 2 T minced green onions
> 1 clove garlic, finely minced
> 1 T lime juice
> 3 T minced fresh cilantro leaves
> 1 T minced fresh epazote leaves, optional
> ¾ t chili powder
> ½ t cumin
> 1 t salt
> ¼ c peeled, seeded and chopped tomato

Process until it is a smooth, firm puree. Taste and add more salt, if desired.

Variations on a Theme:
Stuffed Tomatoes – remove the tops from cherry tomatoes or use small tomatoes cut in half. Scoop out the insides, removing flesh and seeds, leaving only a shell. Lightly salt the insides and drain upside down on a kitchen towel for at least 30 minutes. Fill with avocado mixture. Top with Sour Cream and sliced black olives, if desired.

Avocado Tart – spread filling evenly into a prebaked Pie Crust made in a 9x1-inch tart pan. Cover with a thin layer of Sour Cream. Sprinkle the top with minced fresh cilantro or parsley, and finely chopped pistachios or sunflower seeds.

Beets - delicious with their sweet, earthy taste and very easy to grow in both Spring and Fall. I plant heirloom varieties including Bull's Blood, Detroit Dark Red and Ruby Queen. They can be boiled or baked in their skins like potatoes. Beets also preserve excellently both plain and pickled. The leaves (beet greens) are delicious used young in salads or cooked, if mature.

If buying beets from the grocer, try to choose those with the leaves and tap root still attached. Beets should be smooth and firm with no holes, soft spots, cuts or other blemishes.

To store: beets, leaves trimmed and scrubbed to remove all traces of soil, will keep for weeks in plastic bags in the refrigerator crisper.

To prepare: scrub well under running water. Always cook beets with the root and about one-inch of the leaf stems still attached. Refer to individual recipes for further preparation.

To boil: prepare as above. Cook in a large quantity of boiling, salted water until a knife easily runs through the beets. Drain and let cool until you can easily handle the beets to remove root and stems. The peels will easily rub off.

To bake: prepare as above. Wrap tightly in aluminum foil. Bake at 400 degrees until a knife easily runs through the beets.

Beet Greens

This method works well with other greens (kale, collards, mustard, Swiss Chard, etc.) and young leaves from radishes, kohlrabis and broccoli. Bull's Blood beets provide the best greens. A splash of apple cider vinegar provides a crisp, refreshing flavor to the cooked greens. You can also trim the long, thick stems and cook as for Green Beans II. Greens and stems freeze well in plastic bags.

Wash and remove the stems from:
   3 lb beet leaves

Do not drain or shake the water from the leaves.
Place leaves in a large pot or skillet.
Cover tightly and heat slowly until leaves start to wilt and release their juices.
Gradually increase heat and bring to boiling. Uncover and cook until leaves are just tender.
Cook until any remaining liquid has evaporated
Season to taste with:
   Salt
   Pepper
   Butter or bacon drippings
   A splash of vinegar

Beans, Green and Wax – formerly called string beans because you had to remove the strings which held the two halves together, have in many instances been hybridized so that now they snap clean and need only to have the ends snipped. However, to save time, I remove only the stem end, leaving the tail end intact. We always planted the Contender variety which produced straight, long, tender pods which are good fresh, canned and frozen. Yellow beans, also called wax beans, are delicious, too, and a component of Three Bean Salad. Cherokee Wax is my favored variety. Yellow beans are delicious also served hot or cold like green beans and provide variety to the Summer menu as wells as Fall and Winter menus using the canned or frozen versions. Both green and wax beans are easy to grow and produce abundantly provided adequate moisture and frequent picking.

Rafa, my Black Labrador, loved green beans. When he was young, he would follow me down the row as I picked the beans. I would occasionally toss one to him. He eventually learned to pick the beans himself!

If buying green or wax beans from the grocer or farmers market, select firm beans that do not have any cuts, breaks, brown or soft spots or holes. Store in plastic bags in the refrigerator crisper.

To prepare: wash in cold water to remove any dirt or dust. Remove tops and tails (if desired).

Cooked beans lend themselves to endless variations. There are two ways to cook beans. The first is a long cooking that renders the beans very tender and a dull gray-green or yellow color. The second is a quick blanching that renders the beans just tender, with a bit of crunch, and a bright green or yellow color. Both are equally delicious. Father always preferred his beans cooked the first way which is how we always had them growing up.

Green Beans I

Prepare enough green beans to serve the number being served. I usually allow one-half pound per person. Place beans in a large stockpot. Add water to cover and 1 T salt to each gallon of water. Cover and bring to a boil. Place lid askew of pot and continue to boil until beans are very tender. Depending on the maturity of the beans, this can take from 30 minutes to 1 hour. Drain well and serve hot.

Variations on a Theme: You can add a ham bone or a piece of salt pork to add flavor.

Green Beans II

Prepare green beans. I usually allow one-half pound per person. Bring a large stockpot of salted water (see above) to a boil. Add beans. Immediately begin timing for 5 minutes for beans that will be tender, but firm. Alternately, for softer beans, bring water to a rapid boil again, and boil, uncovered, exactly 5 minutes. Drain immediately and serve hot. If serving cold, drain and plunge immediately into a large bowl or sink full of ice water to stop the cooking. Drain well and turn out onto sheet pans lined with clean towels to drain. Refrigerate if not using immediately. These cooked beans are a great addition to the vegetable-and-dip tray.

Asian Green Beans
My version of a popular Asian Buffet dish.
Heat, in a large skillet, until hot:
    1 T peanut oil
Add:
    2 cloves garlic, minced
Cook until garlic is fragrant, but not browned.
Add and cook until heated through and beans are glazed:
    1 lb Green Beans II
    1 ½ T sesame seeds
    1 T sugar
    2 T oyster (fish) sauce
    2 t soy sauce
    1 t sesame oil

Berries – Raspberries, blackberries, loganberries, Marion berries, tayberries, dewberries, thimbleberries and wineberries are all bramble berries—that is, they grow on bushes, typically with thorns. However, recent developments have provided us with thornless berry bushes. Red and black raspberries and blackberries are what we had growing up. Heritage and Jewel are two good heirloom red and black raspberries, respectively. I have since branched out by growing yellow (gold or amber) and purple raspberries. The blackberries of fond memory were smaller than varieties today. We picked from bushes which grew along the side of the road. They were about the size of the pinky fingertip and well flavored. Raspberries and blackberries make good pies, tarts, jams, jellies and are delicious served fresh with a bit of sugar and cream. Both freeze well. Simply place in a single layer on a rimmed baking sheet; freeze solid; and then transfer to plastic freezer bags or containers.

Blueberries – blue on the outside and green on the inside, cultivated berries are much larger than their wild forebears. The Maine wild blueberry is small but intensely flavored. Blueberries can grow into very large bushes, but need well-drained, acidic soil and lots of organic matter. However, the care they require repays the owner with many luscious berries to use in jams, jellies, sauces, pies, muffins and cakes. Blueberries dry, freeze and can well.
If purchasing blueberries from the grocer or farmers market, choose plump, sound berries covered with bloom, a whitish coating that preserves moisture and extends storage longer than other berries.
To store: refrigerate in a covered container.
To prepare: Wash well and drain before following individual recipe directions.

Fresh Blueberry Filling, Topping or Compote
This method of preparing blueberries retains the tart freshness and juiciness of the blueberries. It is good to use as a filling for tarts, a topping for a butter cake or cheesecake, or served spooned into glasses and layered with Whipped Cream.

Combine in a 1-quart saucepan:
   1 T cornstarch
   1/3 c sugar
Stir in:
   ½ c water
Bring to a boil and cook for 1 minute or until thick and translucent.
Stir in all at once:
   3 c fresh blueberries
Toss until evenly coated with the glaze.
Turn the berries into a colander suspended over a bowl to drain excess glaze.
Variation on a Theme:
Lemon-Blueberry Tart – Preheat oven to 300 degrees. Prepare one recipe Lemon Curd and turn into a prebaked 9-inch Pie Crust. Bake about 8 minutes or until almost set (it should just jiggle when the pan is moved side-to-side). Spoon glazed berries evenly over to top of cooled tart.
Blueberry Tarts – fill Meringue Shells with the blueberries and serve with Whipped Cream.
Blueberry Compote – alternate layers of blueberry mixture and Whipped Cream in glasses; sprinkle the top with graham cracker or vanilla wafer crumbs or toasted coconut.

Broccoli – I plant broccoli in early Spring for an early Summer harvest and then again in late Summer for a Fall harvest. I prefer the Packman variety because it produces large, tender, mild heads and is prolific. I leave the plants to grow side shoots after harvesting the main head. This provides me with broccoli all through the Summer and Fall up until the first hard frost.
If buying from the grocer or farmers market, pick the head with the tiniest buds. You should not see any yellow (which are flowers forming); this is a sign the broccoli is overly mature and likely bitter. If the head you buy has leaves (in fact, I suggest you buy the head with the most leaves), save those and cook as you would cabbage or Beet Greens.
To store: cut a slice from the bottom of the stem and store in a container of water in the refrigerator, covered with a plastic storage bag; otherwise, store in a perforated plastic bag in the refrigerator crisper (set to high humidity).
To prepare for cooking: cut broccoli into individual florets, trim off stem at base of each floret and further cut these to similar size. Peel the fibrous skin off the stem and stem pieces. Cut all to similar size.
To boil: for each pound of broccoli, bring a gallon of water to a boil in large pot with 1 ½ T salt. Drop in the pieces and return water rapidly to the boil. Cook, uncovered, 2-4 minutes, or to desired doneness. Drain well.
Broccoli is delicious served hot or warm as well as raw with dips. I like to serve plain broiled broccoli lightly buttered, or with breadcrumbs browned and crisped in butter. It also good served with a White Sauce, Cheese Sauce or dressed with chopped hard-

cooked eggs.
You can also dip the florets, raw or cooked, into a Fritter batter and fry in hot oil until brown and crisp. Drain on a wire rack or paper towels and keep warm in a 200-degree oven until all pieces are fried.

Broccoli Puff
This recipe uses frozen broccoli.
Preheat oven to 350 degrees. Have ready a deep baking dish.
Cooking according to package directions:
    2 10-oz packages frozen broccoli cuts
Drain thoroughly.
Place in baking dish.
Stir together in a mixing bowl:
    1 can condensed cream of mushroom soup
    4 oz sharp American or Cheddar cheese, shredded
Gradually mix in:
    1/3 c milk
    1/3 c Mayonnaise or salad dressing
    1 egg, beaten
Pour over broccoli.
Combine:
    1/3 c dry bread crumbs
    2 T butter, melted.
Sprinkle evenly over casserole. Bake 45 minutes or until crumbs are lightly browned.

Cabbage – cabbage comes in green and red varieties. I use both interchangeably in the recipes given here. There is also a Chinese Cabbage, also called Napa Cabbage, that can be substituted with satisfactory results. I often use the raw Napa Cabbage leaves as containers for salads.
Cabbage is easy to grow beginning in early Spring and again in late Summer for a Fall crop. Copenhagen and Early Golden Acre are both good for fresh eating and for making Sauerkraut. I leave the plants to grow after harvesting the main head. The plants will produce "baby cabbages" much like Brussels sprouts which are delicious roasted or grilled.
If purchasing cabbage at the grocer or farmers market, select solid heads, heavy for their size and have bright, crisp leaves with no yellowing, cuts or bruises. Heads that are not solid or are light-weight are usually poorly formed, and you will not get much for what you pay.
To store: place in plastic bags or wrap tightly in plastic wrap and store in the refrigerator crisper.
To prepare: remove large outer leaves and wash in cool water then follow directions in individual recipes.

Stuffed Cabbage Leaves
This recipe uses individual cabbage leaves to hold a savory filling.
Preheat oven to 350 degrees. Have ready a 2-quart casserole with sides at least two inches tall.
Combine and mix well in a large bowl:
- **1 egg, beaten**
- **½ c milk**
- **¼ c finely chopped onion**
- **1 t Worcestershire sauce**
- **¾ t salt**
- **Dash pepper**

Add, mixing lightly but thoroughly:
- **1 pound ground beef**
- **¾ c cooked Rice**

Remove from a large head of cabbage:
- **6 large or 12 medium cabbage leaves**

Blanch in boiling water about 3 minutes or until limp. Remove center vein, keeping each leaf in one piece. Drain on clean kitchen towel.
Place ½ c meat mixture on each large leaf or ¼ c mixture on each medium leaf; fold in sides. Starting at unfolded edge, roll up each leaf making sure folded sides are included in roll. Arrange in baking dish.
Combine:
- **1 can condensed tomato soup or tomato sauce**
- **¼ c brown sugar**
- **¼ c vinegar**
- **1 t paprika**
- **½ t coarsely ground pepper**

Pour sauce mixture over cabbage rolls. Bake, uncovered, 1 ¼ hours, basting once or twice with sauce.

Cabbage with Sausage and Apples
This is a quick, easy and tasty one-pan dish. Complete the meal with your favorite bread, rolls, cornbread or biscuits.
Remove large outer leaves, core and slice into medium-sized shreds:
- **1 head cabbage**

Peel, core and slice:
- **1 large onion**
- **1 large apple**

Cut into one-half-inch slices:
- **1 lb Kielbasa or smoked sausage**

Heat in large skillet with a tight-fitting cover:
- **3 T fat**

Add sausage and fry until beginning to brown. Add onions and apples. Cook, stirring

often until these begin to soften. Add cabbage. Mix well. Cover and cook until all are tender, stirring occasionally.
Season with:
- **Salt**
- **Pepper**
- **Herbs or seeds such as parsley or dill, or caraway seeds**

Carrots – easy to grow if you have deeply tilled and rock-free soil. Carrots will produce all season long if planted every two weeks. Among vegetables, carrots are second only to beets in sugar content. These vegetables, available in a rainbow of colors if you grow your own or have access to a farmers market, lend themselves to a many uses from main to side dishes to salads and desserts. The leaves, too, are useful in soups, sautéed or used in place of basil in Pesto. Mashed or pureed carrots are good alone or combined with mashed parsnips, potatoes or turnips.
If purchasing carrots from the grocer or farmers market, avoid those with green spots (which are bitter), those that are cracked (entry points for microorganisms) and those with soft or moldy stem ends. Avoid at all times those that are limp or wilted, rubbery or shriveled. Preferably buy loose carrots which still have their leaves—the best indication of freshness.
To store: place in plastic bags and store in the refrigerator crisper.
To prepare: scrub thoroughly. We always peeled our carrots, but that is not a necessity.
To boil: for each pound of carrots, bring 1 gallon of water to a boil with 1 ½ T salt. Add carrots and cook until desired doneness. Boil a bit longer if carrots are to be mashed to ensure they are thoroughly tender.
To mash: use a potato masher, vegetable mill or ricer to mash carrots. Season with salt, pepper and butter. A bit of brown sugar is always welcome as is a splash of cream.

Glazed Carrots
Cook carrots to desired tenderness. For each pound of cooked carrots:
Melt in a large skillet:
- ¼ c butter

When foaming subsides, add:
- **Cooked carrots**
- **2-3 T brown sugar, honey or maple syrup**
- **Salt and pepper**
- **1 T brandy, optional**

Cook gently until the sugar, honey or syrup caramelizes slightly and glazes the carrots.

Cauliflower – somewhat challenging to grow unless you choose a self-blanching variety.
If purchasing cauliflower from the grocer or farmers market, choose evenly white-colored heads whose curds are firm, have tight florets and are heavy for their size

without a trace of black which is a sign of spoilage.
To store: place in perforated plastic bags in the refrigerator crisper.
To prepare: wash well and follow directions in individual recipes.
To boil: for each pound of florets, bring to boiling 1 gallon of water and 1 ½ T salt. Add florets and rapidly return water to the boil. Cook until just tender at the stem. Drain well.

Baked Cauliflower
This is an unique way to cook and serve cauliflower which everyone seems to enjoy. Preheat oven to 350 degrees. Have ready a casserole just large enough to hold the cauliflower upright.
Boil in a large quantity of boiling water 10-15 minutes or until a thin skewer easily pierces the stem (do not cook so long as to make the curds mushy):
    1 whole head cauliflower, bottom trimmed to sit upright
Drain well and place casserole.
Brush to cover surface of entire head with light coatings of:
    Butter
    Prepared mustard
Cover evenly with:
    Thin cheese slices, or
    Fresh breadcrumbs
Bake 20-25 minutes or until cheese is melted and beginning to brown, or until breadcrumbs are deeply golden brown. Cut into wedges or slices to serve.
Variation on a Theme: the breadcrumb version also works well with a head of broccoli.

Celery – planted in early Spring, celery takes 4 – 5 months to grow before being harvested. Celery is one vegetables I grew for the first time while living in Indiana. Most often used to add flavor to stocks and casseroles, crunch to salads, spreads and dips, and as a quick snack, celery is also good cooked.
If purchasing celery from the grocer or farmers market, choose a bunch that is light in color and shiny. Darker bunches will have a stronger flavor. The bunch should not be limp, wilted or wrinkled, or have any soft or mushy spots, cuts, cracks or trimmed stalks. The leaves should be moist, shiny and alert.
To store: place whole bunches in plastic bags in the refrigerator crisper. You can restore limp celery by separating the stalks and placing in cold water to cover. Let stand a couple of hours and then return to the plastic bag without shaking off the water. Refrigerate in the crisper.
To prepare: separate individual stalks, if not using the entire bunch. Trim ends and wash well. Some celery has pronounced strings. Remove these by snapping the leaf crown toward the round side of the stalk and pulling down to remove the strings. Otherwise, remove leaves where they join the main stalk. Save the leaves to use to flavor stocks, casseroles, etc., or freeze in plastic bags for future use. Follow recipe directions for further preparation instructions.

Braised Celery
This side dish is good served with spicy main dishes as well as more delicately flavored fish dishes.
Arrange in a large skillet with a tight-fitting lid:
>   1 large bunch celery, washed, ends trimmed and stalks cut into 2-inch lengths

Add:
>   1 c chicken stock
>   3 T butter
>   2 T finely minced or grated onion
>   1 t sugar

Bring to a boil. Cover, reduce heat and simmer until celery is barely tender, about 10 minutes.
Remove cover and rapidly boil, stirring occasionally, until the liquid is reduced to a glaze. Season with salt and pepper, if desired.

Cherries – these fruits, available in both sweet and tart varieties, are one fruit shipped ripe to market. Nothing is better in the fruit world than the tart pie cherry—Montmorency being the one most widely grown and available. This cherry makes the most wonderful pies, crisps, jams and jellies. The sweet cherries are wonderful as a fresh-fruit dessert and as additions to dishes both sweet and savory. Cherry season is very short, so be aware of when cherries ripen in your area and are available at your grocer or farmers market. Cherries are easy to grow in the home orchard, but are slow to mature and grow large enough to produce yields of any size.
If you purchase cherries from the grocer or farmers market, you will most likely find sweet cherries readily available. Again, as cherries are shipped ripe to market, you can purchase prepackaged. Tart pie cherries are a rare find. In years when I didn't have productive pie cherry trees, I bought frozen cherries at the local grocer until it went out of business, and then frozen, in bulk, online. Cherries freeze and can well.
To store: place in plastic bags or a covered container and store on the refrigerator shelf.
To prepare: wash under cold running water. Drain well. Remove stems and pits. You can easily remove pits using a hairpin to "scoop" out the pit (seed); however, a vintage or modern cherry pitter is a worthwhile investment.

Corn – today's sweet corn has undergone dramatic change, becoming sweeter every year. However, one of the first sweet corns developed and sold, Golden Bantam, is still my favorite. The newer hybrids are very good, but for those who save their own seed, this heirloom, open pollinated, is by far the best. Also, hybrids do not bear the same result if those seeds are saved from year-to-year.
If purchasing corn from the grocer or farmers market, it is best to buy ears without the shucks so you can see the kernels which should be smooth and shiny and not

shriveled. The ears should be fully filled out except for the very top. If possible, press a kernel with your thumbnail. It should be full of "milk."

To store: sweet corn begins to deteriorate as soon as it is picked. It is best to rush it from the garden to the pot and cook as soon as possible after picking. If you cannot cook immediately, store in the refrigerator still in its husks standing upright in an inch of water. I find it helps a little to add a teaspoon of sugar to the water, although it will never re-gain the "just-picked" flavor. We always removed the shucks and silks from the ears before cooking. I still remember Aunt Mill giving us plastic bags of neatly cleaned and arranged corn when she had a surplus. Today, I prefer to cook the corn in its shucks.

To prepare: you can remove the shucks and silks prior to cooking, but it is not necessary. Drop one ear of corn at a time into rapidly boiling, salted water. Cook 5-8 minutes until heated through. Remove from the water and strip back the shucks (the silks will come off with the shucks), if needed. Serve hot with butter, salt and pepper, lime juice, Mayonnaise or barbecue sauce.

Corn does not have to be cooked before eating. Raw corn kernels are a great addition to salads, salsas, sauces and purees.

Authentic Creamed Corn
Cut off just the tops of the kernels into a bowl. Using the back of your knife, scrape the length of the ear releasing the base of the kernels and the corn "milk." To serve, heat the mixture and about ½ c heavy cream for every five ears of corn in a double boiler over hot, not boiling, water until heated through and thickened. Season with salt, pepper and butter. You can also bake this mixture in an 8x8-inch pan at 325 degrees until set, 30-40 minutes, to make a corn pudding.

Corn Bread Pudding
I developed this recipe one Summer when I had extra corn and heavy cream. You can make it with almost any type of bread, but I especially like to make it with Everyday Bread. This simple dish has a pure, fresh corn taste. It also works well with your own frozen corn (See To Freeze Corn), thawed and drained. You can also slice the bread and cut to fit a 2-quart casserole or baking pan.

Preheat oven to 350 degrees. Have ready a generously buttered 9x5x3-inch loaf pan, preferably metal. If using glass, reduce oven temperature to 325 degrees.

Cut two ¾-inch thick slices lengthwise from:
    1 8x4-inch loaf of bread

Alternately, use sliced bread cutting the slices to fit the pan.
Place bottom slice of bread in bottom of pan.
Melt in large pan:
    ¼ c butter, softened
Add:
    2 c fresh corn kernels (scrape the cobs and add scrapings to kernels)
    1 small onion, grated

Cook slowly until corn and onion are tender, about 8-10 minutes. Cool
Beat:
>   **4 eggs**

Mix in:
>   **2 c heavy cream**

You should have 3 cups total. If not, add more cream to make 3 cups.
Season with:
>   **Salt and pepper**

Pour one-third mixture over bottom slice of bread. Let sit for about 10 minutes or until bread absorbs most of the cream mixture.
Spoon cooled corn mixture over bread in pan. Pour one-third of cream mixture over corn. Butter one side of second slice of bread. Place butter-side up in pan over corn layer. Pour over last third of cream mixture.
Cover tightly and refrigerate several hours or overnight. Bake 50 – 60 minutes or until pudding puffs to fill the pan and a sharp knife inserted into center comes out clean. Let cool in pan 5 minutes before slicing and serving.

Cucumbers - Cucumbers were a Summer and Fall staple from the vegetable garden. We always planted enough to eat fresh daily, and to preserve as pickles and in relishes (see the Canning section for recipes).
Cucumbers are easy to grow either on hills or on trellises. In either case, mulch heavily with straw or grass clippings so the cucumbers don't grow on the ground. Pick often and do not let cucumbers grow too large, or the plants will stop producing. Plant some every two weeks after your frost-free date until early July (depending on variety) to have fresh cucumbers throughout Summer and into early Fall. Straight Eight is a prolific all-purpose cucumber good both fresh and preserved. If purchasing cucumbers from the grocer or farmers market, select firm fruits with a shiny skin and no cuts, wrinkled skins, bruises or soft spots.
To store: keep in the refrigerator crisper with humidity set to "high."
To prepare: wash well. Always peel cucumbers you buy in a grocery store. These have been coated with wax to prevent dehydration. The slender fruits seem to have less seeds than larger ones.

Cucumbers I

Everyone's favorite way to fix cucumbers during the Summer was in a refreshing vinegar brine. Slice cucumbers to your desired thickness (peel or not to your taste). Place in a large glass bowl with a tight-fitting lid.
Combine equal parts of white vinegar and white sugar and a large pinch of salt. Mix well until sugar is dissolved. Pour over cucumbers and refrigerate several hours before serving. These are also delicious with sliced onions added in.

Cucumbers II
Another way to serve cucumbers is to dress them in Sour Cream and/or Mayonnaise. You want the dressing a bit thick because the cucumbers will give up some of their water during refrigeration. Slice cucumbers (and onions, if you like). Use Everyday Salad Dressing. Taste and adjust seasoning to your liking. Pour over cucumbers and mix well. Refrigerate until serving time.
If preparing several hours ahead of time, slice cucumbers and then toss with several pinches of salt and sugar, and let drain in a colander for an hour or more. Omit salt from dressing.
Variations on a Theme: Fresh or dried dill, caraway seed, celery seed and/or poppy seed can be added to vary the flavor. To accompany chicken dishes, add chopped tarragon; fennel or anise seed accompanies fish dishes well, too.

Sautéed Cucumbers
Not common fare, but hot cucumbers are delicious. These are especially good in the Fall as the last of the cucumbers ripen when the weather cools. They are good with both fish and chicken dishes. Prepare cucumbers by peeling and cutting in half lengthwise. Use a spoon to scrape out any seeds (the skins and seeds turn bitter when heated). Cut the flesh into 1-inch pieces. For a reason I can't remember, I always cut the cucumbers into triangle shapes. In a large skillet over medium heat, melt 3 T butter. When butter has melted and stopped foaming, add in the cucumbers and sauté quickly until just heated through. They should retain some crunch. Sprinkle with salt, pepper and dill weed (if using dried dill weed, add it at the beginning of the sauté).
Variation on a Theme: Cherry tomatoes are also delicious fixed this way. Substitute basil for the dill, adding it in after cooking to heat through.

Eggplant – this vegetable has two main varieties: native to Africa and most often large and tear-drop shaped in dark purple (almost black) and white varieties; and native to Asia, most often long and slender in light purple, rose or white. Black Knight and Ping Tung are two very good heirloom varieties to grow.
Both are easy to grow in very fertile soil. Plants grow large and can be burdened with the amount of fruit they produce, so it is best to grow in a cage (much like tomatoes), or tied to a very strong stake.
If purchasing eggplant from the grocer or farmers market, choose fruits which are bright and shiny in color, heavy for their size with a bright green cap and with no blemishes, cuts, soft spots or wrinkled skin. Store unwrapped in a cool place, or in the refrigerator crisper.
To prepare: wash well and dry. Cut off the cap (stem and leaves) and then follow individual recipes.
Slices of eggplant (about ½ inch thick), salted and drained to remove excess moisture, and quickly sautéed, grilled or roasted, to brown both sides are a good substitute for noodles in Lasagna. Liberally sprinkle eggplant slices with salt. Let sit on wire racks to

drain for at least 30 minutes and up to 3 hours, turning several times. Wipe slices with a clean dish towel or with a paper towel before cooking. Sauté in butter and olive oil; bread and fry as in Bound Breading; roast as for asparagus; or grill in a grill pan until just tender when pierced with a knife.

Stuffed Eggplant Slices

The cooked slices may be filled, rolled and baked. I like to use the cheese filling for Lasagna, omitting the egg and adding 1 c bread crumbs. Arrange in a baking dish, seam side down, and cover and bake at 350 degrees until heated through and cheese is melted. Serve with a fresh tomato sauce.

Fried Eggplant

Prepare:
>   **Eggplant**

Slice crosswise or lengthwise about ½-inch thick.
Liberally salt both sides of the slices and place on a wire rack set in a sheet pan to drain for at least 30 minutes and up to 1 hour.
Coat the slices with:
>   **Bound Breading**

Let the coated slices rest on a wire rack up to an hour before frying.
In heavy skillet, heat just enough fat to cover the bottom over medium heat until hot. Place each coated slice, in turn, into hot fat in skillet. Fry on each side until deep golden brown and heated through. Remove to a wire rack set over a baking sheet to drain. Keep warm in a 200-degree oven until all are fried.

Variations on a Theme: top with shredded mozzarella cheese and bake at 350 degrees 7-10 minutes or until cheese is melted; serve with your favorite tomato or pasta sauce. Layer two slices with a slice of baked ham for each serving. Use fried slices to replace noodles in Lasagna.

Eggplant Casserole

This delightful casserole is good with all varieties of meat and game. It is delicious served with a fresh tomato sauce.
Preheat oven to 350 degrees. Lightly grease an 11x7x2-inch pan or oval gratin dish.
Peel and cube:
>   **1 medium eggplant**

Boil in salted water until tender. Drain and mash in a large mixing bowl.
Add and mix well:
>   **¾ c saltine cracker crumbs**
>   **2 eggs**
>   **1 can mushroom soup**
>   **2 T minced or grated onion**
>   **¼ c butter, melted**

Bake 30-40 minutes or until knife inserted in the center comes out clean.

Spicy Eggplant
Best made with Japanese eggplants about 1-inch in diameter and cut crosswise into 1-inch thick rounds. If using other eggplant, peel and cut into 1-inch cubes. If you do not have or cannot find red chili paste, make your own paste by crushing a hot pepper (jalapeno, arbol, serrano or habanero—listed in order of amount of heat) with a pinch of salt and sugar until a smooth paste forms, then measure the amount needed.
Combine in a small bowl and set aside:
> 1 T cornstarch
> 2 T water

Combine in another small bowl and set:
> 2 T oyster (fish) sauce
> 2 T soy sauce
> 2 T water
> 1 T white vinegar
> 1 T sugar
> ½ t red chili paste
> ½ t Chinese five spice, optional
> ½ t sesame oil

Peel, finely dice and reserve:
> 2 large garlic cloves

Prepare:
> 1 lb eggplant

Heat to 350 degrees in an electric fryer or large kettle:
> Peanut oil

Fry eggplant, in batches, 1 minute.
Remove to paper-towel-lined pan to drain.
Heat until hot in a large skillet:
> 1 T peanut oil

Add garlic and cook 20 seconds.
Pour in sauce and cook 20 seconds.
Add eggplant and cook 20 seconds.
Dribble in cornstarch mixture, stirring constantly, until sauces thickens as desired.
Serve immediately.
Variation on a Theme: double the sauce and add 2 c thinly sliced and cooked chicken, beef or pork, or 1 lb shelled, deveined and cooked shrimp.

Gooseberries – these berries are tart when green and slightly sweet when ripened to a light pink color. The berries must be stemmed before cooking. I have two memories of gooseberries. The first is my sister Ann's colorful description of helping Aunt Mill, along with our cousin Michelle, to pick and stem gooseberries. The gooseberry bush has thorns. It can be a quite prickly affair picking the berries. Add to that experience the small, fine stems and blossom ends which must be removed before using, and you can imagine what an experience that would have been for two young girls. The second is one of the reasons Aunts Marcelline and Geraldine built the house they lived in when we were growing up which was just around the corner (in the same neighborhood) from their first house. One reason: because all the neighbors could see what they were doing, including stemming gooseberries in the garage!

I like gooseberries in pies, jams and poached to serve with dark game such as pheasant and venison.

If you buy gooseberries at the grocer or the farmers market, do try to select individual berries. These should be plump, firm and glossy with no blemishes and preferably with the stems attached.

To prepare: remove stems and blossom ends and wash under cold running water. Drain and dry before storing in the refrigerator.

Gooseberry Fool

Fools, fruit puree and Whipped Cream, are a classic, easy dessert. The key to a successful fool is to ensure the fruit puree is tart and the Whipped Cream naturally sweet. Do not attempt to make with frozen non-dairy whipped topping. Follow this recipe to use with your favorite fruit.

Cook, in a medium saucepan, over low heat,

3 c gooseberries

Crush the berries with a potato masher and cook until softened, 10-15 minutes. Puree in a blender or food processor.

Blend in:

¼ c sweet wine, such as muscatel or prosecco, optional
2 T sugar

Cover and refrigerate until cold and up to 3 days.

Whip until soft peaks form:

1 ¼ c heavy or whipping cream

Gently fold gooseberry puree into Whipped Cream.
Mound in stemmed glasses and serve immediately.

Poached Gooseberries

A nice accompaniment to game dishes.
Preheat oven to 350 degrees. Have ready a 1-quart shallow baking dish.
Combine in a large mixing bowl:

2 c gooseberries
¾ c sugar
¼ c butter, melted

Mix well and then pour into prepared baking dish. Bake until berries just soften, stirring occasionally, about 30 minutes.

Jicama – this is a native of Mexico. I have never grown jicama. Rose introduced me to jicama at one of our Food Days. The tuber resembles a rough, brown-skinned turnip. The interior is sweet, water-crisp and white. Best used raw in salads and the raw vegetable tray. Jicama can also be cut into coins and used in place of chestnuts in stir-fry.

If purchasing jicama from the grocer or farmers market, select medium-sized tubers, solid and heavy for their size with no blemishes, cuts or soft spots. Store unpeeled and uncovered in the refrigerator crisper.

To prepare: scrub well, then cut a slice from both ends. Use a sharp paring knife to remove the brown skin which removes easily. Next, remove the tough, fibrous layer. You will be able to see a thin, distinct difference between this layer and the flesh. Cut into slices, wedges, cubes, coins or matchsticks.

Melons – whether cantaloupe, honeydew or muskmelon, melons provide a sweet, juicy snack, salad addition or dessert ingredient. Melons are easy to grow, but they take a lot of space—vines can reach several feet in all directions—and it is best to mulch well with straw to prevent melons from sitting on the soil. American cantaloupe and muskmelons have a pronounced netting and should have a pronounced fruity perfume at the smooth (blossom) end.

If purchasing melons from the grocer or farmers market, select those that are heaviest for their size, with no soft spots, mold or cracks and no strong aroma indicating over-ripeness.

To store: wrap cut or ripe melons tightly in plastic bags and store in the refrigerator. To prepare: wash well to remove any dust or dirt. Melons are usually eaten raw. We would cut the melons into four or six wedges, remove the seeds and fibers and serve as-is with salt and pepper. Small melon halves, or a larger melon cut crosswise into ½-inch rings can be filled with cottage cheese, or fruit, vegetable or Chicken Salad and served as a light luncheon or dinner. Melon balls may be served with similar balls of sherbet or ice cream, or in chilled champagne or Prosecco (or sparkling white grape juice) for dessert. Diced melons are a great addition to fresh salsa, too.

Cantaloupe Jam

I made this jam a couple of years before we had a stall at the farmers market. I thought it was a novelty; but a few people told me they, too, had a recipe. Although not a unique offering, I did sell the first batch I took to market. This jam is like Summer-in-a-Jar. I like it on toast, Biscuits, scones, Waffles and with duck (an excellent alternative to the ubiquitous plum sauce).

Whisk together in a small bowl:
>   **½ c sugar**
>   **5 T powdered pectin**

Set aside.

Place in a large stockpot:
>   **6 cups finely diced, very ripe cantaloupe**
>   **2 T lemon juice**

    3 ½ c sugar

Bring to a boil over medium-high heat. Bring to a full, rolling boil that cannot be stirred down (it may take 10-15 minutes).
Whisk in:

    The pectin mixture

Bring mixture back to a full boil, and boil hard for 2-3 minutes, or until the mixture looks thickened and is set. (Remove pot from heat. Test by putting a small amount on a spoon and placing it in the freezer for a few minutes. If it's jelly-like when it's cold, it's set. If not, boil a few more minutes and test again.)
When finished cooking, remove from heat, and stir in:

    1 t vanilla

    1 ½ t sea or coarse kosher salt (if using regular table salt, reduce to 1 t)

Ladle jam into 8 half-pint jars. Seal and process 10 minutes in a boiling-water bath (see Canning and Preserving chapter).

Melon with Shrimp

I like this best made with honeydew melon, but cantaloupe or muskmelon work well, too. Thinly sliced chicken, either sautéed or fried in a Fritter batter also works well. This dish reaches perfection when the melon balls are icy cold (but not frozen) and the shrimp and sauce are very warm. The Glazed Walnuts are optional but provide a crunchy contrast to the other ingredients (use Glazed Pecans with chicken).
Using a melon baller or small spoon, make into balls:

    1 small honeydew melon, cantaloupe or muskmelon

Place balls on freezer-safe tray and freeze while proceeding with the recipe. Do not allow the balls to freeze.
Have ready:

    1 lb shrimp, boiled, sautéed or fried in a Fritter batter

Keep shrimp warm in a 200-degree oven (cover the boiled or sautéed shrimp; place fritters on a wire rack over a sheet pan).
Combine in a small saucepan:

    ½ c coconut milk

    ¼ c cane syrup (preferably Lyle's Golden Syrup)

    1 T Mayonnaise, heaping

    1 ½ T rice wine vinegar

    ¼ t turmeric

    Dash of celery salt

    Dash ground ginger

Bring to a simmer.
Combine:

    1 T cornstarch

    2 T coconut milk

Stir into coconut milk mixture. Cook until sauce thickens.
Combine sauce with shrimp. Fold in melon balls.

Serve immediately with:
> **Rice**

Topped with the Glazed Walnuts, if desired.

Mushrooms – I once bought a mushroom growing kit—a cardboard box filled with compost and mushroom spawn. I grew the mushrooms in a closet and had so many I canned several pints that year. You can buy several varieties of mushrooms in a kit. It's a fun experiment for kids and adults alike.

There are many varieties of mushrooms available fresh, dried and canned. Explore all the varieties. Thyme and nutmeg are excellent paired with mushrooms.

If purchasing mushrooms from the grocer or farmers market, select mushrooms that are heavy for their size without any blemishes, soft spots or other signs of damage and spoilage. The top should be tightly closed around the stem with no gills showing. Exposed gills are a sign of age. Store in a paper bag, or the original packaging, on the refrigerator shelf—not in the crisper because the moisture accelerates spoilage.

To prepare: wipe with a clean soft cloth or paper towel to remove any dirt or sand. If extremely sandy, swish quickly in water—never soak mushrooms. When adding to a cooked dish, always pre-cook mushrooms by quickly browning in butter/oil over high heat.

Sautéed Mushrooms

In a large skillet, over high heat, melt:
> **3 T butter or oil (a combination of half butter and half oil is superb)**

Add:
> **1 lb mushrooms, wiped clean and sliced**

Cook, tossing constantly, until beginning to brown.

Season with:
> **Salt and pepper to taste**
> **Fresh or dried thyme leaves, if desired**

Deep-fried Mushrooms

Wipe clean and slice off stems even with bottom of caps:
> **1 lb mushrooms**

Coat the mushrooms with Bound Breading.

Place breaded mushrooms on a wire rack while breading all mushrooms.

Heat oil in an electric frying machine according to manufacturer's instructions, or heat about 3 inches of oil in a large pan to 365 degrees.

Add mushrooms, a few at time to avoid crowding, and fry until a deep golden brown on all sides. Remove to paper-towel-lined pan to drain. Keep warm in a 200-degree oven while frying remaining mushrooms.

Creamed Mushrooms
To Sautéed Mushrooms, add:
>½ c heavy cream
>1 clove garlic, minced
>1 ½ t fresh thyme leaves, or ½ t dried
>Salt and pepper, to taste

Cook until cream thickens and coats the mushrooms. Taste and adjust seasoning.

Stuffed Mushrooms
I like to serve these as an appetizer, or as a side dish with a salad and bread for luncheon or dinner, or with sausages, ham or tongue for a light supper. I most often use cream cheese as the base, but you also get good results using ricotta cheese. Some of my favorite fillings, for 24 mushrooms, follow. You can also use the fillings to stuff jalapeno peppers which have had seeds and ribs removed for delicious alternatives to the normal fried poppers.

Preheat oven to 350 degrees. Have ready a foil-lined baking sheet large enough to hold the quantity of mushrooms.

Wipe clean and remove stems from:
>**24 large mushrooms**

Use a small spoon to remove the gills and hollow out the caps.
Heat over medium-high heat:
>**3 T butter**
>**3 T oil**

After the butter has melted and stopped foaming, add the mushrooms, hollowed end down. Cook until browned. Turn mushrooms and brown the top side of the caps. Remove to a rack or pan lined with paper towels to drain, hollow end down.
Prepare:
>**One of the following fillings**

Turn caps hollowed end up. Sprinkle with salt and fill. Place on prepared baking sheet. Bake about 15 minutes or until heated through and filling is lightly browned.

Fillings:

Basic: Combine 8 oz cream cheese, softened, with ½ t each dried onion flakes, coarsely ground black pepper, paprika (smoked paprika is especially good), and dried parsley.

Sausage and Apple: Cook ½ lb sausage until browned, breaking into small pieces. Remove to colander to drain. Cook 2 c peeled and finely chopped apples in ¼ c butter. Add 1 T sugar. Cook until apples are golden. Add 4 oz cream cheese. Cook and stir until cheese has melted. Remove from heat and stir in sausage. Used minced ham in place of sausage and pears in place of apples; or chorizo in place of sausage and potatoes in place of apples.

Walnuts and Cheese: Place in bowl of food processor 5 oz St. Andre, Brie, Camembert, all with rind, or cream cheese. Process until smooth and creamy. Add in ¼ c each finely chopped walnuts and dry bread crumbs.

Herbed Cheese: Combine 8 oz cream cheese, softened, ¼ c each Mayonnaise and Sour Cream and ¼ amount of seasonings for Rose's Dip.
Bacon and Tomato: Fry until crisp 6 slices bacon. Drain and cut into fine crumbles. Combine with 8 oz cream cheese, softened, ½ c finely diced dried tomatoes, 2 T finely chopped fresh basil, and salt and pepper to taste.
Dressing Filling: Use leftover Dressing or Cornbread Dressing. Especially good for Christmas or New Year's parties.
Potato Stuffed Mushrooms: Stuff mushroom caps with Garlic Mashed Potatoes and bake.
Creamed Filling: Fill mushroom caps with Creamed Corn, Spinach or Peas made with a Thick White Sauce.

Nectarines – these fruits are similar to peaches, but have a smooth skin like plums. Select, store, prepare and use as for peaches.

Onions

Onions are related to lilies. How can one argue the most beautiful of flowers is related to the most versatile of vegetables? We grew only one onion on the farm. The varietal name is Miss Society. It is a white, very sweet onion bred and sold by the Earl May Seed Company (and is still available today). It is an easy-to-grow variety and stores very well into the Fall and Winter months. In later years, we turned to the Candy variety—a large, sweet, yellow onion that stores from late Summer through Spring. I still plant both today. We always planted enough to eat fresh, use in various canned items and to store for use until we planted more in the Spring. Onions are used in many ways to flavor meats, casseroles, etc.

If purchasing onions from the grocer or farmers market, select onions which are heavy for their size and with tight skins. Avoid any with bruises, soft spots or areas with a black mold. Sweet onions (Vidalia, Bermuda, Walla Walla are common varieties) in perforated bags in the refrigerator crisper. Store cured onions (most yellow, white and red onions sold in stores) spread out (cardboard trays from the grocer work well) in a cool, dry, dark place away from potatoes.

To prepare: Cut a thin slice from the top. Peel off skin and the first layer, if shrunken and wrinkled. Cut off the root last (purported to prevent tears). Cut, slice, chop, etc. according to individual recipes.

Onion Rings

A large, round, rather flat onion is best for these rings. I usually use the Candy variety, but Vidalia, Walla Walla or another sweet onion will suffice. It is easier to separate into rings if you soak the cut onions in warm water. You must remove the inner skin from the rings so the coating does not fall off when frying. It is also easier to remove this skin if you soak the separated rings in warm water for a few minutes. Peel, cut off top and bottom of each to create flat surfaces, and cut into ¾- to 1-inch slices:

    6 onions

Place cut onions in warm water for several minutes which will make separating into rings easier. Do not let the water cool.
Separate each slice into rings. Reserve center for another use. Soak separated rings in warm water for several minutes. Do not let the water cool.
Remove the inner skin from each ring by using the point of a paring knife. Insert the point into the edge of the ring between the onion and the skin. Peel off the skin which should separate in one piece. Place the skinned rings in a large bowl of ice water.
Make one recipe:
> **Pancakes**

Increasing milk by 1/3 c.
Alternately, combine in a medium bowl:
> **1 c packaged pancake mix**
> **½ t salt**
> **1 ¼ c water**

Place in a shallow bowl:
> **1 c flour**

Place in another shallow bowl:
> **6 c fresh bread crumbs**

Remove one ring at a time from the ice water. Coat in flour, shaking off excess. Dip flour-coated ring into batter, letting excess drip off. Place ring into bread crumbs, coating evenly and pressing gently to ensure bread crumbs adhere and completely coat the ring. Place the ring onto a baking sheet.
Coat all rings. Let all coated rings sit at room temperature for at least 1 hour. Coated rings may be refrigerated, loosely covered with foil or plastic wrap, up to 24 hours before frying.
Pour into large, heavy pan, preferably cast iron, to a depth of two inches:
> **Peanut, vegetable, corn or canola oil**

Heat to 375 degrees. Place onion rings into hot oil. Do not crowd. Fry until golden, turn and fry until golden on other side. Place fried rings on towel-lined rack to drain. Keep warm in 200-degree oven as you fry remaining rings.

Baked Onions

These onions go with just about any meat entrée. Leftovers are good to use in Hash.
Preheat oven to 350 degrees. Have ready a shallow casserole dish just large enough to hold all the onions.
Peel and place in the casserole:
> **6 onions**

Pour evenly over the onions:
> **3 T oil, preferably light olive oil**

Season with:
> **Salt**
> **Pepper**

Bake, uncovered, until a skewer inserted into an onion meets with just hint of resistance, about 60 minutes.
Sprinkle around the onions:
> ½ c dark raisins

Bake an additional 15 minutes or until raisins are plumped.

Creamed Onions I
I like to use a package of boiling onions for a substantial side dish, and frozen pearl onions for a casserole as part of a buffet.
Preheat oven to 350 degrees. Have ready a buttered 1 ½-quart casserole.
Prepare according to package directions:
> **1 pkg. boiling onions, or**
> **2 pkgs. frozen, pearl onions, thawed (just thaw, do not cook)**

Prepare, using ½ c of the water used to boil the onions and 1 ½ milk or cream:
> **2 c medium White Sauce**

Combine onions and sauce. Turn into prepared casserole. Bake 25-30 minutes until heated through, bubbly and lightly browned on top.
Variation on a Theme: top with one of the following before baking:
> **1 c fresh bread crumbs and 2 T melted butter, or**
> **1 c grated Swiss cheese, or**
> **A combination of both**

Creamed Onions II
A simple recipe using heavy cream instead of a White Sauce.
Prepare onions as above.
Pour over the onions in a heavy wide saucepan or skillet:
> **1 ½ c heavy cream**

Cook at a slow simmer until cream is reduced to a sauce that coats the onions.
Season with:
> **Salt and pepper**
> **¼ c chopped fresh parsley**

Glazed Onions
A good accompaniment to hearty meats like venison or other game and field birds (pheasant, etc.), but goes well with many dishes.
Place in skillet large enough to hold in one layer.
> **1 lb boiling onions, peeled, or fresh Spring onions (about 1-inch diameter), peeled**

Slice and distribute over onions:
> **¼ cup butter**

Sprinkle over all:
> **½ t salt**

Add enough water to come ½-inch deep in pan. Cover and bring to rapid boil.

Remove cover and cook until water evaporates and onions are tender, stirring frequently.
Sprinkle over all:
2 T brown sugar or maple syrup
Reduce heat and stir until the butter and brown sugar form a glaze that coats the onions.
Season with black pepper and serve.

Onions Stuffed with Sauerkraut
A nice dish to serve as an alternative to cabbage with corned beef or a pork pot roast. Do use a seeded rye bread as described, or add additional caraway seed to the stuffing mixture, if desired. You can vary the dish by using a different seed or a combination of seeds such as dill, celery, poppy, sesame, juniper berries (crushed), etc.
Preheat oven to 400 degrees. Have ready a casserole dish just large enough to hold the onions.
Peel and place in boiling water about 10 minutes:
6 large onions
Drain well. Cut a slice from the bottom, if needed for onions to sit level. Cut a slice from the top (I cut at the "shoulder" where the onion begins to curve down the side) and remove all but three-quarter inch of shell. Chop the removed onion.
Combine the chopped onion pulp with:
1 c drained Sauerkraut
½ c soft bread crumbs (preferably a seeded rye bread)
¼ t pepper
Heap the mixture into the onion cases. Sprinkle the tops generously with buttered bread or cracker crumbs. Bake the onions in the pan with a little water until well heated and tender, about 35 minutes.
Variation on a Theme: These onion cases lend themselves to various fillings. One of my favorites is to stuff and bake like Stuffed Peppers, using one of the Meatloaf mixtures. Bake these at 350 degrees 45-60 minutes or until the onions are tender, the meatloaf mixture is done and the juices run clear.

Peaches – this quintessential American fruit is most available July and August; however, depending on where you live, or if you grow your own, are available late June to late September. For the most part, peaches have been bred to eliminate the heavy, hoary fuzz of original peaches. You should, of course, rub off any fuzz under cold running water. Peaches freeze, can and dry well.
If purchasing peaches from the grocer or at the farmers market, select those that are free of spots, bruises or shriveled skins. They should have a bright, fresh peach fragrance when smelled at the stem end.
To store: keep at room temperature and use within a day or two of purchasing. For longer storage, can, freeze or dry.
To prepare: wash under cold running water while rubbing off the fuzz. To peel,

following the directions in Formulas and Foundations. Place peeled, pitted peaches in a bowl of cold water to which you have added 2 T lemon juice (to prevent browning).

Peppers – the words "pepper" and "chili" are used interchangeably. This section addresses sweet (also called bell) and hot (also called chili) peppers. There are so many varieties of chilies, with varying degrees of heat.
Bell peppers are sweet and come in a range of colors including green, yellow, red, orange, purple and, relatively recently, white. They usually have four lobes and thick walls. These can be used in soups, stews, salads, casseroles, the raw vegetable tray and stuffed. Peppers also have a substantial role in relishes, pickles and other condiments. See the Canning section for those recipes. California Wonder and Chinese Giant are two very good heirloom peppers to grow.
Fresh and dried chilies I use most often are arbol, jalapeno, poblano and ancho.
If purchasing fresh peppers from the grocer or farmers market, select peppers that are firm, heavy for their size, unblemished, have a solid stem (not shriveled or wrinkled) and a bright, glossy color. Store in perforated plastic bags in the refrigerator crisper where they will keep up to 2 weeks. Diced peppers freeze well and are good to have on hand to add to soups, casseroles and other cooked dishes.
You can buy dried peppers prepackaged from most grocers. I avoid these because they can be old and infested with weevils or gnats. It is much better to select your own from the bins of a Mexican grocer. The peppers you select should be shiny and dry, but pliable.
To prepare fresh peppers: remove stem, seed heart and white ribs before cutting into rings, strips, cubes or dice. If stuffing, it is well to cut a thin slice from the bottom so peppers sit level. You can remove the seeds and ribs from chilies for less heat. Follow recipe directions for further preparation.
To prepare dried peppers: wash under running water. Soften by covering with boiling water and weighing down to submerge completely. Let sit 15-20 minutes or until peppers have softened. Remove stems and seeds. Use the soaking liquid to rinse off the seeds. Strain soaking liquid through a cheesecloth-lined strainer and use for making sauces, etc. Follow recipe directions for further preparation.

Stuffed Peppers I
These two recipes feature a meat-based stuffing which you can vary by using sausage, ground turkey or chicken, lamb, venison or ham. You can also stuff with Rice Pilaf, Macaroni and Cheese, Creamed Vegetables or a mixture of cooked beans and corn for vegetarian options.
Preheat oven to 350 degrees. Have ready a casserole just large enough to hold the peppers. Add water to the depth of about ¼ inch.
Prepare by cutting off the top and a thin slice from the bottom if they do not sit level:
    6 medium sweet peppers
Remove seeds and ribs. Precook prepared peppers in boiling salted water for 5

minutes (after water returns to boil). Remove from boiling water and turn upside down on rack to drain. Sprinkle insides generously with salt. For crisper shells, omit this step.

Fry in a small amount of fat until done:
> **1 lb ground beef**
> **1/3 c onion, diced**
> **The pepper caps, stems removed and diced**

Season with:
> **½ t each salt and black pepper**

Add:
> **1 15-oz can diced tomatoes**
> **½ c water**
> **½ c uncooked long-grain rice**
> **1 t Worcestershire sauce**

Cover and simmer, storing occasionally, about 15 minutes or until rice is tender Stir in:
> **4 oz shredded cheese (about 1 cup)**

Combine rice and meat mixtures. Stuff peppers. Stand upright in casserole. Bake uncovered 20-25 minutes.

Stuffed Peppers II

Preheat oven to 350 degrees. Have ready a casserole just large enough to hold the peppers.

Prepare six peppers as in Stuffed Peppers I.

Fry until done, breaking into small pieces:
> **1 ½ lb ground meat (hamburger, sausage, pork, venison, buffalo, turkey, or a combination)**

In:
> **2 T fat**

Drain and combine, in a mixing bowl, with:
> **1 c cooked Rice**
> **½ t each salt and pepper**
> **1 egg**
> **½ T chopped parsley**

Fill peppers. Place in casserole.

Combine:
> **1 15-oz can tomato sauce**
> **¼ c prepared mustard**
> **¼ c vinegar**
> **½ c brown sugar**
> **1 T Worcestershire sauce**

Pour over and around peppers. Bake 25 minutes.

Top each pepper with:

Sliced or shredded cheese
Return to oven for about 5 minutes or until cheese is melted. Serve with sauce.

Stuffed Pepper Rings
Cut peppers into ¾- 1-inch rings. Place on serving plates and stuff with one of the Salad/Sandwich fillings, Pimento Cheese, Guacamole or any combination of chopped meat and your preferred vegetables, diced. Serve as-is, or napped with Mayonnaise, Thousand Island or Ranch dressings.

Jalapeno Popper Casserole
This casserole is easier to make than individual poppers, but with every bit the flavor and texture. Equally delicious hot, warm or room temperature, it makes an excellent addition to a potluck, tailgating or picnic buffet. Note: use more cheese if you like your poppers really cheesy.
Preheat oven to 350 degrees. Have ready a lightly greased 2-quart casserole.
Wash, cut in half lengthwise, and remove stem end, seeds and ribs from:
16 large jalapeno peppers
Layer in the casserole with:
8 oz Monterrey Jack cheese, shredded
Melt in a large skillet:
½ c butter
When the butter is melted and stops foaming, add:
1 tube butter crackers crushed into crumbs.
Stir well to evenly moisten crumbs.
Sprinkle crumbs evenly over top of casserole.
Cover loosely and bake 15 minutes.
Uncover and continue to bake until peppers are tender, cheese is melted and bubbly and crumbs are deep golden brown.

Potatoes – now available year-round, we began harvesting potatoes around July 4 for new potatoes, leaving the majority of the tubers to mature before digging and storing for use throughout Winter and early Spring. Some would argue it is more economical to buy potatoes, but then you can't experience the pleasures of just-harvested potatoes.
I still grow the heirloom Kennebec variety of potato. It has white flesh, a thin skin and is good baked, boiled, mashed, or fried.
If purchasing potatoes from the grocer or farmers market, select potatoes that are firm and heavy for their size with taut skin and no blemishes, soft spots, wrinkles, sprouts, green spots or mold. Avoid those that are green or have green spots. These have been exposed to the sun and will be bitter (and evenly mildly toxic to some). Store unwrapped and unwashed in a cool, dark, dry, well-ventilated place, preferably in a single layer—avoid bunching or piling when possible and do not store near onions or apples. After storing, should you find any with green spots or sprouts, just

remove before preparing.

To prepare: retain peels whenever possible. When needing to peel, remove as thinly as possible. I like to use a harp peeler or a sharp paring knife. You can also use a common swivel peeler (I avoid those after an accident in my early cooking years which resulted in almost peeling off half a thumb). See individual recipes for additional preparation instructions.

Potatoes have an interesting place in our family history. My sister, Ann, was named Home Economics Student of the Year in high school. I teased her she won without ever having peeled a potato! I think she was 25 or so when she did peel her first potato.

Mashed Potatoes

I love Mashed Potatoes!! How something so simple can be so delicious and satisfying is a miracle. Such special foods should be prepared with particular care. Growing up, I always used a potato masher to mash the potatoes and a wooden spoon, which I still have, to beat in the butter and cream. Now, however, I use an antique vegetable ricer to mash the potatoes. The result is light, fluffy potatoes with no lumps. I do sometimes, depending on the meal, serve rustic "smashed" potatoes with plenty of lumps. When preparing Mashed Potatoes, I usually allow one potato per person plus "one for the pot." Also, I find it best to cook in salted water. You can, of course, omit the salt from the cooking water and season when mashing, but I find a marked difference between the two methods.

Peel and slice:

2 lb (6-7 medium) potatoes, scrubbed

Place in large saucepan and cover with cold water. Add:

1 ½ t salt

Cover and bring to boil over medium heat. Skim off any scum that forms. Cook until potatoes are tender when pierced with a fork.

Drain potatoes (reserve cooking water to make Gravy). Press potatoes through ricer or food mill into warm pan, or use a potato masher to mash the potatoes. Add:

1 c hot heavy cream, half-and-half or whole milk

Beat until light and fluffy. Add:

4 T butter, softened

Continue to beat until butter is melted. Generously season with lots of:

Ground black pepper

Variations on a Theme:

Cream Cheese Mashed Potatoes: reduced cream or milk to ½ c; add 8 oz cream cheese with the butter. Mash potatoes. Beat in hot heavy cream, half-and-half or whole milk, if needed, to make light and fluffy.

Garlic Mashed Potatoes: Add 6-8 peeled garlic cloves (or more, if you love garlic) to potatoes and salted water. Follow instructions to cook and mash.

Cheesy Mashed Potatoes: A quick alternative to Scalloped Potatoes. Add ½ - 1 c of your favorite cheese, shredded, and follow the instructions to finish mashing. I like to coarsely mash the potatoes, add the cheese and stir gently until melted.

Potato Pancakes
Delicious served with Sour Cream and/or applesauce.
Using the large holes on a box grater, grate:
>   **4 medium white potatoes**

I usually do not peel the potatoes; either way produces acceptable results. You should have about 4 cups.
Grate:
>   **1 medium onion**

You should have about ¾ c.
Place potatoes and onion on clean kitchen towel and wring out as much liquid as possible. Place in large bowl.
Add and mix well:
>   **2 eggs, beaten**
>   **1 t salt**
>   **½ t pepper**
>   **2 T flour (optional)**

Heat ¼ inch of fat in a cast-iron skillet over medium-high heat. Scoop ½ c potato mixture and shape into patties. Working in batches, carefully place patties into hot fat, and fry until golden brown on both sides. Lay cooked pancakes on baking sheet lined with paper towels. Place in 200-degree oven to keep warm while frying remaining pancakes.

Variation on a Theme:
Vegetable Pancakes
Follow the instructions for Potato Pancakes using half (two cups) shredded potatoes and half (two cups) of shredded vegetables (squash, zucchini, cooked and chopped spinach, turnips, beets, kohlrabi and cabbage all work well).

Meat and Vegetable Pancakes (Patties)
Use half shredded potatoes and half ground meat (beef, lamb, venison, bison, pork, chicken, turkey or ham all work equally well). Use one egg. After browning on both sides, add 1 c tomato juice to the skillet. Simmer, covered, until done, 20-25 minutes. Remove patties and keep warm. Combine 1 T flour in ¼ water. Add to tomato juice. Cook, stirring constantly, until thickened. Spoon sauce over patties and serve.

A lighter version
Omit eggs and flour. Form and fry as above.

Fried Potatoes
We often had fried potatoes for breakfast on Sundays. This is one popular way of cooking them.
Scrub, peel dice or cut into strips like French fries:
>   **3 medium sized potatoes**

Place potatoes in single layer in large, heavy skillet. Pour in enough oil to barely cover potatoes (about 2 ½ cups). Turn heat to medium and cook until potatoes are done and have turned a very light golden color. Drain on a layer of paper towels that has been laid on top of several sheets of newspaper.

Variation on a Theme:
Scrub, peel and dice:
> **3 medium sized potatoes**

Cook in boiling, salted water until just tender. Drain.
Combine potatoes with:
> **1 c finely chopped onion**
> **(2 finely diced jalapeno peppers), or**
> **½ c each finely diced onion and finely diced sweet bell pepper.**

Heat heavy pan over medium heat until hot.
Add:
> **3 T fat**

Heat until fat is hot. Add potato-onion mixture. Cook quickly until potatoes are browned, turning several times. Serve hot.

Oven French Fries

These fries are easier to make than those fried in oil. They are also low-fat for those battling the bulge, but need their potatoes. You can use sweet potatoes with equally delicious results.

Preheat oven to 400 degrees. Have ready a large, shallow baking sheet lined with foil and sprayed with oil or cooking spray, or lined with a silicone baking mat.
Scrub well, dry, peel, if desired, and cut into wedges or traditional French fries, about ½-inch thick:
> **4 large potatoes**

Beat until frothy in a large mixing bowl
> **2 egg whites**

Add prepared potatoes. Toss to coat evenly. Place in a single layer, with space between each piece on baking sheet. Sprinkle with salt.
Place in oven. Bake, turning once, 15-20 minutes depending on size, or until well browned and tender.

Scalloped Potatoes

A basic dish which can easily become overcomplicated and distracting from the good potato flavor. I prefer to keep this dish as simple as possible; however, the variations are well worth making for special occasions.

Preheat oven to 350 degrees. Have ready a buttered 9x13x2-inch casserole or baking dish.
Peel and thinly slice:
> **3 lb baking potatoes**

Place in three layers in a prepared casserole.

Dust each layer with:
   3 T flour, in total (use 1 T for each layer)
Dot each layer with:
   3 – 6 T butter, total (use 1-2 T for each layer)
Sprinkle each layer with:
   Salt and pepper
   Paprika, optional
   Dry mustard, optional
Heat until hot:
   2 c milk or half-and-half
Pour over potatoes to cover.
Cover casserole and bake 30 minutes. Uncover and bake 50-60 minutes or until potatoes are fork-tender and top is well browned.
Variations on a Theme:
Loaded Scalloped Potatoes – add to each layer (except the top): finely diced ham; fried bacon or chorizo, crumbled; or finely chopped and sautéed mushrooms; and finely chopped chives or green onion or thinly sliced green pepper; and your favorite cheese, shredded.
Potatoes Scalloped with Cream and Wine - Sprinkle each layer with a total of 2 - 2 ½ t dried herb and 1 ½ c grated Gruyere cheese. Replace the milk or half-and-half with 1 c heavy cream and 1 c dry white wine. Bake at 400 degrees about 45-50 minutes. (Note: I like to use different herbs to complement the main course - sage is good with pork and lamb; tarragon with chicken and salmon; thyme with ham; marjoram with beef).
Quick Scalloped Potatoes – Cube the potatoes instead of slicing; measure into a large pot; cook in boiling salted water until just tender. Drain and combine with half as much Medium White Sauce. Place in prepared pan. Top with shredded cheese, if desired, or dust with paprika. Bake about 30 minutes or until bubbling and beginning to brown. Good served with any type of sausage.
Easy Scalloped Potatoes – Combine the cooked cubed potatoes with ¼ c butter, 2 c shredded cheese, a big squirt of the mustard bottle and pepper. Cover and let sit until cheese melts. Stir to combine. Goes well with meatloaf or as a substitute for Macaroni and Cheese.

Squash and Zucchini – all varieties of these vegetables, which grow on vines or bushes, are easy to grow and prolific. Many are the jokes about the abundance of zucchini and what to do with the mother load. Both are very versatile and suitable to many seasonings and parings with other vegetables, meats, beans, etc. Summer squash and zucchini also may be used interchangeably in pies, cakes, muffins and quick breads.
Zucchini should be picked young and small. You should be able to pierce the skin with your fingernail.
If purchasing from the grocer or farmers market, the same rules, above, apply and

avoid any that are shriveled, wrinkled, or have soft spots, cuts or bruises.
To store: small, young, thin-skinned fruits in perforated plastic bags in the refrigerator crisper. More mature fruits, best suited for relishes, can be stored at cool room temperature for several days.
To prepare: if young, there is no need to peel or to remove the seeds. If yours are not, do both.
An eccentric professor-type woman once told us at the farmers market that zucchini is for creative people to make "stuff." It is one vegetable which has a myriad of uses. Zucchini is so versatile a vegetable that it is used in main dishes, relishes, breads and desserts. See the Bread and Canning chapters for additional recipes. The following are the main vegetable dishes, breads and cakes we enjoyed featuring zucchini.

Stuffed Zucchini
Preheat oven to 350 degrees. Have ready a shallow casserole just large enough to hold the zucchini.
Trim ends and slice in half horizontally:
   1 medium zucchini
Scrape out seeds leaving border. Salt generously. Place upside down on rack to drain for at least 1 hour.
Prepare:
   1/3 c Rice
Heat in a skillet over medium heat:
   2 T fat
Add:
   2 stalks celery, finely chopped
   1 small onion, finely chopped
Cook slowly until tender. Remove to bowl.
Crumble into skillet and cook until done:
   ½ pound sausage
Drain and add to onion mixture.
Mix in rice and:
   1 ¼ c tomato sauce
Combine gently. Taste and correct seasoning.
Wipe cut side of zucchini dry with a clean towel. Place in baking dish. Stuff with sausage mixture. Cover tightly and bake about 30 minutes or until zucchini is tender. Remove from oven. Combine:
   ½ c fresh bread crumbs
   ½ c grated cheese
Sprinkle tops of zucchini with bread crumbs and cheese. Return to oven for about 15 minutes to brown crumbs and melt cheese.
Variation on a Theme: Stuff the zucchini with one of the Meatloaf mixtures. Bake 40-45 minutes or until done.

Fried Zucchini
Prepare:
>**Zucchini**

Slice about ½-inch thick.
Liberally salt both sides of the slices and place on a wire rack set in a sheet pan to drain for at least 30 minutes and up to 1 hour.
Coat the slices with Bound Breading. Let the coated slices rest on a wire rack up to an hour before frying.
In heavy skillet, heat just enough fat to cover the bottom over medium heat until hot. Place each coated slice, in turn, into hot fat in skillet. Fry on each side until deep golden brown and heated through. Remove to a wire rack set over a baking sheet to drain. Keep warm in a 200-degree oven until all are fried.

Stewed Zucchini
Delicious made with either young or mature zucchini. Peel the zucchini and do remove the seeds, which can turn bitter when cooked, if using mature fruits. This is also good made with eggplant, either alone or with zucchini, which has been peeled, cubed, salted and drained. Brown the eggplant in hot fat (you'll need approximately twice the amount) before cooking the onions, pepper and celery.
Heat in a large pan until hot and fragrant:
>¼ c fat

Add and cook until translucent:
>1 medium onion, coarsely chopped
>1 medium bell pepper, coarsely chopped
>½ c coarsely chopped celery

Add:
>4 cups zucchini, cubed or cut into thick rounds (about 1/3 inch thick)
>2 large tomatoes, peeled and seeded, or 1 15-oz can diced tomatoes, drained
>3 T brown sugar
>3 T white or apple cider vinegar

Bring to boil. Reduce heat, cover and simmer about 10 minutes or until zucchini is just tender, but not mushy.
Taste and correct seasoning with:
>**Salt**
>**Pepper**

Add and simmer 1-2 minutes before serving:
>Herbs (¼ c fresh basil, coarsely chopped; or 2 T fresh oregano, chopped, or 2 T fresh cilantro, chopped)--use what will complement the main dish you are serving.

Zucchini Bread I
Quick bread doesn't get any better than this. Cinnamon is the only spice in this

bread. It gives a clear, bright flavor to the bread that really accents the rather plain-Jane zucchini. I encourage you to try the chocolate variation, if you don't like the regular variety—people will never guess they are getting a partial serving of vegetables with their chocolate! It has been a best-seller at the Atchison Farmers Market for years.

Two hints to great success: use the best cinnamon you can find. I like McCormick's brand Saigon Cinnamon; use olive oil (I prefer extra virgin) if you have it—otherwise use an unflavored vegetable oil. Make this bread the day before serving as it improves if allowed to rest several hours tightly wrapped.

The baked bread freezes particularly well if wrapped tightly in plastic wrap, then in aluminum foil and placed in a freezer bag. The frozen bread will keep throughout Fall and Winter if stored this way. Thaw, wrapped in plastic, in the refrigerator.

Preheat oven to 350 degrees. Grease and flour two 8x4x2-inch loaf pans (or one 9x5x3-inch).

Sift together:
- **3 c flour**
- **1 t baking soda**
- **1 T cinnamon**
- **½ t baking powder**
- **1 t salt**

In large bowl, beat until well blended:
- **3 eggs**

Add:
- **1 c oil, preferably olive oil**

Blend well and then beat in:
- **2 c sugar**
- **2 t vanilla**
- **2 c shredded zucchini** (use the large holes of a box grater or the grating attachment of a food processor)

Stir dry ingredients into egg mixture. Mix well. Pour into pan(s), dividing evenly. Bake 60-65 minutes or until knife inserted in center comes out clean (begin testing at 55 minutes as ovens vary). Remove from oven and let bread sit in pans for 5 minutes before turning out onto a wire rack to cool until just tepid. Wrap tightly in plastic wrap or place in airtight container to rest for several hours, preferably overnight.

Variations on a Theme: I particularly like adding one of the following:

1 c. toasted English walnuts, pecans, almonds, pistachios or hazelnuts, chopped
½ c diced crystalized ginger
1 - 2 c. mini chocolate chips; omit cinnamon
1 c fruitcake mix; omit cinnamon
1 c dried dates, apricots or prunes, chopped, or raisins; cinnamon optional
Replace ½ c flour with ½ c unsweetened cocoa powder (I prefer extra dark cocoa and extra virgin olive oil.); omit cinnamon.
Replace cinnamon with an equal amount of packaged Pumpkin Spice mix.

Replace an equal amount of sugar with one large box butterscotch cook-and-serve pudding. Reduce flour by 2 T. Sprinkle top of loaf lightly with sea salt after removing from pan, if desired.

Zucchini Bread II

From Aunt Mill's recipe collection. This is like a "fruit bread" with the addition of pineapple, nuts and dried fruits. It makes a fine addition to coffee or tea or snack time throughout Fall and Winter. Make ahead several loaves and freeze for future use.
Preheat oven to 350 degrees. Grease and flour two 9x5x3-inch loaf pans.
Combine:
- **3 large eggs**
- **2 c sugar**
- **2 t vanilla**
- **1 c oil**

Add:
- **2 c grated zucchini**
- **1 c crushed pineapple, drained**

Combine:
- **3 c flour**
- **1 t baking soda**
- **1 t baking powder**
- **1 t cinnamon**
- **½ t allspice**
- **3 c nuts and raisins, chopped dates or candied fruit, or a combination**

Add dry ingredients to egg mixture. Stir until just mixed. Spoon evenly into prepared pans. Bake 1 hour or until knife inserted in center comes out clean. Let cool in pans on rack 10 minutes before removing from pans. Let cool until just tepid. Wrap tightly and let sit overnight before serving. Loaves can be wrapped and frozen.

Squash Casserole I

This is a good side dish with any meat entrée. It is equally good hot or at room temperature which makes it good to serve in the Summer. I usually add one medium onion, sliced, with the squash for added flavor. Either sauté separately and add to boiled squash or boil with the squash.
Preheat oven to 325 degrees. Butter 8 4-oz ramekins.
Cut in half lengthwise, remove seeds and membranes and slice ½-inch thick:
- **3 lb squash** (yellow summer squash or zucchini work best)

Place squash in a large pot of boiling, salted water. Reduce heat; simmer 5 minutes. Drain well and cool.
Combine:
- **½ c unseasoned saltine crackers ground fine (about 16), or dry breadcrumbs**

    4 T butter, melted
    1 T sugar
    2 t kosher salt
    1 t ground black pepper
    2 eggs
Add squash. Fill ramekins.
May be made one day ahead at this point. Cover and refrigerate until needed. If refrigerated, bring to room temperature before continuing.
Sprinkle each ramekin with a total of:
    1 T finely ground unseasoned saltine crackers, or dry breadcrumbs
    1 ½ T melted butter
Place ramekins on baking sheet. Bake about 30 minutes or until heated through and tops are golden brown.

Squash Casserole II

This recipe uses convenience foods (canned soup, Sour Cream and packaged stuffing mix). It is particularly good for a light supper in Fall accompanied by a small salad and Baked Apples with cream for dessert.
Preheat oven to 350 degrees. Butter a 2-quart casserole dish.
Cook until crisp-tender, about 6 minutes:
    6 c sliced squash (¼-inch thick)
    1 small onion, halved and sliced
In:
    ¾ c water
    ¼ t salt
Drain well.
Brown:
    ½ lb ground sausage, crumbled
In:
    2 T fat
Combine cooked sausage with:
    1 can cream of mushroom soup
    1 c Sour Cream
Stir in:
    1 pkg. (6-oz) stuffing mix
Fold in squash and onion.
Turn into casserole dish.
Sprinkle with:
    1 c shredded Cheddar cheese
Bake 25-30 minutes or until bubbly and cheese is browned.

Zucchini Casserole I

Preheat oven to 350 degrees. Have ready a greased 1-quart casserole dish.

Cook in saucepan until just tender, about 15 minutes:
- **4 c chopped zucchini**
- **1 c chopped onion**
- **¼ c water**

Drain well.
Mash with:
- **2 T butter**
- **½ t salt**
- **¼ t pepper**
- **1 T grated Horseradish**

Cool. Then add, mixing thoroughly:
- **1 egg, slightly beaten**

Pour into prepared casserole.
Melt in a small skillet:
- **3 T butter**

Add and cook until browned:
- **1 c cracker crumbs**

Sprinkle over casserole. Bake for 30 minutes or until heated through.

Zucchini Casserole II

Preheat oven to 350 degrees. Have ready a greased 2-quart casserole dish.
Cook in a large pot of rapidly boiling water until tender, about 5 minutes:
- **3 c chopped zucchini**
- **1 medium onion, chopped**
- **1 large potato, peeled and shredded**
- **2 carrots, shredded**

Drain well.
Cook in skillet until done, breaking into small crumbles:
- **1 lb hamburger**

Drain off excess grease.
Place in bottom of prepared casserole.
Layer on top the vegetable mixture.
Top with:
- **Your favorite cheese, sliced**

Stir until pourable:
- **1 can cream of mushroom soup**

Pour over vegetable layer.
Toast and then make into crumbs:
- **4 slices bread**

Sprinkle evenly over casserole. Bake 25-30 minutes or until heated through.

Zucchini Casserole III

Preheat oven to 350 degrees. Have ready a greased 2-quart casserole.
Cook in boiling, salted water until just tender:
> 2 lb zucchini, chopped
> ¼ c chopped onion
> 1 c shredded carrot

Drain well.
Add:
> ½ c butter, melted
> 8 oz Sour Cream
> 1 can cream of chicken soup
> 1 box chicken stuffing

Turn into prepared casserole.
Sprinkle top with:
> 8 oz mozzarella cheese, shredded

Bake 40 minutes or until heated through and cheese is melted.

Zucchini Rounds

This recipe is from Aunts Marcelline and Geraldine. I like these rounds to serve with baked ham, chicken or fish (a good substitute for hush puppies).
Grate and place into a colander to drain while continuing:
> 2 c grated zucchini

Mix together:
> 1/3 c packaged biscuit mix
> ¼ c grated Parmesan cheese
> 1/8 t pepper
> 1 onion, grated
> 2 eggs, slightly beaten

Shape into 12 patties. Fry in hot fat until browned on first side.
Place ½ t butter on top of each round before turning to brown on second side.

Zucchini Pineapple Cake

This cake is baked in a loaf pan. Serve this plain, frosted with a Cream Cheese or Seven Minute frosting, or simply topped with pineapple or apricot preserves.
Preheat oven to 325 degrees. Grease and flour a 9x5x3-inch loaf pan.
Beat in a large mixing bowl until light and fluffy:
> 3 eggs

Add:
> 2 c sugar
> 2 t vanilla
> 1 c oil
> 2 c peeled and grated zucchini
> 1 c crushed pineapple, drained

Blend well.
Sift together:
- **3 c flour**
- **1 t baking powder**
- **1 t soda**
- **1 t salt**

Add to dry ingredients and toss to cover:
- **½ c raisins**
- **1 c chopped nuts**

Add dry ingredients to zucchini mixture. Mix well. Pour into prepared pan. Bake 60-65 minutes or until cake tests done. Let stand in pan 10 minutes before turning out onto wire rack to cool.

Chocolate Zucchini Cake

Preheat oven to 325 degrees. Have ready a greased and floured 9x13x2-inch cake pan. In a large mixing bowl, cream until light and fluffy:
- **½ c butter, softened**
- **½ c oil**
- **1 ½ c sugar**
- **2 eggs**
- **1 t vanilla**

Sift together in a separate bowl:
- **2 ½ c flour**
- **¼ c cocoa**
- **½ t baking powder**
- **1 t soda**
- **½ t ground cloves, optional**
- **½ t cinnamon, optional**

Add dry ingredients to butter mixture alternately with:
- **1 c milk**
- **2 c finely diced (not shredded) zucchini**

Mix only until combined.
Pour batter into prepared pan.
Sprinkle top with:
- **1 c miniature chocolate chips**

Bake about 40 minutes or until a knife inserted in center comes out clean.

Zucchini Cookies

A not-too-sweet cookie with a spicy accent.
Preheat oven to 375 degrees. Have ready cookie sheets.
Cream until light and fluffy:
- **1 c sugar**
- **1 c butter, softened**

    1 egg, beaten
Add:
    1 c grated zucchini
Mix well.

Sift together:
    2 c flour
    1 t soda
    ½ t cloves
    1 t cinnamon
    ½ t salt
Add and toss to coat evenly:
    1 c raisins
    1 c chopped nuts
Add to butter mixture. Mix thoroughly.
Drop onto cookie sheets by tablespoonful.
Bake about 15 minutes. Do not over bake. Remove to rack to cool.
Variation on a Theme: Replace the cloves and cinnamon with 1 T chopped fresh rosemary and raisins with golden raisins or chopped dried cranberries; use these cookies as a base for an appetizer with sliced ham or chicken.

Stuffed Acorn Squash

Preheat oven to 425 degrees. Have ready a rimmed baking sheet line with lightly oiled aluminum foil, or a silicone baking mat.
Place on a microwave-safe plate and cook 5 minutes:
    4 small acorn squash, washed
Cut squash in half; scrape out seeds and fibers.
Rub squash with:
    2 T olive oil
Sprinkle with:
    ¾ t salt
Place cut side down on baking sheet.
Scatter over squash:
    10 springs fresh herbs such as sage and thyme
Roast until squash is tender, 30-35 minutes.
Fry until crisp:
    10 slices bacon
Break bacon into pieces.
Reserve:
    2 T bacon grease
Just before squash is done, heat in a small saucepan:
    1 ¼ c maple syrup
Whisk in reserved bacon grease and simmer until mixture is thick like honey, 10-12

minutes.
Stir in:
> ½ c heavy cream
> 3 ½ c unsalted mixed nuts such as pecans, walnuts, cashews, hazelnuts and almonds
> **Bacon**

Fill roasted squash with nut mixture; drizzle with any remaining maple syrup and a sprinkling of sea salt.

Swiss Chard – this member of the beet family, which has nothing remotely to do with the Swiss, has leaves which are milder than spinach, some as mild as lettuce with stems that have an earthy celery or mild beet flavor.
If purchasing Swiss chard from the grocer or farmers market, select stalks that are firm with no blemishes and leave that are not torn, ragged or have holes (from bugs feasting on the leaves).
To store: place in perforated bags in the refrigerator crisper.
To prepare: wash in several changes of water to remove all traces of dirt, dust and grit. Strip leaves from stems and trim stem ends.
To cook: prepare leaves like Beet Greens; roast stalks, whole or cut into pieces, like asparagus with oil, salt, pepper and cumin. Whole leaves are good to make wraps.

Tomatillos – also known as the Mexican husk tomato, tomatillos are in the same family (nightshade) as tomatoes, potatoes, eggplants and peppers. The fruits can be green or purple and are enclosed in a papery husk. You can harvest tomatillos at any stage, but I prefer to pick them when the fruits have filled the husk and the husks has started to dry and break open.
If purchasing tomatillos from the grocer or farmers market, select those that are firm, heavy for their size and have no holes, cuts, bruises or wrinkled skins.
To store: in the refrigerator crisper set to high humidity.
To prepare: remove husk and wash well to remove the sticky coating from the fruits. See individual recipes for further preparation instructions.

Tomatillo or Green Tomato Salsa
Also called Salsa Verde (Green Salsa). A nice alternative to tomato-based salsa and a good base for Green or Chicken Chili. Simply add chopped cooked chicken, white or black beans and thin to soup consistency with chicken stock; heat and serve.
Have ready 6 glass pint canning jars, lids and rings prepared according to manufacturer's directions.
Combine in a large kettle:
> **5 c chopped tomatillos or green tomatoes**
> **1 ½ c seeded, chopped long green chilies**
> **½ c seeded, finely chopped jalapenos** (remove ribs and seeds for less heat; leave in for more heat)

4 c chopped onions
1 c bottled lemon juice
6 cloves garlic (or more to taste), finely chopped
1 T ground cumin
3 T oregano leaves, chopped
1 T salt
1 t pepper

Stir frequently over high heat until mixture begins to boil, then reduce heat and simmer for 20 minutes, stirring occasionally.

Ladle hot salsa into prepared jars, leaving ½-inch headspace. Seal and process in boiling water bath 15 minutes.

Variation on a Theme: for a quick salsa to use freshly made, using the amounts above, roast the tomatillos in a dry pan on the stovetop until browned to your liking (alternately roast on a foil-lined baking pan in a 400 degree oven). Working in batches, place in a food processor with garlic, salt and pepper and pulse until coarsely chopped. Stir in the other ingredients, if desired, reducing the lemon juice to 2 T, or to taste.

Tomatoes

Growing up on the farm, tomatoes were the familiar round, all-purpose variety. We grew the variety named Rutgers. The Campbell's Soup Company developed this tomato with Rutgers University in the 1930s. At one time, it was the most popular tomato variety in the world. It is a great all-purpose tomato that is equally good fresh and canned. It makes the most wonderfully flavored soup, paste, sauce and juice, and is also good sliced to use in sandwiches, salads, etc.

A frost will stunt or kill tomato vines. Fortunately, tomatoes ripen well after being picked while green. You can ripen tomatoes two ways. The first method is to pull the vines with the fruits still attached before the frost and move to a sheltered area, with temperatures above 55 degrees, such as a garage or basement, and allow the fruits to ripen on the vine. Harvest the fruits as they ripen. The vines will eventually dry completely at which point it is best to burn the vines to control disease.

The second method is to harvest the fruit before the frost and either wrap individual fruits in newspaper, or layer the fruits between layers of newspaper in bushel baskets or cardboard boxes. Avoid metal or plastic containers as these do not "breathe," trapping moisture which can cause mold and rotting. Sort the fruits according to their stage (green, some color, mostly ripe) and store accordingly. Check the fruits weekly and use as the tomatoes ripen.

These ripened tomatoes are best used in cooked dishes. However, a good preparation to use in salads, sandwiches, wraps, pizza, or to layer on crackers or toast for appetizers is to slice the tomatoes about ½-inch thick. Place on a baking sheet lined with foil, parchment paper or a silicone baking mat. Combine one part salt, half part each sugar and freshly ground black pepper. Sprinkle over tomato slices. Bake at 200 degrees about one hour, turning half-way through, or until the tomatoes are cooked through, shrunken and the juices have slightly caramelized.

Green tomatoes are useful for many things, including fried, in salsa or even a pie as well as a variety of pickles and relishes.

If buying tomatoes from the grocer or farmers market, select tomatoes heavy for their size and unblemished, preferably with the stem attached.

To store: keep tomatoes at room temperature as refrigerating will change the texture and the taste which you can never restore.

To prepare: wash and follow preparation instructions for individual recipes.

Green Tomato Pie

This pie is a result of having an abundance of green tomatoes one year. I had to make the pie several times before finding a solution that resulted in a not-overly-juicy pie. First, use a mandolin to cut the tomatoes into even, thin slices. Toss the tomato slices with the salt and sugar and let sit in a colander to release some of their juices. The addition of chopped candied ginger really enhances the green tomato flavor. The assembled pie freezes wonderfully for several months. To freeze: place completed pie in freezer until frozen solid; wrap tightly in plastic wrap and then in aluminum foil; return to freezer.

Preheat oven to 400 degrees. Have ready a 9-inch pie plate, preferably glass, and one recipe Pie Crust.

Combine:
- **3 c washed, hulled and thinly sliced green tomatoes**
- **1 t salt**
- **¼ c sugar**

Mix well and turn into a colander and leave to drain into a wide saucepan or skillet for a minimum of 30 minutes and a maximum of 3 hours. Turn the tomato slices into a bowl.

Add:
- **½ c golden raisins**
- **¼ c chopped candied ginger**
- **1 T cider vinegar**

Toss lightly to mix well.

Rapidly boil the juices until slightly thickened. Set aside.

Roll and fit pie crust into bottom of pie plate. Trim edges.

Combine:
- **3/4 c sugar**
- **½ c flour**

Sprinkle about 1/3 of mixture evenly onto bottom crust.

Layer on half the tomato mixture and pour over half the thickened juices. Repeat layers, ending with flour mixture. Then dot with:
- **1 T butter**

Roll and cover with top crust, sealing and fluting edges as desired. Cut steam vents into top crust. Cover lightly and refrigerate for about 30 minutes to let the dough

relax. (Or freeze until solid, then wrap tightly to freeze).
Bake pie 10 minutes. Lower heat to 350 degrees and continue baking about 50 minutes or until crust is golden, tomatoes are tender and the juices bubble thickly at the center. Cover the edges with foil or a silicone cover if browning too quickly. Remove to wire rack to cool thoroughly before serving.
If baking a frozen pie, bake the entire time at 350 degrees for about 90 minutes. Cover with a sheet of foil if browning too quickly.

Fried Green Tomatoes
A classic dish often maligned with a hard crust, gritty cornmeal and slimy innards. Use solid, firm green tomatoes, heavy for their size.
Core and remove a thin slice from the top and bottom of:
> **4 medium to large green tomatoes**

Slice about ½-inch thick.
Liberally salt both sides of the slices and place on a wire rack set in a sheet pan to drain for at least 30 minutes and up to 1 hour.
Coat the slices with:
> **Bound Breading**

Let the coated slices rest on a wire rack up to an hour before frying.
In heavy skillet, heat just enough fat to cover the bottom over medium heat until hot. Place each coated tomato slice, in turn, into hot fat in skillet. Fry on each side until deep golden brown and heated through. Remove to a wire rack set over a baking sheet to drain. Keep warm in a 200-degree oven until all are fried.
Variations on a Theme: Use ripe tomatoes. Let drain on a clean kitchen towel (omit salting step) for at least 30 minutes and up to 1 hour. Bread and fry immediately. Top each fried slice with ½ t brown sugar before serving, if desired.

Baked Tomatoes
Baked tomatoes make a welcome addition to breakfast, dinner or supper. Two versions are offered here. Both are equally delicious made with vine-ripened fruits or late-season fruits that have ripened after picking. Baked Tomatoes II are also good using canned or stewed tomatoes.

Baked Tomatoes I
Preheat oven to 350 degrees. Have ready a shallow casserole just large enough to hold the tomatoes.
This recipe is for one tomato per serving.
Core and remove the seeds, if desired, from:
> **Tomatoes**

If tomatoes do not sit level on their own, cut off a small slice from the bottom. Place in casserole.
Sprinkle liberally with:
> **Salt**

Pepper
Sugar
Top with:
About ¼ - 1/3 cup fresh or dried bread crumbs
Drizzle with:
Melted butter or olive oil
Bake 20-25 minutes until heated through and crumbs are golden brown.

Baked Tomatoes II
Preheat oven to 350 degrees. Soften ½ c butter. Have ready an 11x7x2-inch casserole or baking dish.
Butter one side each of:
8 slices bread, preferably Everyday Bread
Use bread, buttered side down, to line baking dish (bottom and sides), cutting slices to fit.
Bake 15-20 minutes or until bread begins to brown.
Core and remove seeds from:
4 large tomatoes
Slice or cut into medium-sized pieces.
Add to taste:
Salt
Pepper
Sugar
Pour into bread-lined baking dish. Top with additional slices of bread, buttered-side up. Bake 40-45 minutes or until heated through and top bread is toasted to golden brown.

Watermelon – unlike other melons, there is only one type of watermelon with a honey-sweet taste and flesh that can be red, pink, white or yellow. Watermelons are easy to grow, but require a lot of space and a regular supply of water.
If purchasing watermelons from the grocer or farmers market, select one with a sweet watermelon fragrance, the flesh should you be able to see it should be dense and firm and the seeds dark (although a seedless watermelon may have small white "seeds"). If buying a whole melon, it should have a waxy sheen on the rind and a yellowish patch on the underside—a sure sign it was ripened on the vine.
To store: refrigerate as soon as possible after picking or purchasing.
To prepare: wash well. Cut in half and then into slices, or peel and cube the flesh or cut with a melon baller.

Watermelon Chiffon Pie
Chiffon pies are light, airy and remind me of deliciously flavored clouds. Ethereal. It is a great Summertime pie. If the rind is unblemished and the white part is thick, be sure to save to put up a batch of Watermelon Pickles.

Have ready a 9-inch graham cracker crust.
Cut into cubes, discarding rind and seeds:
>   **3 ½ pounds ripe watermelon**

Process watermelon in blender or food processor until smooth. Strain juice into clean measure. You should have 1 ½ c juice. Treat the chickens to the pulp.
Pour juice into saucepan and add:
>   **1/3 c sugar**
>   **1/8 t salt**

Sprinkle over top:
>   **1 envelope unflavored gelatin**

Let stand 5 minutes. Stir over medium heat until gelatin is dissolved, then add:
>   **2 t lemon juice**

Cover and refrigerate 1 hour or until mixture thickens and mounds slightly when dropped from a spoon.
Whip to soft peaks:
>   **2 egg whites**

Fold into gelatin mixture.
Whip to stiff peaks:
>   **½ c whipping cream**

Fold into gelatin mixture. Spoon into pie shell. Chill 6-8 hours or overnight in refrigerator.

Watermelon Rind Pickles

Resourceful is the one who uses all parts of the fruits, vegetables, grains, meats, fish and fowl at hand. There are several examples throughout this book in that regard. These pickles make use of the white part of the watermelon rind and are a good alternative to the usual pickles. You can use green or red food coloring if you want to color the pickles. I'm not a fan. These have a spicy flavoring from the cloves and cinnamon that goes especially well with game meats like bison, venison, pheasant and the like.
Have ready a number of pint glass canning jars, lids and rings prepared according to manufacturer's directions. The number will depend on how large your watermelon and how may cups of rind you get.
Peel and remove all the green and pink portions from the rind of:
>   **1 large watermelon**

Cut the white part into 1-inch cubes.
Soak overnight covered in:
>   **Salt water (1/4 c canning salt to each quart of water)**

Drain, cover with fresh water and cook until almost tender. This will only take 3-5 minutes.
Drain.
Make a syrup of:
>   **8 c sugar**

4 c vinegar
8 t whole cloves
16 cinnamon sticks
1 t mustard seed

Tie the spices in a piece of cheesecloth.

Heat to boiling and allow to sit for 15 minutes. Remove spice bag.

Add the drained watermelon and let stand overnight.

Remove rind. Reboil syrup and pour over rind.

Let sit overnight as before.

On the third day, pack the rind into the prepared jars, leaving 1-inch headspace.

Bring syrup to boiling (add the food coloring now, if using).

Cover with boiling syrup, leaving ½-inch headspace. Seal and process in a boiling-water bath 10 minutes (see Canning and Preserving chapter).

Salads

This section features a variety of salads which are good accompaniments to dinners and suppers, or a main dish for a luncheon. Each is a good addition to a buffet, and several together could comprise a complete buffet. I recall one of my cousins had a salad buffet for his wedding reception.

Tomato and Onion Salad

This salad is so simple and so delicious. Both qualities depend on the garden-fresh tomatoes and onions. Aunt Mill served this salad often during the Summer when we visited her and Grandmother on Sundays.

Arrange in individual serving bowls or on plates:
- **Tomato slices**
- **Onion Slices**

Sprinkle to taste with:
- **Salt**
- **Pepper**
- **Sugar**

Splash on:
- **Vinegar**

Three-Bean Salad

Many variations of this salad have surfaced through the years, including those with more than three varieties of beans. I prefer tradition. Canned vegetables vary in weight from 14.75 – 16 ounces. This recipe calls for those size cans.

Drain:
- **1 can cut green beans**
- **1 can cut yellow wax beans**
- **1 can dark red kidney beans**

Combine the beans in a large bowl with:
- **1 onion, thinly sliced**

Combine in a small saucepan:
- **½ c sugar**
- **2/3 c vinegar**
- **½ c salad oil**
- **1 t salt**
- **¼ t pepper**

Heat until warm and sugar and salt are dissolved.
Pour over beans and onions. Let cool. Cover and chill overnight.

Variation on a Theme: add ½ c each chopped green or red pepper and celery. Add 1 t mustard seed and ½ t celery seed.

Sauerkraut Salad – substitute 1 pint sauerkraut, drained and rinsed, for the beans, adding the *Variation* ingredients.

Preserving: This also preserves well by canning in pint glass canning jars. Omit the oil. Make enough of the sugar-vinegar mixture to cover the vegetables. Process in a boiling water bath for 15 minutes (see Canning and Preserving chapter).

Hot Three-Bean Salad
In a large skillet, cook until crisp:
    8 slices bacon
Drain bacon, reserving ¼ c drippings in skillet.
Combine:
    2/3 sugar
    2 T cornstarch
    1 ½ t salt
    Dash pepper
Blend into drippings in pan.
Stir in:
    ¾ c vinegar
    ½ c water
Cook and stir to boiling.
Add the same amount of vegetables as in Three-Bean Salad.
Cover and simmer 15-20 minutes, stirring occasionally. Turn bean mixture into serving dish. Crumble the bacon and sprinkle over top.

Frozen Cherry Salad
Have ready a 9x13x2-inch pan.
Combine in a large bowl:
    1 21-oz can cherry pie filling
    1 14-oz can sweetened condensed milk
    1 20-oz can crushed pineapple
Fold in:
    1 9-oz container frozen whipped topping, thawed
    ½ c chopped pecans
Pour into pan. Freeze until firm. To serve, thaw a few minutes, then cut into squares.

Carrot Salad I
One of Father's favorite salads is also easy to make and delicious with many main dishes.
Have ready a 6-cup mold.
Combine in a large bowl:
    1 ¾ c boiling water
    ½ t salt
    1 small package orange-flavored gelatin

Stir until gelatin is dissolved. Chill and when gelatin is about to set, stir in:
> **2 c grated raw carrots** (use the small holes of a box grater)
> **1 c canned crushed pineapple, drained**
> **1 c shredded Cheddar cheese (optional)**

Rinse mold with cold water, but do not dry. Pour gelatin mixture into mold. Sprinkle on top:
> **½ c finely chopped pecans**

Chill until firm.

Carrot Salad II
Peel and slice:
> **2 lb carrots**

Cook in boiling, salted water, until just tender.
Drain well.
Add:
> **1 onion, thinly sliced**
> **1 green pepper, cut into strips**

Pour over:
> **1 ½ c French Dressing, heated to boiling**

Mix well. Cool. Chill overnight.

Cabbage Salad
Good made with fresh cabbage, or drained Sauerkraut. Omit the salt if making with Sauerkraut.
Combine in a large bowl:
> **10 c shredded cabbage**
> **1 green pepper, diced**
> **2 medium carrots, diced**

Bring to a boil:
> **½ c vinegar**
> **½ c oil**
> **½ t celery seed**
> **1 c sugar**
> **2 t salt**

Pour over vegetables. Cool, tossing several times. Chill overnight.

Spinach, Chicken and Orange Salad
A perfect salad for a Spring or Summer luncheon or light supper.
Measure into a jar with a tight fitting lid:
> **3 T oil**
> **3 T orange juice, preferably freshly squeezed**
> **1 T sugar**
> **¼ t dry mustard**

> ½ t poppy seed
> 1 t grated orange rind

Cover and shake well to combine. Let sit at least 2 hours for flavors to blend.
For two servings, arrange half the following on each of two plates:
> ½ lb fresh spinach
> ½ c mandarin orange sections
> 2 Baked Chicken Breasts, thinly sliced
> 2 c sliced strawberries

Divide dressing evenly between plates and serve.

Basic Gelatin for Fruit Salad

Absolutely fresh fruit is a delight when served in a gelatin salad. The salads make either a good accompaniment to the main course or a dessert when served with Whipped Cream.
Have ready a mold or serving dish large enough to hold the gelatin mixture.
Soak until softened, about 5 minutes:
> **1 T gelatin**

In:
> **½ c cold water**

Dissolve this mixture in:
> **1 ¼ c boiling water**

Add:
> **4-6 T sugar**
> **A pinch salt**

Chill, and when it is about to set, combine with 1 ½ c prepared fruit.
Variation on a Theme: white grape juice may be substituted for the water. Delicious with fresh raspberries, peaches or canned pineapple is to steep ½ c mint leaves in the boiling water or white grape juice for 15 minutes. Drain and use this infusion in the basic recipe. The mint-pineapple version is a good addition to meals with lamb or game birds, especially duck.

Molded Cabbage Salad

This salad is refreshing anytime of the year—especially now that fresh cabbage, celery and green peppers are available year-round.
Have ready a 6-cup mold or serving dish with a cover.
Sprinkle:
> **2 envelopes unflavored gelatin**

Over:
> **1 c cold water**

Let stand 1 minute.
Add:
> **1 ½ c boiling water**

Stir about 5 minutes or until gelatin is completely dissolved.

Stir in:
> ½ c sugar
> ½ c vinegar
> 2 T lemon juice
> 1 t salt

Chill, stirring occasionally, until mixture is consistency of unbeaten egg whites, 45-50 minutes.
Fold in:
> 1 ½ c finely grated cabbage
> 1 ½ c finely chopped celery
> ¼ c finely diced green bell pepper
> ¼ c diced pimentos

Turn into mold and chill 3 hours or until firm. To serve, unmold onto serving plate and garnish, if desired, with salad greens.

Pistachio Salad
Combine in a large mixing bowl:
> 1 3 ¾ oz package pistachio instant pudding mix
> 1 16-oz can crushed pineapple with juice

Fold in:
> 1 9-oz container frozen whipped topping, thawed
> 2 c miniature marshmallows
> ½ c chopped pecans or pistachios, preferably toasted

Transfer to mold or serving dish. Refrigerate until set.

Orange Salad
Have ready a 6-cup mold or serving dish.
Combine in a large bowl:
> 1 4-oz package orange gelatin
> 1 24-oz carton cottage cheese

Fold in:
> 1 9-oz container frozen whipped topping, thawed
> 1 15-oz can mandarin oranges, drained
> 2 c miniature marshmallows
> ½ c chopped pecans

Transfer to mold or serving dish. Refrigerate until set.

Orange Pineapple Salad
Have ready a 6-cup mold or serving dish.
Combine in a medium saucepan:
> **1 large can crushed pineapple**
> ½ c sugar

Heat to boiling. Add and stir to dissolve:
>   **2 3-oz packages orange gelatin**

Add:
>   **2 c cold water**

Refrigerate until mixture begins to jell.
Fold in:
>   **1 c shredded Cheddar cheese**
>   **1 ¼ c frozen whipped topping, thawed**

Pour into mold, smooth top and sprinkle evenly on top:
>   **½ c finely chopped pecans**

Transfer to mold or serving dish and refrigerate until firm.

Apricot Salad

Combine in a large mixing bowl:
>   **1 small box apricot gelatin**
>   **1 24-oz carton small curd cottage cheese**
>   **1 16-oz can crushed pineapple with juice**

Fold in:
>   **1 9-oz container frozen whipped topping, thawed**
>   **1 c chopped toasted walnuts**
>   **1 c finely diced celery**

Transfer to mold or serving dish. Refrigerate until set.

Cherry Pineapple Salad

Have ready a 6-cup mold or serving dish.
Drain, reserving juice for another use:
>   **1 large can crushed pineapple**

Place in large mixing bowl. Sprinkle over evenly:
>   **1 3-oz box cherry gelatin**

Add:
>   **1 24-oz carton small curd cottage cheese**

Mix well. Fold in:
>   **1 8-9-oz container frozen whipped topping, thawed**

Transfer to mold or serving bowl and cover. Refrigerate until firm.

Coconut Salad

This is a salad I invented myself while living in Alexandria, Virginia. Toasting the coconut is key to this salad. It provides a bit of crunch in addition to the pecans, and an intense coconut flavor results.
Have ready a 6-cup mold or serving dish.
Combine in a large mixing bowl:
>   **1 3 ¾-oz pkg. coconut or vanilla instant pudding mix**
>   **1 24-oz carton small curd cottage cheese**

Fold in:
- **1 9-oz container frozen whipped topping, thawed**
- **1 ½ c coconut, toasted**
- **2 c miniature marshmallows**
- **½ c chopped pecans**

Transfer mixture to mold or serving dish. Refrigerate until set.

Lemon Walnut Salad

The first time I had this salad, I marveled at the flavor combination. Who knew lemons and black walnuts are so good together? It is a rather sweet salad, so a little goes a long way, and serve it with savory and/or spicy dishes to balance the meal. Have ready a lightly oiled 6-cup mold or serving dish. Inez, a co-worker at Fort Leavenworth gave this recipe to me. She was a delightful lady who loved to dance. We attended a conference one year in St. Louis. I still remember dancing with her to "Twist and Shout." Needless to say, she could do both better than I.

Dissolve:
- **1 3-oz pkg. lemon gelatin**

In:
- **1 c boiling water**

Chill until syrupy. Whip on high speed of electric mixer until fluffy.

Beat in:
- **1 15-oz can lemon pie filling**

Fold in:
- **1 c frozen whipped topping, thawed**
- **1 c black walnuts, finely chopped**

Transfer to mold or serving dish. Chill until firm.

Coconut Cherry Salad

Have ready a lightly oiled 3-cup mold.

In medium saucepan, soften:
- **1 envelope unflavored gelatin**

In:
- **½ c cold water**

Stir over low heat until gelatin is dissolved. Remove from heat.

Blend in:
- **2 c Sour Cream**

Mix well.

Add:
- **½ c sugar**
- **3 ½ oz flaked coconut**

Turn mixture into mold. Chill until firm.
Unmold onto serving dish. Serve topped with:
- **1 21-oz can cherry pie filling**

Additional coconut

Variation on a Theme: substitute 1 c cooked Rice for the coconut.

Bacon and Egg Salad/Sandwich Filling

Especially good served on croissants or biscuits.
Combine in a mixing bowl:
- **10 Hard-boiled Eggs, chopped**
- **8 slices bacon, fried crisp, drained and chopped**
- **½ c shredded Cheddar cheese**
- **½ c Sour Cream**
- **½ c Mayonnaise**
- **2 T grated onion**
- **¼ t salt**
- **¼ t pepper**

Cover and refrigerate at least 2 hours.

Crab Salad/Sandwich Filling

Try this on toasted English Muffin Bread slices; broil until bubbly; top with sliced Cheddar cheese and broil until cheese is melted.
In large bowl, combine:
- **2 8-oz pkgs. crab meat, flaked**
- **1 c finely chopped celery**
- **1 c Mayonnaise**
- **1 2-oz jar diced pimientos, drained**
- **¼ c finely chopped pecans**
- **2 T grated onion**

Shrimp Salad/Sandwich Filling

For salad, combine the dressing and shrimp (whole or chopped) and serve on shredded lettuce or mixed greens. For sandwiches, spread the dressing on two slices of bread; top with lettuce, tomato, avocado and whole shrimp, peeled, deveined and butterflied (split in half lengthwise, but not cutting all the way through to separate halves). This is enough for 6 large shrimp.
Combine:
- **1/3 c Mayonnaise**
- **1 t lemon juice**
- **¾ t grated lemon peel**
- **¼ t ground coriander**
- **1/8 t each salt and pepper**

Chicken Pecan Salad
Use only fresh tarragon in this recipe. Works equally wells as a salad, a sandwich filling or for appetizers served on cucumber slices, or on Pumpkin Bread, Zucchini Bread or Apple Cheese Bread slices.
Combine in a large mixing bowl:
- 1 c chopped cooked white chicken meat
- 2 t chopped fresh tarragon
- ¼ c Mayonnaise
- ¼ c Sour Cream
- ¼ c finely diced celery
- ¼ c finely chopped pecans
- Salt and pepper to taste

Green Goddess Dressing
A bright, herbal dressing that is also useful as a dip. I included this recipe in this section because I always have it on-hand to mix with bits of leftover, chopped roast beef or pork, ham, chicken, turkey or fish to make a quick sandwich.
- ½ cup Sour Cream
- ¼ cup Buttermilk
- ¼ cup fresh dillweed
- ⅓ cup fresh parsley, preferably flatleaf
- ¼ cup fresh chives
- ¼ cup fresh basil
- 2 tablespoons fresh tarragon
- 2 anchovies
- Zest and juice of 1 lemon
- 1 shallot, minced
- Salt and freshly ground black pepper

Canning and Preserving

Preserving the foods we grew on the farm enabled us to enjoy the results of our labors throughout the year. We most often froze sweet corn, and canned tomatoes, green beans and pickles. We stored fresh onions, potatoes and sweet potatoes in the basement. Father would also buy a quantity of plums which we froze and a bushel or two of Jonathan apples which we kept in the basement to use during Winter.

This section includes the recipes I make most often, usually each year. What was preserved as well as how much was always subject to the weather and what the garden produced. The great thing is you don't have to have bushels or buckets of produce to put up food for later. Small batch canning works well for all of these recipes. Simply adjust the recipes to the amount of produce you have to preserve. Follow manufacturer's directions for preparing glass canning jars, lids (flats) and screw bands (rings). Be sure to use salt labeled "canning salt" as it does not contain iodine which may discolor some foods.

Boiling Water Bath: This process is safe for high-acid vegetables like tomatoes, pickles, jams and jellies and Sauerkraut. You can find large kettles with a rack to hold jars at most department stores, grocers and hardware stores. The rack is necessary to keep jars from touching the canner bottom and to allow heat to reach all sides of the filled jars. Fill the canner about half full with water and ½ cup vinegar (to prevent hard-water deposits on cooled jars). Cover and place over high heat before you begin preparing the individual recipe. The actual canning session begins by putting filled jars into the canner of boiling water. Add boiling water, if needed, to bring water at least 1 inch above the tops of the jars. Place a tight-fitting lid on the canner. Bring water to the boil. Set a timer for recommended processing time only after the water returns to the boil. Watch closely to keep water boiling gently and steadily (if the jars are sloshing about, you're boiling too hard). Add boiling water if necessary to keep jars covered. Turn off heat and remove cover from the canner. Let jars sit 5 minutes before removing the jars from the canner. Put jars on a rack or cloth, spacing so air can circulate around them. Don't use a fan and avoid cold drafts. Do not retighten screw bands after processing. Test each jar the day after canning. Jars are sealed if the lid is curved down in the center and does not move when pressed down. If not sealed, refrigerate contents and use as soon as possible. You can reprocess, but the quality diminishes significantly. Remove the ring before storing your canned goods in a cool, dark, dry place.

Pressure Canning: A pressure canner is a worthwhile investment which will quickly pay you back for what one costs. The pressure canner is required to can and preserve low-acid vegetables (beans, corn, etc.), meats, sauces, etc. I defer you to the manufacturer's directions to operate and maintain the pressure cooker because these differ in the operation and maintenance of each.

Tomato Soup
I remember the first time Aunt Mill gave several pints of this homemade soup to me. It was better than the famous canned variety in all aspects (that, however, does have its uses). It is a treat with a grilled cheese sandwich for a light luncheon, Lenten meal or late-night cap. Be sure to cook the ingredients until very tender. Doing so makes putting the tomato mixture through a food mill much easier. Tie the bay leaves and whole cloves in cheesecloth for easy removal before putting tomato mixture through a food mill. I prefer to omit the butter when canning and add a tablespoon to a pint of soup when heating to serve.

Have ready 24 pint canning jars, lids (flats) and rings prepared according to manufacturer's directions.

Cook in a large stock pot, tying the herbs and spices in a piece of cheesecloth, until very tender:
- **3 ga chopped tomatoes**
- **14 stalks celery, finely chopped or grated**
- **8 medium onions, finely chopped or grated**
- **14 sprigs parsley**
- **12 bay leaves**
- **10-15 whole cloves**

Put through a food mill. Discard the skins, etc. or add those to the compost pile or feed to the chickens. Return the tomato mixture to a large kettle.

Stir together:
- **1 ½ c flour**
- **1 c sugar**
- **3 T salt**
- **¾ t pepper**

Slowly whisk into tomato juice and bring to full boil, stirring constantly. Add:
- **¼ c butter**

Stir until melted and mixed in.

Pour hot soup into prepared jars, leaving ½-inch headspace. Wipe rims, cover and seal. Process in a boiling water bath for 20 minutes.

Tomato Paste
This paste doesn't require long cooking to reduce the tomatoes to a firm, thick paste. It turns out beautifully red with a fresh tomato taste. Note: because tomato paste is so dense, it is best to pressure can according to manufacturer's directions. Do save some or all of the liquid that drains from the pureed pulp. It is delicious chilled and served as a drink plain or with spirits (think Bloody Mary without the pulp), and makes a great base for a boiled beef or chicken dinner, or soups.

Wash tomatoes, cut out stem end and remove any other blemishes. Quarter tomatoes and place into a large pot. Cook gently until all tomatoes are heated through and slightly softened. Put tomatoes through a food mill. Then pour the resulting pureed pulp into a colander lined with a clean white cloth (an old, laundered t-shirt is the best) that has been moistened with clean water. Let the puree drain until most of the liquid has drained. The remaining pulp will be so thick a spoon will stand up in it. You can adjust the consistency of the paste by adjusting the time you let the pulp drain. Heat the finished paste to boiling, stirring constantly. (I find that heating the paste in a large, microwave safe bowl, covered with plastic wrap, and stirring every 3 minutes, is preferable to boiling on the stove which can lead to scorched paste if you are not diligent stirring and watching.) Fill half-pint jars, leaving ½-inch headspace. Wipe rims and seal. Can according to manufacturer's directions (for pressure canner) or freeze in half-pint jars.

Variations on a Theme: After draining the cooked tomatoes, you can make a variety of sauces, salsas, Ketchups, etc. from the puree. Use the drained liquid to make the tomatoes the desired consistency. The benefits of this method are you don't have to boil for hours to reduce the tomatoes to the desired consistency, and you have the very flavorful juice for other uses, including canning Tomatoes.

Ketchup

Ketchup. Catsup. Either one typically refers to a tomato-based sauce. Variations are endless from there, including many different flavors, degrees of spiciness, etc. There is even a version made with immature black walnuts—only for the adventurous. I develop a method over the years that uses the tomato pulp, from Tomato Paste, and a mini-fermentation process as described, below.

Have ready 8 pint glass canning jars, lids (flats) and rings prepared according to manufacturer's directions.

Place into a large heavy kettle or Dutch oven:

    8 c tomato pulp
    1 t salt
    1 t pepper
    1 t paprika
    1 c vinegar
    ¾ c brown sugar
    2 T Pickling Spice, tied in a small square of cheesecloth

Heat mixture to boiling, stirring constantly. Reduce heat and simmer, uncovered, 20 minutes, stirring occasionally. Remove from heat. Let cool completely. Cover and let sit overnight.

Repeat process two more times; however, just bring to boiling point.

On the fourth day, the mixture should mound slightly when a small spoonful is placed on a plate. The mixture should not "weep," that is the mound should stay in shape and not leak any liquid. If it does, repeat process one or two more times.

Bring mixture to a boil. Ladle into prepared jars, leaving a ½-inch headspace. Wipe rims, seal and process in a boiling water bath 15 minutes. Remove to rack or clean towel to cool.

Spaghetti Sauce

Have ready 6 glass pint canning jars, lids and rings prepared according to manufacturer's directions.
Combine in a mixing bowl:
- **8 c tomato pulp (see Tomato Paste)**
- **3 T brown sugar**
- **2 T coarse salt**
- **1 T vinegar**
- **1 t coarsely ground pepper**

Measure mixture into a large kettle or Dutch oven.
Add enough reserved drained tomato liquid to make 11 cups of total mixture.
Bring to boiling. Reduce heat and simmer until mixture reaches desired consistency.
Remove from heat. Add:
- **2 c fresh basil leaves, minced**
- **½ c fresh oregano leaves, minced**
- **½ c fresh flat-leaf parsley leaves, minced**

Add to each jar:
- **1 T lemon juice**

Fill jars with sauce, leaving ½-inch headspace.
Seal and process in a boiling-water bath 35 minutes.

Variations on a Theme:
Add up to 1 T crushed red pepper flakes to base recipe.
Use a good quality Merlot wine in place of the reserved drained tomato liquid in the base recipe.
Vary the herbs by using thyme, tarragon, etc. snipped.
Add 6 heads Roasted Garlic to the base recipe after measuring and adding liquid to make 11 cups.
Add 2 sweet onions, 4 fresh poblano peppers and 2 sweet red peppers, roasted and coarsely chopped after measuring and adding liquid to make 11 cups. (Tip: cut onions into ½-inch slices and grill, broil or roast on a foil-lined baking sheet in a 400-degree oven until well browned.) Increase lemon juice to 2 T.

Canned Tomatoes

A variety of canned tomatoes in the pantry is worth its weight in gold.
Heavy ready glass quart canning jars, lids and rings prepared according to manufacturer's directions.
To peel tomatoes, bring to boil a large quantity of water in a large kettle. Working in batches and not crowding the pot, plunge tomatoes into boiling water for 12-15 seconds. Remove to a large bowl of ice and water. Remove core and skin. Place prepared tomatoes into a bowl until ready to use.

Whole Tomatoes – add 2 T lemon juice and 1 t salt to each glass quart canning jar. Pack in tomatoes, pressing so all spaces between tomatoes fill with their own juice. Leave ½-inch headspace. Seal and process boiling-water bath 45 minutes. Alternately, pack tomatoes in jars with lemon juice and salt. Add boiling water, tomato juice or liquid from Tomato Paste to cover, leaving ½-inch headspace. Seal and process in a boiling-water bath 45 minutes.

Crushed Tomatoes – Crush enough peeled, cored and quartered tomatoes to cover bottom of large kettle. Coarsely chop remaining tomatoes and add to the kettle, stirring and crushing to desired consistency. Simmer 5 minutes. Add 2 T lemon juice and 1 t salt to each glass quart canning jar. Fill with hot tomatoes, leaving ½-inch head space. Seal and process in a boiling-water bath 45 minutes.

Diced Tomatoes – best made with a paste-type tomato. Remove seeds from cored and peeled tomatoes. Cut into ½-inch dice. Pack into prepared pint jars with 1 T lemon juice and ½ t salt and ¼ t calcium chloride (optional, to maintain firmness), leaving 1-inch headspace. Add boiling tomato juice or liquid from Tomato Paste to cover, leaving ½-inch headspace. Seal and process in boiling-water bath 35 minutes.

Stewed Tomatoes – For each quart, place in prepared jars 2 T chopped green pepper and onion, 3 T chopped celery, 1 t salt, 1 T sugar, 2 T lemon juice. Fill with tomatoes cut in chunks, leaving 1-inch headspace. Fill jars with boiling water, tomato juice or liquid from Tomato Paste to cover tomatoes, leaving ½-inch headspace. Seal and process in boiling-water bath 45 minutes.

Salsas

Salsas are very much the product of individual taste, including the base (tomatoes, tomatillos, etc.), herbs and spices, heat level, etc. The best way to develop your favorite salsa is to experiment. The recipes that follow are those I make most often, subject to available produce.

Tomato Salsa

Use this recipe as a guide to personalize your own salsa by varying the vegetables, herbs and seasonings.

Have ready 6 quart canning jars, lids and rings prepared according to manufacturer's directions.

Combine in a large kettle:
>7 qt. peeled, cored, chopped tomatoes (preferably a paste-type such as Roma or Amish Paste)
>4 c seeded, chopped long green chilies
>5 c chopped onion
>½ c finely chopped jalapeno peppers (remove ribs and seeds for less heat; leave in for more heat)
>6 cloves garlic, chopped
>2 c bottled lemon juice
>2 T salt

    4 T pepper, optional

Bring to a boil, stirring frequently. Reduce heat and simmer 10 minutes.
Add:
    2 T ground cumin
    3 T oregano leaves
    2 T fresh cilantro

Simmer 20 minutes, stirring occasionally.

Ladle hot mixture into prepared jars, leaving ½-inch headspace. Seal and process in boiling water bath 20 minutes.

Arbol Salsa

A recent annual favorite and best-seller at the Atchison Farmers Market. This delicious salsa uses canned (preferably home-canned) tomatoes and dried arbol peppers. Start with five arbol peppers then adjust to your personal heat level.
Bake in a 350-degree oven on a foil-lined baking sheet until lightly roasted and fragrant:
    5 dried arbol peppers

Place in a blender jar:
    1 qt. tomatoes, drained
    The roasted peppers
    1 head Roasted Garlic
    1 medium onion, peeled and chopped
    ½ t salt

Blend until all ingredients are liquefied. Taste and add more salt, if desired.
Pour into a covered container and store at least overnight in the refrigerator to let flavors meld.

Tomato Juice

If ever there was an elixir made from garden produce, this is it. Aunt Mill's tomato juice was beyond compare. It had a bright, fresh tomato flavor heightened with a judicious amount of celery, onion, sugar and salt. Tomato crops vary from year to year, so you really need to be mindful of how your tomatoes taste and adjust the seasoning accordingly. Of course, your own particular tastes should rule.

Have ready 8 glass quart canning jars, lids and rings prepared according to manufacturer's directions.

In a large pot, bring to a boil:
    1 ga. tomatoes, cored and blossom end removed

Add:
    1 – 2 large onions, finely chopped or grated
    4-5 celery stalks, finely chopped or grated

Cook until vegetables are tender.

Push mixture through a sieve or food mill, casting aside skins, seeds, and remains of onion and celery.

Add to taste:
>**Salt and sugar**

Bring to a boil. Pour boiling juice into clean, sterilized jars, leaving one-half inch headspace. Cover, seal and process in a boiling water bath 15 minutes for pints, 20 minutes for quarts.

Larry's Taco Sauce

Cousin Larry was the town barber well into 2020. The following recipe is one he created himself. The first time I tasted this I could not get enough. In fact, one semester at university I used the dorm kitchen to cook up a batch using canned tomatoes—not 20 quarts, though! It is delicious with chips, vegetables, meats, etc. I now make this with 10 pints of tomato pulp made as in Tomato Paste. I prefer to grate the vegetables; finely chop if you prefer a chunkier sauce.

Have ready 12 pint canning jars with lids and rings prepared according to manufacturer's directions.

Wash, core, peel and squeeze out seeds:
>**20 qts. tomatoes**

In a large canner or stockpot, cook until they are reduced to about 10 pints. Stir often so the tomatoes do not stick and burn on the bottom.

When cooked down, add:
>**1 qt. vinegar**
>**2 c sugar**
>**4 large onions, finely chopped or grated**
>**4 large green peppers, stem, ribs and seeds removed, and finely chopped or grated**
>**6 t garlic salt**
>**6 t chili powder**
>**6 oz jalapeno peppers, minced (remove seeds and ribs for less heat)**
>**3 t ground black pepper**
>**6 t salt**

Cook until thick. Test a small spoonful by placing on a plate. If the mound releases juice around its edges, continue cooking until it doesn't. Fill jars with boiling mixture, leaving ½-inch headspace. Cover, seal and process in a boiling water bath 15 minutes.

Sauerkraut

Aunt Mill taught me to make Sauerkraut before I was out of high school. She would let me borrow her kraut cutter and wooden pestle for several years. I always planned to make Sauerkraut on July 4—a day off work and early Summer when the cabbages had matured. Aunt Mill packed her Sauerkraut into jars to ferment. I started out that way, but because you can no longer buy canning rubbers and zinc lids, have transitioned to packing it into a large food-grade bucket with lid to ferment and then canning in individual jars. I have an antique crock weight I use to keep the fermenting Sauerkraut under the brine. It takes a bit of time to prepare, and can be messy. Be

sure to put down newspapers on your work surfaces and floor to ease cleanup.
Use good, sound heads of mature cabbage. Harvest and wash the night before.
Use 1 pound salt for 40 pounds of cabbage; 2 ounces (3 ½ T) for 5 pounds of cabbage.
Remove outer green leaves and dirty leaves. Quarter the cabbage and cut out the core. Shred finely using a kraut cutter, a mandolin or a very sharp knife.
Put 5 pounds of cabbage and 2 ounces of salt into a large pan and mix with hands. Pack gently into a large crock or food-grade plastic bucket. Pack gently, but tightly, with a potato masher. Repeat until crock or bucket is nearly full. Cover with a cloth, a plate and a weight (a clean milk jug filled with water works well).
Place filled crock or bucket in a cool, dark, dry place to ferment. Choose a place that maintains 65 degrees; too cool and fermentation will take longer; too warm and the cabbage will spoil. Fermentation will take 10-12 days. During this time, check daily. Remove any scum that forms, and wash and scald the cloth, plate and weight to keep those free from scum and mold.
After fermenting, pack into prepared glass pint canning jars, packing tightly and adding kraut juice to fill jars leaving ½-inch headspace. Use a brine of 2 T salt to a quart of water if you do not have enough kraut juice for all jars.
Put on lid, screwing band firmly tight. Process in boiling water bath 15 minutes.

Horseradish

This fiery condiment is good with hot or cold meats. Horseradish is easy to grow, very prolific and will live for years. Be sure to grind the Horseradish in a well-ventilated area. I stand with my back to a fan so the air blows the fumes away. The fumes can cause eye and nose irritations as well as choking. A meat grinder with a medium blade provides the best texture; however, you can use a food processor to grind the Horseradish.
Wash under running water, scrubbing well:
    1 lb fresh horseradish roots
Use a paring knife or vegetable peeler to remove skins. Cut away any soft or dark spots, if needed. Cut the roots into pieces 1-2 inches long.
Grate or grind the Horseradish.
To each cup of ground Horseradish, add:
    ½ t salt
    2 T vinegar
Stir well.
Add just enough to bind the Horseradish to a spreading consistency:
    Heavy cream
Cover and chill for several hours before serving.

Dill Pickles

Also delicious made with green tomatoes—sliced, quartered or left whole (cherry or pear varieties).

Have ready pint or quart canning jars, lids and bands prepared according to manufacturer's directions.

Slice large cucumbers, quarter medium cucumbers or leave small cucumbers whole. Place into the bottom of each jar:

> **Garlic clove(s)**
> **Fresh dill (flower heads and leaves, or dill seed [1 t for pints; 2 t for quarts])**
> **Salt (½ t for pints; 1 t for quarts)**

Fill jars with:

> **Cucumbers**

Pack tightly, leaving 1-inch space between top of contents and jar rim:
Bring to a rolling boil:

> **Vinegar**

Pour vinegar into jars to cover contents and to within ½-inch of top of jar. Wipe rims, cover, seal and process in a boiling water bath 15 minutes for pints, 20 minutes for quarts.

Variation on a Theme:
Dilly Green Beans

Use pint jars and replace the cucumbers with whole green or yellow wax beans cut to fit into the jars.

Pickled Beets

Pick, wash and trim beets so only ½ inch of stems remain. Do not trim tap root. Place beets in large kettle and add water to cover. Bring to boil over high heat. Reduce heat and gently boil until tender. Drain and let cool until easy to handle. Trim stems and roots; remove skins.

Slice or quarter beets into large kettle. Combine equal parts of vinegar and sugar to cover beets. Bring to boiling. Ladle beets into canning jars and add vinegar-sugar mixture, leaving ½-inch headspace. Cover and seal. Process in a boiling water bath 15 minutes for pints, 20 minutes for quarts.

Dill Tomatoes

Prepare pint or quart jars, lids and bands according to manufacturer's directions.
Fill jars with:

> **Green tomatoes (slice or quarter large ones; use whole cherry or pear tomatoes)**

Add to each jar:

> **2 heads fresh dill**
> **2 cloves garlic**
> **1 hot red pepper, optional**

Boil in a large kettle:
- **2 qts. white vinegar**
- **2 qts. distilled water**
- **2 c pickling salt**
- **2 c sugar, optional**

Pour over tomatoes in jars. Wipe rims, cover, seal and process in a boiling water bath 15 minutes for pints or 20 minutes for quarts. Let cure 6 weeks before using.

Crab Apples

Crab apples are a lovely treat if you are fortunate to have them. They are too hard and tart to eat without cooking. However, pickling turns them into a divine accompaniment to a wide variety of meats and main courses.

Have ready pint canning jars, lids and bands prepared according to manufacturer's directions.

Bring to a boil in a large, narrow stockpot:
- **3 c sugar**
- **1 c water**
- **1 c vinegar**

Add until the liquid just covers them:
- **Crab apples, with stems, that have been washed (about 2 qts.)**

Cook gently just until the skins break.

Ladle hot apples into jars and cover with syrup, leaving ½-inch headspace. Wipe rims, cover, seal and process in a boiling water bath 15 minutes.

Sweet Pickles

Of all the produce we put up, Sweet Pickles have always been my favorite. We always had some type of pickle at each meal—sweets, bread and butter, beets, etc. All were delicious and reminded us of the bounty of the garden. My first recipe was much worn after many years, so I asked Aunt Mill for this recipe again. She enclosed it in a card with the following: "Dear Jim, I hope you can make this out. I think it is wrote up kinda dumb but that is the way I got it. I use a plastic bucket (I suppose it had pickles or some food in it). My stone jars gave out. Good Luck. As ever—Mill." If you are fortunate to have them, do use the old-fashioned stoneware crocks. There is just something about them.

Have ready 12 pint canning jars, lids and rings prepared according to manufacturer's directions.

Wash, slice about ¼-inch thick and place into a clean stone jar:
- **2 gallons of cucumbers**

Dissolve:
- **2 c canning salt**

In:
- **1 ga. boiling water**

Pour over cucumbers, weight down and cover. Let sit in a cool place for 7 days.

On 8th day:
Drain and pour over pickles in crock:
>   **1 ga. boiling water**

Cover and let sit 24 hours in cool place.
On 9th day:
Drain well.
Combine until dissolved and then pour over pickles in crock:
>   **1 ga. boiling water**
>   **1 T powdered alum**

Cover and let sit 24 hours.
On 10th day:
Drain and pour over pickles in crock:
>   **1 ga. boiling water**

Let sit 24 hours. Drain well.
On 11th day:
Drain well.
In large pot, combine:
>   **10 c vinegar**
>   **10 c sugar**
>   **4 T Pickling Spice (tied in a cheesecloth bag)**

Pour over well-drained pickles.
On 12th and 13th days:
Drain off syrup, reheat syrup (do not boil), adding each day:
>   **1 c sugar**

Pour over pickles. Let sit 24 hours.
On 14th day:
Scald pickles in syrup. Pack into prepared jars. Pour hot syrup over pickles in jars leaving ½-inch headspace. Wipe rims, cover, seal and process in a boiling water bath 15 minutes.

Modern Sweet Pickles

I titled these Modern Sweet Pickles because it is a variation of pickles made with lime (the mineral, not the fruit). The original method left the pickles lacking in taste and texture. I created this method to achieve the same results as the original Sweet Pickles recipe in less time.
Slice into an enamel or crock container:
>   **7 lb cucumbers, washed, ends trimmed and sliced ¼-inch thick**

Combine and pour over cucumbers:
>   **Cold water**
>   **1 c pickling lime**

Let sit 24 hours, stirring occasionally as the lime settles to the bottom of the container.
Drain, rinse with cold water and then cover with clear cold water. Let sit 24 hours.

Drain. Then follow the directions for Sweet Pickles picking up on the 11th day.

Sweet Dill Pickles

This recipe, from Aunts Marcelline and Geraldine, is perfect for those who like "half sours"—pickles that are not as sour (or sweet) as other recipes. The amount of brine provided is sufficient for 5-6 pint jars. It can be easily multiplied for as many cucumbers you have to be canned.

Have ready pint canning jars, lids and rings prepared according to manufacturer's directions.

Place into each jar:
- **2-3 garlic cloves**
- **1 head of fresh dill or ½ t dill seed**

Fill jars, to within 1-inch of top, with:
- **Cucumbers, cut into desired shape (sliced, cubed, lengths, etc.)**
- **1 small hot red pepper, optional**

Combine in a large kettle:
- **1 quart vinegar**
- **1 c water**
- **1 c sugar**
- **½ c salt**

Bring to boiling.

Pour mixture into filled jars to cover vegetables, leaving ½-inch headspace. Cover, seal and process in a boiling water bath 15 minutes.

Pickled Peppers

Chilies, jalapeno, bell, banana and pimiento peppers all preserve well. I have been canning jalapeno peppers (and serrano, when available) for several years. Note the oil is optional. Extra virgin olive oil is best for this product.

Have ready quart canning jars, lids and rings prepared according to manufacturer's directions.

Into each jar, place:
- **1 clove garlic, peeled**
- **1 t salt**
- **1 bay leaf**
- **2 T oil, optional**

Layer in:
- **Jalapeno peppers which have had a slit cut into one side**
- **Onions, peeled and cut into wedges**
- **Carrots, peeled and sliced ¼-inch thick on the diagonal**

Pack vegetables leaving 1-inch headspace.

Fill jars with:
- **Boiling vinegar**

Leaving, ½-inch headspace.

Wipe rims, cover, seal and process in boiling water bath 20 minutes.

Pickling Spice
A good basic mixture. Use to make pickles and your own Corned Beef.
Combine in an airtight container:
- 2 T yellow mustard seeds
- 2 T coriander seeds
- 1 T black peppercorns
- 1 T whole allspice
- 1 T whole cloves
- 8 whole cardamom pods
- 2 cinnamon sticks, broken into pieces
- 4 bay leaves, crumbled
- 1 t ground ginger
- 1 t crushed red pepper (optional)

Zucchini Relish
What to do with the abundance of zucchini each year? Make this relish! It is fantastic with hot dogs and hamburgers, added to potato and tuna salads, on cold roast beef sandwiches and perfect with all kinds of pork dishes. I use a metal meat grinder (the kind that bolts onto a table or other work surface) to grind the zucchini and onions. You can use a food processor, but the texture will not be the same.

Prepare 16 half-pint canning jars, lids and rings according to manufacturer's directions.

Combine in a large non-reactive bowl and let sit overnight, loosely covered:
- 10 c ground zucchini
- 4 c ground onions
- 5 T pure salt

Drain well. Rinse in cold water and drain well again. Put in a kettle with the following:
- 2 ¼ c white vinegar
- 4 ½ c sugar
- 1 T nutmeg
- 1 T dry mustard
- 1 T turmeric
- 1 T cornstarch
- ½ t ground black pepper
- 2 t celery salt
- 1 green pepper, finely chopped
- 1 red pepper, finely chopped

Bring to a boil and then reduce heat and simmer uncovered, stirring occasionally for 30 minutes. Pour hot relish into jars, leaving ½-inch headspace. Wipe rims, cover, seal and process in a boiling water bath 10 minutes.

Sweet Meat Relish

This relish is also zucchini-based and is a recipe Aunt Mill gave to me in the early 1980s.

Have ready 12 half-pint glass canning jars, lids and rings prepared according to manufacturer's directions.

Put through a food grinder or chop, in batches, in a food processor:
- 10 c chopped unpeeled zucchini
- 4 c chopped onion
- 1 large green pepper, stem, seeds and ribs removed

Place in large non-reactive container. Cover with water. Add:
- 2 qts. ice
- 3 T canning salt

Let stand 3 hours. Drain well.

Turn vegetables into a large kettle. Add:
- 2 ½ c apple cider vinegar
- 5 c sugar
- 1 t ground black pepper, preferably freshly ground
- 1 t turmeric
- 2 t dry mustard
- 2 t celery seed

Bring to a boil, reduce heat and cook for 30 minutes. Ladle mixture into jars, leaving ½-inch headspace. Wipe rims, cover, seal and process in a boiling water bath 10 minutes.

Cucumber Relish

A good use of surplus cucumbers, especially those which may have grown too large for other uses. If you use this type, be sure to remove the seeds (and skins if bitter). Prepare 12 half-pint jars, lids and bands according to manufacturer's directions.

Put through a food grinder:
- 8 c chopped cucumbers
- 2 c chopped onion
- 3 medium green or red peppers

Place in large non-reactive container. Add:
- 1 T canning salt

Let stand 10 minutes. Drain well.

In large non-reactive kettle, combine:
- 2 c white vinegar
- 3 c sugar
- 1 T canning salt
- 1 t cinnamon
- 1 t celery seed

    1 t turmeric
    1 t allspice

Heat until sugar dissolves. Add vegetables. Bring to a boil. Reduce heat and simmer 20 minutes. Ladle into jars, leaving ½-inch headspace. Wipe rims, cover, seal and process in a boiling water bath 10 minutes.

Bread and Butter Pickles

These seem to be regional favorites and the recipes vary by the region. I prefer to use small cucumbers and onions and for these to be sliced very thin. I use a mandolin, but a sharp knife and a steady hand will work, too.

Prepare 12 pint canning jars, lids and rings according to manufacturer's directions. Combine in a large non-reactive container:

    1 ga. sliced cucumbers
    8 sliced onions
    ½ c canning salt

Mix well and add:

    1 qt. ice cubes

Cover and weight down. Let sit 3 hours. Drain well.
In a large kettle, combine:

    5 c sugar
    1 ½ t turmeric
    ½ t ground cloves
    1 t celery seed
    2 T mustard seed
    5 c vinegar

Add cucumbers and onions. Place over low heat and paddle occasionally, using a wooden spoon. Heat mixture to scalding, but do not boil. Pour hot mixture into sterilized jars, leaving ½-inch headspace. Seal and process in a boiling water bath 15 minutes.

Freezing Fruits and Vegetables

If you plan to freeze fruits and vegetables, you should know the basics.

Most fruits can be frozen whole (strawberries, cherries, berries) with or without sugar. I prefer to freeze berries on a rimmed sheet until frozen solid and then pour into plastic freezer bags. This makes it easy to remove the quantity needed. Other firmer fruits such as apples and pears should be poached in a light sugar syrup and frozen in the syrup. The stone fruits (peaches, apricots, plums, nectarines, etc.) can be peeled (except for apricots and plums), sliced and frozen with or without sugar. Place all fruits in cold water into which you have added some lemon juice to prevent discoloring.

You must blanch vegetables to be frozen if you want to enjoy them at the same peak of flavor upon thawing. The only exception is sweet (bell) peppers which do not need to be blanched, but blanching for 2 minutes does soften them to enable you to pack more in individual containers. I like to remove the top, seeds and ribs from sweet peppers, place in a casserole dish so they stand upright, fill with water and then freeze. After freezing solid, I store these in plastic freezer bags. This prevents from pepper cases from cracking and breaking. I thaw and use to make Stuffed Peppers. Fortunately, the process of blanching is quite easy. It's little more than boiling an ingredient for a designated amount of time (see list below). Be sure to begin timing as soon as you place the vegetables in boiling water. Set a timer for accuracy.

Blanching Vegetables
Fill a large saucepan or kettle with enough water to cover vegetables and bring to boiling.
Add produce, cover and boil for the time indicated, below.
Once finished, drain and immediately place produce in ice water for the same amount of time to stop the cooking process.
Drain and place produce in a single layer on clean kitchen towels to dry the surface.
Place in a single layer on a waxed paper- or foil-lined baking sheets and freeze until frozen solid.
Transfer frozen produce to a heavy-duty freezer bag. Label and date bag.

Vegetables and Blanching Times
Green Beans – 3 minutes
Peas, green, shelled – 5 minutes
Peas, sugar snap – 1-2 minutes
Corn on the cob – 7, 9 or 11 minutes for small, medium, large ears
Carrots, whole baby – 5 minutes
Carrots, sliced – 3 minutes
Broccoli spears – 5 minutes
Onions – 4 minutes
Button Mushrooms – 4 minutes
Asparagus – 3 minutes
Cauliflower florets – 2 minutes
Summer Squash – 1 ½ minutes

To Freeze Corn
Every year while I was at university and then living in Kansas City, Aunt Mill would give me several containers of frozen fruits and vegetables as well as jars of pickles, beets, green beans and other items. I always treasured those gifts. I found this recipe, written in pencil on a piece of an envelope in Aunt Mill's recipe box.
This same treatment works well with green peas, too.
Combine in a large kettle:
    1 qt. water
    4 t salt
    1 c sugar

Add:

4 qts. corn, cut from cobs

Bring to a rolling boil. Cool and then fill freezer containers, leaving 1-inch headspace. Freeze.

Ice Creams and Sherbets

I bought my first ice cream maker in the late 1980s from a now defunct mail order book club which also offered several non-book items. It is one of many rare finds of a quality product from an unexpected source which has been worth every penny of the investment. It has certainly paid for itself many times over given how much ice cream I have made with it through the years. Mother enjoyed ice cream very much. In fact, she had a bowl—not a scoop or cup or cone, but a B-O-W-L—of ice cream every day. She did go through phases of adding various things to her ice cream—dill pickles, Peanut Butter, chocolate syrup, marshmallow cream to name a few. This chapter honors her.

The ice cream base recipe is one I worked out over the years to achieve a repeatedly rich, full-tasting ice cream with many variations. It makes 4 cups (1 quart) of ice cream, which is the size of my trusty ice cream maker. If you have not made ice cream before, or do not have experience scalding milk or making an egg-based custard, it is well to invest in an instant-read thermometer to assist you in these endeavors. You can, if you choose, to slightly lower the fat content by using equal amounts of cream and milk (and using fat-free, skim or 2% milk) and three whole eggs instead of all egg yolks. However, the texture will be different. It will be more icy than the higher-fat version. You can achieve a slightly less-icy version if you use the optional Cobasan--an emulsifier from Germany and available at some stores and online. You can also eliminate the vodka or other alcohol as suggested. However, the alcohol (including that in vanilla) act as antifreeze which keeps the ice cream from freezing rock-hard. Add the optional vodka and the vanilla once the ice cream begins to harden in the ice cream maker.

Ice Cream
In large saucepan, scald:
> **3 c heavy cream**
> **1 c milk**

The mixture should register 175 degrees on an instant-read thermometer.
Combine in a medium, heavy-bottomed saucepan:
> **6 egg yolks**
> **1 c sugar**
> **Pinch of salt**

Beat until thick and pale yellow in color.
Add, stirring constantly:
> **About 1 c of the scalded milk/cream.**

Mix well and then stir in remaining milk/cream mixture.
Cook mixture, stirring constantly and reaching all areas of the pan, over medium heat, DO NOT boil, until thickened. The mixture will start to form small bubbles

around the edge of the pan and release steam. The mixture will evenly coat the back of a spoon, and a finger drawn through the custard will leave a definite path. The temperature should be 160 degrees on an instant-read thermometer.
Remove from heat and pass through a fine strainer into a bowl.
Stir in:
> **Liquid or solid flavorings (see Variations)**
> ½ t Cobasan, rounded, optional

Mix well. Place bowl in larger bowl of ice and water, and stir until cooled.
Cover by placing a piece of plastic wrap directly onto the surface of the custard. Refrigerate at least 2 hours, preferably overnight.
Pour mixture into ice cream maker and freeze according to manufacturer's directions. When ice cream begins to harden, add:
> **2 T vodka, or other optional alcohol flavoring (see Variations)**
> **Vanilla or other extract flavoring (see Variations)**

Remove frozen ice cream to a tightly covered container and let ripen in the freezer at least 2 hours before serving. Store up to 1 week.

Variations on a Theme:

French Vanilla – scrape the seeds from two vanilla beans and combine with the sugar. Add the vanilla bean pods to the milk mixture before cooking. Add 1 t pure vanilla extract to the base.

Lemon, Lime or Orange – omit eggs. Scald 1 ½ c milk, add ¼ c sugar and let cool. Combine cooled, scalded milk with 1 c Lemon, Lime or Orange Curd and 1 ½ c cream. Follow base recipe to chill custard and freeze ice cream.

Pistachio – finely grind ½ c whole unsalted pistachios in a nut grinder or food processor. Combine with milk, eggs and sugar and cook as in base recipe. Tint custard with green food coloring, if desired. Add 2 T Pistacha (pistachio liqueur) instead of vodka, if desired.

Peanut Butter – whisk ½ c creamy Peanut Butter into hot milk mixture after straining and before adding cream. Add 2 T Amaretto instead of vodka, if desired.

Chocolate – bring milk to boiling and slowly stir into 1/3 c cocoa. Let cool and then proceed with recipe. Add 1 t vanilla. Replace vodka with chocolate liquor, if desired.

Chocolate Chip – add ½ c mini chocolate chips to chilled custard before freezing.

Coffee - add 2-3 T instant espresso coffee powder to hot cream/milk mixture. Stir to dissolve. Replace vodka with 3 T Kahlua, if desired.

Mint Chocolate Chip – add ½ c mini chocolate chips to chilled custard before freezing; add 2 T peppermint schnapps instead of vodka; tint with green food coloring, if desired.

Cherry Nut – add 2 T maraschino cherry juice to cooled custard; add ½ c chopped maraschino cherries and ½ c toasted, chopped pecans before freezing. Replace the vodka with kirsch or cherry brandy, if desired.

Butter Pecan – replace ¼ c cream with ¼ c butter in the custard base; add ½ c toasted, chopped pecans before freezing. Replace the vodka with butterscotch schnapps, if desired.

Fruit Ice Cream – scald 1 ½ c cream and ½ c milk as in master recipe. Let cool. Combine in a blender the scalded cream/milk, ¾ c sugar and 2 c fresh blueberries, strawberries, red or black raspberries, blackberries or mulberries. Blend until pureed. Replace vodka with cassis or Chambord, if desired. Chill and freeze as in master recipe.

Lemon Sherbet
This is the first ice cream/sherbet I made. It is still one of my favorites. I like to add 1 T vodka to this recipe so the sherbet doesn't freeze into a solid mass. Now, you can use lemon-flavored vodka to intensify the flavor!
Combine in a 1-quart saucepan:
- ¾ **c sugar**
- **Dash salt**
- **1 c water**

Bring to boiling, simmer 5 minutes. Cool.
Add:
- **½ c cream**
- **½ c lemon juice (preferably fresh-squeezed)**

Pour into refrigerator tray or 9x9x2-inch metal baking pan; freeze until firm.
In glass bowl, beat:
- **2 egg whites to soft peaks**

Gradually add:
- **¼ c sugar**

Beating to stiff peaks.
Break frozen mixture into chunks with wooden spoon; turn into chilled bowl. Beat with electric mixer until smooth. Add vodka, if using. Fold in beaten egg whites. Return quickly to cold tray. Freeze until firm.

Fruit Sherbet
Father remarked often about how good two of Aunt Mill's recipes were: fruitcake and this fruit sherbet. I was thrilled when I found both in the box of her recipes I received.
- **1 lemon**
- **2 oranges**
- **1 c sugar**
- **4 bananas, mashed**
- **1 c pineapple tidbits**
- **½ c maraschino cherries with juice, cut into pieces**
- **1 c cream**

Juice lemon and oranges. Remove seeds from pulp. Add pulp to juices. Add rest of fruit and sugar. Mix well. Whip cream until stiff. Add to fruit. Freeze in an ice cream maker according to manufacturer's instructions.

5 FALL

Fall has always been my favorite season of the year. The blue of the September skies in Kansas is unlike anywhere else in the land. The change of seasons from the heat of Summer to the cool of Fall seems to make work easier even though there is a lot to do to ready the garden and orchard to rest over the Winter and to prepare for the livestock to return to the farm from the pastures. Fall is a time of harvesting, preserving and planning. There's always much activity as the last of the fruits and vegetables ripen, and need to be harvested before the first frost. It is satisfying to see the results of putting up your own food to enjoy through deep Fall and Winter and into early Spring. With this final round of preserving comes an opportunity to plan for holiday gifts, too.

We started school in late August and were in the classroom the entire Fall season through the first couple of weeks of Winter. Grade school (grades one through eight) were the most enjoyable to me. The year was filled with learning and with special events, including: a Christmas play and program; a carnival; and an end-of-year picnic. In addition to those, we also had Halloween and Valentine's Day parties. These would rotate between the classes (we had two grades in each classroom). The students would provide the treats and games for these parties. Father Roberts treated all students to ice cream bars on St. Joseph's Day (March 19) to celebrate our patron saint's feast day. Sister Verona made many ceramic plaques and statues which the seventh- and eighth-grade students could purchase and paint. We spent several hours over a couple of weeks to paint what we bought.

Fall was also the time when we harvested the corn and soybeans, and the sows farrowed the fall litter of pigs. Father farmed with his brothers, Harold and Jack, for many years. They worked together like a well-oiled machine, each with his own primary role.

During haymaking season: Father and Harold would mow the hay or straw; Jack would rake it; Harold ran the baler; and Jack would drive the wagons through the fields while Father along with our older cousins would stack the bales on the wagons. During harvest season: Harold and Jack ran the combines; Father ran the trucks either to the elevators in Nortonville and Atchison, or to each of the farms to store the grain. As the fields were cleared, one of them would break off to disc under the stalks which would break down during the Winter adding nutrients to the soil for the next year.

Fruitcakes

Fruitcake is often maligned. However, I understand why given some of the recipes which exist that include a potent mix of spices, mincemeat, jam or jelly and other ingredients which make good door stops or a replacement for that brick which fell off the side of the house. Properly made, however, fruitcake can be quite delicious. Use the best lard (or butter), fresh eggs and candied fruit to make these fruitcakes. I have been making fruitcake annually since about 2010 and have a few vintage remains from several years stored for prosperity. Make the cakes at least one month before serving to allow the flavor to mature and mellow. If you don't want to use brandy to moisten the cakes, you can use orange juice; however, you will need to store the cakes in the refrigerator. Start with half as much orange juice as brandy to prevent the cakes from becoming soggy. Let come to room temperature before serving to heighten the flavors.

White Fruit Cake I

Both Father and Aunt Mill claimed their sister, Aunt Dorothy, made a splendid fruit cake. I was fortunate to find the recipe among the many Aunt Mill accumulated over the years. Interestingly, the recipe card is definitely Aunt Dorothy's handwriting, but a recipe from our parish cookbook includes a recipe titled "Dorothy's Fruit Cake" which has a similar batter but includes more fruits and nuts. I've included both recipes: the first exactly as written; the second with a modified mixing method (which I now use to mix all cake and cupcake batters).

Preheat oven to 325 degrees. Have ready a 10-cup tube pan that has been lined with brown paper (grease paper after lining pan). Alternately, use two paper-lined 9x5x3-inch loaf pans.

Cream together:
- ½ c lard
- 1 t vanilla
- 1 c sugar

Mix together in a large bowl:
- 1 c flour
- 1 c chopped nuts (your choice)
- ½ pound citron, chopped
- ½ c candied pineapple, chopped
- 1 c white or golden raisins
- 1 c mixed red and green candied cherries

Sift together:
- 1 c flour
- ½ t salt
- ¼ t soda

    2 t baking powder

Beat to soft peaks:
    5 egg whites

Add dry ingredients and fruit/nut mixture to lard mixture. Fold in egg whites.

Pour into prepared pan(s).

Bake for 2 hours or until cake tests done. If browning too quickly, cover with a sheet of foil.

Remove to wire rack. Let cake cool in pan 10 minutes. Remove cake from pan and let cool completely. When cool, remove paper.

Slowly pour evenly over cake:
    1 c brandy

Moisten clean, lint-free cloth with additional brandy. Wrap cake in cloth and store in an air-tight container for at least 1 month to let flavors mellow.

White Fruitcake II

This recipe is from Aunt Mill's little red recipe book. The addition of Sour Cream makes me wonder if the aunts strove to improve the cake over the years.

Preheat oven to 325 degrees. Have ready a 10-cup tube pan that has been lined with brown paper (grease paper after lining pan). Alternately, use two paper-lined 9x5x3-inch loaf pans.

Sift together:
    1 ½ c flour
    ¼ t salt
    ¼ t soda
    2 t baking powder
    1 c sugar

Combine in a glass measure:
    ½ c Sour Cream
    5 egg whites
    1 t vanilla

Mix together in a large bowl:
    ½ c flour
    1 c chopped nuts (your choice)
    1 c white raisins
    ½ lb citron, chopped
    ½ c candied pineapple, chopped
    1 c mixed red and green candied cherries

Sift flour mixture into large mixing bowl.

Add:
    ½ c lard, room temperature
    ½ cream mixture

Mix on low speed to combine then mix for 1 minute at medium speed. Scrape down sides of bowl. Add remaining cream mixture in three additions, beating 20 seconds

after each addition.
Pour batter over fruit and nut mixture. Combine well.
Spoon into prepared pan(s).
Bake for 1 ½ hours or until cake tests done. If browning too quickly, cover with a sheet of foil.
Let cool in pan 5 minutes. Turn out onto wire rack to cool. When cool, remove paper.
Slowly pour evenly over cake:
> 1 c brandy

Moisten clean, lint-free cloth with additional brandy. Wrap cake in cloth and store in air-tight container for at least 1 month to let flavors mellow.

White Fruitcake III

This recipe is from Aunts Marcelline and Geraldine. Similar to White Fruitcake II, but with the addition of cake flour and a different proportion of nuts and fruits. Also, the original recipe card has white raisins lined out and replaced with dates.

Preheat oven to 325 degrees. Have ready a 10-cup tube pan that has been lined with brown paper (grease paper after lining pan). Alternately, use two paper-lined 9x5x3-inch loaf pans.

Sift together:
> 1 c cake flour
> ¼ t salt
> ¼ t soda
> 2 t baking powder
> 1 c sugar

Combine in a glass measure:
> ½ c Sour Cream
> 5 egg whites
> 1 t vanilla

Mix together in a large bowl:
> 1 c flour
> 2 c chopped nuts (your choice)
> 1 c white raisins (or dates)
> 1 c candied pineapple, chopped
> 1 c mixed red and green candied cherries

Sift flour mixture into large mixing bowl.
Add:
> ½ c lard, room temperature
> **Half of the cream mixture**

Mix on low speed to combine then mix for 1 minute at medium speed. Scrape down sides of bowl. Add remaining cream mixture in three additions, beating 20 seconds after each addition.

Pour batter over fruit and nut mixture. Combine well.

Spoon into prepared pan(s).
Bake for 1 ½ hours or until cake tests done. If browning too quickly, cover with a sheet of foil.
Let cool in pan 5 minutes. Turn out onto wire rack to cool. When cool, remove paper.
Slowly pour evenly over cake:
>   1 c brandy

Moisten clean, lint-free cloth with additional brandy. Wrap cake in cloth and store in air-tight container for at least one month to let flavors mellow.

Dorothy's Fruit Cake
Preheat oven to 325 degrees. Have ready a 10-cup tube pan that has been lined with brown paper (grease paper after lining pan). Alternately, use two paper-lined 9x5x3-inch loaf pans.
Sift together:
>   1 ½ c flour
>   ½ t salt
>   ¼ t soda
>   2 t baking powder
>   1 c sugar

Combine in a glass measure:
>   ½ c heavy (whipping) cream
>   5 egg whites
>   1 t vanilla

Mix together in a large bowl:
>   ½ c flour
>   4 c chopped nuts (your choice)
>   2 c citron, chopped
>   2 c candied pineapple, chopped
>   2 c red candied cherries
>   2 c green candied cherries

Sift flour mixture into large mixing bowl.
Add:
>   ½ c lard, room temperature
>   ½ cream mixture

Mix on low speed to combine then mix for 1 minute at medium speed. Scrape down sides of bowl. Add remaining cream mixture in three additions, beating 20 seconds after each addition.
Pour batter over fruit and nut mixture. Combine well.
Spoon into prepared pan(s).
Bake for 1 ½ hours or until cake tests done. If browning too quickly, cover with a sheet of foil.
Let cool in pan 5 minutes. Turn out onto wire rack to cool. When cool, remove paper.
Slowly pour evenly over cake:

1 c brandy

Moisten clean, lint-free cloth with additional brandy. Wrap cake in cloth and store in air-tight container for at least 1 month to let flavors mellow.

Thanksgiving Dinner

We began having Thanksgiving Dinner in the evenings and invited Aunts Mill, Marcelline and Geraldine in the early 1980s when I started cooking in earnest while in high school. The first few years Grandmother also joined us. She died in 1984. The typical menu included turkey, Mashed Potatoes and Gravy, Dressing, Egg Noodles, Broccoli and Rice Casserole, Cranberry Sauce, Waldorf Salad, a selection of rolls and Pumpkin Pie. Over the years, we would rotate between our house, Aunt Mill's, and Aunts Marcelline's and Geraldine's. I got several of the recipes in this section from them, and those have become tradition over the years.

Dressing

We always baked our dressing separate from the chicken or turkey (technically the definition of "dressing," whereas "stuffing" is baked inside the bird). This version depends on onion, celery, fresh eggs, and a rich stock for its hearty flavor. Several days before making the dressing, lay out the bread slices on several racks to dry. The bread must be thoroughly dry to make this dressing. Do not attempt to make this with fresh bread. The results will be disastrous (Aunt Mill referred to it as "snotty."). Once dry, cut the bread into ½-inch cubes. The apple and raisins are optional, but give a wonderful flavor to the dressing that pairs well with poultry, ham and game birds. You can add one cup of diced fresh or canned pineapple (well drained). I made that one year and thought it was delicious with the ham for Christmas dinner. I was the only fan. This dish is rather like a pudding. It starts out very liquid, but bakes up into the consistency of well-Mashed Potatoes.

Preheat oven to 350 degrees. Have ready a 2 ½-quart baking dish (I prefer an enameled roaster), heavily buttered and:

1 24-oz loaf plain, white sandwich bread (24 slices), thoroughly dried and cut in ½ inch cubes

Place in a 2-quart saucepan with tight fitting lid:

½ c butter
2 large onions, finely chopped or grated
2 c celery, finely chopped or grated
1 large apple, peeled, cored and finely chopped (optional)

Cook, covered, over low heat until very soft, about 1 hour. Remove from heat and stir in, if desired:

1 c raisins (optional)

Let cool until just warm.
Place bread cubes in large mixing bowl. Add onion mixture. Mix well.
Stir in, 1 cup at a time, and stirring well:

4 cups (or more) richly flavored stock (chicken or turkey)

Let mixture sit until all liquid is absorbed. Beat well until the mixture is uniform in texture (no large bread crumbs remain). You may need to add additional stock. The mixture should be very liquid and well mixed.
Add:
> **4 large eggs**

Beat well. You should end with a very moist, homogenous mixture with the consistency of cooked oatmeal. Pour the very liquid mixture into the prepared baking dish. Bake at 350 degrees about 45 minutes, stirring every 10 minutes. When stirring, move the cooked outer portion (scraping sides and bottom of casserole) into the center. When done, the mixture will be steaming hot throughout and firm like Mashed Potatoes—a spoonful will softly hold its shape on the plate. Do not over bake.

Note: leftovers freeze remarkably well if covered tightly. Let thaw in refrigerator before reheating. I prefer to re-heat as if baking fresh—in a buttered casserole dish. The crispy, browned parts from the pan sides and bottom are delicious!

Sweet Potato Pie

This pie gets it special flavor from leftover mashed sweet potatoes. I prefer the filling to be coarse rather than perfectly smooth. You'll get the perfect texture if you use a wooden spoon to stir and smash the potatoes versus using a potato masher or ricer. If cooking sweet potatoes especially for this pie, you'll need 2 ½ cups. You'll also want to add 1 T brown sugar, ¼ t ground black pepper, ½ t salt and 2 T butter. Mix well.

Preheat oven to 350 degrees. Have ready one 9-inch partially pre-baked Pie Crust. Combine in a mixing bowl:
> **2 ½ c mashed sweet potatoes**
> **1 14-oz can sweetened condensed milk**
> **2 large eggs**

Mix well. Pour into pre-baked pie crust. Bake 35-40 minutes, or until knife inserted into center of pie comes out clean. Remove to a wire rack to cool completely.

Pumpkin Pie

Use 1 16-oz can pumpkin puree and follow the directions for Sweet Potato Pie. I prefer pumpkin pie without spices; however you can add 1 t pumpkin pie spice or cinnamon, if desired.

Crumb Topping for Pumpkin or Sweet Potato Pie

A recipe from Aunts Marcelline and Geraldine who made a pumpkin pie one year when we would celebrate Thanksgiving with them and Aunt Mill. The three sisters chose to live the single life and never married. I remember one time my sister, Ann, asked Aunt Mill why she never married. Her response: she could help more people if she didn't marry. She cared for Grandfather and Grandmother, and was a second mother to many of us. They always helped when new babies were born, or people were sick. They also helped other farming families during threshing season. They were saints.

Mix together in a small bowl:
- **1/3 c butter, softened**
- **1/3 c flour**
- **½ c brown sugar**
- **½ c coconut**
- **½ c chopped pecans**

Sprinkle over top of pie 15 minutes before the end of recommended baking time. If pie does not test done and topping is browning quickly, cover pie with a piece of aluminum foil to complete baking.

Streusel Topping

Use this as a topping for pies, coffee cakes and muffins. This is enough for a 9-inch pie or coffee cake or 12-18 muffins. Use cake flour, if you have it, to make an exceptionally crispy, crumbly streusel. You can vary this by using light, golden or dark brown sugar, by adding more, less or no cinnamon, and by using various nuts and/or spices. The black walnut version is splendid on a rhubarb pie.

In a food processor, fitted with a metal blade, pulse until nuts are coarsely chopped:
- **1/3 c brown sugar, firmly packed**
- **2 T sugar**
- **1 c pecans, English walnuts or black walnuts**

Add:
- **1 t cinnamon, optional**
- **½ c flour**
- **4 T butter, softened**
- **½ t vanilla**

Pulse briefly to make a coarse, crumbly mixture. Remove to a bowl and pinch mixture into small lumps.

Egg Noodles

There is nothing more simple to make than egg noodles—and nothing as delicious as hot, buttered noodles. Aunt Mill would always make noodles for Christmas and Easter dinners. The family loved them, and the noodles were always the first to go. Aunt Mill rolled and cut her noodles by hand which gave them a rustic, rough cut, but they were always thin and narrow. A pasta machine makes quick work of rolling and cutting the noodles. My machine has settings from 1 to 7. I prefer setting 6 in most cases.

The dough must be stiff, but not dry. Allow the dough to rest in a bowl of flour and covered with an inverted bowl for about an hour after mixing and kneading. This will make the noodles easier to roll as the gluten will relax, and the flour will have absorbed the liquid from the egg yolks.

Frozen egg yolks work beautifully in this recipe. If using thawed frozen yolks, you will need to add one or two tablespoons of warm water to the thawed yolks to make them fluidly liquid.

Mix until smooth and creamy then proceed with the recipe. Use the provided ratio of flour to yolks, adding additional flour, if needed to make a smooth, stiff dough.

Note: Noodles and Angel Food Cake have a ying-yang relationship: you can save and freeze the whites and yolks from each, respectively, to make either later if you wish. A ratio that has always worked for me is one egg yolk and ¼ cup of flour. I generally use about ½ t salt for 6 egg yolks. Mix the yolks well, but do not beat them excessively. Add the salt and mix until dissolved. Then add in the flour and beat well until all flour is moistened. If you have extra dry flour at the bottom of the bowl, sprinkle on water ½ teaspoon at a time until the flour is moistened. Stir into rest of dough. Knead dough until it is smooth, uniform in color and is slightly elastic when stretched. Place in a bowl of flour and cover with an inverted bowl. Let rest 1 hour. Cut dough into pieces about the size of an egg. I place the pieces in a bowl of flour as I work. Remove one piece of dough and roll thinly on a lightly floured surface or with a pasta machine. If using a pasta machine, roll though the widest setting, fold in half, turn 180 degrees and roll again. Do this several times, lightly flouring dough each time, until the dough rolls without adding additional flour. Then proceed to roll through the various settings until as thin as you desire. Lay rolled dough on lightly floured surface or hang on a rack (I use an antique wooden laundry rack reserved especially for this purpose) and let sit until the top feels dry to the touch. Turn dough over and let dry again before cutting. The strips should be pliable. If they are stiff and crack, they are too dry; however, do not discard the dough. It will be perfectly delicious when cooked. Follow manufacturer's directions for cutting if using a pasta machine. If cutting by hand, do not turn dough over to dry on second side, rather roll dough into a loose cylinder and use a sharp knife to cut slices to your desired size. For both methods, separate strands and place on lightly floured sheet pans to dry thoroughly if not cooking immediately. Dried noodles keep several months in an airtight container. Freeze in plastic freezer bags for extended storage.

Cranberry Dessert Quiche

Cranberries are one of my favorite fruits, and this is my absolute favorite holiday dessert. I have two spiral notebooks full of hand-written recipes (and one with a chapter which contains the start of the Weishaar family tree), and this recipe is in one of those as well as a good many of the recipes in this book. I first made this pie in the mid-1980s for Thanksgiving dinner. I make it at least once a year, every year—thanks to frozen cranberries. It is easy, beautiful and tasty. Note: It is very important to slice the apples very, very thin so that they soften a bit when placed in the hot cranberry mixture.

Preheat oven to 325 degrees. Have ready one 9- or 10-inch pre-baked Pie Crust.
Mix on very low speed until thoroughly combined:

 2 8-oz pkgs. cream cheese, softened at room temperature
 ½ cup sugar

Slowly add, one at a time:
> **3 eggs, room temperature**

Add:
> **1 t grated orange rind**

Pour into pastry crust.
Bake 40 minutes, or until a knife inserted halfway between edge and center comes out clean.
Remove from oven to a wire rack. Let cool.
Meanwhile, in a saucepan, combine:
> **1 cup sugar**
> **1 cup water**

Bring to a boil and add:
> **2 c cranberries**

Cook gently until most of the berries have popped.
Remove from heat and fold in:
> **1 ½ c apples, peeled and sliced very thin**
> **1 T grated orange rind**

Cool and then spoon over baked quiche. Chill thoroughly before serving.

Variations on a Theme: use pears in place of the apples. Replace apples with 1 c raisins; reduce sugar to ¾ c and cook raisins with cranberries. Replace apples with 1 c frozen sour cherries, thawed; increase sugar to 1 ¼ c; add cherries, tossed with 2 t cornstarch after cranberries have popped; cook an additional 2 minutes to cook cornstarch.

Waldorf Salad

Mother made this salad for a number of occasions, including the family Thanksgiving and Christmas dinners, and the annual Church Picnic. It is easy and delicious: the apples and celery are crisp; the walnuts crunchy; and the raisins chewy.
Combine and chill well before serving:
> **4 apples, cored, peeled and chopped medium**
> **1 small bunch seedless green grapes, halved**
> **1 c raisins**
> **1 c chopped walnuts, preferably toasted**
> **1 c sliced celery**
> **1 9-oz container frozen whipped topping, thawed**

Cranberry Salad

This salad is easy to make in the food processor. Alternately, you can use a food grinder. Vary the salad by adding: toasted, chopped walnuts or pecans; miniature marshmallows; peeled, cored and chopped apple; or raisins.
Wash, dry and cut into eighths:
> **1 large orange**

Working in small batches, pulse orange sections in a food processor until coarsely

chopped.
Return coarsely chopped oranges to the food processor bowl, again in batches, and add a similar amount of:
- **1 12-oz bag fresh cranberries**

Pulse until evenly chopped.
Transfer pulsed mixture to a large mixing bowl.
When complete, mix in:
- **1 c sugar, or to taste**
- **One or more of the additions listed above, if desired**

Transfer mixture to a storage container. Cover and refrigerate for several hours or overnight before serving.

Cranberry Sauce

Combine and bring to a boil in a medium saucepan:
- **1 c water**
- **1 c sugar**

Add:
- **1 12-oz pkg. cranberries**

Return to the boil and cook, stirring occasionally, until berries begin to burst.

For whole sauce: pour into a serving dish; let cool before covering and refrigerating.

For jellied sauce: continue to cook until most berries have popped. Remove from heat and mash with a potato masher. Press mixture through a sieve into a mold. Let cool before covering and refrigerating. Discard solids in sieve (or add to one of the treats in "For the Boys"). Recipe can be multiplied to make more, if needed.

Fall Fruits and Vegetables

Fall culminates in the harvest of fruits, vegetables, nuts and grains after planting in the Spring and cultivating throughout the Summer. It is also a time to preserve this bounty for use throughout the year. The preserved items and the recipes in this section are perfect to share with family and friends.

Apples - Although apples are in the market the year round, they are not at their peak from January to June. While several varieties of apples begin to ripen in June, the windfall applies—so called because high winds will knock apples off the trees—are prefect for making applesauce. I always gather these from the ground and cook them into applesauce.

If purchasing apples from the grocer or farmers market, select apples with flesh that feels firm and tight beneath the skin. Fruits should not have any soft or dark spots, bruises or holes. Preferably, the apples will have the stem still attached.

To store: keep apples at room temperature if using within a few days; otherwise, store in the refrigerator in perforated plastic bags. Bulk apples can be stored in a dark, dry, cold place (like an unheated garage or basement).

To prepare: wash and dry. Refer to individual recipes for further preparation.

Applesauce

If you have your own apple trees, use the apples the tree drops of its own accord or that blow off the tree in a high wind. Turning these "green" apples into applesauce makes use of what would otherwise be waste. Cooking the apples with the skin on adds considerable flavor to the finished sauce. However, if you want a chunkier sauce, it is better to peel the apples. Use apples with white flesh and very red skins, such as Romes, Macouns and Ida Reds, to obtain a naturally pink applesauce. Adjust the amount of sugar to make a sauce that is sweeter or more tart.

Wash, quarter, core and remove seeds from:
> **3 lb apples**

Place in a bowl with:
> **2/3 c lemon juice**

Toss well to coat.
Place the apples, drained of any remaining lemon juice in a large kettle along with:
> **2 c water**
> **1 ¼ c sugar**

Bring to a boil, reduce heat and simmer, stirring occasionally, until apples are soft. Press through a sieve, colander or food mill to remove skins.
Place in covered container and chill until serving.
Applesauce freezes well in plastic or glass freezer containers. You can also can it by packing boiling sauce into pint glass canning jars, leaving ½-inch headspace and

processing in a boiling-water bath 25 minutes (see Canning and Preserving chapter).

Red Hot Apples

These easy-to-prepare apples are one of Father's favorites. Use a good baking apple that will retain its shape when cooked through. We always used Jonathans.
Preheat oven to 350 degrees.
Halve, peel and core enough apples to fit in a single layer in a 9x13x2-inch pan.
In a medium saucepan, bring to boil:
> **2 c water**

Add in:
> **2 pkgs. cinnamon candies ("red hots")**

Stir over low heat until completely melted. Pour mixture over apples in pan. Bake, basting often, until tender when pierced with the tip of a knife.
Let apples cool in syrup.
To serve, drain apples and serve with:
> **Whipped Cream**
> **Sharp Cheddar cheese, finely grated**

Baked Apples

This is another favorite and easy way to prepare apples. The apple flesh will be tender and almost caramelized while the peels will be a deep mahogany color and very delicious. We almost always had these as a snack during the days when we butchered. Father and Uncle Harold would visit with Aunt Mill on Wednesday evenings while we children attended Catechism classes, and Aunt Mill often served these as a special treat in the Fall.
Preheat oven to 350 degrees.
Halve, remove the stem and blossom ends, and core enough:
> **Apples**

To fit in a single layer in a 9x13x2-inch pan. Place in pan cut side up. Dot each apple with:
> **A thin slice of butter**

Combine:
> **1 ½ c sugar and 2 t cinnamon**

Sprinkle evenly over apples.
Bake, basting often with accumulated juices until apples are tender and caramelized. Remove to a lightly buttered platter to cool.

Apple Cake

Fall in a Bundt pan! You can use any variety of apples available, but a mixture of apples provide the best flavor and texture. The standard for us was the Jonathan variety. Father would always order a couple of bushels from the local apple orchard in early Fall. We made many pies, cakes, baked apples, Fried Apples and Red Hot Apples.

This cake remains moist and fresh for several days. It is best to store the cake in a pie safe or other similar type of cupboard that is not airtight (don't store in a plastic container) as the cake has a very moist interior that contrasts nicely with a firm, golden-brown crust. The crust goes soft when the cake is stored in an airtight container.

Preheat oven to 350 degrees. Have ready a greased and floured 10-inch Bundt pan.
Combine in a mixing bowl and set aside:
- **4 apples, peeled, cored and coarsely chopped**
- **¼ c sugar**
- **2 t cinnamon**

Combine in a large mixing bowl:
- **3 c flour**
- **2 ¼ c sugar**
- **1 T baking powder**
- **1 t salt**

Beat in another mixing bowl until well combined:
- **4 eggs, room temperature**

Add and mix well:
- **1 c oil (preferably light olive oil)**
- **7 T orange juice**
- **1 t vanilla**

Add to dry ingredients and mix only until all dry ingredients are moistened and batter is relatively smooth throughout.

Fold in apple mixture, and pour into pan.

Bake 1 hour and 15 minutes (begin checking after 1 hour) or until cake tests done. Let cool in pan 10 minutes. Loosen cake from sides and center tube and turn out onto platter. Let cool. May be dusted with powdered sugar before serving.

Apple Dumplings

These dumplings feature apples in a biscuit-like dough which are baked in a buttery, spiced syrup. You can make these also with small Seckel pears or Asian pears. For a special, alternative dessert for Thanksgiving or Christmas, stuff the cores with fresh cranberries.

Preheat oven to 375 degrees. Have ready a 13x9x2-inch pan.
Make the syrup by combining in a medium saucepan:
- **2 c water**
- **1 ½ c sugar**
- **¼ t cinnamon**
- **¼ t nutmeg**

Bring to boil. Reduce heat and boil slowly 5 minutes. Remove from heat and stir in until melted:
- **¼ c butter**

Set aside while you make the pastry.

Combine in a mixing bowl:
- **2 c sifted flour**
- **2 t baking powder**
- **1 t salt**

Cut in, until mixture resembles coarse crumbs:
- **¾ c butter, lard or shortening**

Stir in all at once:
- **½ c milk**

Stir just until moistened.
Turn out on a lightly floured surface. Knead gently just until the dough is smooth. On lightly floured surface, roll dough to 18x12" rectangle. Cut into 6 six-inch squares.
Peel and core, but leave whole:
- **6 small apples**

Place one apple in center of each square. Sprinkle apples generously with:
- **Sugar and cinnamon**

Dot with:
- **Butter**

Moisten edges of pastry. Bring corners to center and pinch edges together. Place one inch apart in the pan. Pour syrup over dumplings. Bake 35-40 minutes or until apples are tender. Serve warm with cream or Whipped Cream.

Fried Apples

A good accompaniment to pork, venison and game dishes.
Stem, core, peel and cut into ¼-inch slices:
- **6 apples**

Melt in a large skillet:
- **¼ c butter**

Add in apples when the butter stops foaming. Stir well.
Cover skillet and cook over low heat about 15 minutes or until apples begin to soften and release their juices. Stir occasionally.
When apples begin to release their juices, add:
- **¼ c sugar**
- **¼ t salt**
- **½ t cinnamon, optional**
- **A dash of pepper, optional**

Continue to cook, stirring occasionally until apples are tender and juices thicken and begin to caramelize.

Brussels Sprouts - these miniature cabbages are juicy with a nutty-sweet cabbage flavor and are in season late Fall through Winter. In fact, Brussels sprouts become sweeter if touched by a light frost. They are easy to grow from seed, and require less room than cabbages because they grow along a stalk which can be up to 2-feet tall, depending on variety.

If purchasing Brussels sprouts from the grocer or farmers market, try to buy those still on a stalk. If sold loose, pick those that are solid and tightly closed, heavy for their size and with no yellowish coloring or blemishes. If sold packaged, I open and inspect the contents before purchasing.

To store: in perforated plastic bags in the refrigerator crisper.

To prepare: pull off stalk, if needed, remove loose leaves and trim stalks. Rinse and drain. If boiling or steaming, cut an X in the bottom of each so they cook quickly and evenly. If roasting or sauteeing, cut in half from top to bottom.

To boil: for 1pound of sprouts, bring 16 cups water and 2 T salt to a rapid boil. Drop in prepared sprouts and bring rapidly back to the boil. Boil uncovered until easily pierced through, 6-10 minutes for whole sprouts. Drain. If desired, return to hot pan and shake over high heat 30-60 seconds until dry.

To steam: place in a single layer in a steamer basket and steam over 1 – 2 inches of water until easily pierced, 8-15 minutes for whole sprouts.

To roast: you can pre-boil for 5 minutes, if desired, but I prefer to roast raw sprouts. Preheat oven to 400 degrees. Prepare 1 pound sprouts and cut in half lengthwise. Place in bowl and toss with 2 T olive oil, coarse salt and freshly ground pepper. Turn onto a large rimmed baking sheet lined with foil or a silicone baking mat. Roast 15-20 minutes or until tender and well browned. Excellent also roasted with: poppy or sesame seeds; minced garlic and Parmesan cheese (add cheese after roasting); or roasted and served with toasted nuts (chopped hazelnuts, almonds or pecans).

Cranberries – these tart berries come in varying shades of red, from light pink to almost black. This is just a sign of various varieties, not degrees of ripeness. Cranberries store well in the refrigerator and the freezer. I always buy extra bags and freeze to use throughout the year. One of my favorite sayings of Father's is, "You have more trouble than a cranberry merchant." He would usually say this to Mother when she was having some type of difficulty.

To store: short-term in their bag in the refrigerator crisper; long-term, transfer to plastic freezer bags or containers and freeze.

To prepare: rinse well; remove any bits of leaves or twigs, and any shriveled berries.

Cranberry Dressing

This dressing uses both cornbread and white bread crumbs for the base. It is hearty enough to serve as a main course for a light supper accompanied by a salad and fruit for dessert. The turkey liver is optional, but a fine addition.

Preheat oven to 350 degrees. Have ready a lightly buttered 2-quart casserole. Spread in an single layer on a large rimmed baking sheet:

  1 ½ c diced (½-inch squares) **Cornbread I**
  3 ½ c diced (½-inch squares) **white bread, preferably Everyday Bread**

Bake until evenly toasted, about 8 minutes. Transfer to a large mixing bowl.

In a large skillet, cook over medium heat:
- **1 lb sausage**
- **1 c chopped onion**
- **½ c chopped celery**

Stir often to break up the sausage and cook until evenly browned.
Add:
- **2 ½ t dried sage**
- **1 ½ t dried rosemary, crushed**
- **½ t dried thyme**

Cook, stirring to blend, 2 minutes
Pour mixture over bread crumbs.
Add:
- **1 apple, chopped**
- **1 c dried cranberries**
- **1/3 c minced flat-leaf parsley**
- **1 cooked turkey liver, minced (optional)**

Drizzle with:
- **¾ c turkey or chicken stock**
- **4 T butter, melted**
- **2 T brandy, optional**

Toss to mix well.
Turn into prepared casserole, cover.
Bake 30 minutes; uncover and bake until top is golden.

Kohlrabi – "cabbage turnip" in German. We usually planted these in late Summer for a Fall harvest. The kohlrabi is actually a swollen stem tasting of a delicate, sweet, nut-flavored cabbage.
If purchasing kohlrabis from the grocer or farmers market, select small kohlrabis, with leaves attached, if possible, and that are firm and unblemished. Strip off stems and leaves and store in perforated plastic bags in the refrigerator crisper.
To prepare: wash and remove the thin peel. Kohlrabi are best in the raw vegetable tray, or shredded for salad (kohlrabi slaw is delicious). Kohlrabi can also be boiled or steamed until crisp tender. Toss with butter, black pepper and grated fresh Parmesan cheese for an interesting side dish.

Parsnips – While living in Indianapolis, I grew a number of vegetables for the first time, including parsnips, peanuts, celery, carrots, and pinto, black and navy beans. Parsnips looks like large, white carrots. Their cooked textured is much like potatoes. These are a Winter vegetable and become sweeter after a light frost.
If purchasing parsnips from the grocer or farmers market, select medium-sized roots which are crisp, plump and unblemished.
To prepare: peel, and remove the core if tough, before cooking. Cut into cubes or slices.

Parsnips can be boiled and mashed like potatoes (either alone or combined with potatoes, carrots or turnips). They are also good creamed or glazed like onions, or roasted like other root vegetables or Brussels sprouts.

Pears – pears are one fruit which must ripen off the tree. Once ripe, they are highly perishable and last only a couple of days. The exception is Asian pears which are deliciously crisp and juicy fresh from the tree. Similar to apples, pears are available year-round, but are at their peak August – October. I planted a pear tree in the early 1980s, and it is still producing today. Pears freeze very well. Simply peel, core and slice. Cook in water to cover and with sugar sufficient to sweeten. Cook gently until just tender. Cool. Pack into freezer containers, leaving 1-inch headspace.

If purchasing pears at the grocer or farmers market, select ripe pears (they will smell like a pear and yield to gentle pressure). Avoid any with bruises, dark or soft spots or shriveling. You can finish ripening pears by placing in a paper bag, not too tightly packed, and rotating the bag daily until ripened.

To store: place in perforated plastics bags—not airtight bags or containers—in the refrigerator.

To prepare: generally, wash well, and peel, core and remove stem. See individual recipes for further preparation instructions.

Use pears in pies (delicious combined with cranberries); poached pear slices are good in Upside Down Cake.

Poached Pears

These make a refreshing change for dessert. You can serve them plain, with ice cream, cream, a splash of brandy, the centers filed with Chocolate Ganache, or a mixture of nuts and coconut, or stuffed with a cheese such as Brie, Camembert or Blue.

Combine in a large kettle:
> **2 c sugar**
> **1 qt. water**

Bring to a boil and stir until sugar is dissolved.
Lower heat and add:
> **Rind of one orange (colored part only)**
> **1 vanilla bean**
> **1 cinnamon stick**

Simmer for 10 minutes.
Add:
> **6 medium pears**, peeled and cored from the bottom; leave the stem intact and cut a small slice off the bottom so the pears sit upright.

Add additional water, if needed, to cover pears.
Cook gently, rotating and turning pears, until just easily pierced with a sharp knife.
Remove from heat. Allow pears to cool in poaching syrup.
Store, covered, in the syrup in the refrigerator until serving.

Remove pears from syrup and let stand upright on a rack to drain before filling and serving.
Reserve poaching liquid to poach additional pears. Remove rind, vanilla bean and cinnamon stick. The poaching liquid will keep for several weeks in the refrigerator or freezer.

Pumpkins – these Winter squash come in all shapes and sizes from petite to gargantuan, and in several colors including white, orange, pink, blue, green and all may be solid, striped, spotted or mottled. Pumpkins, like most Winter squash are heirlooms and are easy to grow if you have the room. Pumpkins can grow great vines several feet long in all directions.
If purchasing pumpkins from the grocer or farmers market (or picking your own at a pumpkin patch), choose pumpkins that are heavy for their size, with a thick, hard shell showing no soft spots, mold, cuts or bruises.
To store: keep whole pumpkins in a cool, dry, dark place with good ventilation. You can preserve pumpkin, cut into 1-inch cubes, using a pressure cooker to can; however, the cooked, mashed flesh freezes very well and is easier to process.
To prepare: scrub well. Remove the stem. Cut the pumpkins in half to start with. If very large, it is best to cut into several manageable pieces. Remove seeds and fibers, then peel, if boiling.
To boil: cut the flesh into 1-inch cubes and cook in boiling, salted water until just tender, 12-15 minutes. Drain well.
To roast a whole pumpkin: deeply pierce in four or five places around the top to prevent the pumpkin from exploding. Place on a large rimmed sheet and roast at 375 degrees 45 minutes to 1 ¼ hours or more, depending on size. Pumpkins are done when a knife or skewer easily penetrates shell and flesh. Cut in half, remove stem, seeds and fibers.
To bake pumpkin pieces: cut into pieces and remove seeds and fibers. Place cut side down on rimmed baking sheet. Add ¼ inch of water to pan and cover with foil. Bake at 400 degrees until tender.

Pumpkin Nut Bread
This bread make a good base for appetizers if you use half white flour and half wheat flour. Slice and top with Ham or Chicken Salad/Sandwich Spread, or spread with softened cream cheese and top with sliced summer sausage, sliced smoked sausage or ham, or crisply cooked and crumbled bacon. You can substitute 1 t cinnamon for the ginger and cloves with good results.
Preheat oven to 350 degrees. Grease and flour a 9x5x3-inch pan.
Sift together:
    2 c flour
    2 t baking powder
    ½ t salt
    ½ t ground ginger

    ¼ t soda
    ¼ t ground cloves
    ½ c chopped walnuts
    ½ c raisins, golden or dark, optional
In large mixer bowl, cream:
    1 c packed brown sugar
    1/3 c butter, lard or shortening
Beat in:
    2 eggs
    1 c canned or mashed pumpkin
    ¼ c milk
Add flour mixture, folding well only until dry ingredients are evenly moistened. Do not beat.
Pour batter into pan.
Bake 50-60 minutes or until tester inserted into center comes out with moist crumbs attached. Cool in pan 10 minutes before turning out onto wire rack to cool.
Wrap tightly in plastic wrap and store overnight before slicing.

Pumpkin Bars
A good alternative to Pumpkin Pie on the Thanksgiving or Christmas buffet. These also make a nice hostess gift, or a gift for distant loved ones.
Preheat oven to 350 degrees. Have ready a 10x15x1-inch pan.
Combine:
    2 c flour
    2 t baking powder
    2 t ground cinnamon
    1 t soda
    1 t salt
In bowl, beat together:
    4 eggs
    1 16-oz can or 1 ¾ c mashed pumpkin
    1 ½ c sugar
    1 c oil, preferably light olive oil
Add dry ingredients, blending well. Pour into pan, spreading evenly.
Bake 25-30 minutes.
Let cool before cutting into bars.
Zucchini Bars: Prepare Pumpkin Bars as above except substitute 2 c shredded unpeeled zucchini for the pumpkin.

Sweet Potatoes – these can either be yellow-gray or brown-skinned with yellowish to white, dry, mealy flesh, or copper or purple skins with very sweet, moist, orange flesh. The recipes provided use the latter which I still grow, planting in late Spring after the possibility of frost and harvesting just before the first frost in Fall. Sweet potatoes, with a little care, will produce abundantly and store well throughout the Winter through the following Fall.

If purchasing sweet potatoes from the grocer or farmers market, select firm tubers with uniformly bright skin, heavy for their size and free of all blemishes, cuts or soft spots.

To store: keep in a well-ventilated, cool, dark, dry place. Do not wrap.

To prepare, wash well, peel or not. Follow recipe directions for further preparation.

To boil: Peel and cut into slices or cubes. Cook in boiling salted water to cover until easily pierced with a fork. Drain well.

To bake: Wrap potatoes in aluminum foil and bake at 400 degrees about 1 hour or until easily pierced with a fork. Alternately, cook in a microwave on high power about 12 minutes or until flesh gives when gently pressed, rotating potatoes top-to-bottom half-way through. Remove from oven and wrap in a clean dish towel and let sit 5 minutes.

Mashed Sweet Potatoes

Use either boiled or baked potatoes.

Mash sweet potatoes to desired consistency with either a vegetable ricer, potato masher or wooden spoon depending on if you want a smooth, mashed or chunky mashed consistency, respectively.

Add for each potato:
- **2 T butter**

Mix well.

Season to taste with:
- **Salt**
- **Pepper**
- **Brown sugar (about 1 T per potato)**

Sweet Potato Casserole I

Preheat oven to 350 degrees.

Place in a 2-quart casserole, lightly buttered:
- **6 cooked, mashed sweet potatoes**

Season the potatoes with:
- **Butter**
- **Salt**
- **Pepper**
- **2 T bourbon**

Top with the following streusel:
- **½ c brown sugar**
- **½ c chopped nuts (pecans, walnuts or black walnuts are especially good)**
- **4 T butter, softened**
- **½ t chipotle chili powder, optional**

Sweet Potato Casserole II
Preheat oven to 350 degrees. Have ready a 2-quart casserole, lightly buttered.
Combine in a large mixing bowl:
- **3 c peeled and cubed sweet potatoes**
- **3 c peeled, cored and cubed apples**
- **¼ c brown sugar**
- **½ t salt**

Turn into prepared casserole.
Pour over:
- **¼ c apple juice or water**

Cover tightly and bake about 30 minutes or until just tender. Uncover and continue to bake, stirring every 5 minutes, about 15 minutes more or until vegetables are caramelized and liquid has evaporated.
Serve seasoned to taste with black pepper.

Sweet Potato Casserole III
This casserole is not overly sweet.
Preheat oven to 350 degrees. Have ready a 2-quart casserole, lightly buttered.
Boil until nearly tender when pierced with a knife, about 20 minutes:
- **2 lb sweet potatoes**

Drain and let stand until cool enough to handle.
Peel and cut potatoes into ¼-inch rounds. Layer into prepared casserole, seasoning each layer with:
- **Salt**
- **Pepper**
- **Paprika**
- **1 T butter, melted**
- **3 T pure maple syrup**
- **1 T balsamic vinegar**

Dot the top layer with:
- **2 T butter**

Cover and bake until well glazed and very tender, about 45 minutes.

Turnips
Oh, the turnip! A member of the Mustard family, turnips are crisp and peppery sweet when raw but meltingly soft and slightly sweet when cooked. Easy to grow and best if planted in late July for a Fall harvest.

If you purchase turnips from the grocer or farmers market, buy small, unblemished roots, heavy for their size—usually, the smaller, the sweeter, although larger turnips are good for mashing and combining with other vegetables.

To store: place in plastic bags and store in the refrigerator crisper. Turnips, scrubbed and leaves removed, will keep for several weeks.

To prepare: remove peel with a vegetable peeler and then use a knife to remove the fibrous layer beneath the peel. You will see a definite line between the fibrous layer and the flesh. Cut into the shape indicated in individual recipes.

Cooked turnips can be mashed, seasoned and served in any way you do potatoes. Especially delicious is a blend of equal parts of cooked, Mashed Potatoes or sweet potatoes and turnips. Season turnips with cream, butter, lemon, nutmeg, garlic, spicy cheeses, crisp bacon, thyme, parsley or chervil. In addition to raw and mashed, the following are my favorite recipes.

Turnip Casserole I

The casserole goes especially well with baked ham.

Preheat oven to 350 degrees. Have ready a 1 ½-quart casserole.

Cook in salted, boiling water until tender:

1 ½ pounds turnips, peeled and cubed (about 4 cups)

Drain well.

Fold cooked turnips into:

2 c medium White Sauce

Turn into prepared casserole.

Sprinkle evenly over the top:

1 c fresh or dried bread crumbs

Bake 20-25 minutes or until bubbling all over and crumbs are lightly browned.

6 WINTER

I believe we should be good stewards of what God has given us: land, animals, resources, etc. Among the resources? Time. I know people who don't like Winter for several reasons. However, we should make good use of all our time. Winter is a time to relax, regenerate and plan. We can relax and enjoy time with family and friends during the several Winter holydays, holidays and just days: Advent, Christmas, New Year's, Valentine's Day, Lent, St. Patrick's Day. We can regenerate because it seems there is less work to do (depending on the weather), by reviewing the previous year and looking forward to the next. Blustery Winter days are a good time to plan the garden, sort through what we have, and donate what we don't need or use anymore to charity. Winter can be what we make it!

Father's sisters—Dorothy, Ruth, Mill, Marcelline and Geraldine—were known for their individual talents. Aunt Dorothy made the most intricate and beautiful "fancywork" like crocheted tablecloths and doilies. Aunt Ruth's specialty was ceramics, and she made some very beautiful and detailed figurines. Aunt Mill was known for her cooking. She worked for several years as a cook at a Nortonville restaurant, the Youth Center in Atchison, and the nursing home in Nortonville. Aunts Marcelline and Geraldine were well-known seamstresses. Their first job off the farm was at the Horton Garment Factory in Atchison (along with Aunt Mill) where they made clothes sold in department stores across the country. They also worked at the Atchison Leather Works. They continued this work after they "retired" and made custom bedding for Nell Hill's as well as altar linens and vestments for St. Benedict's Church and the monks.

This section contains many recipes for cakes, cookies, breads, muffins, etc. Why? They make perfect gifts! Also, with the slower pace of Winter, you may find you have time to make and freeze some of these for later. You'll have a delicious dessert or treat at the ready for unexpected guests or events.

Christmas Dinner

Christmas dinner through the years have changed from large gatherings of all the grandparents, aunts, uncles and cousins to immediate families. The Christmas season starts much too early, in my opinion. The crass commercialization of Christmas is insulting to those who celebrate its true meaning—the birth of Christ. This unattributed quote beautifully describes, for me, Christmas: "While all things were in quiet silence and the night was in the midst of her course, Thy almighty Word, O Lord, leapt down from heaven from Thy royal throne."

I'll admit there was a time when I followed the crowd and bought endless presents, decorated the day after Thanksgiving and took down the decorations the day after Christmas. However, for the last 20 years or so I have become more traditional. I don't buy lavish presents, nor do I put up a tree or any decorations until Christmas Eve. I prefer to observe Advent – that period of four weeks between Thanksgiving and Christmas—preparing spiritually and temporally for the coming of Christ. In the same Traditional manner, I like to have a simpler meal on Jan. 6, the Epiphany—also called the Little Christmas—which commemorates when the Savior was manifested in visible form and revealed to the Magi. I extend Christmas to Feb. 2, which is the end of the Christmas cycle in the Traditional Catholic calendar and is the feast of The Purification of the Blessed Virgin Mary, and today The Presentation of the Lord.

Turnip Casserole II

This is Aunt Marcelline's recipe. Turnip casserole is now a standard dish for Christmas dinner.

Preheat oven to 350 degrees. Have ready a 1 ½-quart casserole dish.
Cook in boiling, salted water until tender:
> 1 ½ lb turnips, peeled and cubed (about 4 cups)

Drain well.
Melt in a medium saucepan:
> 2 T butter

Blend in:
> ½ t salt
> 2 T flour

Add all at once and cook until thickened and bubbly:
> 1 c milk or cream

Reduce heat and stir in until melted:
> ½ c shredded sharp Cheddar cheese
> 2 T chopped parsley

Combine with turnips. Turn into casserole.
Sprinkle top with:
> **Paprika**

Cover and bake 15-20 minutes or until bubbling all over.

Cornbread Dressing

I did not make this until just a few years ago after having a surplus of leftover corn bread I had frozen. You can use the stock from whatever meat you are serving.
The day before:
Cut into one-half-inch cubes and place on a rimmed baking sheet, in a single layer, to dry overnight.
>   **1 recipe Corn Bread, baked and cooled**

The cubes will not be completely dry.
Combine in a tightly covered saucepan:
>   **1 large onion, grated**
>   **4 large stalks celery, grated**
>   **½ c butter**

Cook over medium heat until very tender and onions begin to caramelize. Cool, cover and refrigerate.
The day of serving:
Preheat oven to 350 degrees. Generously butter a 2-quart baking dish.
Place bread cubes in a large mixing bowl.
Reheat the onion-celery mixture until warm. Add to the bread cubes. Toss to mix.
Combine in a large measuring cup:
>   **2 eggs**
>   **1 c chicken, turkey or pork stock, plus more if needed**
>   **½ t dried sage**
>   **Salt and pepper, to taste**

Add to crumbs, tossing gently to combine. The mixture should be evenly moistened, but not wet. If some crumbs are still dry, add additional stock 2 T at a time and toss gently after each addition until evenly moistened.
Turn mixture into prepared pan. Bake about 30 minutes or until the top is evenly browned and the dressing is heated through.

Yule Log

I made this for the American Society of Military Comptrollers Christmas luncheon which I catered when I operated MillRose. I received several orders for this delicious cake from those who attended the luncheon. You can replace the whipping cream with one 8-9-oz container frozen whipped topping, thawed.
Prepare as for Jelly Roll using the following ingredients:
>   **½ c flour**
>   **¼ c unsweetened cocoa powder**
>   **1 t baking powder**
>   **¼ t salt**
>   **4 egg yolks**
>   **½ t vanilla**

    1/3 c sugar
    3 egg whites
    ½ c sugar
For the filling, whip until it holds stiff peaks:
    1 c whipping cream
Fold in:
    ½ c butter mints, finely chopped
Frost with Chocolate Ganache. Use a fork to make lines in the frosting to resemble tree bark.

Yeast Breads and Rolls

There are many wonderful bread recipes in existence today. I present here those baked most often. They are all easy to make and delicious. Bread making is like anything else: the more you do it, the better you become. Once you master the basics, you will have the skills to make endless variations of the master recipes. I find that making bread is more satisfactory for me if I make it by hand rather than in a bread machine. I usually begin the basic dough in a heavy-duty mixer and then finish by hand.

In my early years of learning to cook and bake, I would make a fresh batch of cinnamon rolls each Sunday. My brother, cousins and I would then have them as a snack after a day of fishing, hunting or sports.

Note in the following recipes the flour is measured using the dip-and-sweep method, and warm refers to a temperature between 105 and 115 degrees.

Angel Biscuits

Some biscuits made with yeast have an overwhelming yeasty taste—and not the good kind associated with good bread. This biscuit recipe was among many I received from Aunt Mill. The origin is lost, however, because the recipe was written on a piece of paper that was originally a form letter from a magazine. Aunt Mill subscribed to many magazines. Note: dissolve the yeast in the warm water, and let cool before adding to the dough. The yeast will proof somewhat; however, the mixture needs to cool, otherwise the warm liquid will activate the baking soda prematurely and melt the fat. Alternately, use instant yeast which requires no proofing. Fast-rising yeast is not the same as instant yeast. Be sure to plunge the biscuit cutter straight down and do not wiggle when removing it from the dough. Doing so preserves the straight-cut edges of the biscuits which will help them rise neatly and higher.

Preheat oven to 400 degrees. Have ready a lightly greased, heavy baking sheet.
Mix in a small bowl:
>   **1 pkg. active dry yeast**
>   **½ c lukewarm water**

Stir until yeast is dissolved. Cool.
Sift in a large mixing bowl:
>   **5 c flour**
>   **3 T sugar**
>   **1 t baking soda**
>   **1 t baking powder**
>   **1 t salt**

Cut in to make fine crumbs:
>   **¾ c fat (butter, lard or shortening)**

Add:
> **The proofed yeast**
> **2 c Buttermilk**

Mix until all flour is moistened. Let dough rest 2-3 minutes. It will firm slightly. The dough can be refrigerated at this point.

When ready to bake, gently knead dough until smooth, roll on floured board to about ½" thick. Cut out biscuits using a floured cutter, or cut with a knife. Place on prepared pan.

Place pan in oven and immediately turn oven to 450 degrees. Bake 5 minutes. Lower heat to 400 degrees and bake about 7 minutes longer.

English Muffin Bread

I have made English Muffins one time in my life, just to get the experience and to say I have done it. It is not a complicated process, but it is time-consuming. You cook the muffins on a griddle and need to have some type of ring mold to hold the batter while it cooks. Traditional English muffin batter is very light, spongy and full of bubbles which when cooked results in the craggy, pock-marked surface when the muffins are split. This, of course, is what makes them so delicious. The surface toasts to a crispy brown while the holes remain moist—perfect for holding butter, jam, honey, etc. This bread is quick and easy to make. You can use either an 8x4x2-inch pan or a 9x5x3-inch loaf pan. The bread baked in the smaller pan will be more dense, but still delicious.

Have ready one or two greased loaf pans.

Combine in a bowl of electric mixer:
> **3 c flour**
> **1 T sugar**
> **2 t salt**
> **¼ t baking soda**
> **2 pkgs. active dry yeast**

Mix well.

Heat just until warm:
> **2 c milk**
> **½ c water**

Add to dry mixture. Beat well.

Add:
> **1 ½ - 2 c flour**

Stir to make a not-too-stiff batter. The batter should be soft enough to fall easily from the spoon, but not stiff enough to hold its shape or to have to be removed with another spoon or spatula.

Divide batter evenly between pan(s), smoothing tops.

Let rise until batter is even with tops of pans.

Meanwhile preheat oven to 400 degrees.

Bake loaves 25 minutes. Remove immediately from pans to wire rack to cool.

Basic Bread Receipt

I remember the first time I tasted rolls made from this dough. It was during a Winter butchering that Aunt Mill brought several of these for snacking. She called them "kolaches." She formed the dough into small ovals and formed an indentation in the center. After baking, she filled them with homemade jellies and drizzled them with confectioners' sugar icing. They were exquisite, and I immediately asked for the recipe. You can use this dough to make many kinds of rolls from "kolaches" to cinnamon to dinner rolls. I provide the recipe just as she wrote it out for me.
Combine:
1 ¾ c warm water, 1 T sugar, 1 ½ T yeast and 2 c flour. Mix well, cover and set in warm place for 15-20 minutes to proof.
Meanwhile, cream ½ c shortening or lard. Add ¼ c sugar, 1 ½ t salt, 2 eggs, room temperature and ¼ c flour. Beat well and add to yeast mixture. Gradually add 3 ¼ c flour, kneading in last cup of flour for 5 minutes or until a soft, but not sticky, dough forms. If sticky, add a small amount of flour. Let rise to double. Shape, place in greased pans and let rise until doubled. Bake at 350 degrees for about 20 minutes or until done.

Raisin Bread

I especially like the addition of nutmeg to this bread. It perfectly complements the raisins. Cardamom is also good with raisins in place of the nutmeg.
Have ready two greased 9x5x3-inch loaf pans.
Scald:
> **2/3 c milk**

Add:
> **1/3 c sugar**
> **1 t salt**
> **½ c butter**

Set aside to cool to lukewarm.
Meanwhile, combine until dissolved in a large mixing bowl:
> **½ warm water**
> **2 pkgs. active dry yeast**

Add:
> **Milk mixture**
> **3 eggs, beaten**
> **¼ t nutmeg**
> **3 c flour**

Beat until smooth.
Add to make a soft dough:
> **1 ½ c seedless raisins**
> **3 c flour**

Turn out onto a floured surface; knead until smooth and elastic, about 8 minutes.
Place dough in greased bowl, turning to grease all sides.
Cover and let rise in warm place until doubled in bulk, about 1 hour.
Punch down; let rise again until almost doubled, about 30 minutes.
Turn out onto floured surface and divide in half. Cover; let rest 10 minutes.
Shape into loaves. Place into prepared pans. Cover and let rise until tops of loaves are slightly higher than sides of pan, about 45 minutes.
Meanwhile, preheat oven to 350 degrees.
Bake 40-45 minutes.
Remove loaves to wire rack to cool.

Pizza Crust
This simple dough is remarkable for making both thin- and thick-crust pizzas, calzones (stuffed pizzas) and pizza rolls.
In a large mixing bowl, combine:
- **1/3 c water**
- **1 pkg. active dry yeast**
- **A pinch of sugar**

Stir until yeast and sugar are dissolved.
Dust the top with flour to completely and evenly cover. Cover bowl and let sit until yeast is bubbly and breaks through the flour covering.
Add:
- **1 c water**
- **¼ c olive oil, preferably extra virgin**
- **1 T sugar**
- **1 t salt**
- **1 c flour**

Mix until combined and then beat at medium speed for 2 minutes.
Add:
- **2 c flour**

Beat until dough comes together and leaves the sides of the bowl. Add up to another ½ c flour, if needed.
Knead, using electric mixer, or by hand on a floured surface, for about 7 minutes or until dough is smooth and springs back when gently pulled.
Place in greased bowl, cover and let rise until doubled, about 1 hour.
Punch down dough and knead a few times on a lightly floured surface. Let rest, covered, 10 minutes.
Meanwhile, preheat oven to 400 degrees.
If making a thick-crust pizza, place dough on a greased 10x15x1-inch pan. Roll and stretch to fit into pan.
If making thin-crust pizzas, place one-half dough on each of two greased 10x15x1-inch pans. Roll and stretch to fit into pans.
Let rolled dough rest, covered with a clean towel, 15 minutes.

Prebake crusts 10 minutes before topping with your choice of toppings.
Bake topped pizzas about 25 minutes or until done.
Let rest 5 minutes before cutting and serving.
Variations on a Theme:
Stuffed Pizzas (Calzones) – divide dough into 12 even pieces. Shape into balls. Roll each ball into an 8-inch round. Place pizza ingredients on one half of dough, leaving a ½-inch border. Fold over unfilled half of dough. Seal edges by pinching together and then pressing with a fork. Place on greased baking sheets. Let rest, covered with a clean towel, for 15 minutes. Bake in a 350-degree oven 25-30 minutes or until dough is done and filling is hot.
Pizza Roll - divide dough in half. Roll each half into a thin rectangle about 11x13 inches. Use pizza sauce sparingly to cover the top of each piece of rolled dough, leaving a 1-inch border. Layer on pizza toppings (this works best if the toppings are diced to a uniform size). Roll, from the long side. Pinch to seal seam and edges. Transfer to greased baking sheets. Let rest, covered with a clean towel, for 15 minutes. Bake at 350 degrees for about 60 minutes or until dough is baked and filling is hot. Cover with foil if browning too quickly. Remove from oven and let stand 5 minutes before cutting and serving.

Long Johns
These treats are easy to make. The plain dough is cut into rectangles, baked and then covered with a rich, caramel glaze.
Soften in a large mixing bowl:
>**1 pkg. yeast**

In:
>**¼ c warm water**

Combine in a small saucepan:
>**¾ c milk, scalded**
>**¼ c shortening**
>**¼ c sugar**
>**1 t salt**

Cool to lukewarm then add to yeast mixture.
Beat in:
>**1 egg**

Add enough to make a soft dough:
>**3 ½ - 3 ¾ c flour**

Mix well and then turn out onto a floured surface and knead about 8 minutes. Place in greased bowl and let rise until doubled in size.
Punch down. Let rise until doubled again.
Preheat oven to 350 degrees.
Roll dough about ¾-inch thick. Cut into 1x3-inch rectangles. Place 1 inch apart on a greased baking sheet.
Bake until done, about 20 minutes.

Remove to rack and then cover evenly with the following glaze.
Boil for 1 minute:
> **½ c butter**
> **1 c brown sugar**

Cool and add:
> **¼ c milk**
> **3 ¼ c powdered sugar.**

Beat until smooth and creamy.

Cream Cheese Fruit Rolls

These charming rolls are a bit involved to make, but rival a good cheese Danish. Use your favorite preserves for the filling—a variety makes for a colorful breakfast or brunch buffet on Christmas Day—the following recipe includes directions to shape these into Christmas wreaths. Alternately, you can form these into 24 simple rounds or ovals. Make an indentation in center to hold the filling.

Have ready a large greased baking sheet.

Soften in electric mixer bowl:
> **1 pkg. active dry yeast**

In:
> **¼ c lukewarm water**

Set aside.

Combine in a small saucepan:
> **¼ c milk**
> **¼ c sugar**
> **¼ c butter**
> **¾ t salt**

Heat until warm and butter almost melts.
Add to yeast mixture along with:
> **1 c flour**
> **1 egg**

Beat at low speed 30 seconds, then at high speed for 4 minutes.
Stir in to make a moderately stiff dough:
> **1 – 1 ½ c flour**

Turn out onto floured surface and knead until smooth and elastic. Shape into ball. Turn into greased bowl, turning to coat surface. Cover with damp towel and place in warm place to rise until doubled.

Meanwhile prepare filling by beating in a bowl until light and fluffy:
> **6 oz cream cheese, softened**
> **2 T sugar**
> **1 egg**
> **½ t vanilla**

Set aside.

Punch down risen dough. Divide in half and cover and let rest 10 minutes. On lightly

floured surface, roll out half of the dough to ¼-inch thick. Cut with a 2-inch round cutter into 12 rounds. Place rounds 3 inches apart on prepared pan.
Add scraps to remaining dough and shape into ball. Divide ball into fourths and each fourth into 6 pieces making 24 pieces in all. On lightly floured surface, roll each piece of dough into an 8-inch rope. For each roll, twist two ropes together, sealing ends.
Brush top edge of each circle of dough with:
- **1 egg white, beaten until frothy**

Coil each twist around a circle, pressing ends to seal.
Spoon about 1 T of filling into center of each roll.
Brush edges of roll with:
- **1 egg white**, beaten until frothy

Let rise, uncovered, in a warm place until doubled.
Meanwhile, preheat oven to 375 degrees
Bake for 12-15 minutes or until done. Remove to a wire rack to cool.
Spoon into center of each roll:
- **Preserves, jam or jelly, or your favorite pie filling**

Raspberry Rolls

This is a most unusual recipe and uses convenience foods. The clipping I have is much tattered and faded, so I don't know where I got this recipe, but I do remember when I first found it, I was intrigued and skeptical. It's like a fruity Monkey Bread. Raspberry fans will enjoy these rolls. I enhanced the recipe by adding fresh raspberries after sprinkling with nuts. These make a good alternative to cinnamon rolls for a breakfast buffet.
Grease a 9x13x2-inch pan.
Thaw:
- **2 loaves frozen bread dough**

Cut each loaf into 8 slices, then each slice into 4 pieces. Place in single layer in pan.
Combine in a mixing bowl:
- **½ c brown sugar**
- **½ c white sugar**
- **1 t cinnamon, optional**
- **1 3-oz package raspberry gelatin**
- **1 c chopped nuts**

Sprinkle evenly over dough along with 1 c fresh red raspberries.
Cut into thin slices:
- **½ c butter**

Distribute evenly over dough.
Cover and let rise until light and nearly doubled.
Meanwhile, preheat oven to 350 degrees.
Place pan on foil-lined cookie sheet to catch drippings.
Bake 30 minutes or until done.
Let sit 5 minutes and then turn out onto a serving platter to cool.

Batter Bread

This bread is delicious used in sandwiches with a variety of fillings. It is also great for picnics—make the sandwiches and then return to the can in which the bread baked to transport. While this bread is delicious plain and just baked, you can customize this to your taste by adding 1 T of chopped fresh herbs and/or seeds. My favorite is to add 1 ½ t crushed black peppercorns. You can also poach several cloves of garlic, minced, in the butter. The possibilities are endless. Do not overfill the cans; otherwise the bread will rise too high and fall out. If not eating within a day or two, it is wise to freeze it immediately and reheat in a 350-degree oven to restore the just baked flavor and texture.

Have ready two generously greased 1-pound coffee cans.
In a large mixing bowl, dissolve:
>   **1 pkg. active dry yeast**
>   **½ t sugar**

In:
>   **¼ c warm water**

Let stand until bubbly and proofed, 5-10 minutes.
Blend in:
>   **2 t sugar**
>   **2 eggs, room temperature**
>   **½ c milk, room temperature**
>   **1 t salt**
>   **Herbs, seeds and/or spices (see headnote)**
>   **6 T unsalted butter, melted and cooled**

Add:
>   **2 c flour**

Beat 4 minutes at medium speed of electric mixer or 400 vigorous hand strokes.
At low speed or by hand, beat in:
>   **½ - ¾ c all-purpose flour**

You should have a smooth, thick batter that is quite sticky.
Cover bowl with plastic wrap and let rise in a warm place until doubled.
Stir down risen batter and spoon into cans, filling slightly less than half full. Cover with buttered plastic wrap and let rise in a warm place until batter is within ¾ inch from top of cans.
Meanwhile, preheat oven to 375 degree.
Bake until tops rise above pans, are golden brown and cake tester inserted in center comes out clean, 30-35 minutes. Loosen edges with a slim knife, if necessary and turn out of cans onto rack. Cool completely before attempting to slice. Store in cans covered with the accompanying lid, or with plastic wrap and then foil.

Cinnamon Crisps

Snickerdoodle fans will like these "rolls." These are delicious with coffee, tea or milk in the morning, afternoon or evening. Good made with pecans or walnuts. A bit involved to make, but rewarding for special guests. I like to make these ahead on a free day and freeze to have at a moment's notice. Refresh and re-crisp in a 350-degree oven for about 5 minutes. Remove to a wire rack to cool.

Measure into a bowl:
- **4 c flour**

Combine in an electric mixer bowl:
- **2 c of the measured flour**
- **1 pkg. active dry yeast**

In saucepan, heat until just warm:
- **1 ¼ c milk**
- **¼ c sugar**
- **¼ c butter, lard or shortening**
- **1 t salt**

Add to flour mixture along with:
- **1 egg, room temperature**

Beat at low speed of mixer 30 seconds, then at high speed 4 minutes.

By hand, stir in as much remaining measured flour as you can mix in with a spoon. Scrape dough out of bowl onto a lightly flour surface, knead in enough of remaining flour to make a moderately soft dough that is smooth and elastic. Shape into a ball and place in lightly greased bowl; turn once to grease surface; cover and let rise until doubled.

Meanwhile make the filling by combining in a small bowl:
- **½ c packed brown sugar**
- **½ c sugar**
- **¼ c butter, melted**
- **½ t ground cinnamon**

Set aside.

Punch down dough; gently knead a few times, and divide in half. Cover; let rest 10 minutes. Roll half of dough into a 12-inch square. Spread half of filling over dough. Roll up, beginning from one side; seal edges. Cut into 12 rolls. Place on greased baking sheets 3-4 inches apart. Flatten each to about 3 inches in diameter. Repeat with remaining dough and filling. Cover and let rise to until nearly doubled, about 30 minutes.

Meanwhile, preheat oven to 400 degrees.

Cover rolls with waxed paper. Use rolling pin to flatten to 1/8-inch thick; remove paper.

Brush rolls with:
- **¼ c butter, melted**

Combine in a small bowl:
- **1 c sugar**
- **½ c finely chopped nuts**
- **1 t ground cinnamon**

Sprinkle evenly over rolls.
Cover with waxed paper; roll flat. Remove paper.
Bake 10-12 minutes. Remove immediately to wire rack to cool.

Variation on a Theme:
Make a filling with the following:
- **1/3 c butter, softened**
- **¾ c brown sugar**
- **1 egg**
- **1/3 c milk**
- **1 t vanilla**
- **1 t cinnamon**
- **3 c walnuts, finely chopped**

Roll dough into approximately 30x20-inch rectangle (dough will be thin) on a floured towel.
Using rubber spatula, spread filling evenly over dough right to edges. Starting at wide side, lift towel and let dough roll up like a jelly roll. Pinch edges to seal.
Coil roll loosely on greased baking sheet, cover and let rise until nearly doubled, about 45 minutes.
Bake at 350 degrees 40-45 minutes or until done. Remove from pan to rack to cool.

Jelly-filled Coffee Cake

This is a delightful coffee cake that you can customize to the season by the jelly or preserves you use to fill the cake. Shaped like a flower, it can be the centerpiece of a breakfast buffet or coffee service.

Measure into a bowl:
- **3 c flour**

Combine in an electric mixer bowl:
- **1 pkg. active dry yeast**
- **1 c of the measured flour**

In a saucepan, heat until warm and fat is almost melted:
- **2/3 c milk**
- **¼ c sugar**
- **¼ c shortening, butter or lard**
- **1 t salt**

Add to flour mixture along with:
- **1 egg, room temperature**
- **1 t finely shredded lemon or orange peel**

Beat at low speed of electric mixer for 30 seconds, scraping sides of bowl constantly. Beat 4 minutes at high speed. Stir in as much of remaining flour as you can mix in with a spoon.
Turn out onto lightly floured surface. Knead in enough of remaining flour to make a moderately stiff dough that is smooth and elastic. Shape into ball. Place in lightly greased bowl; turn once to grease surface. Cover; let rise in warm place till double.

Punch down. Cover; let rest 10 minutes. Roll out into a 10x8-inch rectangle. Place a glass or other small round dish into the center of the baking pan. With a 2 ½-inch round doughnut cutter, cut into 12 pieces; arrange in a circle around the glass on the greased baking sheet. Stretch the rings slightly with fingers to elongate. Remove glass. Cluster "doughnut holes" in center; cutting additional "holes" from dough scraps. Let rise till light and almost doubled, about 1 hour.
Preheat oven to 375 degrees.
Bake 20-25 minutes or until golden brown and done.
Carefully remove from baking sheet. Cool on rack then transfer to a serving platter. Fill rings with a spoonful of:
> **Your favorite jelly, jam or preserves**

Stir together in a mixing bowl:
> **1 ½ c powdered sugar**
> **3 T lemon juice**
> **¼ t vanilla**

Drizzle over coffee cake. Sprinkle center with:
> **¼ c chopped toasted pecans or toasted slivered almonds**

Sweet Bread

This dough comes to together very easily. The recipe in Aunt Mill's collection was written in Aunt Dorothy's style. I present it here just as written. It uses water left over from cooking potatoes. If using, adjust the amount of salt. It makes two 8x4x2-inch loaves. It lends itself well to toast, French Toast, tea sandwiches or a cheese tray when sliced thin and toasted until dry, but not browned. I find it too sweet to accompany savory dishes.
> **¾ c potato water, warm**
> **¼ c lukewarm water mixed with 1 t sugar and 1 pkg. yeast**
> **1/3 c sugar**
> **1 ½ t salt**
> **1 T, rounded, lard**
> **2 eggs**

Put potato water in bowl; add salt, sugar, lard and eggs and beat. Add 1 to 2 c flour until thick. Then add yeast mixture to this. Stir well. Add more flour to made soft dough (about 1 ¾ - 2 c). Knead until smooth and slightly springy. Let rise. Form loaves. Let rise again. Bake at 350 degrees about 40 minutes until done. Let sit in pan about 5 minutes before turning out onto wire rack to cool.

Whole Wheat Bread

Some whole wheat breads are extremely dense and sometimes dry. This bread is neither. The addition of olive oil and honey provides moisture. Those and the dried milk extend the shelf life. If you like a larger-sized loaf, you can make 1 ½ times the recipe and use a 9x5x3-inch loaf pan. In this case, use 3 ¼ t yeast.
Have ready a greased 8x4x2-inch loaf pan.

Dissolve in a large mixing bowl:
> **1 pkg. yeast**

In:
> **2 T water**

Dust the top to cover evenly:
> **Flour**

Cover and let sit until yeast proofs (it will bubble and break through the flour). Add:
> **1 1/3 c lukewarm water**
> **¼ c olive oil**
> **¼ c honey**
> **3 ½ c whole wheat flour**
> **¼ c dried milk**
> **1 ¼ t salt**

Stir until dough starts to leave sides of bowl. Transfer dough to a lightly greased surface. Oil hands and knead 6-8 minutes or until it becomes smooth. Transfer to lightly greased bowl; cover and let rise until almost doubled. Punch down dough. Shape into 8-inch log. Place in prepared pan. Cover with lightly greased plastic wrap or a moistened kitchen towel. Let rise until the dough rises about 1 inch above edge of pan.

Meanwhile, preheat oven to 350 degrees.

Bake bread about 40 minutes or until done. Tent with foil if browning too quickly. Remove from oven. Turn bread out onto wire rack to cool.

Quick Breads

A number of quick breads-those whose leavening is baking powder and/or baking soda vice yeast—in your repertoire is a good thing. You'll have many options for buffets, breakfasts, coffee and tea, and gifts throughout the year. These breads freeze well, either as whole loaves or individual slices.

One year I made a basket of breads for the gift exchange at the Christmas party at work. Someone joined the gift exchange without bringing a gift, so the last person was left without a gift. I made a second basket and presented it the next day.

This section contains the quick breads I rely on most often. I have switched to using olive oil when making quick breads which include oil. Start by using a light olive oil. I like how it complements the fruits, nuts and chocolate used to flavor the breads.

Tips: grease and flour the pans; measure flour by lightly spooning into the measuring cup or spoon; do not overmix—just until dry ingredients are moistened; use shiny metal pans (if using glass pans, reduce oven temperature by 25 degrees and begin checking for doneness 5 minutes before recommended minimum baking time), do not overbake; let cool on a wire rack until just lukewarm; wrap in plastic wrap and then aluminum foil; let sit overnight before slicing and serving.

Dumplings

Dumplings are a quick and easy way to turn a soup or broth into a hearty, filling meal. There are many varieties of dumplings and the possible additions are endless. This recipe is very basic; therefore, it works well with any variety of soup or broth.

Have heating to boiling in a large kettle your soup or broth of choice.
Measure, then sift:
- **1 c cake flour**
- **2 t baking powder**
- **½ t salt**
- **1 T fresh or 1 t dried herbs (to complement the soup or broth), optional**

Break into a measuring cup:
- **1 egg**

Add to make ½ cup:
- **Milk**

Beat well and stir liquid mixture into dry. Keep the batter as stiff as possible.
Dip spoon into boiling liquid, then dip spoon into batter to fill it. Drop batter into the soup. Continue doing so until all batter is used and dumplings are just touching each other. Cover tightly and simmer 10 minutes. Serve immediately.

Hush Puppies

Well-made hush puppies are not greasy, and have a crisp, golden-brown crust enclosing a moist and tasty corn-and-onion flavored center. I like to serve these with

barbecued meats as well as the traditional fish.
Whisk together in a large mixing bowl:
- 1 2/3 c cornmeal
- 1/3 c flour
- 1 T minced fresh parsley or 1 t dried parsley flakes
- 2 t baking powder
- 1 t sugar
- 1 t coarsely ground black pepper
- ¾ t salt
- ½ t baking soda

Whisk together in another bowl:
- 2 large eggs
- 1 c Buttermilk
- ½ c grated onions

Add to flour mixture and stir just until dry ingredients are moistened.
Pour into a deep skillet or Dutch oven:
- **1 inch vegetable or peanut oil**

Heat to 365 degrees.
Use a small cookie or ice cream scoop (about 1 T capacity) or a measuring spoon to drop batter into the hot oil.
Fry several hush puppies at a time, without crowding. Turn with a slotted spoon to brown all sides. Transfer to a baking sheet lined with paper towels to drain. Keep warm in a 200-degree oven until all are fried.

Apricot Nut Bread I

I present two versions of this delightful bread. Father always enjoyed apricots: fresh, canned or dried, and just about anything which contains this exquisite fruit. This bread makes a great base for appetizers, especially when added to a cheese board. I particularly like this with a creamy blue cheese or warm Brie.
Preheat oven to 350 degrees. Have ready a greased and floured 9x5x3-inch loaf pan.
Sift together in a large mixing bowl:
- 2 ½ c flour
- 1 c sugar
- ½ t salt
- ¼ t baking powder
- ¼ t baking soda

Stir in, tossing to coat evenly:
- 1 c finely diced dried apricots soaked in 1 T hot water
- 1 c chopped walnuts, toasted

Mix together in a large glass measuring cup:
- 2 large eggs, beaten
- 1 c Buttermilk
- ¼ c apricot nectar

3 T melted butter

Combine with dry ingredients until just mixed.
Pour into prepared pan. Bake 60-70 minutes or until tester inserted in center comes out clean. Tent with foil if browning too quickly.
Cool in pan 10 minutes. Turn out onto rack to cool. Wrap in plastic wrap and then in aluminum foil. Store overnight before slicing.

Apricot Nut Bread II
Follow the directions for making Apricot Bread I, using these ingredients.
- 2 ¾ c flour
- ¾ c sugar
- 1 T baking powder
- ½ t baking soda
- ½ t salt
- 2 eggs
- ¼ c oil
- 1 c Buttermilk
- 1 ½ c dried apricots, cut into thin strips
- 1 c chopped toasted nuts

Poppy Seed Bread
Of all the seeds which can be added to various foods and dishes, I like poppy seeds the most. This bread is crunchy with the poppy seeds and has a subtle almond flavor. The exception: use a flavorless oil to let these flavors come through.
Preheat oven to 350 degrees. Grease and flour two 8x4x2-inch loaf pans. Combine and mix well in a large mixing bowl:
- 2 c sugar
- 1 ¼ c milk
- ¾ c oil
- 3 eggs
- 2 T poppy seeds
- 1 ½ t vanilla
- 1 t almond extract

Sift together into another bowl:
- 3 c flour
- 1 ½ t baking powder
- ½ t salt

Stir dry ingredients into sugar mixture. Mix until just combined.
Turn batter into prepared pans. Bake 65 minutes or until tester inserted into center comes out clean. Let cool in pans 10 minutes. Remove and cool on wire rack. Wrap and store overnight before slicing.

Banana Bread

Preheat oven to 350 degrees. Have ready a greased and floured 8x4x2-inch loaf pan.
Sift together in a large mixing bowl:
- 1 ¾ c flour
- 1 ¼ t baking powder
- ¾ t salt
- ½ t soda
- ¼ c chopped nuts, preferably toasted

Stir together in another bowl:
- 2/3 c sugar
- 1/3 c oil

Add, one at a time, beating well after each addition:
- 2 eggs, beaten

Mix in:
- 2 T milk
- 1 c mashed ripe banana
- 1 t vanilla

Turn batter into prepared pan. Bake 60-65 minutes or until wooden pick inserted into center comes out clean. Cool in pan 10 minutes. Remove from pan to wire rack to cool. Wrap in plastic wrap and then aluminum foil and store overnight before slicing and serving.

Cherry Nut Bread

A nice bread for the holidays. Fans of Cherry-Nut Ice Cream (something Aunt Mill always had in the freezer for an instant treat) will enjoy this.
Preheat oven to 350 degrees. Have ready two greased and floured 8x4x2-inch pans.
Sift together in large mixing bowl:
- 2 ½ c flour
- ¾ c sugar
- 1 T baking powder

Mix together:
- 1 egg
- 1 ¼ c eggnog
- 1/3 c oil

Stir into dry ingredients.
Fold in:
- ½ c chopped walnuts or pecans, preferably toasted
- ½ c chopped maraschino cherries

Turn into prepared pans. Bake 45-50 minutes or until done. Cool in pan 10 minutes before turning out onto wire rack to cool. Wrap in plastic wrap and then aluminum foil and store overnight before slicing and serving.

Homemade Eggnog: Beat together 2 eggs, 1 c light cream, ¼ c sugar and ¼ t ground nutmeg. Makes 1 ¼ cups.

Cranberry Orange Bread

Another good base for appetizers, especially spread with cream cheese and topped with smoked turkey or ham.

Preheat oven to 350 degrees. Have ready two greased and floured 8x4x2-inch loaf pans.
Remove and finely shred peel from:
- **3 oranges**

Juice oranges, measuring ¾ c juice and reserving any remainder
Combine:
- **¾ c orange juice**
- **1 t orange peel**
- **1 beaten egg**
- **2 T oil**

Sift together in a large mixing bowl:
- **2 c flour**
- **¾ c sugar**
- **1 ½ t baking powder**
- **1 t salt**
- **½ t soda**

Add juice mixture, mixing until just blended.
Fold in
- **1 c coarsely chopped cranberries**
- **½ c chopped toasted walnuts**

Turn batter into prepared pans. Bake 50-60 minutes or until done. Cool in pan 10 minutes before turning out onto wire rack to cool. Glaze, if desired, with a mixture of 1 T orange juice and 1 c powdered sugar.

Variations on a Theme: Prepare as above except substitute 1 c snipped dried apricots, dates, dried figs or raisins for the cranberries. Pour boiling water over apricots, figs or raisins; let stand about 15 minutes to plump. Drain well before folding into batter. Use half cranberries and half peeled, diced pears.

Apple Cheese Bread

Preheat oven to 350 degrees. Have ready one greased and floured 8x4x2-inch loaf pan.
Combine in a large mixing bowl:
- **½ c oil, preferably olive oil**
- **1/3 c sugar**

Add:
- **1/3 c honey**
- **2 eggs**

Sift into mixture:
- **1 c whole wheat flour**
- **1 c flour**

    1 ½ t baking powder
    ½ t baking soda
    ½ t salt
Combine well and add:
    1 ½ c peeled, cored and grated Granny Smith apples
    ½ c grated Swiss cheese
    ½ c toasted walnuts, chopped
Turn into prepared pan. Bake 50-60 minutes or until done. Turn out of pan onto a wire rack to cool. Wrap in plastic wrap and then aluminum foil and store overnight before serving.

Cocoa Coffee Cake

When I think of old friends in the kitchen, those recipes and dishes we turn to time and again for special occasions and special people, the first two that always come to mind are this recipe and White Velvet Muffins. Both the coffee cake and the muffins have been perennial favorites of family, co-workers and friends for years. This cake and Apple Cake are great entries for an old-fashioned cake walk.
Preheat oven to 350 degrees. Have ready a well-greased and floured 10-inch Bundt or tube pan.
Cream in an electric mixer bowl:
    1 ½ c sugar
    1 c shortening or butter
Add:
    4 eggs
Sift together:
    3 c flour
    4 t baking powder
Add alternately to fat mixture with:
    1 1/3 c milk
Beat smooth after each addition.
Spoon one-third mixture into prepared pan.
Top with half of the following mixture:
    2/3 c presweetened cocoa powder (i.e., chocolate milk mix)
    2/3 c chopped nuts, preferably toasted
Repeat layers, ending with batter.
Bake 50-60 minutes or until done. Cool in pan 10 minutes; turn out onto wire rack to cool. Dust with sifted powdered sugar, if desired, before serving.

Corn Breads

Corn bread is as diverse as those who make it. I find it varies by region. This simple, straight-forward recipe for cornbread is good for many uses. I like cornbread best baked in a cast iron skillet (it's well worth the effort to search for an antique cast iron mold to make the muffins). The heat of the iron ensures a crisp, brown crust, yet the bread stays light and moist. Use an 8- or 9-inch cast iron skillet, and preheat in the 400-degree oven while gathering and measuring the ingredients. Delicious served hot with plenty of butter and jam, honey or maple syrup.

Cornbread I

Preheat oven to 400 degrees. Place an 8- or 9-inch cast iron skillet or other baking pan in oven to preheat heat while mixing batter.
You will need ¼ c oil, or melted butter, lard, shortening or drippings. Melt the solid fats in the preheating pan.
Meanwhile, in a medium bowl, whisk together:
- **1 ¼ c flour**
- **¾ c cornmeal**
- **¼ c sugar**
- **2 t baking powder**
- **½ t salt**

Meanwhile, combine:
- **1 beaten egg**
- **1 c milk**

When fat is melted, remove pan from oven, swirl fat in pan to coat evenly. Return pan to oven, and then pour fat into milk mixture, beating constantly. Mix liquid mixture into dry only until combined. Remove pan from oven, pour batter into pan, spread evenly, and then bake 20-25 minutes or until knife inserted into center comes out clean. Let sit in pan 5 minutes before serving.

Cornbread II

Preheat oven to 400 degrees. Have ready a greased and heated 8-inch pan.
Cream in a mixing bowl:
- **½ c lard, butter or shortening**

Beat in until light and fluffy:
- **¼ c sugar**
- **2 eggs**

Whisk together:
- **1 c cornmeal**
- **1 c flour**
- **½ t salt**
- **1 T baking powder**

Add alternately to creamed mixture with:
- **1 c milk**

Turn into prepared pan. Bake 20 minutes or until knife inserted in center comes out clean.

Cornbread III

Add 1 c cooked, mashed or pureed squash, pumpkin or sweet potatoes to egg/milk mixture. Follow instructions for Cornbread I, above. Bake 25-30 minutes.

Rhubarb Bread I

A dear coworker, Dawn, gave this recipe to me. She is originally from Iowa and would always return home in the Spring just to get fresh rhubarb!

Preheat oven to 350 degrees. Have ready two greased and floured 8x4x2-inch loaf pans.

Sift together into a large mixing bowl:
- 2 ¼ c flour
- 1 c whole wheat flour
- 2 t baking soda
- 1 t baking powder
- 1 t salt
- 2 t cinnamon
- ½ t ground nutmeg
- ½ t ground allspice

Beat in electric mixer bowl on high until fluffy and smooth (about 5 minutes):
- 3 eggs, beaten
- 1 ¾ c firmly packed brown sugar
- 2 t vanilla
- 1 c oil

Stir in dry ingredients.

Fold in:
- 2 ½ c diced rhubarb
- ¾ c chopped toasted walnuts

Turn into prepared pans. Bake 50-60 minutes or until knife inserted in center comes out clean.

Cool in pans 10 minutes and then turn out on wire racks to cool.

Wrap in plastic wrap and then in foil; let sit overnight before serving.

Rhubarb Bread II

This recipe is from Aunts Marcelline and Geraldine and features black walnuts. To sour milk: place 1 T vinegar in a glass measuring cup; add milk to the required measure; and let sit 15 minutes.

Preheat oven to 325 degrees. Have ready a greased and floured 9x5x3-inch loaf pan.

Sift together into a large mixing bowl:
- 2 ½ c sifted flour
- 1 t baking soda
- 1 t salt

Combine in a mixing bowl:
- 2/3 c oil
- 1 ½ c firmly packed brown sugar

Blend in:

    1 egg, beaten
    1 t vanilla
    1 c sour milk
Stir in dry ingredients.
Fold in:
    1 ½ c diced rhubarb
    ½ c chopped black walnuts
Turn into prepared pan.
Top with the following mixture:
    ½ c brown sugar
    ½ t cinnamon
    1 T butter, melted
Bake 40 minutes or until knife inserted in center comes out clean.
Cool in pan 10 minutes and then turn out on wire racks to cool.
Wrap in plastic wrap and then in foil; let sit overnight before slicing and serving.

Muffins

Muffins were a best seller when I operated MillRose. They make great additions to a breakfast buffet and are good snacks. Muffins also ship well and are perfect fillers for gift baskets any time of year. Muffins freeze well and taste just-baked when defrosted and reheated. I offer here the recipes I have turned to time and time again when an event or occasion called for muffins.

Muffin recipes vary greatly in the mixing methods and ingredients. However, I have developed a uniform method which always provides reliable results: combine dry ingredients; melt the fat; combine liquid ingredients, including mashed fruits or vegetables; combine both mixtures quickly and gently only until dry ingredients are moistened. Tips: measure flour by lightly spooning into the measuring cup or spoon; always sieve the baking soda to ensure there are no lumps (there is nothing worse than biting into a lump of baking soda). Fill muffin cups about two-thirds full so the tops round evenly above the muffin cups. You can top muffins just before baking with a number of different toppings, too, which are at the end of this chapter.

Master Mixing Method

Unless otherwise indicated in individual recipes, use this master mixing method to make the following recipes. Note the ingredients for each recipe are listed in the order each is used in the following steps.

Step 1 - Preheat oven to 400 degrees.

Step 2 - Line muffin pan cups with papers, or spray with non-stick cooking spray.

Step 3 - In large bowl, combine dry ingredients. Stir in solid additions (chocolate, nuts, dried fruits, etc.). Set aside.

Step 4 - In separate bowl, whisk together moist additions (bananas, pumpkin, sweet potatoes, etc.), melted fat (butter, lard, shortening, etc.) or oil, sugar or other sweeteners, egg(s), liquid flavoring (vanilla, etc.) and other liquid ingredients until smooth.

Step 5 - Add the liquid ingredients to the dry ingredients all at once and fold only until evenly moistened, being sure to scrape bottom of bowl. Do not over mix.

Step 5 - Divide batter evenly among muffin cups, filling about two-thirds full--a bit fuller if you like "muffin tops."

Step 6 - Sprinkle on optional topping.

Step 7 - Bake until tops are golden and a toothpick inserted into center comes out clean, 20-25 minutes.

Step 8 - Cool for about 5 minutes in the pan on a wire rack before removing from the pan.

Caraway Rye Muffins

A good selection to serve with corned beef.
Exceptions to Master Mixing Method: Bake 20-23 minutes. Makes 10 muffins.

    1 c rye flour
    ¾ c flour
    2 ½ t baking powder
    ½ t salt
    2 t caraway seed
    ¾ c shredded Cheddar cheese
    1 egg, beaten
    ¾ c milk
    1/3 c oil
    ¼ c sugar

Corn Muffins

Exceptions to the Master Mixing Method: Bake 17-20 minutes. It is best to spray the muffin tins with non-stick cooking spray or to grease them. Cupcake papers will stick to the muffins if served straight from the oven; however, the papers release well from warm or cooled muffins. The Sour Cream provides for an exceptionally fine crumb; however, the cornmeal remains a bit crunchy because of the absence of other liquid to soften it during baking. I like the crunch, but you can use finely ground cornmeal, if desired. Fresh corn kernels are best for this recipe, but thawed frozen kernels or drained canned kernels will work.

    1 ½ c flour
    1 c yellow cornmeal (regular or finely ground, see headnote)
    2 t baking powder
    ½ t baking soda
    ¾ t salt
    ½ c corn kernels
    1 1/3 c Sour Cream
    3 large eggs
    ½ c sugar
    ½ c butter, melted

Variations on a theme:
Blueberry – add 1 – 1 ½ c fresh blueberries, washed and dried.
Jalapeno Cheese – reduce sugar to 2 T. Add 1 c shredded Cheddar, Monterrey Jack or Cotija cheese to the dry ingredients. Sauté ¼ c finely chopped onions until golden in the butter. Add 1 T seeded and finely chopped fresh jalapeno pepper, cool and mix with other liquid ingredients.
Raisin – add 1 c golden raisins.
Bacon – add 4 strips bacon, fried crisp, drained and crumbled to dry ingredients.

Raisin Bran Muffins
A back-of-the-box recipe that cannot be beat. I modified the recipe which follows to double the benefits of these muffins from the fiber of bran and Vitamin D from lard. Plain fiber flake cereal can be used and substitute diced dried dates or prunes for the raisins.
The exception to the Master Mixing Method: combine the milk and bran cereal and let stand until softened before mixing with other moist/liquid ingredients. Best served warm or reheated.
    1 ¼ c all-purpose flour
    1 T baking powder
    ½ t salt
    ½ c raisins (optional, but if you like raisins this is a good addition)
    3 c bran cereal with raisins
    1 ¼ c milk
    1 large egg, room temperature
    ½ c firmly packed brown sugar
    1/3 c oil or, preferably, melted lard or bacon grease

Nutmeg Muffins
Fragrant, cream-crumbed nutmeg muffins are the best of their kind, but you must grate one and a half nutmegs to make these perfect creations. Although whole nutmegs feel like rocks, they are easy to grate, and the flavor of freshly grated nutmeg is incomparable. These muffins are good with fruit, or butter, or all by themselves. The exception to the Master Mixing Method: bake 15-20 minutes.
    2 c all-purpose flour
    1 T baking powder
    1 ½ t freshly grated nutmeg
    ½ t salt
    1 large egg, room temperature
    ¾ c heavy cream
    ¾ c milk
    ¾ c sugar
    5 T butter, melted and cooled

Banana Muffins
    2 cups flour
    2 t baking powder
    1 t baking soda
    1 t salt
    ½ c chopped walnuts, preferably toasted
    1 ½ c mashed ripe banana (about 3 ½ bananas)
    2/3 c packed light brown sugar
    1/3 c unsalted butter, melted and cooled

1 large egg, room temperature
1 t vanilla

Pumpkin Muffins
You can substitute 1 ½ t pumpkin pie spice for the individual spices. I also like to add ¼ t freshly ground black pepper. Canned, or freshly cooked and mashed pumpkin work equally well in this recipe.
- 2 c flour
- 2 t baking powder
- 1 t baking soda
- 1 t ground cinnamon
- ½ t ground ginger
- ½ t salt
- ¼ t ground cloves
- ½ c packed light brown sugar
- 1 c mashed pumpkin or pumpkin puree
- ½ c unsulphured molasses
- 1 large egg
- 1 t vanilla

Sweet Potato Muffins
Of all the muffins I've enjoyed over the years, these are my all-time favorite. The pure sweet potato flavor comes through, and they are not-too-sweet making them perfect for breakfast with butter and preserves, or for an afternoon snack with tea—even late night with a glass of milk. Delicious with Pecan Topping.
The exception to the Master Mixing Method: makes 18 muffins.
- 2 ½ c flour
- 2 t baking powder
- 1 t baking soda, sieved
- ½ t salt
- 1 c cooked and mashed sweet potatoes (from 2 medium sweet potatoes)
- 1/3 c packed dark brown sugar
- 1 1/3 c Buttermilk
- ½ c unsalted butter, melted
- 2 large eggs

Chocolate Chip Muffins
These are like the best chocolate chip cookies in muffin form. You can use regular chocolate chips, but I like to use mini chips (use the entire package if you like really chocolatey muffins). The exceptions to the Master Mixing Method: Bake 15-20 minutes or until toothpick inserted into center comes out clean. Remove from oven and cool 5 minutes before removing from pan to wire rack to cool.
- 2 c flour

2 t baking powder
1 t baking soda
1 t salt
12 oz chocolate chips (or 1 ½ c mini chips)
½ c chopped walnuts or pecans, toasted (optional)
2/3 c milk
½ c unsalted butter, melted and cooled
1/3 c granulated sugar
1/3 c packed brown sugar
2 eggs, room temperature and slightly beaten
1 ½ t vanilla

Brownie Muffins

The exceptions to the Master Mixing Method: Melt the semisweet chocolate and butter together and cool; then combine with sugar, milk, etc. Bake 16-18 minutes or until cake tester inserted in center comes out clean.

1 ½ c flour, sifted
¼ c unsweetened cocoa powder
2 t baking powder
1 t baking soda
¼ t salt
9 oz mini chocolate chips
1 c coarsely chopped walnuts (optional)
4 oz semisweet chocolate, coarsely chopped
8 T unsalted butter
2 large eggs, lightly beaten (at room temperature)
2/3 c sugar
½ c milk

Cranberry Muffins

The exceptions to the Master Mixing Method: Preheat oven to 425 degrees. In small saucepan, bring to a boil the milk and oatmeal; remove from heat and stir in butter until melted; cool; beat in eggs. Bake 20-22 minutes.

1 1/3 c flour
2 t baking powder
1 t baking soda
½ t salt
1 ½ c fresh or frozen cranberries
½ c raisins, optional
1 ½ c milk
1 1/3 c old-fashioned rolled oats
1/3 c butter, cut into pieces
¾ c packed light brown sugar

2 large eggs

White Velvet Muffins

These were the first muffins I ever baked myself, and the only ones I baked for years. They are light, delicate and richly flavored. They make great gifts, too. These do not use the Master Mixing Method, but rather are made like a cupcake batter. Do not overmix the batter, otherwise you will have muffins with a coarse texture and holes throughout rather than a fine, even crumb (hence the name "velvet").

Preheat oven to 350 degrees. Have ready a 12-cup muffin tin lined with paper cups. Sift:

- 1 ½ c flour
- 1 ½ t baking powder
- ¼ t ground nutmeg

In mixer bowl, cream:

- ½ c sugar
- 1/3 c shortening

Add:

- 1 egg

Beat well until light and fluffy.
Add alternately with flour mixture:

- ½ c milk

Spoon batter into muffin cups, filling 2/3 full. Bake for 18-20 minutes or until done. Combine:

- ½ c sugar
- 1 t ground cinnamon

Dip each muffin, one at a time, in:

- 6 T butter, melted

Then dip in sugar mixture till coated. Serve warm.

Blueberry Poppy Seed Muffins

When I operated MillRose, muffins were one of the most popular baked goods I sold. Especially popular were the Blueberry Poppy Seed Muffins. I declined to share the recipe when asked because I used a very good blueberry muffin mix which has since been discontinued. When I learned it was no longer available I set out to develop my own recipe of which this is the result. The topping took the longest to work out, but one day when making a Fruit Crisp the solution came to me. You can use regular blueberries if the wild Maine blueberries, which are smaller and more intensely flavored are not available. You can find these canned or frozen at most grocers and on-line. Drain the canned variety; do not thaw the frozen variety.

Preheat oven to 400 degrees. Have ready a 12-cup muffin tin lined with cupcake papers and one recipe topping for Fruit Crisps. Follow the Master Mixing Method using these ingredients:

- 3 c flour

1 T baking powder
½ t baking soda
½ t salt
10 T butter, melted and cooled
2 eggs
1 ½ c plain yogurt, preferably full-fat
1 c sugar
2 T poppy seeds
1 T grated lemon rind, optional
1 ½ c blueberries (see headnote)

Sprinkle top of each muffin with 1 – 1 ½ t crumb topping.

Muffin Toppings
Use one of the following mixtures to top your muffins.
Almond Topping – Combine 1/3 c chopped almonds, ¼ c brown sugar, ¼ c flour and 2 T butter, melted.
Cinnamon Topping – Combine with a fork until well blended ½ c brown sugar, ¼ c butter, softened, ¼ c flour and 2 t cinnamon.
Pecan Topping – I. Cream together 3 T butter, softened, 1/3 c flour, 1/3 c brown sugar. Add 1 c chopped pecans. II. Combine ¼ c brown sugar and ¼ chopped pecans.
Streusel Topping – Mix until crumbly 3 T butter, softened, ¼ c brown sugar, ¼ c old-fashioned oats, ¼ c flour, ¼ c chopped walnuts and ½ t cinnamon.

Cookies

Cookies are typically categorized as drop or bar cookies. Drop cookie dough is mixed and then either scooped onto the baking sheet using a cookie scoop (similar to an ice cream scoop) or by the tablespoon or teaspoon. Bar cookies are baked in a sheet or other pan with sides and cut into squares, rectangles or diamonds. Some bar cookies have a crust of graham cracker crumbs, shortbread or other mixture. Drop cookie dough can also be baked as bars with quite acceptable results. Spread evenly in a 9x13x2-inch pan and bake 20-25 minutes or until done.

I have further categorized drop cookies as either creamed or quick-mix. Creamed cookie doughs are made by creaming the fat and sugar(s) until light and fluffy. Then eggs and liquid flavoring (e.g., vanilla) are added. The dry ingredients are sifted together and additions (chocolate chips, etc.) are mixed with the dry ingredients. The dry ingredients are added to the creamed mixture and mixed well.

Quick-mix cookie doughs are made by melting the fat before adding to the sugar(s). Eggs, dry ingredients and additions are added as in creamed cookie doughs. See the Master Mixing Method in the Quick-mix Cookies section.

It is well to chill both doughs for about an hour before forming and baking, unless baking as bar cookies. Both doughs also freeze well. Scoop or drop cookies onto a cookie sheet lined with waxed or parchment paper or aluminum foil. Freeze solid and then store in airtight freezer containers or bags. Remove as many as needed at a time. Bake at 400 degrees for 8 minutes, rotate pans and then bake at 350 degrees until the edges and tops are lightly browned, about 5 minutes.

Bar Cookies are easy to make and easy to serve. The cookies make great gifts as well as additions to a coffee bar, luncheon, dinner or supper buffet, or just to have on hand for unexpected guests. It is easier to remove the cookies from the pan and cut if you line the pan with aluminum foil letting a couple of inches extend beyond the short sides. Simply lift the foil after the cookies have cooled in the pan to remove them to a cutting board to cut in squares, rectangles or diamonds.

Bar Cookies

What could be a better first recipe in this section than one with this title from Aunt Mill's recipe box?

Preheat oven to 325 degrees. Have ready one 9x13x2-inch pan, either lightly greased, or lined with aluminum foil and the foil lightly greased.

Combine in a large mixing bowl:
- ½ c shortening
- 1 c brown sugar, packed
- 3 T milk

Beat on medium speed until well mixed and creamy.

Beat in:
> **1 egg**

Sift together into a bowl:
> **2 c flour**
> **¼ t salt**
> **¾ t soda**

Stir in:
> **½ c each chocolate chips, coconut, nuts, raisins and cereal (rice or corn flakes)**

Mix well.
Spread into prepared pan.
Bake about 20 minutes or until tester inserted in center comes out clean. Cool cookies in pan on rack before cutting into bars.

Fruitcake Bars

Preheat oven to 350 degrees.
Melt in a 9-inch square pan:
> **6 T butter**

Mix in:
> **1 ½ c graham cracker crumbs**

Press mixture evenly over bottom of pan.
Layer on:
> **1 c coconut**
> **1 c chopped nuts**
> **2 c candied fruit, chopped**
> **½ c chopped dates**
> **1 c raisins**

Pour evenly over all
> **1 14-oz can sweetened condensed milk**

Bake for 20 minutes. Let cool in pan before cutting into bars.

Sour Cream Cranberry Bars

I first discovered dried cranberries while in college. Cranberries, fresh or dried, are my favorite fruit, and I use them in both savory and sweet dishes. This is one of my favorite cookies.

Preheat oven to 350 degrees. Have ready a 9x13x2-inch pan lined with foil and foil overhanging the short ends of the pan.
Cream in a mixing bowl:
> **1 c butter, softened**
> **1 c brown sugar**

Stir in:
> **2 c oats**
> **1 ½ c flour**

Set aside 1 ½ cups. Press remaining mixture evenly into prepared pan. Bake for 10-12 minutes or until just beginning to color.
Combine in a mixing bowl:
- **2 c dried cranberries**
- **1 c Sour Cream**
- **¾ c sugar**
- **1 egg**
- **1 T grated lemon peel**
- **1 t vanilla**

Spread this mixture over the crust. Sprinkle with reserved oat mixture.
Bake 20-25 minutes. Remove from oven. Cool on rack. Remove by lifting the foil on the short ends of the pans. Cut into bars before serving.

Lemon Bars

These bars have been a favorite of mine for years. They are easy to make, and the combination of the variations make a perfect hostess, birthday or holiday gift as well as a wonderful dessert buffet for a dinner party, tea or just because.
Preheat oven to 350 degrees. Have ready a 9x13x2-inch pan lined with foil and the foil overhanging the short ends.
Blend together in a mixing bowl to make a soft dough:
- **1 c butter, softened**
- **¼ t salt**
- **½ powdered sugar**
- **2 c flour**

Press evenly into the prepared pan. Bake 15-20 minutes or until golden.
Meanwhile, combine:
- **4 eggs**
- **1 T grated lemon peel**
- **5 T lemon juice**
- **2 c granulated sugar**
- **¼ c flour**

Beat until smooth. Pour over baked crust.
Reduce heat to 325 degrees and bake 25 minutes or until firm.
Cool. Remove from pan by lifting overhanging foil. Place on cutting board. Dust with powdered sugar before slicing into bars to serve.

Variations on a Theme:
Lime Bars
Substitute lime juice for lemon juice and replace lemon peel with 2 T lime peel.
Orange Bars
Substitute orange juice and peel for lemon juice and peel.

Almond Bars
Substitute Amaretto liqueur for lemon juice. Omit lemon peel. After pouring filling over crust, sprinkle with 1 c finely chopped almonds (I chop the almonds because it makes slicing and serving much easier than sliced almonds).

Coconut Bars
Preheat oven to 350 degrees. Have ready a 9x13x2-inch pan lined with foil and foil overhanging short ends.
Cream in a mixing bowl:
> **12 T butter, softened**
> **½ c sugar**
> **½ t salt**

Stir in:
> **2 c sifted all-purpose flour**

Press dough into pan. Bake 12-15 minutes or until set and just beginning to brown. Remove from oven and set aside.
Beat well in mixing bowl:
> **4 eggs**
> **2 t vanilla**

Add:
> **2 c brown sugar**
> **¼ c flour**
> **1 t salt**

Mix well. Stir in:
> **2 c flaked coconut**
> **1 c walnuts, chopped, optional**

Spread coconut mixture evenly over pre-baked crust.
Bake an additional 25-30 minutes or until knife inserted in center comes out clean. Remove to wire rack to cool in pan before removing by lifting foil at short ends. Place on cutting board. Cut into diamond shapes.

Apricot Bars
Preheat oven to 350 degrees. Have ready a 9x13x2-inch pan lined with foil hanging two inches over short ends..
Mix well:
> **½ c butter, softened**
> **½ c brown sugar**
> **1 ¼ c flour**

Press into prepared pan.
Bake 10 minutes. Remove from oven and set aside.
Meanwhile, blend together:
> **1 c brown sugar**
> **2 eggs**

    1 c finely chopped dried apricots
    ¾ c coconut
    ½ c chopped pecans or pistachios, preferably toasted
    3 T flour
    ½ t vanilla
    ½ t lemon juice
    ¼ t salt

Spread over baked crust.
Bake 25 minutes or until knife inserted in center comes out clean.
Remove to wire rack to cool before cutting.

Fudge Brownies

These are the first brownies I baked and that I return to again and again. Be careful not to overbake. Begin testing as soon as you can smell the brownies. A tester inserted into the center should have a few moist crumbs clinging to it—begin checking even before the minimum baking times, below. These brownies do not contain any leavening, hence the fudgy texture. See the variation for brownies that are thicker and more cake-like.

Preheat oven to 350 degrees. Have ready a greased 8x8x2-inch pan.
Melt together in a medium saucepan:
    ½ c butter
    2 oz unsweetened chocolate

Remove from heat. Stir in:
    1 c sugar

Add, mixing until smooth and glossy:
    2 eggs
    1 t vanilla
    ¼ t salt

Fold in:
    ¾ c flour

Spread evenly in pan. Bake about 25 minutes or until toothpick inserted into center comes out with wet crumbs. Cool on wire rack before cutting into rectangles or squares.

Variation on a Theme: for those who like thick, cakey brownies, use the following ingredients and the mixing method, above:
    6 oz semisweet chocolate
    10 T butter
    1 ¼ c sugar
    3 eggs
    2 t vanilla
    ½ t salt
    2/3 c flour
    ½ t baking powder

Bake about 35 minutes until toothpick inserted into center comes out with wet crumbs.

Pecan Pie Bars
Preheat oven to 350 degrees. Have ready an 11x7x1 ½-inch pan.
Stir together in a mixing bowl:
> 1 ½ c flour
> 2 T brown sugar

Cut in to make fine crumbs:
> 6 T butter

Pat into pan.
Bake about 15 minutes or until just pale golden. Remove from oven. Set aside.
Beat lightly in a bowl:
> 2 eggs

Stir in:
> ½ c packed brown sugar
> ½ c chopped pecans
> ½ c dark corn syrup
> 2 T butter, melted
> 1 t vanilla

Pour over baked layer. Bake about 25 minutes or till done. Cool slightly on wire rack; cut into bars.

Drop Cookies (Creaming Method)
These cookies are made with the traditional creaming method. I prefer to use an air-insulated cookie sheet on which to bake these. However, a heavy gauge aluminum sheet will work. A silicone baking mat is well worth the investment when it comes to baking and cleanup—no need to worry if you need to grease the sheet or not.

Apricot Chocolate Chip Cookies
Another of my favorite fruit-chocolate combinations in a cookie form.
Preheat oven to 350 degrees. Have ready several cookie sheets, ungreased or lined with a silicone baking mat.
Cream together in an electric mixer bowl:
> ¼ c butter, softened
> ¼ c shortening
> 1/3 c sugar
> 1/3 c brown sugar

Beat in:
> 1 egg
> ½ t vanilla

Combine in another bowl:
> 1 c flour

    ½ t salt
    ½ t baking soda
    2/3 c chopped dried apricots
    ½ c chocolate chips
    ½ c chopped toasted walnuts

Add dry ingredients to creamed mixture. Mix well.
Drop by rounded tablespoonful onto ungreased cookie sheet. Bake 10-12 minutes or until done. Remove to rack to cool.

Pineapple Chocolate Chip Cookies

Preheat oven to 350 degrees. Have ready several cookie sheets, greased or lined with a silicone baking mat.
Cream in an electric mixer bowl:
    1 c shortening
    1 c sugar
    1 c packed brown sugar

Beat in:
    2 eggs
    2 8-oz cans crushed pineapple, well drained
    2 t vanilla

Combine in another bowl:
    4 c flour
    2 t soda, sieved
    2 t baking powder
    ½ t salt
    1 c chocolate chips
    1 c chopped toasted nuts

Stir into creamed mixture.
Drop by tablespoon onto cookie sheet. Bake 10-12 minutes or until done. Remove to rack to cool.

Chocolate Covered Cherry Cookies

This is my version of a cookie of which the original recipe provided mediocre results; however, with some tweaks, you will produce very delicious results. Note: save the juice you drain from the cherries, and after draining, spread the cherries on paper towels to absorb excess moisture that otherwise will make the cookies damp. Do seek out maraschino cherries used for drinks (a well-stocked liquor store will have these) as the usual ones in the grocery store have declined in quality over the years, and the so-called "natural" or "organic" maraschino cherries are abysmal.
Preheat oven to 350 degrees. Have ready several lightly greased cookie sheets or cookies sheets lined with a silicone baking mat.
Drain, reserving juice from:
    1 10-oz jar maraschino cherries

Placed drained cherries on paper towels to dry.
Sift into a large bowl:
- 1 ½ c flour
- ½ c unsweetened cocoa powder
- ½ t salt
- ¼ t baking powder
- ¼ t baking soda

In a mixer bowl, cream:
- ½ c butter, softened
- 1 c sugar

Beat until light and fluffy and sugar has dissolved.
Beat in:
- 1 egg
- 1 ½ t vanilla

Gradually add dry ingredients and beat until well blended.
Shape dough into 1-inch balls. Place on cookie sheet. Press down center of ball with thumb to make an indentation.
Place in the indentation a:
- **Drained maraschino cherry**

Heat over low heat until melted:
- 1 12-oz package semisweet chocolate chips
- 1 14-oz can evaporated milk

Stir in:
- 8 t reserved cherry juice

Spoon about 1 teaspoon over each cherry, spreading to cover cherry. (Frosting may be thinned with additional cherry juice, if necessary).
Bake for 10 minutes or until done. Remove to wire rack; cool.
Spread cooled cookies with additional frosting, recovering cherry.

Chocolate Cookies

Preheat oven to 400 degrees, with racks in upper and lower thirds. Line two baking sheets with parchment paper or a silicone baking mat.
In medium bowl, sift together:
- 2 ¼ c flour
- ½ c cocoa
- 2 t cream of tartar
- 1 t baking soda
- ½ t salt

Melt:
- 1 c butter

Add:
- 1 ½ c sugar

Mix well.

Add:
>   **2 large eggs**
>   **1 t vanilla**

Using heaping tablespoons, form balls of dough. Place about 3 inches apart on prepared pans.

Bake until cookies are set in center and begin to crack, about 10 minutes, rotating sheets halfway through.

Let cookies cool on sheets 5 minutes, then transfer cookies to racks to cool completely.

Store in airtight container up to 1 week.

Variations on a Theme:

Roll the cookies in powdered sugar, granulated sugar or cinnamon-sugar before baking.

Chocolate Espresso Cookies

Add 2 t instant espresso powder to the dry ingredients. Roll balls in granulated sugar.

Mexican Hot Chocolate Cookies

Roll balls in a mixture of ¼ c sugar, 2 t cinnamon and ½ t chipotle chili pepper powder before baking.

Carrot Cookies

We grew up with these not-too-sweet cookies. Mother made them frequently during the years she baked. They are light and delicate with a cake-like texture. They are best made small--do not over bake.

Preheat oven to 300 degrees. Have ready greased cookie sheets or line with a silicone baking mat.

Cream until light and fluffy:
>   **1 c shortening**
>   **¾ c sugar**

Add and beat well:
>   **1 egg**
>   **1 t vanilla**

Stir in:
>   **1 c grated raw carrot (use the small holes of a box grater)**

Sift together:
>   **2 c flour**
>   **2 t baking powder**
>   **½ t salt**

Drop by teaspoonful onto cookie sheets. Bake for about 10 minutes or until set and pale golden. Remove to rack to cool.

Variations on a Theme: turn these into an appetizer base by adding 1 T minced fresh herbs such as rosemary, sage or thyme.

Crackle Cookies
Deeply chocolate flavored with a crackly topping of powdered sugar.
Preheat oven to 350 degrees. Have ready a large cookie sheet, preferably lined with a silicone baking mat.
Combine in a mixing bowl:
>	½ c sugar
>	2 T oil
>	1 oz unsweetened chocolate, melted

Mix well.
Combine:
>	½ c flour
>	½ t baking powder
>	1/8 t salt

Add to sugar mixture. Mix well.
Chill dough, covered, 2 hours. Form into 1-inch balls. Roll in powdered sugar, covering completely.
Bake 10-12 minutes. Let sit on cookie sheet about 5 minutes. Remove to rack to cool.

Cream Cheese Chocolate Chip Cookies
Preheat oven to 350 degrees. Have ready cookie sheets, preferably lined with a silicone baking mat.
Cream until light and fluffy:
>	1 c butter
>	1 c sugar

Beat in well:
>	1 3-oz pkg. cream cheese, softened

Add:
>	2 eggs
>	1 t vanilla
>	½ t lemon extract, optional

Combine in a separate bowl:
>	2 ½ c flour
>	1 t baking powder
>	½ t soda
>	1 c chopped nuts
>	1 c semi-sweet chocolate chips

Stir into creamed mixture.
Drop by teaspoonful onto cookie sheet. Bake 12-15 minutes. Let cool on sheet 1 minute before removing to wire rack to cool.

Peanut Butter Chocolate Chip Cookies
Peanut Butter and chocolate have always been a favorite pairing of mine.
Preheat oven to 350 degrees. Have ready a large cookie sheet, lightly greased, or lined

with a silicone baking mat.
Beat in a large mixing bowl until light and creamy:
- ½ c sugar
- 1/3 c packed brown sugar
- ½ c butter
- ½ c Peanut Butter
- ½ t vanilla
- 1 egg

Combine in a separate bowl:
- 1 c flour
- ½ c quick-cooking oats
- ½ t baking soda
- ¼ t salt
- 1 c chocolate chips

Stir into butter mixture. Mix well.
Drop dough by tablespoon onto prepared sheet.
Bake 10-12 minutes. Remove to rack to cool.

Date Oatmeal Cookies

Preheat oven to 350 degrees. Have ready a large cookie sheet, lightly greased or lined with a silicone baking mat.
Sift into a bowl:
- 1 ½ c sifted all-purpose flour
- 1 t baking powder
- ½ t salt
- 1 t each cinnamon and allspice

Add:
- 1 c chopped dates
- ½ c coconut
- ½ chopped nuts

Cream until light and fluffy:
- ½ c butter
- 1 c sugar
- 3 eggs

Add:
- ½ c milk
- 2 c rolled oats

Stir in flour-date-nut mixture.
Drop by small tablespoon onto prepared sheets.
Bake for 10-12 minutes or until delicately browned.

Teatime Cookies

Preheat oven to 375 degrees. Have ready a large cookie sheet, greased or lined with a silicone baking mat.
Combine:
- ¾ c flour
- 1 t baking powder
- ¼ t salt
- 1 c quick oats
- 1 c wheat flakes (cereal)
- ½ c walnuts, chopped
- ½ c coconut

Cream until light and fluffy:
- ½ c shortening
- ½ c brown sugar
- ½ c sugar

Beat in:
- 1 t vanilla
- 1 egg
- 1/3 c milk

Stir in dry ingredients.
Drop by teaspoons onto greased baking sheet.
Bake 8-10 minutes or until golden brown.
Let cool 1 minute on baking sheet. Remove to wire rack to cool completely.

Cream Wafers

Melt-in-your-mouth goodness. Not a drop cookie, but one made with the creaming method. Tint the filling for different occasions.
Preheat oven to 375 degrees. Have ready cookie sheets, ungreased or lined with a silicone baking mat.
Cream together:
- 1 c butter, softened
- 1/3 c heavy cream
- 2 c flour
- ¼ t salt

Refrigerate for several hours or until firm.
Remove dough to a lightly floured surface.
Roll dough to about 1/8-inch thick. Cut into rounds using a floured 1 – 1 ½-inch biscuit cutter.
Dip cut cookies into:
- **Sugar**

Place on baking sheet 1 inch apart. Prick each cookie with a fork four times.
Bake 7-9 minutes or until just set. Cookies should not start to color.
Remove to a wire rack to cool completely.

Cream:
- ¼ c butter
- ¾ c powdered sugar
- 1 t vanilla
- Food coloring, if desired

Mix in water 1 t at a time, if needed, to make spreading consistency.
Spread frosting on the bottom of one cookie and then top with a second cookie, top side up.

Quick-mix Cookies

These can be made as drop cookies or as bar cookies. If making as bar cookies, use a 9x13x2-inch pan and bake 22-25 minutes.

Master Mixing Method:

Step 1 – Combine dry ingredients (sieve baking soda to remove any lumps).
Step 2 – Stir dry, solid additions (chips, nuts, etc.) into flour mixture.
Step 3 – Melt fat; set aside until cool but still liquid.
Step 4 – Beat eggs; add liquid flavorings and salt.
Step 5 – Combine in large mixing bowl the sugar(s) and fat. Stir until well mixed.
Step 6 – Add egg mixture and stir until well combined and creamy.
Step 7 – Stir in flour mixture until evenly combined.
Step 9 – Chill 1 hour before forming and baking.

Chocolate Chip Cookies

For several years, Father (who I learned has an insatiable sweet tooth) baked his own cookies when Mother stopped baking. His cookies (which he always baked in a sheet pan and cut into bars) had the most interesting texture which was at the same time crisp and crumby. I discovered his method when on a home visit when I was living in Indiana. He melted the butter and just dumped everything into one bowl and mixed it together. I refined his method just a bit. This method of making cookie dough works for almost all cookie recipes as does the freezing method. You can freeze cookie dough balls and bake as many when needed following this procedure. I like to use 14 T butter and 2 T light olive oil for 1 c butter.

Preheat oven to 350 degrees. Have ready several cookie sheets, ungreased or lined with a silicone baking mat.

- 2 ¼ c flour
- 1 t baking powder
- ½ t soda
- 12 oz chocolate chips
- 2 eggs
- 1 t vanilla
- ¾ t salt
- 1 c butter, melted and cooled

¾ c sugar
¾ c brown sugar, packed

Spread batter evenly into a 9x13x2-in pan. Bake about 25-30 minutes. Or, use an ice cream scoop to form balls on baking sheet. Bake 12-15 minutes or until set and golden around the edges.

You can also freeze the balls on a baking sheet and then store in a plastic freezer bag. When ready to bake, place frozen cookies on baking sheet. Bake at 400 degrees for 8 minutes. Rotate pans and bake at 350 degrees about 5 minutes or until edges are golden brown. Remove to wire rack to cool.

Variations on a Theme:

Butterscotch Cookies – substitute butterscotch chips for chocolate chips.

Cranberry Chocolate Chip Cookies
I especially like this version for the Thanksgiving and Christmas holidays. Decrease chocolate chips to 8 ounces. Add 1 ½ c. fresh cranberries, and ½ c toasted English or black walnuts, both coarsely chopped, to the batter. Note: frozen cranberries do not work well in this version.

Ranger Cookies
Aunt Mill called these and the Cowboy Cookies a "health cookie." This was years before we knew the health benefits of nuts, chocolate and coconut. Healthy or not, this and all cookies in this book are delicious. Enjoy with a glass of ice-cold milk, or your favorite tea or coffee—hot or cold.

Shape into tablespoon-size balls and flatten. Bake at 350 degrees on cookie sheet for 10-12 minutes or until golden around edges.

 2 ¼ c flour
 1 t baking powder
 1 t soda
 1 t nutmeg
 1 t cinnamon
 1 c old-fashioned oats
 1 c crisp rice cereal
 1 c coconut
 ¾ c chopped dates
 ¾ c nuts
 ¾ c raisins
 ¾ c chocolate chips
 2 eggs
 1 t vanilla
 1 t salt
 1 c butter, melted
 1 c sugar
 ½ c brown sugar

Pumpkin Chocolate Chip Cookies

Another of Aunt Mill's "health cookies." The pumpkin provides fiber and vitamin A to one's diet.

Preheat oven to 375 degrees.
- 2 c flour
- 2 t baking powder
- 1 t cinnamon
- ½ t salt
- 1 c chocolate chips
- ½ c chopped nuts
- 1 egg
- 1 t milk
- 1 t vanilla
- ½ c butter, melted
- 1 c pumpkin
- 1 c sugar

Drop from teaspoon onto lightly greased baking sheet. Bake 10-12 minutes, until golden brown.
Cool 2 minutes on baking sheet. Remove to wire rack to cool.

Everything Cookies

Bake at 350 degrees on greased baking sheets, 10-12 minutes.
- 3 c flour
- 1 t soda
- 1 t cream of tartar
- 1 c oatmeal
- 1 c crisp rice cereal
- 12 oz chocolate chips
- 1 c nuts, chopped, preferably toasted
- 1 egg
- 2 t vanilla
- 1 t salt
- 1 c oil
- 1 c butter, melted
- 1 c brown sugar
- 1 c sugar

Banana Oatmeal Chocolate Chip Cookies

Drop by tablespoon onto lightly greased cookie sheet. Bake at 350 degrees about 12 minutes.
- 1 ½ c flour
- ½ t soda
- 1 t cinnamon

½ t nutmeg
1 ¾ c oatmeal
1 c chocolate chips
½ c nuts, chopped, preferably toasted
1 egg
1 t vanilla
½ t salt
¾ c butter, melted
1 c sugar
1 c mashed, ripe banana

Candies

Mother and Father always bought a selection of Brach's brand candy when they purchased groceries each week. These were always hands-off for me because I became diabetic at age four. However, I would sometimes sneak one or two candies every-now-and-then. It is difficult to find Brach's candies in stores these days. However, some of the candies are available to purchase on-line.

Fudge

One of the few candies we had during Christmas, and the one Mother enjoyed most, was fudge, and more often than not, it was homemade. Making good candy is not difficult, but it does take time and precision. The following fudge gets its best flavor from the freshest ingredients: whole milk, unsalted butter, fresh nuts, quality chocolate, and the best vanilla—I find the best vanilla is the brand available at Mexican grocery stores and indigenous to that country. Juan gave this recipe to me. Have ready two buttered 8x8x2-inch pans or one 9x13x2-inch pan.
Combine in a large saucepan:
- **4 c sugar**
- **1 c butter**
- **1 c milk**

Stir constantly over medium heat until sugar is dissolved. Bring to boil over medium-high heat and boil, stirring constantly, for 2 minutes. Turn off heat. Add:
- **25 large marshmallows, quartered**

Continue stirring until completely melted.
Gradually add:
- **12 oz semi-sweet chocolate, chopped**
- **13 oz milk chocolate, chopped**
- **2 oz unsweetened chocolate, chopped**

Stir until completely melted.
Stir in:
- **1 t vanilla**
- **1 c chopped nuts, optional**

Pour into prepared pan(s). Let set until thoroughly cool before cutting. Store in airtight containers. Note: you can use any size pan for this fudge depending on how thick you want it. 10x15x1-inch, 9x13x2-inch and 8-inch square pans all work well, and the thickness will range from ½ to 1 inch.

Marshmallows

At once thought an exclusive recipe, marshmallow recipes abound across cookbooks and the Internet. I have yet to create marshmallows from the root of the plant of the same name, but when I do it will be in the second edition of this book. This is a basic recipe. You can create your own variations by using different spices, flavorings, chocolate, peppermint candies, etc. You will need a large heavy-duty electric mixer and bowl (4-5 quart) to make these.

Oil a 3-quart glass baking dish with vegetable oil. Line the dish with aluminum foil. Lightly coat foil with oil.

In large bowl of electric mixer, soften:

    4 envelopes unflavored gelatin

In:

    ¾ c water

Place in a heavy saucepan:

    ¾ c water
    3 c sugar
    1 ¼ c light corn syrup
    ¼ t salt

Bring to a boil and cook over high heat until the syrup reaches 234-238 degrees or the soft ball stage on a candy thermometer.

With the whisk attachment, beat the hot syrup into the gelatin mixture. Stop mixer; pour in a small amount of syrup; beat at high speed; repeat until all syrup is added to the gelatin mixture. Then beat until very stiff, white, glossy and cool to the touch about 15 minutes at high speed.

Beat in:

    2 t vanilla

Pour mixture into prepared pan and smooth with an oiled spatula. Allow to rest, uncovered, at room temperature, 10-12 hours.

Have ready about:

    1 ½ c powdered sugar, sifted

Using a fine sieve, sprinkle a fine coating of powdered sugar over top of marshmallows. Evenly coat with more powdered sugar a wooden cutting board large enough to hold the marshmallows. Turn stiffened marshmallow mixture onto board, and using a lightly oiled cookie cutter, cut into shapes. Dip all cut edges in additional powdered sugar to prevent sticking. Store in an air-tight container up to 3 days.

Variations on a Theme:

Chocolate Marshmallows I – Combine equal parts of confectioner's sugar and cocoa powder. Replace the confectioner's sugar for dusting and rolling with this mixture.

Chocolate Marshmallows II – Cut into small circles or squares. Dip in melted chocolate. Place on a foil-lined sheet until chocolate is set.

Peppermint Marshmallows – Replace the vanilla with 1 t peppermint extract. Roll the edges of the cut marshmallows in finely crushed peppermint candies.

Peanut Butter Fudge

I created this recipe for Mother who also enjoyed Peanut Butter sandwiches—with jelly or honey or brown sugar or dill pickles. This is for Peanut Butter lovers everywhere. You can use creamy Peanut Butter, if desired. For added decadence, dip individual squares into melted semi-sweet or dark chocolate; place on a parchment-paper-lined sheet pan and refrigerate until chocolate is set.

Have ready a lightly greased 9-inch square pan.
Bring to a boil in a large, heavy saucepan:
- **2 c sugar**
- **2/3 c milk**

Cook to soft ball stage (234-238 degrees on a candy thermometer)
Pour over the following in a large mixing bowl:
- **1 t vanilla**
- **1 c chunky Peanut Butter**
- **1 7 oz jar marshmallow cream**

Mix well and pour into prepared pan. Let cool before cutting into 1-inch squares.

Aunt Viv's Caramel Corn

Popcorn played a significant role in the Weishaar family history. The farm to the East of the family farm was sold at a tax sale in the early 1940s. Grandfather did not buy it at the time. However, a year later the person who purchased it no longer wanted it. Grandfather bought the 120 acres. He then planted it in popcorn. He was able to pay for the land with the proceeds he received from selling the popcorn. He almost doubled the size of the farm with this purchase. Since then the family farm has consisted of 280 acres. The year Grandfather purchased the land was the only year it was planted. It has been in pasture ever since. "The hundred-and-twenty" as we have always called it also had up to five ponds on it which we often fished.

After the noon meal (dinner to us, lunch to others), Father would head off to his bed or to the couch, or sometimes to the floor, for a nap before the afternoon work commenced. I remember very few times when he did not have his after-dinner nap. It was a time for all of us to relax and refresh ourselves before working all afternoon and into the evening. During that time, Mother and we children would watch reruns of shows popular in the 1950s and 1960s. Mother's favorite was "The Lucy Show," starring Lucille Ball and Vivian Vance. One episode featured the ladies branching into their own business selling "Krazy Krunch" caramel popcorn. The recipe was repeated often during the show. I wrote it down and set to work making "Aunt Viv's Caramel Corn." After only a few tweaks, here is my result:

Cook to the softball stage (234-238 degrees on a candy thermometer):
- **1 ½ c brown sugar**
- **2 T butter**
- **6 T water**

Immediately pour this mixture over:
- **3 quarts popped popcorn**

2 cups mixed nuts (salted nuts provide the best flavor)

Mix well and pour onto buttered sheet or marble slab. Mix lightly again with buttered hands to ensure nuts are evenly distributed. Spread out and let cool. Store tightly covered in a cool, dry place.

Butchering

While I always prefer to use beef, pork, chicken, etc. raised and processed on the farm, a treasure trove of "wild game" such as venison, buffalo, elk, rabbit, squirrel, pheasant, quail, etc. adds variety to menus and to the diet. However, hunting, processing and cooking these are best only for the skilled cook whose partner is a Nimrod. If less well endowed, you can get most of these from specialty shops—either local brick-and-mortar establishments, or "virtual" establishments via mail order and/or online.

Rendering Lard

Lard has been in and out of favor for years. It was a household staple until the advent of hydrogenated vegetable oil products (aka "shortening"). Lard, however, has less saturated fat, more unsaturated fat and less cholesterol than an equal amount of butter by weight. Un-hydrogenated lard contains no trans fats.

If you must purchase lard, it is good to know the different grades of lard based on the type of fat used. Lard can be obtained from any part of the pig that has a high concentration of fatty tissue. The highest grade of lard, known as leaf lard, is obtained from the "flare" visceral fat deposit surrounding the kidneys and inside the loin. Leaf lard has little pork flavor, making it ideal for use in baked goods, where it is valued for its ability to produce flaky pie crusts. The next-highest grade is obtained from fatback, the hard subcutaneous fat between the pig's back skin and muscle. The lowest grade (for purposes of rendering into lard) is obtained from the soft caul fat surrounding digestive organs, such as small intestines.

We rendered lard from what we trimmed from the pork we butchered. It was always creamy white in color, smooth in texture, and never had an overwhelming pork flavor. I have revived rendering lard, and baking and cooking with it since returning to Kansas, and it has been a best-seller at the Atchison Farmers Market.

To render lard, grind or chop very fine the fat. Doing so will make rendering easier and take less time. Pour enough water into a large, heavy pan or skillet to just cover the bottom. Heat to bring the water to a boil, then reduce the heat to low. Add the fat. Let cook until the lard is rendered, stirring occasionally. Cook until all the lard is rendered (liquefied), the water has evaporated and the remains are golden brown and crisp. Be sure to keep the heat low and watch closely. Strain the lard through a double thickness of cheesecloth into sterile containers. Let cool before sealing. Store in a dark, dry, cool area.

The remains, or browned bits, are called cracklins. They are delicious drained well and then salted to eat as a snack. They are also good added to Mashed Potatoes, corn bread or used to top casseroles. Cracklins freeze well in airtight containers or plastic freezer bags.

You can also render chicken, duck and goose fat, including fat trimmed from the birds as well as the skin, in the same way. Partially freeze the fat and skin to make grinding easier (I use a food processor with the metal blade). I like to freeze fat and skin in plastic bags until I have a good quantity to render. It takes longer to render, and I find it easiest to render in a large casserole or roasting pan, uncovered, in a 200-degree oven. Stir occasionally until the fat is rendered and the skins are crisp. Do not overcook, or the fat will taste of the cooked bird. Strain and package as for lard. Store the rendered fat in the refrigerator (Note: goose fat is liquid at room temperature).

Scrapple

For years during the butchering sessions, we made scrapple from the hog heads. We would quarter the heads, after we skinned them and removed the brains, eyeballs, etc. We cooked the cleaned heads until the meat fell from the bones in large kettles on a gas stove in the basement. The meat and broth was particularly rich and well-seasoned. Scrapple is equally good made with either chopped pork roast or sausage. If using sausage, you can use chicken stock in place of the pork broth with equally good results. Scrapple freezes well for several months. Pour the mixture into a lightly greased loaf pan, let cool completely, uncovered, before freezing. If not freezing, omit the flour. The proportion of two pounds bony pork pieces to 1 c cornmeal to 4 cups liquid is easily adjustable for cooking in quantity for freezing. Either way, scrapple makes a delicious breakfast served with any variety of eggs and fruit salad. It also makes a fantastic light dinner or supper with a cabbage or three-bean salad.

Have ready a lightly greased 8x4x3-inch loaf pan.

Place in a large crock pot:

    2 lb pork neck bones or other bony pieces

Add:

    Boiling water to cover
    1 onion, with skins, roots trimmed and halved
    1 small carrot, scrubbed
    2 stalks celery, halved crosswise
    2 t salt
    Several shakes of the pepper can

Cook on high until the meat falls from the bones (6-8 hours).

Strain, reserving the broth. There should be about 4 cups. If not, add enough water to measure 4 cups. Let broth and meat cool.

Chop or grind meat very fine.

Remove fat from stock. To 1 cup of the stock, add:

    1 c cornmeal
    2 T flour

Bring remaining 3 cups of broth to boil. Pour in the cornmeal mixture, stirring constantly. Bring back to boil, then reduce heat to medium low and cook 10-15 minutes or until very thick, stirring often. Remove from heat. Add meat. Mix well. If freezing, pour into prepared pan. Let cool completely, uncovered, before freezing. Wrap tightly in foil and place in a large freezer bag.

If not freezing, pour mixture into prepared pan. Let cool in pan. Cover tightly and refrigerate overnight.

Remove from pan. Slice about ½" thick, coat with flour and fry slowly in melted butter or drippings.

To cook the frozen version, thaw in refrigerator, slice and fry as above.

Summer Sausage

I received this recipe from Mary, one of my supervisors at Fort Leavenworth. She was a very good cook. This is a good item for an appetizer, meat-and-cheese or antipasto tray, or to use as a filler for biscuit sandwiches.

Mix well together:
- **2 lb lean ground beef**
- **1 rounded T curing salt**
- **1 ½ t onion powder, or one small onion, grated**
- **1 ½ t garlic powder**
- **1 ½ T liquid smoke**
- **½ c water**
- **1 T mustard seed**
- **1 T crushed whole peppercorns**

Roll into three sticks the size of a half dollar. Wrap tightly in foil. Refrigerate 24 hours. Unwrap and bake for 1 hour at 300 degrees. Let cool before slicing to serve.

Mincemeat

Mincemeat as it was known in our family was quite different from the mincemeat commonly known that originated in Europe and can be purchased commercially. We used fine cuts of beef, usually a chuck roast or shoulder, and the standard Jonathan apple. To these ingredients were added cinnamon, a few raisins, a bit of sugar and a touch of wine. Use a bold, sweet wine for this recipe. The result is a subtly sweet mixture to serve cold or at room temperature, often as a side to more hearty fare during the Winter months. This recipe is from Aunt Frieda who married Father's brother, Jack. The wine used when this was made in quantity was Morgan David, a sweet wine made from Concord grapes. Homemade grape wine would be especially good.

Cook a quantity of beef until fork tender using the method in Main Dishes. Drain and cool. Reserve stock.

When cool, remove any remaining fat from the meat. Weigh the meat, and then peel, core and weigh an equal amount of tart apples (Jonathan, Granny Smith, etc. or a combination). Chop the apples.

Measure the meat/apple mixture into a large, heavy pot.

To each quart of meat/apple mixture, add:
- **¼ c raisins**
- **1 t. cinnamon**
- **¼ c sugar**

½ c wine

Bring to a boil, then reduce heat to low and cook for 1 hour. When done, cool and then pack into freezer containers. Cover and freeze. Can be frozen for several months.

Tongue

Tongue is one of those foods people either like or hate. Do try it if you haven't. It is a versatile meat which provides variety to your menus. You can special-order a tongue from your local grocer or buy it anytime, it seems, from a reputable Mexican market.

Place the tongue in a large bowl or pan. Add in 2 T salt and cover with cold water. Place in the refrigerator and let soak at least overnight and up to several days (change the water a couple of times). Drain well and place in a slow cooker.

Add:
- **1 onion, stem and root end removed, quartered**
- **1 carrot, scrubbed and halved**
- **2 stalks celery, scrubbed and halved**
- **1 t black peppercorns**
- **2 large bay leaves**
- **2 t salt**

Add cold water to barely cover contents. Cover and cook on high until a fork easily pierces the tongue. It is better (if not impossible) to overcook. Let cool in pot until you can handle it easily.

Transfer the still-warm tongue to a platter or cutting board. Remove the skin and any fat as well as any vessels from the cut end of the tongue. Note: if the tongue cools completely, you will have much difficulty removing the skin. Slice at an angle, beginning with the tip end, about ½-inch thick.

The tongue is now ready to serve. You can let cool and serve cold in sandwiches, or reheat in some of the cooking liquid to serve like a roast with potatoes, vegetables, etc., or sauté briefly in hot oil or lard and serve as a filling for tacos.

Oxtails

I can remember having the oxtails (tails not from an ox, but from the beeves we butchered) only when we butchered. We cooked the oxtails, and used the meat and broth to make a richly flavored soup with rice and mixed vegetables.

Head Cheese

Not a dairy cheese, but a meat terrine or jellied meatloaf. This dish was typically made with the meat from the actual hog head. I can vaguely remember the butchering days of the mid-70s when the family still made this (and Blood Sausage) by quartering the hog head and cooking in large kettles on the vintage gas stove in our basement. You can buy a similar product today in some delis which is labeled "Brawn," or "Souse" if made with the addition of vinegar. This makes a good sandwich filling or cold

luncheon dish. You need cuts of meat with plenty of natural gelatin. I use the hocks or "bones" from butchering. Absent those, you can use ribs.
Place in a slow cooker:
- **3 lb bony pork cuts**
- **2 onions, peeled and quartered**
- **5 celery stalks, halved**
- **1 large carrot, scrubbed and ends trimmed, halved**
- **2 bay leaves**

Cover with cold water and cook on high 8-10 hours or until meat is ready to fall from the bones.
Drain and reserve stock.
Remove meat from bones, discarding fat. Dice the meat.
Reduce the stock by one-half.
Add:
- **Salt and pepper to taste**
- **½ t mace or sage**
- **The diced meat**

Simmer for 30 minutes. Taste again and adjust seasonings, if needed.
Pour into loaf pan. Cover by pressing plastic wrap onto the surface. Cover with another loaf pan and fill the pan with canned goods.
Chill at least 8 hours or overnight. Serve, cut into slices with:
- **French Dressing**

Or use as a sandwich filling.

Blood Sausage

Unless you do your own butchering or can find a meat processor willing to save the blood from a butchered hog for you, it is best to order this from a deli or specialty food source. Many on-line resources sell blood sausage, also called Blood Pudding and Boudin Noir.

I remember the aunts and uncles making this only once when they all joined to butcher for everyone. Grandmother collected the blood from the butchered hog, added a bit of vinegar to prevent it from coagulating and stirred it slowly while she took it to the house to store in the refrigerator until needed. Grandmother also scraped and washed the intestines which were used as the casing for the sausages. Aunt Mill led the production of making the filling, stuffing the casings, tying off the large ropes of stuffed casings into individual sausages and then poaching them in a large kettle of water on the vintage Western Holly gas stove in the basement of the family home.

The poached sausages are delicious broiled, pan-fried or grilled.
Have ready prepared sausage casings.
Cook gently, without browning:
- **¾ c grated onion**

In:
> **2 T lard**

Cool slightly and then combine in a large mixing bowl with:
> **1/3 c whipping cream**
> **¼ c bread crumbs**
> **2 eggs, beaten**
> **1 t salt**
> **½ t coarsely ground black pepper**
> **1 bay leaf, pulverized**

Add:
> **½ lb leaf lard or beef suet, finely diced**
> **2 c fresh pork blood**

Fill casings only three-fourths full. Put sealed casings into a wire basket without crowding.

Bring to a boil a large kettle of water. Remove pan from heat and plunge the basket into the kettle. Return pan to very low heat (about 170-180 degrees) for 15 minutes. Test for doneness by piercing a sausage with a fork; if blood comes out, continue to cook about 5 minutes or until barely firm. If any sausages rise to the surface, prick them to release the air that might burst the skins.

Remove to a platter to cool. Refrigerate until serving or freeze in plastic freezer bags or butcher paper.

To serve: split and fry or grill very gently until heated through.

Liver

People either love or hate liver. I think it all comes down to the preparation. Baby beef, calf, beef (in order with regard to strength of flavor and tenderness), lamb and pork livers are all good sources of iron and B vitamins and are delicious when properly cooked. We always had beef liver. It is commonly available today from the grocer already sliced and most often only available frozen. You can sometimes special order other varieties. The secret to delicious liver? Brine it for several days in milk and salt. This draws out the metallic taste which is sometimes very strong because liver is high in iron. Make sure your liver has the silverskin (the thin membranous outer covering) and any tubes from the interior removed (do this also if you buy liver already sliced). I like liver sliced about ¼-inch thick. Two other important tips: cook quickly and only until just done. In fact, it should be just slightly pink on the inside when you remove it from the heat. It will finish cooking to perfection from the residual heat.

Simplicity is the best approach to cooking liver.

Liver I

Several days ahead of cooking, brine in a glass or other non-metal, covered container, in the refrigerator:
> **1 lb liver, sliced ¼-inch thick and prepared as above**

In:
> **Milk, to cover**
> **1 t salt**

Drain and discard the milk each day. Sprinkle liver lightly with salt and cover with milk. Brine 3-5 days.
Drain liver. Lay slices on a paper-towel lined rack. Wipe slices.
Season with:
> **Pepper**

Heat in a heavy skillet over high heat:
> **2 T fat (lard, oil, shortening or butter)**

Dredge liver in:
> **Flour**

Shake off excess.
Add the liver to the skillet in batches and brown quickly on both sides, 1-2 minutes. Do not crowd the skillet and add more fat as needed. Remove to a warm plate as it is done.

Liver II

This version is poached in butter and results in an amazingly tender, rich and delicious main dish.
Prepare as in Liver I:
> **1 lb liver, sliced ¼-inch thick**

Heat, over medium-high heat, in a heavy pan large enough to hold the liver in a single layer without crowding:
> **2 c butter**
> **½ c lard or light olive oil**

Heat until butter is melted and stops foaming.
Lay in the liver slices in a single layer. Reduce heat to medium-low. Cook gently 6-7 minutes or until liver is just light pink inside.
Remove to a wire rack to drain. Keep warm until serving.

Liver and Onions

A classic dish easily mangled. The fat in which you cook liver can take on a strong taste which makes it terrible for gravy or sauce. If you like a gravy or sauce with your liver and onions, it is best to make a separate Pan or Stock Gravy using beef stock, cream or milk with fresh lard or butter as the fat. To make this dish, I like to prepare Liver II, the cooked onions which follow, and Pan Gravy, using a well-flavored beef stock and butter.
Heat in a large skillet or Dutch oven:
> **3 T fat**

Add:
> **3-4 large onions, halved and very thinly sliced**
> **Generous sprinkling of salt and pepper**

Cover and cook, stirring often, over low heat until the onions are very soft but not colored 20-30 minutes.
Spoon over cooked liver and serve immediately with gravy, if desired.

Corned Beef
Once you make your own corned beef, you will not want to buy one from the grocer. This is easy to do and the results are delicious.
In a large pot, combine:
>   **1 ga. water**
>   **2 c kosher or sea salt (coarse)**
>   **1 T curing salt**
>   **4 cloves garlic, minced**
>   **½ c brown sugar**
>   **¼ c Pickling Spice**

Bring to a simmer and cook until sugar is dissolved. Remove from heat and let sit until room temperature.
Transfer brine to a 2-gallon resealable plastic bag set in a large shallow pan.
Place in brine in bag:
>   **1 3 ½ - 4-lb flat cut beef brisket**

Chill in refrigerator 5 days, turning occasionally.
Rinse well before cooking.

Brains
Brains are the most delicate of organ meats and contain no muscle fiber. These are most often firmed before cooking by poaching and then pressing. It is difficult today to find brains, other than frozen pork brains, at most grocers. That is a shame because, when properly cooked, brains are a delightful dish. Prepare brains by soaking in cold water for 1-2 hours to remove all traces of blood. Then, poach in barely simmering (never boiling!) water to which has been added 2 T lemon juice or 1 T white vinegar, for 10 minutes. Drain carefully. Rinse with cold water. Place the brains on a plate and cover with another plate and weight with canned goods to press out the water and firm them. Refrigerate the weighted brains for 1-2 hours.

Sautéed Brains
A simple, and probably the best, way to prepare and serve brains.
Prepare, as above,
>   **Brains**

Pat dry and season with:
>   **Salt**
>   **Pepper**

Coat with:
>   **Flour**

Melt in a large skillet:

¼ **c butter**
¼ **c lard**

Heat until butter melts and stops foaming.
Add in the brains and cook about 3 minutes on each side. Cover, reduce heat and cook until brains are firmed and browned, 3-4 minutes. Serve with lemon wedges and capers.

Brining

It seems now that brining is all the rage. Poultry, game or fish, is soaked in a salt-water solution, sometimes with flavorful additions, for several minutes or hours (or, even, overnight) to tenderize the meat and make it more flavorful. However, we have been brining since the beginning of time. Brining is especially useful for drawing out the last bits of blood from the meat, reducing an overly "wild" taste of freshly hunted game, and most importantly to preserve the meat for an extended period of time. We would often keep a large catch of fish, or several game birds or animals for several days in a brine in the refrigerator. We were always mindful to change the solution daily. We always brined chicken, game birds and animals, and fish; we never brined beef or pork, except for the tongues.

Desserts

What would life be without desserts? Mother had a weekly routine she followed all the years she could work. Monday and Tuesday were laundry days. Wednesday was baking day. Thursday or Friday were days to catch up on other chores and grocery day when she and Father would go to Atchison to buy groceries and other goods, go to the bank, pay the telephone and electric bills, etc. Saturday was cleaning day. Sunday was observed as the Lord's Day and a day of rest. It was on Wednesdays when Mother would bake a cake, cookies, pies, crisps—many of the recipes in this section. Father told us kids he did not care what classes we took in high school, but we would all take Home Economics. His reasoning: we all needed to know how to cook, sew on a button, etc. because our old fat wives weren't going to do it for us. Needless to say, he was right. I took on cooking and baking for the family in the early 1980s when Mother was hospitalized for an extended period.

Pistachio Dessert
Preheat oven to 350 degrees. Have ready a greased 9x13x2-inch pan.
Combine in a mixing bowl:
- **1 c flour**
- **2 T sugar**
- **½ butter, softened**
- **¼ c chopped nuts**

Press into prepared pan. Bake 15 minutes or until just beginning to turn golden. Remove from oven. Cool.
Beat in mixing bowl:
- **1 8-oz pkg. creamed cheese, softened**
- **2/3 c powdered sugar**
- **½ of a 9-oz tub frozen whipped topping, thawed**

Spread evenly over crust.
Mix together:
- **2 3-oz boxes instant pistachio pudding**
- **2 ½ c cold milk**
- **½ t almond flavoring**

Spread over cream cheese mixture. Top with rest of whipped topping. Sprinkle with chopped pecans. Chill until serving.

Meringue Shells
These shells make a quick dessert filled with ice cream, pudding or fresh fruit.
Preheat oven to 350 degrees. Have ready a large baking sheet lined with parchment paper.
In large bowl of electric mixer, beat 1 minute:

4 large egg whites

Add:
　¼ t cream of tartar

Beat until soft peaks form. Gradually add:
　1 c sugar

Beat until mixtures resembles marshmallow crème, about 5 minutes.
Beat in:
　2 t cornstarch
　½ t apple cider vinegar
　½ t vanilla
　¼ t ground cardamom

Drop meringue onto prepared sheet in six mounds spaced 3 inches apart. Using back of spoon, make depression in center of each.

Place in oven. Immediately reduce temperature to 250 degrees. Bake until meringues are dry outside, pale straw in color and lift easily from parchment, about 50 minutes. Cool on sheet on rack.

Pudding

Mother often made chocolate, vanilla and butterscotch puddings. Hers was a simple cornstarch pudding recipe. I've tweaked it a bit to make it a master recipe and provide several variations. Serve simply with a bit of Whipped Cream. I also prefer to make this with 6 egg yolks rather than 2 whole eggs. It is, by volume, the same, but the all-yolk version produces a richer pudding.

Have ready heated to boiling:
　2 c whole milk, half-and-half, or 1 c milk and 1 c heavy cream

Beat well in a medium, heavy-bottomed saucepan:
　2 eggs (see headnote)

Beat in:
　2 T cornstarch
　½ c sugar
　¼ t salt

Slowly mix in hot milk. Cook, stirring constantly, over medium heat to boiling. Cook 2-3 minutes until thick, stirring constantly. Note: if using all yolks, I prefer to pass the cooked pudding through a sieve into a bowl. Discard any solids left behind.

Remove from heat and stir in:
　1 t vanilla
　2 T butter

Pour into a serving bowl or individual molds. Press plastic wrap directly onto top surface. Cool and then refrigerate several hours or until chilled and set.

Variations on a Theme:

Chocolate – reduce cornstarch to 1 ½ T; stir in 1 ½ - 4 oz bittersweet chocolate, chopped, when adding the vanilla and butter. Stir until melted.

Coffee – stir in 4 t instant espresso or coffee powder with the milk.

Peanut Butter – stir in ½ c creamy Peanut Butter with the butter and vanilla.
Butterscotch – replace sugar with brown sugar. Increase butter to 3 T.
Pistachio – Combine milk and 1 c shelled pistachios (rinse well if the nuts are salted) in a medium saucepan. Bring to a boil. Remove from heat and let stand until cooled. Liquefy in a blender container, in batches if needed. Stain through a sieve lined with cheesecloth or a clean white cloth. Add 1 T Pistacha (pistachio liqueur) in place of the vanilla, if desired.

Lemon Pudding and Pie Filling

This is full of pure lemon flavor and is firm enough to use in Lemon Meringue Pie. You can make this with three whole eggs, if desired, but the consistency and taste will not be as firm or rich as if made with all egg yolks—and you'll need extra eggs to make the meringue!
Whisk together in a heavy-bottomed saucepan:
   1 c sugar
   ¼ c cornstarch
   ¼ t salt
Whisk in:
   6 large egg yolks
Continue whisking until mixture is thick and lemon colored, and the mixture forms a slowly dissolving ribbon when the whisk is raised above the mixture.
Stir in:
   1 ½ c water
   1 T grated lemon zest from 1 lemon
   ½ c lemon juice from 2-3 lemons
Heat mixture, stirring constantly, over medium-high heat until boiling. Continue to cook and stir for 2 minutes until mixture is clear and thick.
Remove from heat.
Stir in until melted:
   2 T butter

To use as a pie filling: do not cool. Pour hot filling immediately into prepared crust. Cover immediately by pressing plastic wrap directly onto top surface to retain heat while making Successful Meringue. Spread meringue over hot filling, reaching to the edge of the crust. Bake at 375 degrees, watching carefully, until meringue browns, about 8 minutes.

To use as a pudding or other filling: Cover immediately by pressing plastic wrap directly onto top surface. Cool to room temperature before refrigerating.

Cakes, Cupcakes, Coffee Cakes

This collection of cakes, cupcakes, coffee cakes and frostings are easy to mix, bake and assemble. You'll get the best results by using quality ingredients, careful measuring and the correct oven temperature. Experiment with various fillings and accompaniments to make your own signature dessert.

Note the recipes in this section are a combination of two different mixing methods: 1) the traditional creaming method, in which fat and sugar are beaten until light and fluffy, then eggs and/or other liquids are added sometimes alternately with dry ingredients; and 2) an easier method, in which the dry ingredients are combined in the mixing bowl, the softened fat and about one-quarter of the liquid is beaten into the dry ingredients for 1 ½ - 2 minutes, and then the eggs combined with the remaining liquid ingredients are beaten into the flour mixture in three additions, beating for 20 seconds after each addition. I prefer the second method because it is easier, quicker and produces consistently superior results. I use it for all cakes, coffee cakes and cupcakes except for Angel Food and Everyday Chocolate cakes, and Jelly Rolls.

Cream Cheese Pound Cake

This is the most delicious pound cake. Ever. Darlene, who worked for me at Fort Leavenworth, gave the recipe to me. She served hers with Butter Pecan Ice Cream. The first time I made it with our eggs was disastrous. I used large to extra-large eggs. The texture was not the meltingly smooth, fine-grained, velvety texture it should have been. Preheat oven to 300 degrees. Have ready a greased and floured 10-inch tube pan.
Cream until smooth, light and fluffy:
>   ½ c butter, softened
>   1 c margarine, softened

Add:
>   3 c sugar

Cream until light, fluffy and sugar has dissolved.
Add:
>   8 oz cream cheese, softened
>   2 t vanilla
>   2 t fresh lemon juice

Cream well.
Add alternately until thoroughly mixed:
>   6 eggs, slightly beaten
>   3 c cake flour

Turn into prepared pan. Bake 1 ½ hours or until knife inserted between side and tube comes out clean. Let cool in pan 10 minutes before turning out onto wire rack to cool. Sift powdered sugar over before serving.

Coconut Cream Ice Cream Cake

We reaped the majority of our food from the farm, and took advantage of emerging "convenience" foods, such as instant pudding mixes, frozen dairy toppings, etc. as they became available at the grocer and to add variety to our diets and menus. However, we most often relied on the home grown, homemade versions because we had the bounty of fresh fruits, vegetables, meats, milk, cream and eggs. Early in my career, I worked with a lady named Ava who also happened to be a fantastic cook and food enthusiast. She often made this for the potluck luncheons our office would have—suitably named "Food Day!" The ingredients list is a bit misleading considering it seems a jumble of oddments for one dish. However, make it once and you'll return to it again and again. This easy dessert is particularly good in Summer when something cool and light is in order.

Crush into fine crumbs:
>**2 tubes butter crackers**

Mix in until well combined:
>**½ c butter, melted**

Press into bottom of 9x13x2-inch pan.
Refrigerate 20 minutes to set.
Combine in a large mixing bowl until well combined:
>**½ ga. vanilla ice cream, softened**
>**2 small boxes instant coconut cream pudding**
>**1 ½ c cold milk**

Pour over prepared crust.
Refrigerate 1 hour to set.
Spread over the top:
>**1 9-oz container frozen whipped topping, thawed**

Sprinkle over the top:
>**Toasted coconut**

Refrigerate overnight. Do not freeze.

Chocolate Roll

Some recipes for this cake call for peppermint extract—up to one teaspoon! Aunt Mill once remarked it's "Enough to knock you off the Christmas Tree." She taught me how to make a wonderfully peppermint-flavored filling that is not overwhelming and perfectly complements the chocolate cake. Her secret: she folded chopped butter mints into Whipped Cream. If you cannot find the traditional butter mints (small, square, pastel-colored soft candies), you can use soft peppermint candies (white with red stripes and shaped like a small barrel) and often sold in large tubs during the Christmas season. Freeze any extras in freezer bags.

Preheat oven to 375 degrees.
Line a lightly greased 10x15x1-inch jelly roll pan with waxed or parchment paper (allow 2 inches to overhang each short end), and grease and flour the waxed paper. Lay out a clean kitchen towel and sift an even layer of powdered sugar over entire

surface.
Sift together in a small bowl:
- **1/3 c flour**
- **1/3 c cocoa**
- **1 t baking powder**
- **½ t salt**

In a separate large bowl, beat until stiff peaks form:
- **4 egg whites**
- **½ c sugar**

In another separate bowl, beat until light in color and mixture forms a slowly dissolving ribbon when beaters are lifted:
- **4 egg yolks**
- **2 T warm water**
- **1 t vanilla**

Fold yolks into whites. Fold in dry ingredients.
Spread batter in prepared pan. Bake for 15-20 minutes or until cake tests done. Immediately turn cake out onto prepared towel. Roll cake and towel together starting at one short end. Place on wire rack to cool.
Unroll cake. Spread with filling to within 1 inch of edges. Roll cake. Frost if desired. Chill until serving.

Variations on a Theme:

Chocolate Peppermint Roll (Yule Log): Combine one 8 – 9-oz container frozen whipped topping, thawed, with ½ c finely chopped butter mints. Fill cake and reroll. Frost with Chocolate Ganache.

Chocolate Lemon Roll: Unusual, but delicious. Fill cake with 1 can lemon pie filling, 1 recipe Lemon Curd, or 1 recipe Lemon Pudding/Pie Filling. Roll and dust with additional powdered sugar.

Chocolate Peanut Butter Roll: Combine until well mixed, light and fluffy 8 oz cream cheese softened, ½ c smooth Peanut Butter, ½ c powdered sugar, 1 t vanilla. Fill and roll cake. Dust with additional powdered sugar, or frost with Chocolate Ganache.

Chocolate Cream Cake

An old-fashioned, simple cake which used to be made with surplus cream. It has a delicate chocolate flavor and should be served simply with a sprinkling of powdered sugar or softly Whipped Cream.
Preheat oven to 350 degrees. Have ready a greased and floured 8-inch cake pan (square or round).
Sift together:
- **1 c + 2 T flour**
- **5 t cocoa**
- **1 t soda**

Beat together:

    2 eggs
    1 c sugar
    1 t vanilla
Slowly add:
    1 c cream
Quickly, lightly and thoroughly mix in dry ingredients.
Bake 20 minutes or until done when a toothpick inserted in center comes out clean. Cool in pan 5 minutes. Remove to a wire rack to cool completely.

White Cake

There are as many variations of white cakes as there are variations of finished cakes which feature white cake layers. A simple meringue is employed in this recipe to give the cake added lightness and a delicate crumb. This cake always served as the base for a refreshingly tart lemon cake, or a sweet and crunchy coconut cake. Both are regal enough for major celebrations and hold up well for buffets, bazaars, cake walks and the like.

Preheat oven to 375 degrees. Grease and flour two 9-inch cake pans.
Sift together:
    2 c sifted cake flour
    2 ½ t baking powder
    ¼ t salt
In medium mixing bowl, beat on high speed until foamy:
    3 egg whites
Add:
    ¼ c sugar
Beat until meringue holds soft peaks.
In large mixing bowl, beat until light and fluffy:
    ½ c shortening
    ¾ c sugar
Sift in dry ingredients alternately with:
    ¾ c milk
    1 t vanilla
Mix gently until well combined. Fold in meringue.
Turn batter into prepared pans and bake 20-25 minutes, or until a tester inserted in center and edge comes out clean. Cool in pan 5 minutes before turning out of pans onto a wire rack to cool.

Variations on a Theme:
Lemon Cake – Fill cake with half a recipe of Lemon Curd. Frost top and sides with Lemon Buttercream.
Coconut Cake – Fill and frost cake top and sides with Seven Minute Frosting or Buttercream. Sprinkle top and sides to thickly cover with Toasted Coconut.

Yellow Cake

The trio of chocolate, white and yellow cakes will give you an endless portfolio of cakes for any occasion by using various fillings and frostings. While you can make a yellow cake with whole eggs, I prefer to use all yolks.

Preheat oven to 350 degrees. Have ready two 9x2-inch round cake pans, greased and floured.

Sift together in a bowl:
- **3 c sifted cake flour**
- **1 T + 1 t baking powder**
- **¼ t salt**

Set aside.

In large bowl of an electric mixer, cream:
- **12 T butter, softened**

Add:
- **1 ½ c sugar**

Beat in:
- **6 egg yolks**

Beat until light, fluffy and sugar has dissolved.

Add flour mixture to creamed mixture alternately with:
- **1 c milk**
- **2 ¼ t vanilla**

Begin and end with flour mixture.
Divide batter evenly among pans, spreading evenly.
Bake 25-35 minutes or until tester inserted near center comes out clean.
Let cakes cool on rack in pans 10 minutes.
Remove cakes from pan to rack to cool completely.

Variation on a Theme: use 4 ½ egg whites in place of the egg yolks to make a white cake. One large egg white should measure 2 T, so use 1 T egg white for the ½ egg white.

Angel Food Cake

Angel Food Cake has always been my favorite. Aunt Mill would sometimes surprise me with one when I was home on holiday from university, or just whenever I visited. She always had one in the freezer and would present it on a vintage melamine plate that had a brown bull's-eye decoration. I have that plate now, and it is one of my most prized possessions. Use the egg yolks to make Noodles. Note: the original recipe instructed to mix in the flour using the mixer on "low or folding speed." I use a large spatula to fold together the batter.

Preheat oven to 375 degrees. Have ready a 10-inch tube pan.

Sift together five times:
- **1 cup plus 2 T sifted cake flour**
- **¾ c sugar**

Measure into large mixing bowl:
- **1 2/3 c egg whites**

>   ½ t salt

Beat on high speed until foamy.
Add:
>   **1 ½ t cream of tartar**

Continue beating until egg whites form stiff, but not dry peaks.
Sprinkle in, beating about 1 minute total:
>   **1 c sugar**

Add:
>   **1 t vanilla**

Mix in flour mixture at low or folding speed.
Pour into prepared pan. Bake for about 35 minutes or until no imprints remain when finger lightly touches top of cake. Cover with foil if browning too quickly.
Invert pan and let cake hang until cold. Remove from pan to a serving plate.
Variation on a Theme : to make Chocolate Angel Food Cake, combine ¼ c plus 1 T cocoa with ¼ c boiling water and the 2 t vanilla until smooth. Remove 1 heating cup of beaten egg whites and fold into the cocoa mixture. Fold this into the batter after adding the flour mixture.

Cake (Chocolate Sheet Cake)

Speaking of variation on a theme: I've seen several of this recipe—a delicious chocolate concoction that is not for the calorie conscious. Despite the high amount of fat in the cake and frosting, it is surprisingly light. It's very easy to overindulge if one is not careful. I've had the best results using butter in this recipe. Some recipes call for margarine and some for shortening—both give unsatisfactory results. I received this recipe, simply titled "Cake," from Bev, a delightful co-worker (she was a dynamo!) at Fort Leavenworth. Powdered buttermilk works very well in this recipe. Use the recommended amount of buttermilk powder per package instructions, mix it with the other dry ingredients, and substitute an equal amount of water or regular milk for the amount of liquid buttermilk called for.
Preheat oven to 350 degrees. Grease and flour a 10x15x1" sheet pan.
Combine in a large bowl:
>   **2 c flour**
>   **2 c sugar**
>   **¼ c cocoa**
>   **1 t baking soda**

Bring to a boil:
>   **1 c unsalted butter, sliced**
>   **1 c water**

Add butter/water mixture to dry ingredients. Mix quickly and then blend in:
>   **½ c Buttermilk**
>   **2 eggs, room temperature**

Bake 25 minutes or until center of cake springs back. Remove from oven and frost while hot with the following frosting:

Melt in medium saucepan:
- **1 stick butter**

Add:
- **¼ c cocoa**
- **1 lb powdered sugar, sifted**
- **1 t vanilla**
- **¼ c Buttermilk**

Mix well and spread over hot cake. Top with:
- **1 c chopped pecans or English walnuts, optional**

Rocky Mountain Slide

I vaguely remember the first time Aunt Mill served this cake at a Sunday supper. Everyone was delighted. It is easy to prepare and can be made with all convenience foods (cake mix, canned pie filling, frozen whipped topping, packaged nuts). However, I prefer to use the Everyday Chocolate Cake recipe, baking it in a 9-inch springform pan. You can use a double recipe and bake in a 9x13x2-inch pan—which is how Aunt Mill made hers. Why the name Rocky Mountain Slide? I have no idea; however, the topping does tend to slide about when cut and served. An unusual, but delicious alternative is to use lemon pie filling and black walnuts. It reminds me of a box of chocolates with crème centers Aunts Marcelline and Geraldine would sometimes give as Christmas gifts to the aunts, uncles and cousins.

- **1 recipe Everyday Chocolate Cake**
- **1 20-oz can cherry pie filling**
- **1 8-oz container frozen whipped topping, thawed**
- **½ to 1 c chopped nuts (pecans, walnuts or almonds), optional**

Prepare cake. Let cool in pan. Spread whipped topping evenly over cake. Spoon pie filling evenly over whipped topping. Sprinkle nuts over all. Refrigerate several hours or overnight. Cut and serve.

Hot Fudge Cake

This is another recipe that has many variations. This one has been in my files for many, many years. I make this in Winter to enjoy warm with Ice Cream and in Summer to enjoy in its cooled state (with Ice Cream, of course—Peanut Butter Ice Cream is superb). Don't forget the Whipped Cream!

Preheat oven to 350 degrees. Have ready an 8x8x2-inch baking pan.

Whisk together in mixing bowl:
- **1 c flour**
- **¾ c sugar**
- **2 T cocoa**
- **2 t baking powder**
- **¼ t salt**

Combine in a glass measuring cup:
- **½ cup milk**

2 T oil

Add to dry ingredients mixing only until moistened. Pour into baking pan.
Combine and sprinkle evenly over top of batter:
　　1 c chopped nuts, toasted, optional
　　1 c brown sugar
　　¼ c cocoa
Pour slowly over all:
　　1 ¾ c hot water
Bake 45 minutes. Cake will form on top with hot fudge below. Cut into squares and invert onto serving plates.

Cranberry Coffee Cake

You can use canned cranberry sauce for this coffee cake, but I prefer to make my own.
Preheat oven to 350 degrees.
Grease a 9-inch springform pan. Sprinkle evenly over the bottom:
　　¼ c chopped almonds
In a medium bowl, stir together until evenly mixed:
　　½ c flour
　　1/3 c sugar
　　¼ c chopped almonds
　　¼ c butter, melted
　　¼ t vanilla
In a large mixer bowl, beat until well mixed and lightly and fluffy:
　　1 c sugar
　　½ c butter, softened
　　1 t vanilla
Add, and mix well:
　　2 eggs
Sift together:
　　2 c flour
　　1 ¼ t baking powder
　　½ t soda
　　¼ t salt
Add dry ingredients to butter mixture alternately with:
　　1 c Sour Cream
Fold together only until evenly blended.
Spoon half of batter into prepared pan. Spoon evenly over batter in pan:
　　1 c whole cranberry sauce
Spoon remaining batter over sauce, spread to cover to edges.
Sprinkle with topping.
Bake 60 - 75 minutes or until wooden pick inserted in center comes out clean. Begin checking for doneness when you can smell the cake.
Cool 10 minutes on wire rack; remove sides of pan. Serve warm or cooled.

Prune Coffee Cake
Don't turn away from this coffee cake because it contains prunes. It is meltingly tender and delicious. If the prunes are not soft, cover with boiling water and let sit until plumped and softened. Drain well before proceeding with the recipe. Be sure to let the cake cool in the pan as directed—the cake is fragile.
Preheat oven to 350 degrees. Grease and flour a 10-inch tube pan.
Combine in a small bowl and set aside for the topping:
   ½ c brown sugar
   1 T cinnamon
   ½ walnuts, chopped, optional
Dice:
   1 ½ c prunes
Combine in a bowl with:
   1 t grated lemon rind
   ¼ c flour
In bowl of electric mixer, combine:
   1 ¾ c flour
   1 t baking powder
   1 t baking soda
   ½ t salt
   1 c sugar
Mix on low speed until blended.
Cut into 16 pieces and add to dry ingredients:
   1 c butter, softened
Combine in a small bowl:
   2 eggs
   1 c Sour Cream
   1 t vanilla
Add half egg mixture to butter and dry ingredients. Beat on low speed to combine and then on medium speed for 2 minutes. Scrape down sides of bowl. Beat in remaining egg mixture in three additions, mixing for 20 seconds after each addition. Fold in prunes. Turn batter into prepared pan. Sprinkle topping evenly over top. Bake 55 minutes or until tester inserted half-way between sides and tube comes out clean.
Let cool in pan 10 minutes. Remove from pan, invert so sugar/cinnamon is on top and cool completely on wire rack or serving plate.

Upside-Down Cake
Most often associated with pineapple, an upside down cake works well with various fruits. See the *Variations on a Theme* for some suggestions. You can bake this cake in a regular cake pan, a cast-iron skillet or, my preference, a springform pan. I developed this recipe for a 10-inch springform pan. You can use the same-sized regular cake pan

or cast-iron skillet. You can use regular corn syrup (the traditional ingredient), but I prefer to use cane syrup.

Preheat oven to 350 degrees. Have ready a 10-inch springform pan. Lightly grease the bottom, but do not grease the sides.

In a small saucepan, combine:
- 1 T water
- 1 T cane syrup
- 1/3 c butter
- 2/3 c brown sugar

Bring to a boil, stirring constantly. Boil 1 minute, or until sugar is completely dissolved.

Pour into prepared pan. Arrange toppings over syrup. Set aside.

Measure:
- ¾ c + 2 T milk, room temperature

Combine in the bowl of an electric mixer:
- 2 ½ c sifted cake flour
- 1 ¼ c sugar
- 3 ¼ t baking powder
- ¾ t salt

Mix on low speed 30 seconds to blend.

Combine in a small bowl:
- 5 egg yolks
- ¼ c of the measured milk
- 2 t vanilla

Add to flour mixture:
- 10 T butter, softened
- The remaining measured milk

Beat on low speed to combine. Then beat on medium speed 1 ½ minutes.

Add, in three additions:
- The egg yolk mixture

Beat 20 seconds after each addition and stop mixer to scrape sides and bottom of bowl.

Pour batter into pan, spreading evenly.

Bake about 1 hour and 15 minutes or until a toothpick or thin knife inserted in the center comes out clean.

Remove from oven. Run a knife around the top edge of the cake to loosen it from the pan. Let cool 10 minutes in pan before removing to a serving plate to cool.

Variations on a Theme: Pineapple rings with a maraschino cherry in the middle is the American classic version of this cake. However, apple, pear, peach, plum, apricot, rhubarb, and banana variations are equally delicious.

Apple or Pear - peel and thinly slice apples or pears. Good combined with cranberries. Arrange apple or pear slices around edge of pan; fill center with fresh cranberries, if desired.

Peach - peel and slice about ½-inch thick. Good combined with blueberries. Arrange peach slices around edge of pan; fill center with fresh blueberries, if desired.

Plum or Apricot - do not need to be peeled; can be sliced about ½-inch thick or place halves cut-side down in the pan.

Rhubarb - should be finely diced; you will need about 2 c.

Banana - should be sliced crosswise about ½-inch thick.

Coconut-Pecan – use this in place of the butter-sugar mixture in the base recipe. In small saucepan melt ¼ c butter. Add ½ c brown sugar. Cook until sugar is dissolved. Spread in pan. Sprinkle with 2/3 c each chopped pecans and shredded coconut. Drizzle over the top ¼ c evaporated milk.

Cherry-Vanilla Cupcakes

These have been a perennial favorite for years and were popular when I had my Service Accommodation business—MillRose—in the early 1990s. A variation, reminiscent of cherry mash candies, is to frost with Chocolate Ganache, using milk chocolate—a darker chocolate overpowers the cherry flavor.

Preheat oven to 350 degrees. Have ready 24 muffin cups lined with cupcake papers.

Drain, reserving juice, and place on a paper-towel-lined plate:
>   **2 jars maraschino cherries with stems**

Sift together in electric mixer bowl:
>   **2 c flour**
>   **1 ½ c sugar**
>   **1 t baking powder**
>   **½ t salt**
>   **¼ t baking soda**

Add:
>   **½ c butter, softened and cut into eight pieces**

Whisk together in a small bowl:
>   **¾ c Buttermilk**
>   **1/3 c maraschino cherry juice**
>   **1 t vanilla**
>   **½ t almond extract**
>   **4 egg whites, room temperature**

Add half of liquid mixture to dry ingredients. Beat on low speed to combine and then on medium speed for 1 ½ minutes.

Scrape sides and bottom of bowl. Beat in remaining liquid ingredients in three additions, beating 20 seconds after each addition.

Spoon batter evenly into cups, filling each about two-thirds full. Bake 15-18 minutes or until tops spring back when lightly touched. Remove from pan and cool in baking cups on wire racks until completely cool.

Make the frosting by beating together in electric mixer bowl:
>   **1 c butter, softened**
>   **2 c powdered sugar**

    3 T maraschino cherry juice
    ½ t almond extract

Beat until well combined.
Beat in until light and fluffy:
    2 c powdered sugar

If necessary, beat in additional juice or milk, one teaspoon at a time, until frosting reaches a spreading consistency.
Frost cupcakes and top with a maraschino cherry with stem.

Variations on a Theme:
Key Lime Cupcakes – for the batter: replace maraschino juice with an equal amount of Buttermilk; omit almond extract; add 2 T grated lime zest. For the frosting: replace maraschino cherry juice with lime juice (preferably Key Lime juice); omit almond extract.

Cheesecake

This is a master recipe with 19 variations, including two savory variations to serve as appetizers, developed through years of baking.
The three secrets to making a terrific cheesecake are:
1. Have all ingredients at room temperature before beginning.
2. Beat at slowest speed possible.
3. Bake in a water bath.

I like to bring cheesecake to room temperature several hours before serving.
Heat oven to 350 degrees. Wrap bottom and sides of 9-inch spring form pan with two layers of aluminum foil. Lightly grease pan. Heat 2 qts. water to boiling.
Combine in a medium bowl:
    7 T unsalted butter, melted
    1 ½ c graham cracker crumbs
    ¼ c sugar

Stir until evenly moistened. Pour into pan, press firmly, forming a ½" crust up the sides of the pan. Bake until set, 12-15 minutes. Transfer to wire rack.
In bowl of electric mixer, beat on lowest possible speed until smooth:
    1 lb cream cheese, room temperature

Slowly add:
    1 c sugar

Drizzle in, stopping occasionally to scrape down sides of bowl and bottom:
    4 large eggs, room temperature and lightly beaten

Beat in:
    1 c Sour Cream, room temperature
    1 t vanilla
    ½ t salt

Pour batter into crust, spreading evenly.
Set cheesecake in a larger pan and set both on oven rack.
Add to the boiling water:

1 t cream of tartar

Pour boiling water into larger pan until it comes half-way up sides of spring form pan. Bake until sides have set, but center appears soft, about 35 minutes, then turn off oven but leave cheesecake in the oven with the door shut for 30 minutes. Do not worry if it looks underdone, it will firm on cooling. Transfer to wire rack to cool. Run a thin-bladed knife or spatula around outside of crust, loosening it from the pan. When cool, cover and refrigerate overnight.

Variations on a Theme:
Chocolate Cheesecake I – melt 4-8 oz semi-sweet chocolate (depending on how intensely flavored you want); let sit until cool but still melted; mix into cream cheese.
Chocolate Cheesecake II – top cooled cheesecake with half recipe of Ganache.
Chocolate Chip Cheesecake – add 1 c mini chocolate chips to the batter after mixing.
Lemon Cheesecake – add 1 T grated lemon peel. Top cooled cheesecake with Lemon Curd. Bake at 300 degrees about 8 minutes or until curd is set.
Lime Cheesecake – add 1 T grated lime peel. Top cooled cheesecake with Lime Curd. Bake at 300 degrees about 8 minutes or until curd is set.
Orange Cheesecake – add 1 T grated orange peel. Top cooled cheesecake with Orange Curd. Bake at 300 degrees about 8 minutes or until curd is set.
Raspberry or Strawberry Cheesecake – top the cooled cheesecake with Raspberry or Strawberry Puree. Garnish with fresh berries, if desired.
Blueberry – top the cooled cheesecake with Blueberry Filling, Topping or Compote.
Cherry Cheesecake – thaw one 12-ounce package tart cherries, reserving juice. Measure juice (you should have 1 cup; add water to make 1 cup if you do not have enough). Combine in small bowl ½ c sugar and 2 ½ T cornstarch. Whisk into juice in a medium saucepan. Bring to a boil and cook, stirring constantly for 2 minutes. Add cherries and stir to combine. Cool. Spread on cooled cheesecake. Refrigerate until set.
Cranberry Cheesecake – follow recipe for Cranberry Dessert Quiche to make topping, omitting apples, if desired. Cool then spread on cooled cheesecake. Refrigerate until set.
Walnut-Caramel Cheesecake – combine one jar caramel ice cream topping and 1 c chopped English walnuts, toasted. Spread over cooled cheesecake.
Peanut Butter Cheesecake – replace sugar with 1 c packed light brown sugar and mix ¾ c creamy Peanut Butter into cream cheese. Top with chopped Peanut Butter cups or toffee candy bars before serving.
Cookies and Cream Cheesecake – make crust with chocolate wafer crumbs (preferably Nabisco Famous Amos brand). Pour half of batter into pan. Top with 15 coarsely chopped crème-filled chocolate sandwich cookies. Top with remaining batter. Sprinkle top of baked and cooled cheesecake with additional chocolate wafer crumbs or sandwich cookies cut in half on top of each slice.
Apricot Swirl Cheesecake – use 1 c. Apricot Filling. Pour half of batter into pan. Drop spoonfuls of half of filling over batter. Swirl with a knife. Top with remaining batter and then filling. Swirl.

Sour Cream Topped Cheesecake – combine 1 c Sour Cream, ¼ c sugar, ½ t vanilla. Preheat oven to 450 degrees. After cheesecake has cooled 30-45 minutes, pour topping over cheesecake. Bake 5 minutes. Cool until it reaches room temperature, then refrigerate.

Pumpkin Cheesecake - add one 1-lb can unsweetened, unseasoned pumpkin puree and 2 T bourbon.

Fiesta Cheesecake - this Mexican-inspired cheesecake makes a surprising appetizer served with corn chips. Make a crust with 1 c ground tortilla chips (grind or crush with rolling pin to the consistency of coarse cornmeal), 2 T melted butter and ¼ c flour. Bake 10 minutes. Omit the sugar and season the batter with: 1 t dried oregano; 1 ½ t cumin powder; ½ t garlic powder; 1 t chili powder; ½ t pepper; ¼ t chipotle chili powder. Mix and bake as for Master Recipe. Serve at room temperature with tortilla chips and your favorite salsa.

Blue Cheesecake – serve this cheesecake as an appetizer with crackers or for dessert with fresh pears. Replace ½ c graham cracker crumbs with an equal amount of ground walnuts for the crust. Reduce sugar to ¼ c. Replace 4 oz of cream cheese with 4 oz of a strong-flavored blue cheese (e.g., Roquefort or Maytag)..

Cream Cheese Frosting

Just four simple ingredients make the most splendid frosting to use on cakes, cupcakes, cookies and even cheesecake.
Melt:
> **8 oz white chocolate**

Let sit until cool but still liquid.
Beat in the bowl of an electric mixer until smooth and creamy:
> **12 oz cream cheese, room temperature**

Beat in the cooled white chocolate until incorporated.
Beat in:
> **1 c butter, softened**
> **1 T lemon juice**

Use immediately, or cover and refrigerate. Bring to room temperature before re-beating, or it may curdle.

Cocoanut Carrot Cake

This is a wonderful recipe. Reprinted here just as I received it from Aunt Mill. Notice the spelling of "cocoanut."

Preheat oven to 350 degrees. Have ready two greased and floured 9-inch round cake pans.
Combine in mixing bowl:
> **2 c flour**
> **2 t soda, sieved**
> **2 t cinnamon**

Mix well in a large mixing bowl:

  2 c sugar
  1 ½ c oil
  4 large eggs
  1 t salt
Add:
  2 c shredded carrots
  1 8-oz can crushed pineapple, well drained
  1 c finely chopped walnuts
  1 c flaked cocoanut
Stir in flour mixture until just combined.
Pour batter evenly into prepared pans. Bake 35-45 minutes or until cake layers test done. Remove to wire rack. Cool layers in pans for 5 minutes. Remove layers from pans to wire rack to cool completely.
Fill with pineapple or apricot preserves and frost with Cream Cheese Frosting, or the following, if desired.
Beat together until light and fluffy:
  12 oz cream cheese, softened
  1/3 c butter, softened
  ½ t vanilla
  2 c powdered sugar
  2 T milk
Stir in:
  ½ c flaked cocoanut
  ½ c chopped raisins
Fill and frost top of cake.

Gingerbread I

This is comfort food at its best. Father remarked several times that Aunt Mill made a wonderful gingerbread using bacon drippings. A bit skeptical at first, I eventually made a gingerbread using bacon drippings. He was right! It offers an incomparable flavor to the bread. I have used both cured bacon drippings and green (uncured) bacon drippings with equally good results. However, I favor the subtlety of the cured bacon drippings. If you want to ease into this recipe, begin by using butter instead of bacon drippings. This bread freezes very well, so you can make ahead and have ready at a moment's notice.
Preheat oven to 350 degrees. Have ready a greased 9x9x2-inch pan.
Melt:
  ½ c bacon drippings
Transfer to a large mixing bowl then add and mix well:
  ½ c sugar
  1 egg, room temperature
Sift together in a separate bowl:
  2 ½ c sifted flour

    1 ½ t baking soda
    1 t cinnamon
    1 t ground ginger
    ½ t salt
Combine in a large glass measuring cup:
    ½ molasses
    ½ c honey
    1 c hot water
Add the sifted and liquid ingredients alternately to the fat mixture until blended. Turn into prepared pan
Bake about 60 minutes or until toothpick inserted into center comes out clean.
Remove to rack to cool.

Gingerbread II
Preheat oven to 350 degrees. Have ready a greased 9-inch cake pan.
Sift into a large mixing bowl:
    2 ½ c flour
    2 t baking soda, sieved
    2 t ginger
    1 ½ t cinnamon
    ½ t cloves
    ½ t baking powder
Combine in another bowl:
    ¾ c fat, melted
    ¾ c molasses
    ¾ c brown sugar
    2 eggs, well beaten
Mix thoroughly until sugar is dissolved.
Add to the dry ingredients:
    Fat mixture
    1 c boiling water
Mix lightly, but thoroughly.
Turn into prepared pan, spreading evenly.
Bake about 30 minutes or until tester inserted in center comes out clean.
Cool in pan on wire rack.

Cake Icing
I got this recipe in Home Economics class in high school. My class ventured into a project to decorate cakes on special order. I forget why we did that and how we used the funds we raised. My cousin, Darlene, a terrific, talented artist, was the best at decorating the cakes. However, we did not use this recipe to decorate those cakes. This is a light icing best spread on cakes or cupcakes.
Combine in a small saucepan:

    1 c milk
    3 T flour
Cook until thick. Let cool.
In large mixing bowl, cream until light and fluffy:
    1 c butter, softened
    1 c sugar
    2 T shortening
There should not be any graininess from the sugar.
Add:
    The milk mixture
    2 T powdered sugar
    1 t vanilla
Beat until smooth, light and fluffy.

Buttercream

Real, authentic buttercream is not anything like what stores, restaurants and bakeries pass off as buttercream. You're lucky if the buttercream they peddle has butter in it at all. Usually, it is a mess of shortening and powdered sugar and who-knows-what else. Real buttercream has five ingredients: butter, egg yolks, sugar, water and flavoring, which can be as simple as vanilla and as complex as the cook desires. This recipe is my own, but based on the classic technique. I have substituted egg whites for egg yolks—only slightly less fat, but very light, smooth and not overly sweet to let the cake take center stage.
Let come to room temperature:
    2 c butter
It should be softened, but still cool (about 65 degrees).
Cut the butter into 1 T sized pieces and set aside.
Beat in a large bowl of an electric mixer until foamy:
    5 egg whites
Add:
    ¾ t cream of tartar
    ¼ t salt
Beat until soft peaks form when the beater is raised.
Trickle in:
    ¼ c sugar
Beat until stiff peaks form. Set aside.
Have ready a heatproof glass measuring cup near the stove and a glass of ice water.
Combine in a heavy saucepan:
    ¾ c sugar
    ½ c light corn syrup
Heat, stirring constantly, until the sugar dissolves and the syrup comes to a rolling boil. Cook 1-2 minute or until large bubbles cover the surface. The temperature on a candy thermometer should register 138-140 degrees (soft-ball stage).

Immediately transfer the syrup to the glass measuring cup to stop the cooking. Beat the hot syrup into the egg whites by pouring a small amount of syrup over the whites with the mixer off. Immediately beat at high speed for about 5 seconds. Repeat until all syrup is added. Continue beating until completely cool.
Beat in the butter, 1 T at a time.
At first the mixture will seem thin, but will thicken by the time all the butter is added. If it looks curdled when adding the butter, increase the speed and beat until smooth before continuing to add more butter. (Note: if your kitchen is really warm or you are making on a hot day, and the mixture does not seem to smooth out, I have found it helpful to add 1 T ice water and beat at high speed until smooth. This amount of water will not affect the final product.)
Reduce speed to low and add one of the flavorings, if desired.

Variations on a Theme:
Vanilla – beat in 2 t pure vanilla extract.
Chocolate Buttercream – beat in 5 oz melted and cooled chocolate (semi, extra bittersweet, bittersweet or white).
Fruit Buttercream – beat in ¾ c lightly sweetened Raspberry or Strawberry Puree or Lemon, Lime or Orange Curd.
Coffee Buttercream – beat in 2 T instant espresso powder (not instant coffee crystals) dissolved in 1 t boiling water. Add 3 T Kahlua, if desired.
Mocha – beat the coffee mixture into Chocolate Buttercream.
Maple – replace the corn syrup with the same amount of pure maple syrup. Beat in 2 t maple extract into the finished buttercream. Dust the frosted cake with maple sugar for a spectacular cake.
Apricot – beat in ½ c Apricot Filling.

Ginger Lemon Pudding Cake

This recipe is similar to the Hot Fudge Cake. It is a soothing and comforting treat for someone who is ill. I like to omit the spices and substitute white sugar for the brown sugar to make a Spring or Summer dessert.
Preheat oven to 350 degrees. Have ready an 8x8x2-inch cake pan.
Sift into a large mixing bowl:
- **1 1/3 c flour**
- **½ c packed brown sugar**
- **1 T baking powder**
- **1 t cinnamon**
- **½ t salt**
- **½ t ground ginger**

Combine in another bowl:
- **½ c water**
- **¼ c light molasses or cane syrup (preferably Lyle's Golden)**
- **¼ c oil**

Mix liquid ingredients into dry. Combine thoroughly.

Spread evenly in pan.
Sprinkle evenly over batter in pan:
   1/3 c chopped nuts
Bring to a boil:
   1 ½ c water
Stir in:
   ½ of a 6-oz can frozen lemonade concentrate, thawed (6 T)
   ½ c packed brown sugar
Pour carefully over batter. Bake, uncovered, till done, 40-45 minutes.
Serve warm with Ice Cream.

Baked Pumpkin Pudding

Preheat oven to 350 degrees. Have ready a greased and floured 6 ½-cup ring mold.
Cream until light:
   6 T butter
   ¾ c packed brown sugar
   ¼ c sugar
Beat in:
   2 eggs
Sift together:
   1 ½ c flour
   ½ t salt
   ½ t soda
   ½ t cinnamon
   ½ t ground ginger
   ¼ t ground nutmeg
Combine and add alternately with dry ingredients to creamed mixture:
   ¾ c mashed cooked pumpkin or canned pumpkin puree
   ½ c Buttermilk
Mix well after each addition.
Fold in:
   ½ c chopped walnuts
Spoon into prepared pan; cover tightly with foil.
Bake at 350 degrees for 1 hour. Let stand 10 minutes. Unmold. Serve with Whipped Cream.

Carrot Cake

This is a recipe I developed myself after having too many carrot cakes that were greasy and unappetizing. I added toasted English walnuts and golden raisins. I also substituted the vegetable oil called for in most recipes with light olive oil. The olive oil gives this cake a truly special flavor while the Buttermilk and fresh ginger balances the sweetness. This cake is delicious on its own, or split and filled with a good-quality apricot preserves, frosted with the Cream Cheese Frosting, and sprinkled with more chopped, toasted English walnuts.

Preheat oven to 350 degrees. Have ready two greased and floured 9-inch cake pans.

Sift together:
- 3 c flour
- 2 t baking powder
- 1 t soda
- 1 t salt
- 1 t cinnamon

Stir in, coating evenly:
- 1 c English walnuts, chopped and toasted
- 1 c golden raisins
- ¼ c finely minced candied ginger

Combine, mixing well, in a large mixing bowl:
- 1 ½ c light olive oil
- 2 c sugar

Add, one at a time, stirring until evenly smooth and glossy:
- 3 large eggs

Add:
- 1/3 c Buttermilk
- 1 t vanilla
- 1 T grated fresh ginger, optional

Stir in:
- 2 ½ c grated carrots
- Flour mixture

Bake 45-55 minutes or until layers test done.

Let cool in pans 10 minutes before turning out onto rack to cool. Split layers. Fill with good quality apricot jam or preserves. Frost with Cream Cheese Frosting and coat with additional chopped and toasted English walnuts.

Chocolate Shortcake

Preheat oven to 400 degrees. Have ready a large baking sheet lined with parchment paper.

Whisk together in a mixing bowl:
- 2/3 c whipping cream
- ¼ c chocolate syrup
- 1 t vanilla
- ½ t instant espresso powder dissolved in 1 T hot water (optional)

Blend together in a large mixing bowl:
- 1 ½ c flour
- ½ c sugar
- 1/3 c unsweetened cocoa powder
- 1 T baking powder
- ½ t salt

Cut in to form fine crumbs:
>	¼ c butter

Add chocolate mixture. Mix until moist clumps form.
Turn dough out onto work surface. Gather dough into ball. Divide into 6 equal pieces. Using lightly floured hands, form each piece into 2-inch-high, 2-inch-diameter mound. Place on prepared sheet. Brush tops with:
>	2 T melted butter

Then sprinkle each with:
>	1 teaspoon sugar

Bake about 15 minutes or until tester inserted in center comes out with some moist crumbs attached.
Let cool on sheet. To serve, split and top with Whipped Cream and berries.

Devil's Food Cake

This was Mother's favorite cake. It is an old-fashioned cake with a not-too-strong chocolate flavor. Traditionally frosted with Seven Minute Frosting, it is equally delicious with a variety of frostings and fillings.

Preheat oven to 350 degrees. Have ready two greased and floured 9-inch round cake pans.
Sift together into a mixing bowl:
>	2 ¼ c flour
>	½ c unsweetened cocoa powder
>	1 ½ t soda
>	1 t salt

Set aside.
In a separate bowl, with clean beaters, whip to soft peaks:
>	3 egg whites

Gradually add, beating until stiff peaks form:
>	¾ c sugar

In another mixer bowl, cream:
>	½ c shortening

Gradually add:
>	1 c sugar

Beat until light and fluffy.
Add:
>	1 t vanilla

Add, one at a time, beating on medium speed for 1 minute after each:
>	3 egg yolks

Add, alternately with dry ingredients, to sugar mixture, beating on low speed after each addition until just combined:
>	1 1/3 c cold water

Fold meringue into batter; blend well. Pour batter into prepared pans, dividing evenly. Bake in 350 degree oven for 30-35 minutes or until done. Place on wire racks to cool for 10 minutes. Remove from pans. Cool. Frost as desired.

Seven-Minute Frosting
In top of double boiler, combine:
- 1 ½ c sugar
- 1/3 c cold water
- 2 egg whites
- 2 t light corn syrup
- Dash salt

Beat on low speed of electric mixer for 30 seconds to combine.
Place over boiling water (water should not touch bottom of pan). While beating constantly on high speed, cook about 7 minutes or until frosting forms stiff peaks. Remove from heat; add:
- 1 t vanilla

Beat 2-3 minutes longer or till of spreading consistency.
Variations on a Theme:
Seafoam Frosting: Prepare Seven-Minute Frosting as above, except use 1 ½ c packed brown sugar instead of sugar.
Mocha Frosting: Prepare Seven-Minute Frosting as above, except beat in ¼ c unsweetened cocoa powder and 1 t instant espresso coffee just before frosting cake.
Peppermint Stick Frosting: Prepare Seven-Minute Frosting as above, except use ¼ t peppermint extract instead of vanilla. Garnish cake with crushed peppermint candy, if desired.

Jelly Roll
I have always enjoyed various jelly roll cakes. In the early days, these were a go-to dessert because families usually had various jellies and preserves on hand to fill cakes when chocolate, sugar, etc. wasn't as readily available to make other fillings and frostings. Plus, these are so easy to pair with the rest of the meal to complement the main dish and provide endless variety to the menu. A jelly roll mixes, bakes and finishes very quickly.
Preheat oven to 375 degrees. Have ready a lightly greased 15x10x1-inch jelly roll pan (a baking sheet with raised sides). Line with waxed or parchment paper, leaving two inches extend over short ends. Grease and flour paper.
Sift together:
- ½ c flour
- 1 t baking powder
- ¼ t salt

In a small mixer bowl, beat at high speed about 5 minutes or till thick and lemon colored:
- 4 egg yolks
- ½ t vanilla

Gradually add:

>   **1/3 c sugar**

Beat until sugar is dissolved and a slowly dissolving ribbon forms when beaters are raised.
In a separate bowl with clean beaters, beat at medium speed till soft peaks form:
>   **3 egg whites**

Gradually add:
>   **½ c sugar**

Beat till stiff peaks forms.
Fold yolk mixture into whites. Sprinkle flour mixture over; fold in lightly by hand.
Spread batter evenly into pan.
Bake 12-15 minutes or till done.
Have ready a clean kitchen towel sprinkled with sifted powdered sugar.
Immediately loosen edges of cake from pan and turn out onto prepared towel.
Starting at narrow end roll warm cake and towel together. Place on wire rack to cool.
Unroll; spread with:
>   **½ c jelly or jam, any flavor**

To within one inch of edge. Roll up. Transfer to serving platter.
Sprinkle with:
>   **Sifted powdered sugar**

Pumpkin Cake Roll

The walnuts sprinkled on top of the cake before baking combined with the powdered sugar from the towel in which the cake is rolled make any additional garnishes unnecessary in my opinion. This is a delightful cake for serving at a Fall luncheon or with afternoon coffee. Extra delicious filled with Cream Cheese Frosting.
Prepare as for Jelly Roll, above, using the following ingredients:
>   **¾ c flour**
>   **2 t ground cinnamon**
>   **1 t baking powder**
>   **1 t ground ginger**
>   **½ t salt**
>   **½ t ground nutmeg**
>   **3 eggs**
>   **1 c sugar**
>   **2/3 c pumpkin puree**
>   **1 t lemon juice**

After pouring batter into pan, top evenly with:
>   **1 c finely chopped walnuts**

For the filling, cream:
>   **2 3-oz pkgs. cream cheese, softened**
>   **¼ c butter, softened**

Beat in until light and fluffy:
>   **½ t vanilla**

1 c sifted powdered sugar

Coffee Cake
We didn't have coffee cakes all that much growing up. When we did, they were often served as snacks at such gatherings as butchering or house painting, etc. It is easy to make, stores well and makes a great gift.
Preheat oven to 325 degrees. Have ready a greased and floured 9x13x2-inch pan.
Cream until light and fluffy:
- ½ c butter
- 1 c sugar

Beat in:
- 2 eggs

Add:
- 1 t vanilla
- 1 ½ c Sour Cream

Sift together:
- 2 c flour
- 1 t soda
- 1 t baking powder
- ½ t salt

Add to creamed mixture.
Place half of batter in prepared pan.
Top with half of the following, mixed together for form a crumbly mixture:
- 4 T sugar
- 2 T flour
- 1 t cinnamon
- 2 T butter, melted

Turn remaining batter into pan and sprinkle with remaining topping.
Bake about 30 minutes or until tester inserted in center comes out clean.

Pies

Pie is my favorite dessert. I especially like a pie that showcases a single fruit. A great pie begins with a great crust. I like the crust to be tender, crisp and flaky and flavorful enough to eat by itself. A good graham cracker or chocolate cookie crust also makes a delicious base for chiffon or cream (pudding) pies and all the Puddings make delicious pie fillings. Use the graham cracker or chocolate cookie crust recipes in Cheesecake and its variations. Top cream pies with Successful Meringue or freshly Whipped Cream.

Pie Crust

Everyone has a favorite pie or pastry crust. The following is one I developed after learning to make countless variations. It is a superb all-purpose crust that is equally good to hold sweet and savory fillings. I suit the crust to the filling by sometimes adding black pepper for savory or sprinkling the top crust with sugar for sweet. The crust is tender, flaky and crisp all at once. You can replace the shortening with an equal amount of unsalted butter. I make it most often with one-half lard and one-half butter (cut in the butter first). I like the flakiness the lard provides and the flavor the butter provides. If using all butter, you may need to adjust the water because butter contains more moisture than shortening and lard. After making this several times, you will come to understand the dough. This is easily made in the food processor using on/off pulses. Use a fork to toss the flour-fat mixture to make sure the fat is evenly distributed.

Combine in a large bowl:
- 2 ¼ c flour
- 1 t salt
- ¼ t baking powder

Chill until cold.
Using a fork, two knives or a pastry blender, cut in:
- ½ c chilled lard, butter or shortening

Until the mixture resembles coarse cornmeal.
Cut in another **½ c chilled lard, butter or shortening** until the largest pieces are about the size of small peas.
Sprinkle over dough **1 T cider vinegar** and then about **5 T ice water**. Toss gently after each addition. Test by pressing together a small bit of dough. The dough should form a solid mass. Turn out onto a large sheet of plastic wrap. Using the wrap, gently knead the dough into a solid mass. Divide into two portions—one slightly larger than the other if making a two-crust pie. The larger piece will become the bottom crust. Chill several hours or overnight to allow the dough to rest.
Let sit at room temperature about 5-10 minutes before rolling. I find rolling between two sheets of lightly floured plastic wrap is the easiest way to handle the dough.

Alternately, roll out on a lightly floured cloth or board. Roll dough to about 1/8" thickness before placing into pan(s).

For a pre-baked crust (baked blind): Roll dough and fit into pan. Crimp edge as desired and chill, loosely covered with plastic wrap for 1 hour. Preheat oven to 375 degrees. Line dough with aluminum foil large enough to completely cover edges. Fill pan with dried beans, pie weights or copper pennies. Bake 20 minutes if you are going to fill and continue baking. Remove from oven. Gently pour weights into another container, carefully remove foil. Immediately patch any cracks or holes, by pressing dough to join. (Note: it is best to then brush the hot crust with one lightly beaten egg white at this point which will ensure the crust stays crisp when filled and baked.)

For a fully baked crust: After 20 minutes, remove foil and weights, as previously described, and continue baking at 350 degrees until crust is thoroughly cooked and light golden brown.

Pecan Pie

A perfect Pecan Pie was one of my earliest culinary quests. The back-of-the-bottle recipe is too cloyingly sweet, and others had cardboard crusts and a medicinal taste to them. I ended up creating my own recipe, which is actually a tart so that the ratio of nuts is high compared to the filling. This makes for a not-too-sweet treat. I prefer to use cane syrup, but you can use an equal amount of corn syrup.

Preheat oven to 350 degrees. Have ready:
>**1 9 ½ x 1-inch pie crust, prebaked**

Toast, until just fragrant, 10-12 minutes, on a baking sheet:
>**1 ½ c coarsely chopped pecans**

Pour into pre-baked tart crust, distributing evenly.
Reduce oven temperature to 325 degrees.
Combine in a heavy-bottomed saucepan:
>**¾ c cane syrup (preferably (Lyle's Golden)**
>**½ c light brown sugar, packed**
>**Pinch salt**
>**4 egg yolks**
>**4 T butter, heated until just melted**

Cook over low heat until sugar has dissolved and mixture is warm.
Pour through a fine strainer into a small mixing bowl.
Stir in:
>**1 t vanilla**

Pour over nuts in crust.
Bake about 30 minutes or until knife inserted half-way between center and edge comes out clean. Cool on rack before serving.

Fritters

Fritters are a vintage dessert made with a batter similar to funnel cakes, but encasing fruit, vegetables, meat or blossoms. The batter profits from resting for at least 2 hours, covered and refrigerated, after mixing. This is the Master Recipe for fruit fritters. See the *Variations on a Theme* for making different fritters.

Beat together in a bowl large enough to dip the items to be frittered:
- **2 egg yolks**
- **2/3 c milk**
- **1 T butter, melted**

Sift before measuring:
- **1 c flour**

Resift with:
- **¼ t salt**
- **1 T sugar**

Combine liquid and dry ingredients. Let rest at least 2 and up to 12 hours. Then beat the mixture well until smooth.

Heat to 375 degrees in a large kettle, Dutch oven or electric fryer:
- **3 inches oil**

Dip prepared fruit into batter. Fry in hot oil, turning to cook and brown evenly. Drain on paper toweling. Keep warm in a 200-degree oven until all are fried. Dust with powdered sugar before serving.

Variations on a Theme:

Fruit Fritters - make sure fruit is ripe, but not mushy. Slice about ½-inch thick. Small berries may be left whole. Increase sugar to 2 T, if desired. Dust fruit slices with powdered sugar before dipping in the fritter batter.

Vegetable Fritters – use firm vegetables and cut into slices, strips or cubes. Omit sugar and add ¼ t pepper.

Meat Fritters – use very thin slices of meat or fish cut into strips. Omit the sugar and add ¼ t pepper. You may replace the milk with an equal amount of flat beer.

Blossom Fritters – use unsprayed elderberry, lilac or unopened squash, pumpkin, or daylily blooms. Pick with the dew on them (i.e., early morning) and dry well. Add 1 or 2 T additional sugar. Fry in deep fat heated to 350 degrees. Elderberry blossom fritters dusted with powdered sugar and sprinkled with kirsch are ethereal.

Chiffon Pie

Wanda, a lady I worked with at Fort Leavenworth, made the most wonderful chiffon pies for Food Day. I could eat an entire pie in one sitting! This is the recipe she gave to me. This makes a perfect dessert for Spring or Summer dinners, or a dessert buffet for showers, weddings, etc. I once served a trio of thin slices (three different flavors) at a catered luncheon—similar to Neapolitan ice cream. Note: a prepared graham cracker pie crust is perfectly acceptable. The challenge I have is finding one that is not cracked (and getting it home in the same state!).

Have ready an 8- or 9-inch graham cracker crust.

In a large mixing bowl, preferably metal, pour:
- **1/3 c boiling water**

Over:
- **1 4-oz pkg. gelatin, any flavor**

Mix at least 2 minutes or until completely dissolved.
Add enough ice cubes to:
- **½ c cold water**

To make 1 c.
Add to gelatin, stir until slightly thickened. Remove and discard any unmelted ice.
Gently stir in with wire whisk until blended:
- **1 8-oz tub frozen whipped topping, thawed**

Refrigerate 15-20 minutes or until mixture is very thick and will mound when dropped from a spoon. Spoon into crust. Refrigerate 4 hours or overnight until firm.

Successful Meringue

Depending on many factors, meringue tends to shrink, weep, etc. This recipe, as the title from Aunts Marcelline's and Geraldine's recipe box indicates, results in a successful meringue. The extra effort is well worth it.

In a small saucepan, moisten:
- **1 T cornstarch**

With:
- **2 T cold water**

Add:
- **½ c boiling water**

Cool until thick and clear. Set aside to cool.
Meanwhile, in a large bowl of electric mixer, beat until foamy:
- **4 egg whites, room temperature**

Add:
- **¼ t salt**
- **1 t cream of tartar**

Beat until soft peaks form then beat in:
- **6 T sugar**

Beat until stiff peaks form.
Beat in:
- **Cooled cornstarch mixture**

Mix thoroughly.
Spread meringue on top of hot pie filling.
Bake at 375 degrees until meringue is golden brown.
Remove to wire rack to cool.

Fruit Crisps

Of the baking Mother did, her fruit crisps were my absolute favorite. The juicy, bubbly fruit melded with the buttery, crisp topping making a sublime dessert. These are delicious served warm or at room temperature, plain, or with cream, Whipped Cream or Ice Cream.

Preheat oven to 350 degrees.
Turn into a 9x13x2-inch baking dish:
- **4 cups sliced or chopped fruit: apples, apricots, peaches, plums, blackberries, raspberries, cherries, rhubarb or a combination**

Sweeten to taste with:
- **1 cup or more sugar**

In large bowl, mix:
- **2 c flour**
- **½ c sugar**
- **½ t salt**

Cut in until mixture resembles fine bread crumbs:
- **12 T butter**

The topping should be light and fluffy. Be careful not to pack it down. Spoon evenly over fruit leaving a bit of an uncovered border around the edges of the pan.
Bake until fruit is tender, mixture is bubbling and topping is light golden brown and crisped, 30-35 minutes

Lemon Meringue Pie

Preheat oven to 375 degrees.
Have ready a 9-inch prebaked pie crust or graham cracker crumb crust.
Make Successful Meringue.
Scrape hot Lemon Pie Filling into pie shell. Cover with Successful Meringue, spreading to edges of crust.
Bake until meringue is well-browned, watching constantly, about 15 minutes.

Fruit Pies

Almost all fruits (and some vegetables) make delicious pies. Our pies were always simple creations that made the most of the fresh fruit available each season. Mother made her pies with quick tapioca. I prefer cornstarch as the thickener. I bake pies at 400 degrees for 15 minutes and then at 350 degrees for 30-45 minutes or until the crust is a deep golden brown and the fruit juices are bubbling thickly at the center. For superior results bake in a glass pie pan and on a pizza stone covered with foil, or on a baking sheet lined with foil on the lowest rack in the oven. Cover the pie with a sheet of foil if browning too quickly; alternately, cover the edges of the crust with an aluminum or silicone ring which you can purchase just for this purpose.
For a two-crust pie, you'll get good, reliable results using the following formula:
- **4 cups chopped fruit or berries**
- **1 c sugar, more or less depending on fruit used and personal taste**
- **¼ t salt**
- **Cornstarch, see below**
- **2 T butter**

For apples, peaches, pears, nectarines: Combine fruit with sugar and salt. Turn into a colander set in a large skillet or wide saucepan. Let sit, stirring occasionally for at least

30 minutes and up to 3 hours. Return fruit to a bowl and toss with the cornstarch (using 2 – 2 ½ teaspoons). Rapidly boil the rendered juices with the butter until thick and syrupy. Fold the juices into the fruit.

For apricots, plums, blackberries, raspberries and rhubarb: Combine fruit with sugar, salt and cornstarch (use 1 – 2 ½ tablespoons). Add fruit and mix gently to combine. Let sit about 15 minutes or until dry ingredients are completely moistened. Dot butter over filling after spooning into crust.

For sour pie cherries, gooseberries and blueberries: Do not use Cape Gooseberries which have a husk. Combine the fruit with sugar, salt and cornstarch (use 2 – 2 ½ T). Let sit at least 10 minutes, and up to 30 minutes, or until juices form. Bring slowly to the boil. Cook 1 minute until fruit begins to soften and juices thicken. Pour into a bowl and cool completely. Cherries and gooseberries; gooseberries and blueberries; and blueberries and elderberries are wonderful together.

Cranberry-Raisin (Mock Cherry) Pie

Culinary history dates this pie back to the early 1900s, and its popularity steady through the end of World War II.

Preheat oven to 375 degrees. Have ready and 8- or 9-inch pie plate and Pie Crust for a double-crust.

Combine in a large saucepan:
  2 c cranberries
  1 c seedless raisins
  1 ¼ c sugar
  ½ c water

Cook over medium heat, stirring often, 10 minutes or until cranberries pop and mixture is very thick. Let cool.

Stir in:
  1 t vanilla

Spoon mixture into crust. Top with crust, crimp and seal edges. Cut four to six slits into the top crust.

Bake pie 10 minutes. Lower temperature to 325 degrees and bake 40-45 minutes until crust is golden brown and filling is bubbly at the center. Cool before cutting.

Crumb Pies

Apple is probably the best-known crumb pie, but all fruit pies make good crumb pies if you prepare Streusel with various nuts and spices. I like walnuts and cinnamon with apple and pear; almonds with peach (and ginger) and cherry; pistachios with apricot and nectarines; pecans and grated lemon rind with gooseberries and blueberries; and black walnuts with rhubarb.

Prepare pies as for Fruit Pies; however, instead of using a top crust, cover the pie with a sheet of foil with a hole cut in the center. Bake as for Fruit Pies. When fruit is tender and juices bubble thickly, return oven temperature to 400 degrees.

Remove foil from pie and sprinkle evenly over the top:

Struesel
Bake 15-20 minutes or until streusel is deeply golden brown and crisp.

Crema Fruit Pie
This easy fruit pie with a simple filling and delightful streusel topping is my own creation. It comes together quickly and is a snap to make if you have pie dough and streusel in the freezer. Note: this does not work as well with "syrup" from low-sugar or no-sugar canned fruits.

Preheat oven to 400 degrees. Have ready a 9-inch, partially baked Pie Crust and half the recipe of Streusel.
Drain, reserving syrup:
> **1 large can fruit in heavy syrup**

Place fruit in pie crust.
Combine:
> **½ c heavy or whipping cream**
> **1/3 c reserved juice**

Pour evenly over fruit in crust.
Sprinkle Streusel over pie.
Bake 15-20 minutes or until Streusel is golden brown. Remove to wire rack to cool completely before serving.

Cream Pies
All of the Puddings make an excellent base for a cream pie. Use an 8-9-inch prebaked pie crust, a graham cracker or chocolate cookie crust, or bake a single, large Meringue Shell to use as a crust. Here are some options:

Banana Cream Pie – use the Vanilla or Butterscotch Pudding and add 2 bananas sliced or cubed. Top with Whipped Cream.

Butterscotch Pecan Pie – use the Butterscotch Pudding and add 1 ½ c chopped toasted pecans. Top with Whipped Cream.

Coconut Cream Pie – use the Vanilla or Butterscotch Pudding and add 1-1 ½ c coconut. Top with Whipped Cream and a sprinkling of Toasted Coconut.

Chocolate Cream Pie – use the Chocolate Pudding and top with Whipped Cream and grated semi-sweet chocolate, or top with Successful Meringue.

Peanut Butter – the Peanut Butter Pudding makes a good cream pie topped with Whipped Cream. Alternately, beat until light and fluffy 8 oz cream cheese, softened, 1 c Peanut Butter, 1/2 c light brown sugar. Whip 1 ½ c cream to soft peaks. Beat 1 c softly whipped cream into peanut butter mixture. Fold in remaining 2 c whipped cream. Spoon into crust and chill. Top with Chocolate Ganache, made with milk chocolate, if desired.

Main and Side Dishes

Macaroni and Cheese
Some make macaroni and cheese a main dish itself, and as the variations suggest, you can add various meats and vegetables to make it a one-dish meal. There are so many variations of this dish, but I prefer to keep it simple: make it on the stovetop; use sharp Cheddar cheese; no breaded topping. The evaporated milk and eggs makes this dish rich and creamy, and the sharp Cheddar cheese gives it a very cheesy flavor.
Cook in boiling, salted water, according to package directions until slightly underdone (the macaroni will finish cooking in the following steps):
 1 lb elbow or shell macaroni
Drain well and return to pot.
Add:
 ¼ c butter, cut into pieces
Stir until butter is melted and macaroni is evenly coated.
Meanwhile, heat until hot:
 1 can evaporated milk
Lightly beat in a small bowl:
 2 eggs
 ½ t pepper
 1 T prepared mustard
 ¼ t paprika, optional
Mix in all but ¼ c of the heated milk.
Stir egg mixture into macaroni along with:
 8 oz sharp Cheddar cheese, shredded
Cook over very low heat, stirring constantly until cheese melts and sauce thickens. If the sauce is too thick, use the reserved milk to thin. Reserve any unused milk to reheat leftovers.
Quick Macaroni and Cheese – combine cooked macaroni with half as much Medium White Sauce, adding the mustard and cheese to the sauce; cook until cheese is melted.
Easy Macaroni and Cheese – combine the cooked macaroni with ¼ c butter, 2 c sliced cheese, a big squirt from the mustard bottle and pepper. Cover and let sit until cheese melts. Stir to combine.
Macaroni and Cheese with Ham and Cauliflower – add 1 c chopped cooked ham and 1 small head cauliflower florets, cooked, to any of these recipes for a complete meal. Top with toasted, buttered bread crumbs.

Spicy Sweet Potato Casserole

I have to add this most recent recipe to this collection because it features sweet potatoes and the spicy taste is really delicious. This dish freezes well for several months and can be made with various meats, adding variety to the menu.

Melt in a large skillet:
- **3 T butter**

Add:
- **1 large onion, finely diced**

Cook until beginning to brown.

Add:
- **1 lb ground beef (or lamb, pork, venison, or bison)**

Cook until done.

Add:
- **1 T curry powder**
- **1 t each salt, pepper, cinnamon, ginger, turmeric, and garlic powder**

Add:
- **1 can diced tomatoes, drained**
- **3 medium sweet potatoes, peeled and cut into small cubes**
- **1 lb green beans, fresh or frozen, cut into 1-inch pieces**

Cover pan and cook until sweet potatoes are tender, about 20 minutes. Add water or chicken stock, if needed, after 10 minutes of cooking.

Baked Beans

Family legend has it Aunt Mill once made baked beans and Uncle Andy (Aunt Ruth's husband) remarked those were the best baked beans he ever had—much to Aunt Ruth's chagrin. Aunt Mill's baked beans were simply white beans cooked in her homemade tomato juice. The beans were not overly sweet and the juice glazed the beans perfectly. I like baked beans to be more substantial.

Preheat oven to 350 degrees. Have ready a 2-quart casserole and:
- **1 lb cooked navy or Great Northern beans**

Fry or bake until crisp:
- **1 lb bacon**

Cut bacon into 1-inch pieces. Set aside.

Cook, until tender, in the bacon drippings:
- **1 large onion, chopped**

Combine beans, bacon, cooked onion and drippings in a large mixing bowl.

In a separate bowl, combine:
- **2 c Ketchup**
- **1 c brown sugar**
- **½ c molasses**
- **½ c prepared mustard**
- **½ c vinegar**
- **¼ c Worcestershire Sauce**

    1 T paprika
    1 ½ t coarsely ground black pepper
Pour sauce over bean mixture. Mix well. Turn into casserole.
Bake, uncovered, for about 45 minutes to 1 hour or until sauce is reduced and beans are thickly glazed.
Variations on a Theme: substitute 1 ½ c maple syrup for the brown sugar and molasses.

Barbecued Beans

Another recipe from a co-worker and also a surprise entry in Aunts Marcelline's and Geraldine's recipe box!
Preheat oven to 350 degrees. Have ready a 1 ½ quart casserole.
Cook until done and well-browned:
    1 lb ground beef
    ½ c onion, chopped
In:
    2 T fat
Drain well. Add, mixing well:
    ½ t salt
    ¼ t pepper
    1 (1-lb 12-oz) can pork and beans
    ½ c catsup
    1 T Worcestershire sauce
    2 T vinegar
    ½ t tabasco sauce (optional)
Bake 30 minutes or until hot.
Variation on a Theme: to make Sweet Barbecue Beans, omit vinegar increase catsup to 1 c and Worcestershire sauce to 3T and add 1 c brown sugar.

Braised Rice

Rice was something of a staple growing up. We had it just plain, or combined with browned hamburger and a cheese or tomato sauce. One favorite way of cooking rice is the following which flavors the rice deliciously depending on what type of liquid is used. Sometimes, we would make a sort of pilaf by adding nuts and dried fruit—especially delicious with game and pork.
Preheat oven to 350 degrees.
In large oven-proof skillet with a tight fitting lid, heat:
    3 T oil
Add in:
    1 finely chopped onion
Cook about 3 minutes, and then stir in:
    1 c long-grain rice
Cook and stir for 2 minutes before adding:
    2 c chicken or beef stock, or

>   **1 qt. whole tomatoes with juice and 1 c stock**

Bring to a boil, cover tightly with aluminum foil and then pan cover. Bake about 30 minutes. The rice should be perfectly cooked and have absorbed all the liquid. Remove from heat and let stand, covered, for 5 minutes before serving.

Variations on a Theme: for "pilaf", add ½ c chopped dried fruit (apricots, cranberries and cherries, or a combination, are particularly good). After cooking and resting, stir in ½ c chopped toasted nuts (pecans, walnuts, almonds, hazelnuts and pistachios are all good choices).

Macaroni Casserole

A quick casserole which uses several convenience foods.
Preheat oven to 350 degrees. Have ready a 1 ½-quart casserole.
In medium skillet, melt:
>   **2 T butter**

Add:
>   **½ c chopped onion**

Cook until tender but not brown.
Stir in:
>   **1 10 ¾ oz can condensed cream of celery soup**
>   **1 8-oz can tomatoes, cut up**
>   **¼ t dried thyme**
>   **Dash of pepper**

Add:
>   **1 c macaroni, cooked and drained**
>   **1 12-oz can luncheon meat, ham or corned beef, cut into 1x1/2" strips**
>   **¼ c chopped green pepper**

Turn into casserole.
Top with:
>   **1 c shredded cheese**

Bake uncovered 35-40 minutes or until bubbly throughout, cheese is melted and lightly browned.

Fiesta Salad

The first time I had this salad was at a "Food Day" at work at Fort Leavenworth. This was a time when we presented awards, years-of-service certificates, etc. My co-worker, Judy, made this and shared the recipe. This is also good made with the "French Dressing" in this book.
Cook until done:
>   **1 ½ lb hamburger**
>   **1 envelope taco seasoning**

In:
>   **2 T fat**

Drain and cool.

Combine beef mixture with:
- **1 head lettuce, thinly sliced or shredded**
- **1 can red beans, drained**
- **2 or 3 tomatoes, diced, or 1 large can diced tomatoes, drained**
- **1 small red onion, chopped**
- **8 oz sliced black olives**
- **8 oz grated Cheddar cheese**

Can make up to this point; cover and chill until serving time.
At serving time, add:
- **1 12 – 16-oz bag corn chips**
- **1 bottle Catalina style salad dressing**

Toss gently to mix together.

Meat, Fish, Poultry and Game

This chapter addresses the basics related to meat, fish, poultry and game. It doesn't go into endless narratives of different grades, cuts or cooking methods. For treatises on those detailed topics, I defer to the United States Department of Agriculture (USDA) and the various resources available through libraries, bookstores and online venues. Sadly, we are left with these since the neighborhood butcher, for the most part, has been replaced by an unseen presence that mysteriously produces sliced, ground and packaged meats straight from processing plants. In the past, meat was shipped to market as hanging carcasses, sides or large pieces. It was the neighborhood butcher who relied on his knowledge of each animal's anatomy to further butcher these into retail cuts like steaks, chops, roasts, stew meat and ground meat. I can still remember our local butcher who also owned one of two grocery stores in Nortonville behind the counter cutting up meat and packaging it for sale. Much ado has been made in the last few decades about the use of pesticides, antibiotics and steroids used to control disease and promote growth. It is always best to procure your meat locally, if possible. However, if your only source is the local grocer, be aware of two terms used to label meats today. The first is natural—this has no bearing on how the animal was raised. It refers, rather, to meat that has been minimally processed and free of artificial flavorings, colorings, preservatives and other synthetic ingredients. The second is organic—this refers to meats raised on certified organic farms without antibiotics, pesticides or steroids, and processed by certified entities in ways that minimally affect the environment.

Much ado has also been made about the diet of the animals—mostly if the animals were raised on a grass-fed or grain-fed diet. Each has its own proponents and opponents. We pastured (grass-fed) our animals, but "finished" them on grain before butchering. In all my years having eaten at hundreds, if not thousands, of restaurants and other food establishments, I have never had better meat than from our own farm.

Dry-aging Meats - this works well for beef, pork, lamb, goat, and bison as well as game such as venison, elk, etc. Wipe the meat dry and place on a rack over a paper-towel lined plate or baking sheet. Place on a shelf at the back of the refrigerator and let age for up to a week. Trim dried meat before cooking. Expect to lose up to a pound of weight through moisture loss and trimmings.

Cooking Meats
The term "meat" refers to the muscles of cattle, pigs, sheep and goats as well as bison, venison, elk, etc. Whatever the beast, cooking methods are similar for all—the only difference is in timing and the temperature of various degrees of doneness.

There are basically two cooking methods: 1) the dry-heat method for tender cuts of meat with a coating of fat and/or marbled fat throughout the cut; and 2) moist-heat, in which liquid is used, for less-tender cuts of meat and those with little fat covering or marbling. The following includes an extensive listing of cuts of meat available from most grocers and meat processing shops. We have a much simpler system for the meat we butcher: beef included roasts, soup bones, ribeye, T-bone and minute steaks, and hamburger; pork included roasts, hams, chops, pork steak (sliced shoulder), cutlets, loins, ribs, sausage, bacon, hocks and pork burger.

We cooked roasts as described in "Cooking in Liquid," pan-fried steaks and sliced meats, and made burgers, meatballs and meat loaves from ground meat.

Dry-heat Cooking Methods
Use these methods for the following cuts of meat:
Beef – Rib Roast, Boneless Rib Roast, Rib Eye, Boneless Top Loin (New York Strip or Strip) Steak, Tenderloin Steak, Rib Eye (Delmonico) Steak, T-Bone Steak, Top Loin Steak, Porterhouse Steak, Sirloin (bone-in and Boneless) Steak, Bottom Round Steak, Round Bone, Top Round Steak.
Pork – Blade Boston Roast, Blade Steak, Smoked Arm Picnic Roast, Canned Arm Picnic, Smoked Hocks, Rib Crown Roast, Center Loin Roast, Rib Chops, Sirloin Roast, Whole Tenderloin, Loin Chop, Loin Blade Roast, Back Rib, Country-Style Ribs, Rib Chop, Canadian-Style Bacon, Sliced Canadian-Style Bacon, Boneless Top Loin Roast, Loin Butterfly Chop, Spareribs, Salt Pork, Bacon, Smoked Ham: Shank Portion; Rump Portion; Center Slice, Boneless Smoked Ham Roll, Country-Style Ham Shank Portion, Canned Ham.
Lamb – Whole Shoulder Roast-Square Cut, Boneless Shoulder Roast, Boneless Cushion Shoulder Roast, Boneless Blade Chops, Blade Chop, Arm Chop, Frenched Rib Roast, Rib Chops, Frenched Rib Chops, Spareribs, Stuffed Chops, Loin Roast, Loin Chop, Loin Double (English) Chop, Boneless Loin Double Roast, Boneless Loin Double (English) Chop, Leg Sirloin Half Roast, Leg Sirloin Chop, Leg Center Slice, Leg American-Style Roast, Leg Frenched-Style Roast, Boneless Leg Roast.

Roasting – Season meat. Insert meat thermometer. Place roast, fat side up, on rack in shallow roasting pan just large enough to hold the meat. Do not cover, add water or baste. Meat will brown as it cooks. Roast at 325 degrees to desired doneness. Let meat sit 15 minutes before carving to allow juices to retreat into meat. Carve across the grain.

Broiling – This is best for steaks, chops, etc. up to 1 inch thick. For thicker cuts, use the Broil-Roast method. Preheat your broiler or do not preheat your broiler according to manufacturer's directions. Slash fat edge of meat. Place meat on cold rack of broiler pan. Add a little water to cover the bottom of the broiler pan to prevent drippings from burning. Broil to desired doneness, using a meat thermometer. Let meat rest 5 minutes before cutting or carving to allow juices to retreat into the meat.

Broil-Roast – Broil as above until both sides are well-browned. Transfer meat to oven-safe pan and place in 375-degree oven and roast until desired doneness, using a meat thermometer. Baste with butter or oil and turn once during roasting. Let meat rest 5 minutes before carving or cutting to allow juices to retreat into meat.

Pan-broiling – Place meat in a heavy skillet or on a griddle. Do not add fat or water. Brown slowly on both sides. Cook, uncovered, over medium heat to desired doneness; turn occasionally. Remove fat as it accumulates.

Pan-frying – In heavy skillet, brown slowly in a small amount of hot fat. Season. Cook, uncovered, over medium heat, turning occasionally.

Moist-heat Cooking Methods
Beef – Boneless Chuck Eye Roast, Arm Pot Roast, Blade Roast, Corned Beef Brisket, Short Ribs, Shank Cross Cuts, Scored Flank Steak, Rolled Flank Steak, Flank Steak Rolls, Round Tip Roast, Bottom Round Steak, Top Round Steak, Boneless Rump Roast, Rump Roast.
Pork – Smoked Shoulder Roll, Blade Steak, Smoked Arm Picnic Roast, Smoked Hocks, Hocks, Center Loin Roast, Rib Chops, Whole Tenderloin, Loin Chop, Back Ribs, Country-Style Ribs, Rib Chops, Spareribs, Salt Pork, Smoked Ham (Shank Portion and Rump Portion), Country-Style Ham (Shank Portion).
Lamb – Boneless Shoulder Roast, Boneless Blade (Saratoga) Chops, Blade Chop, Arm Chop, Lamb Shanks, Riblets, Spareribs, Stuffed Chops.

Braising – Coat meat with flour, if desired. Brown slowly on all sides in hot fat. Pour off fat. Season. Add a small amount of water, stock, wine or other liquid. Cover tightly. Cook at low temperature or in a slow oven. Liquid should just simmer. Cook to desired doneness. Let sit 15 minutes to allow juices to retreat into meat.

Cooking in Liquid – this is the method we most often used and which I still use today. It works well with various cuts of roasts, whole poultry and game. If you question the age and tenderness of your roasts, fowl or game, this will alleviate any anxiety. It is a fool-proof method to deliver tender, succulent and flavorful results. We most often cooked the meat in an enameled roasting pan in the oven with just salt and pepper for seasoning. Today, I prefer to use the slow cooker (except for a whole turkey) and flavorful additions to make a rich stock to use for soup, gravy, etc. You may need to double or triple the ingredients if cooking a large turkey. Either method works well, but you do need to watch the oven method so the meat doesn't boil dry. Some swear by browning the meat well on all sides before braising; however, I find the following method (known in culinary land as "a blanc") to deliver perfectly delicious results.

Whichever method you choose, use the following for each beef, pork, bison, lamb, goat or venison roast, or whole chicken, turkey, pheasant, rabbit or squirrel:
>   **1-2 onions, root and stem trimmed, peel or dried skins intact, halved or quartered**
>   **1-2 large carrots, stem and root end trimmed, scrubbed, halved**
>   **4-6 stalks celery with leaves, halved**
>   **2 bay leaves**
>   **1 t black peppercorns**
>   **2 t salt**
>   **Water to barely cover the meat**

Cook on high 3-8 hours or on low 5-12 hours depending on roast, fowl, etc. Timings are approximate, for there are many factors that make precision impossible such as the temperature of the meat at the beginning of cooking, its shape and thickness, the fat and bone content, and aging. It is best to use a meat thermometer for accurate results. You can purchase instant-read thermometers with markings for various meats, fowl, etc. and temperatures marked ranging from rare to medium to well-done.

If not serving immediately, let meat cool in broth. Then remove meat, remove bones, skin and fat. Place meat in covered storage container and refrigerate. Strain broth, pour into storage container and refrigerate until fat solidifies. Remove fat before using broth. Adjust salt for both meat and broth before serving or during further preparation.

Variation on a Theme:
Poultry and Meat Stock - save and freeze poultry wing tips, backs and necks until you have 3-4 quarts and then use this method to make stock. For beef, pork, and other meats, use boney pieces, hocks, or less-tender cuts of meat.

Stewing – Cut meat into uniform 1- 2-inch cubes. Coat with flour. Brown slowly in hot fat, if desired. Season. Add liquid just to cover meat. Cover pan tightly and simmer. Add vegetables long enough before serving to be cooked. Remove meat and vegetables and thicken juices, if desired.

Soup-making – Follow directions for stewing, but add more water or other liquid. Cover and simmer 2-3 hours. Add vegetables, as desired, and cook until done.

Beef

Beef has eight different grades, but the average consumer need only be aware of three: prime; choice; and select. If you find prime at the grocer, you'll pay for the abundant marbling the meat has from young, well-fed cattle. Choice is usually the highest grade sold at most grocers, meat markets and processing shops. Much of the meat at these is select which has less marbling and less juiciness than prime or choice.

It is quite acceptable when cooked properly. Beef used to be dry-aged, but storing beef halves in refrigeration or meat lockers is expensive so today most meat is wet-aged. We always let our beeves hang for a week after butchering. Dry-aging removes some of the moisture, concentrates the flavor and tenderizes the meat. You can dry-age roasts and other cuts of meat in your refrigerator (ensure it does not register above 40 degrees). See Dry-aging Meats for more information.

When buying beef, select meat that is a good, deep-red color, with no more than ¼ inch of smooth, white external fat. The cuts should be even and well-shaped with no signs of discoloration.

Beef is cooked rare at 140 degrees; medium at 160 degrees; and well done at 170 degrees.

Oven Swiss Steak

I've modified this recipe over the years to increase the amount of vegetables and make the dish more flavorful. You can greatly reduce the cooking time if you use minute steaks and start cooking the sauce before cooking the meat. Good served over Rice or wide Egg Noodles.

Preheat oven to 350 degrees. Have ready a 2-quart baking dish.
Cut into 6 serving pieces:
   1 ½ lb beef round steak, about ¾–inch thick
Combine and pound into the meat slices:
   2 T flour
   1 t salt
Melt in a skillet over medium-high heat:
   2 T fat
Brown meat on both sides in hot fat. Remove to a baking dish.
Blend into the fat in skillet:
   2 T flour
Add:
   16-oz can whole tomatoes, cut up, or diced tomatoes
   ½ c Tomato Juice, beef stock or water
   1 c finely chopped celery
   1 c finely chopped carrot
   1 t Worcestershire sauce
   1 bay leaf
Cook and stir until thickened. Pour over meat in baking dish. Cover and bake about 1 hour or until meat is done and vegetables are tender. If sauce is too thick, thin with additional Tomato Juice, stock or water to desired consistency.

Mushroom Steaks

Aunt Mill introduced these to me at a Sunday dinner. I passed them off as something "French" in Home Economics class for my project! This recipe uses cooked ground beef in a recipe similar to meatloaf.

Preheat oven to 375 degrees. Have ready a 10x15x1-inch rimmed baking sheet lined with foil (lightly grease the foil).
Brown in a skillet:
> **2 lb ground beef**
> **1 onion, finely chopped or grated**

In:
> **2 T fat**

Add a little water. Cook until done. Drain well. Cool.
Beat in a large mixing bowl until well combined:
> **2 eggs**

Add:
> **2 T milk**
> **2 pieces of bread (shredded into crumbs)**
> **Salt and pepper**

Let sit until bread absorbs liquid. Beat well.
If the bread does not absorb all of the liquid, add another slice, mix well and let stand again until liquid is absorbed.
Add:
> **Meat mixture**

Combine gently until well mixed.
Using a ½ c measuring cup, divide mixture into mounds onto prepared pan; flatten to shape into patties about ½-inch thick. Bake until lightly browned with a crispy crust, about 30 minutes. Serve with a sauce made with a can of cream of mushroom soup and one-half the liquid specified in the directions (you want it to be thick like a gravy or sauce). Season with minced parsley, a dash of nutmeg and a pinch of pepper. Serve also with Rice, Mashed Potatoes or Egg Noodles.

Salisbury Steak

Salisbury Steak is typically made with minced, not ground meat. However, unless you mince your own meat, you will need to use ground—which makes a perfectly acceptable Salisbury Steak. Use ground venison, elk or buffalo for variety (1 lb of one of these meats with ½ pound ground beef gives excellent results). Serve these with Egg Noodles or Rice.
In a large bowl, combine:
> **1 egg, beaten**
> **1/3 c strong beef stock**
> **1 small onion, grated**
> **½ c dry bread crumbs**
> **½ t salt**
> **¼ t pepper**

Add:
> **1 ½ pounds minced or ground beef**

Mix gently, but thoroughly.

Using ½-cup measure, form into six patties about ½ inch thick.
Brown patties in a skillet over medium heat until well-browned, 3-4 minutes on each side.
Remove patties and set aside. Discard drippings and wipe skillet clean.
In skillet, cook until translucent:
> **2 T butter**
> **1 medium onion, grated**

Add:
> **1 T flour**

Stir until blended.
Add:
> **¼ c water**
> **¼ c Ketchup**
> **1 c strong beef stock**
> **1 t Worcestershire sauce**
> **½ t prepared mustard**

Bring to boil. Cook and stir for 2 minutes.
Return patties to skillet.
Cover and simmer 15 minutes or until meat is no longer pink.
Serve patties with gravy.

Meat Loaf Ring

This version has a bit more flavoring and is cooked in a ring. Fill the ring with Macaroni and Cheese, Baked Beans or Creamed Peas after baking, omitting the glaze. Can also be baked in a greased loaf pan.

Preheat oven to 350 degrees. Have ready a 5 ½ cup ring mold and a rimmed baking sheet lined with foil (grease foil)
Combine in a large mixing bowl:
> **2 eggs, beaten**
> **¾ c milk**
> **½ c fine dry bread crumbs**
> **¼ c finely chopped onion**
> **2 T snipped parsley**
> **1 t salt**
> **½ t ground sage**
> **¼ t ground pepper**

Mix well and let sit until crumbs are evenly moistened.
Mix in gently until well combined:
> **1 ½ lb ground beef**

Rinse mold with cold water, but do not dry. Pat mixture into ring mold. Unmold onto baking sheet. Bake 50 minutes.
Combine:
> **¼ c Ketchup**

>   2 T brown sugar
>   1 t dry mustard

Spread over loaf during last 10 minutes of cooking. Let sit 5 minutes and fill center, if desired, before serving.

Hamburger Casserole
Preheat oven to 350 degrees. Have ready a 9x13x2-inch baking dish or pan.
Cook until done:
>   **2 lb ground beef**

In:
>   **2 T olive oil**

Drain off excess fat. Return beef to pan along with:
>   **2 t sugar**
>   **2 t salt**
>   **½ t pepper**
>   **2 ½ c Tomato Sauce**

Simmer 15 minutes.
Cook according to package directions.
>   **3 oz egg noodles**

Drain. Place in prepared baking dish.
Beat until smooth:
>   **2 3-oz packages cream cheese, softened**

Stir in:
>   **1 16-oz carton Sour Cream**
>   **1 large onion, finely chopped**

Spread over noodles in pan. Cover with meat mixture. Top with:
>   **1 c sharp Cheddar cheese, grated**

Bake for 30 minutes or until heated through.

Meatballs and Gravy
Some might call these Swedish Meatballs, and maybe they are. All I know is they have the most wonderful flavor and are delicious served over Rice or with Egg Noodles.
Have ready a large skillet with tight-fitting lid.
Cook until soft and golden brown:
>   **½ chopped onion**

In:
>   **1 T butter**

In mixing bowl, combine:
>   **1 egg, beaten**
>   **1 c light cream**

Stir in:
>   **1 ½ c soft bread crumbs**
>   **Cooked onions**

>   ¼ c finely snipped parsley
>   1 ¼ t salt
>   **Dash pepper**
>   **Dash ground nutmeg**
>   **Dash ground ginger**

Add:
>   **1 ½ pounds ground beef**

Shape into 1-inch balls.
Brown meatballs in:
>   **2 T butter**

Remove from skillet.
Stir into pan juices:
>   **2 T flour**

Combine and then add to flour mixture:
>   1 ¼ c water
>   **1 t instant beef bouillon granules**
>   **½ t instant coffee crystals**

Cook and stir until thickened and bubbly. Add meatballs; cover and simmer about 30 minutes, basting occasionally.
Serve with Rice or Egg Noodles.
Variations on a Theme: make the meatballs using other ground meat or a combination (beef, pork, bison, venison, elk, veal, turkey or chicken.

Pork – today's pork is not what it used to be; it is both tenderer and leaner. Pork producers have bred much of the fat out of pigs today so the pork you find at the grocer or meat market is prone to becoming dry, tough and tasteless if overcooked. Gone, too, are the days when people feared eating undercooked pork because of the risk of trichinosis. Fortunately, modern production practices have improved the safety and wholesomeness of pork (and at any rate, the trichinosis organism is destroyed at 137 degrees).

When buying pork, select meat that is moist and attractively pink, not gray or red and with a fine-grained texture. Any external fat should be smooth and white, not chalky or discolored.

Pork is cooked well done at 170 degrees, but it is recommended to cook to 150-160 degrees (for slightly rosy, tender and juicy roasts and chops).

Pork Loin with Fruit

This also works well with venison, bison and lamb loin.
Preheat oven to 350 degrees.
Place on a large sheet of aluminum foil:
>   **1 pork loin**

Season on all sides with:
>   **Salt**

Pepper

Sprinkle over and around:
> **1 onion, finely diced**
> **1 c dried fruits (apricots, cranberries, cherries or a mixture)**

Cover with another sheet of foil. Fold over and seal all edges.
Place on a baking sheet.
Bake for 45 – 60 minutes, depending on size or until meat registers 165 degrees on a meat thermometer. Let rest 10 minutes before carving and serving.

Lamb – American, Australian and New Zealand lamb are widely available throughout the year thanks to new breeding techniques. I prefer American lamb because the individual cuts are larger with more meat in proportion to bone. Lamb is graded prime, choice and good. Unlike beef, marbling with fat is not a factor in grading lamb. The highest grade goes to lamb with thick, well-shaped eye muscles in the loin and rib cuts. Most lamb sold in grocers and meat markets is choice.
When buying lamb, select meat that is moist and bright, but not slimy or sticky, pinkish to pale red in color and with fat that is waxy white and not discolored, brittle or chalky.
Large cuts of lamb are covered with a white, papery membrane called the fell, which must be removed before cooking because it is indigestible and prevents seasonings and heat from penetrating the meat. Ask your grocer or butcher if this has been removed. Beneath the fell is a fair amount of fat which should be trimmed away as it can have a strong, tallow-like taste that will overpower the delicate flavor of the meat. Leave only a few streaks of fat to baste the meat as it cooks.
Lamb is cooked rare at 130-135 degrees; medium at 140-150 degrees and well done at 170 degrees.

Roasted Lamb on a Vegetable Rack

This method works well with loins, roasts and even thickly cut steaks or chops-beef, pork, lamb, venison, bison, etc.
Preheat oven to 400 degrees. Have ready a shallow roasting pan lined with foil.
Arrange in the bottom of the roasting pan, forming a rack (lay vegetables first in one direction and then in the other):
> **4 large carrots, ends trimmed and peeled, and halved lengthwise**
> **4 large celery stalks, ends trimmed**
> **2 large onions, peeled and cut into eighths**
> **4 heads of garlic, roots removed and quartered**
> **Several sprigs of herbs such as rosemary, thyme, marjoram or a combination**

Sprinkle with salt and pepper.
Wipe dry with a paper towel:
> **A roast, loin, steak or chops**

Coat lightly with:

Olive oil or melted butter

Place meat on top of vegetable rack.
Insert meat thermometer into thickest part of meat.
Roast to desired doneness.
Remove meat to a platter or carving board. Tent with foil and let rest 10 minutes to allow juices to retreat into meat.
Test vegetables. If not tender, return to oven and roast until tender.
Carve meat and serve with vegetables.

Buffalo (Bison) – today, buffalo is raised on numerous ranches in the United States. I can buy fresh or frozen buffalo at a local grocer. There are also several good on-line sources for buffalo as well as other large game meats like venison, elk and moose. Buffalo, as compared to beef, is a high-protein, low-fat and low-calorie source of meat. Because of its low-fat content, it should be cooked at lower temperatures than beef. It is recommended to cook only to rare or medium-rare because of this also. However, I have never had bad results cooking to well-done. It is a matter of patience and attention. I worked for eight months one year in Atlanta, GA. I stayed in a hotel close to a national restaurant which served several buffalo items from nachos to chili to steaks to hamburgers and meatloaf. But of all those, after eating my way through the entire menu, the short ribs were the best. Tender, juicy and well-flavored.

When buying buffalo, select meat that is moist and bright red. It should have little if any fat. Trim any external fat from the meat before cooking. Use in any recipe calling for beef, just mind the temperature and timing (because it is low-fat it will cook quicker than beef).

Rabbit – it's smooth-textured white meat with a mild, delicate, slightly sweet taste is very much like that of chicken. Commercially raised rabbit today has a much higher ratio of meat to bone. You can find it is some grocers, usually frozen, and through various on-line resources both fresh and frozen. Rabbit can be used in any dish as chicken, using the saddle as breast meat and the hind legs as drumsticks. The forelegs have little meat and should be used in the stockpot or when rabbit is braised or stewed. Be careful not to overcook it and dry it out as it has much less fat than chicken. We fried rabbit when it was available.

Smothered Rabbit

A simple way to prepare rabbit with delicious results. Thyme is a particularly good seasoning for rabbit.
Preheat oven to 300 degrees.
Coat:
> **2 rabbits, cut into 6 pieces each**

In the following mixture:
> **1 c flour**

   1 t salt
   ½ t pepper
   ¼ t thyme, optional
Let sit on a wire rack for 20 minutes and up to 1 hour.
Heat in a large skillet until it foams:
   ½ c butter
   2 T lard
When foaming, add:
   2 slices bacon, cut into ½-inch pieces
Cook until bacon is browned. Remove bacon to paper towel-lined plate.
Add the rabbit to the pan and cook until browned on both sides.
Sprinkle on the bacon and:
   1 onion, finely diced
Add:
   ¼ c water or white vermouth
Cover tightly and bake for 45 minutes.

Slow Cooker Rabbit

You can also bake this in the oven, but the slow cooker is an excellent tool to use to obtain moist, tender and excellent results.
Place into a slow cooker:
   1 3-4-lb rabbit
Rub over the entire surface:
   3 T butter, softened
Season with:
   Salt
   Pepper
   Thyme
Cover with:
   2 – 3 slices bacon
Add:
   1 onion, thinly sliced
   1 c water
Cover tightly and cook on high for 4-5 hours or until done.

Venison – most often associated with deer meat, venison (of which the Latin root word means "to hunt") actually refers to all large antlered game animals like deer, elk, moose, antelope, etc.—most of which are commercially raised in the United States. These have a less-gamey taste than their wild relations. I've had all of these different meats, but have only cooked deer and elk; the others I had at a fantastic restaurant in Indianapolis, which sadly went out of business. All venison is processed into cuts much like beef and pork. I encourage you to try these various meats. You will find antelope is delicate like veal; caribou is juicy and flavorful; and elk is a close second to prime beef. Like buffalo, you can find these meats via various on-line retailers if not available in your area.

These meats also have little intermuscular fat so they tend to dry out and become tough if overcooked or cooked at too high of a temperature. However, with attention to temperature and timing even well-done venison can be tender and juicy. Cook chops, loins, roasts and ground venison like you would beef or pork.

Poultry (Chicken, Turkey, Duck, Goose, Pheasant and Quail)

The term poultry refers to farm-raised birds raised for meat and eggs. At one time it did not apply to game birds such as quail, guinea hen, partridge and pheasant. However, by federal law, any bird offered for sale in the United States must be farm-raised. If you do not have access to the bounty of the wild or do not raise your own, you can buy the latter from several on-line sources.

I'll leave the debate of "free-range" and "organic" to others. I do know the quality of poultry available at the common grocer has declined in quality over the years. I have often found the birds still have pin feathers, the giblets (liver, heart, gizzard) mangled and pre-cut pieces (legs, thighs and breasts) are often ragged and the skin so badly damaged it doesn't cover the pieces. If your only source is the local grocer, I recommend you purchase whole birds and learn to cut those into pieces yourself. It is not difficult; it just takes practice. Second to raising your own, is to seek out local farmers who raise and sell poultry.

When buying poultry at the grocer (and often you will only find unfrozen chicken while virtually all turkey, duck and goose is frozen), check the sell-by date first. If the package contains a seemingly large amount of liquid, feels sticky or has even a faint off-odor, the poultry will be inferior regardless of sell-by date. Avoid also poultry with ice or frozen sections. Most poultry arrives at the grocer already frozen, so in this state the poultry has effectively been frozen twice. Not good for any poultry or meat.

Chicken comes in many sizes from small (1-3 pounds) poussins up to large 10-pound capons. All these can be roasted as can Cornish hens—in fact all poultry roasts well. Braising and Cooking in Liquid also work well with poultry.

Dark meat is done at 170-180 degrees; white meat at 160 degrees.

Fried Chicken

It was heaven in your mouth. Words cannot do justice to describe the perfect melding of flavor, texture and aroma. But, if ever there existed the possibility of tasting heaven, it was surely Aunt Mill's fried chicken.

Of course, everyone has his or her favorite, but nothing ever came close to hers— richly flavored, juicy meat, a flour-egg-milk coating that fused with the skin to become one—never soggy and never crunchy. The whole thing melted in your mouth. And, was delicious hot or cold.

It was something I could eat every day. In fact, Father tells how, growing up on the family farm in the 1930s-1960s, the family and help ate fried chicken twice a day from

Easter until Thanksgiving. I envy that! Fried chicken was always on the menu when we visited Aunt Mill and Grandmother on Sundays. I recall only twice having something other than fried chicken. It was also the centerpiece of family gatherings at Easter and Christmas (Easter was fried; Christmas was baked).

Grandmother raised up to 400 chickens at one time. She sold the eggs to the local grocer. The former chicken coop, transformed decades ago into a shed for livestock, is still used today. I have a picture of Grandmother (one of only a few pictures of her) standing in front of her chicken coop.

As I mentioned, everyone has his or her own favorite fried chicken and there are many good versions. Mother's fried chicken with a crust, pale and golden from just a dusting of flour, was delicious, too. But, nothing was as special or remembered quite like Aunt Mill's fried chicken.

I watched many times as she prepared the chicken, and I thought I could somehow, someday, someway duplicate it. That never happened. I had always wanted to ask Aunt Mill to teach me, one-on-one, step-by-step how, but I didn't. Alas, one day it was too late. I never learned to fry chicken. Maybe that's for the better since some things really cannot be duplicated, and often some things are so closely tied to or identified with one person that when that person is no longer living it's best to consign those things to the happy memories associated with that person.

I never learned to fry chicken, but I did learn so much more, and for that I am forever grateful.

Pressed Chicken

This is a great recipe for sandwiches or cold salads for a light luncheon or Summer picnic. Pressed Chicken is equally good served with Mayonnaise or a tart jelly.
Day before, place in a large, covered pot or kettle:

- **2 4-lb ready-to-cook roaster chickens**
- **5 cups water**
- **2 carrots, scrubbed well and ends removed**
- **2 celery stalks, scrubbed well and ends removed**
- **1 onion, quartered**
- **2 bay leaves**
- **½ t whole black peppercorns**
- **1 T salt**

Gently simmer, tightly covered, about 2 hours, or until very tender. Drain chicken in colander, reserving cooking liquid. Refrigerate cooking liquid until fat solidifies.

Let chicken sit until cool enough to handle then remove skin and bones from chicken. Finely cut up chicken..

Remove fat from liquid. Heat until just liquefied. Strain broth through fine sieve or piece of cheesecloth into a large saucepan. Boil, uncovered, until reduced to 2 c. Add chicken to broth; simmer, covered, 10 min. Stir in:

- **3 T snipped parsley**

Turn chicken and broth into lightly oiled 9"x5"x3-inch loaf pan. Cool to room

temperature. Cover with plastic wrap. Weigh down chicken with another 9"x5"x3" loaf pan partially filled with water or canned goods.
Refrigerate overnight or until firm.
To serve: Remove weight and plastic wrap. With spatula, loosen pressed chicken from pan; unmold. Cut with sharp knife into ¾-inch slices.

Chicken and Rice Casserole
An excellent use of rice and chicken as a plan over, or worth cooking both just for this casserole. You can vary this casserole by using different meats, cheeses, herbs and peppers. Keep the measurements the same.
Preheat oven to 350 degrees. Have ready a lightly greased 2-quart casserole.
Combine in a large mixing bowl:
  2 c cooked Rice
  2 c shredded cheese (your choice)
  1 ½ c cooked, chopped chicken
  1 12-oz can evaporated milk
  ½ c finely chopped onion
  2 large eggs, lightly beaten
  ¼ c finely chopped cilantro
  2 T butter, melted
  1 T diced jalapeno pepper, optional
Stir well. Bake 45-50 minutes or until knife inserted in center comes out clean.

Baked Chicken Breasts
This is a dish that was always welcome and could be served with just about any type of vegetable, starch and other accompaniment. Nothing could be easier, or more versatile. These are equally delicious served hot right from the oven, used in numerous casseroles, pizza, fajitas and stir-fry, or chilled in a variety of salads or sandwiches. This method also works well with thighs.
Preheat the oven to 350 degrees. Have ready a pan just large enough to hold the quantity of breasts you are cooking.
Place in a single layer in a baking dish:
  Chicken breasts, skin and bones removed
Dot each breast with several pieces of:
  Butter
Or drizzle with:
  Olive oil
Sprinkle liberally with:
  Salt and ground black pepper
  Any fresh herbs you may wish to use
Cover tightly with foil. Bake until done, usually 1 ½ hours or so. Err on the side of over baking. If you under bake for even a few minutes, the breasts will be tough and stringy, not meltingly tender and juicy.

If serving immediately, let rest, covered, in pan juices for 5 minutes.
If not serving immediately, uncover, turn over breasts and let cool in pan in juices before refrigerating.

Oven-fried Chicken

I like to oven-fry chicken breasts, legs and thighs. This method works well with both skin-on and skinless chicken. It is best to grind the crackers into very fine crumbs, using a food processor; however, more coarsely crushed crumbs work well, too, and provide a different texture to the coating.

Preheat oven to 400 degrees. Have ready a 10x15x1-inch pan, lined with foil, with a wire rack. Spray rack with cooking spray or grease with lard or shortening.

Grind or crush into crumbs:

Butter crackers

You need about 2 c crumbs for 8 pieces of chicken.

Place the crumbs in a shallow bowl or pie plate.

Add:

1 t salt
½ t pepper
½ t paprika, optional

In a second shallow bowl or pie plate, whisk together:

4 eggs

In third shallow bowl or pie plate, place:

2 c flour

Dip chicken pieces into flour, shaking off excess, then in egg, letting excess drain off, then in crumbs, pressing crumbs to adhere.

Place coated chicken pieces on rack in pan.

Bake 45-60 minutes total, turning chicken half-way through, until golden brown and juices run clear.

Variation a Theme: if you like your fried chicken spicy, replace the salt with garlic salt and add to the crumbs 1 t dried oregano leaves, ½ t rubbed sage and ¼ t ground cumin and increase pepper to ¾ t.

Duck and Goose

Two of Father's sayings that are favorites of mine involve the goose. For years when the geese traveled south in late Fall, covered the fields and filled the skies with their honking, Father would comment, "I bet those geese are so tough you couldn't stick a fork in the gravy." Now in his later years, an oft-quoted saying is, "I feel like I don't have the strength to pull the smoke off a goose turd."

My experience is duck and goose, especially wild-caught, are relegated to jerky. However, both are delicious when properly prepared and a good alternative to chicken or turkey. Goose is not a tender fowl like chicken. It has a certain texture and chewiness, and its own special flavor. Duck can be a problem child when trying to achieve a perfect breast and tender legs. The challenge is winning the battle of the fat that comes with both. Usually, moist-heat cooking (steaming, braising, simmering) is used for meats with little natural fat or marbling while dry-heat cooking (pan frying, broiling, roasting, grilling) is used for meats with a covering of fat or that are well-marbled. In the case of duck and goose, it is best to use the reverse. Steaming the fowl will render out a quantity of fat. Then braising it will render even more fat. Finally, roasting, uncovered will crisp the skin. This three-pronged approach renders out the most fat, crisps the skin and results in the most succulent flesh. This technique applies to both a 9 ½-11-lb roasting goose and a 5-lb duckling, only the timing and roasting temperature differ. Times and temperatures are provided for the goose [and the duck].

To prepare your bird: pull all loose out from the cavity of the bird, checking both ends. Chop off wings just below the elbow. Rub inside and out with lemon juice and lightly salt the inside of the cavity.

Place the prepared bird, breast UP, on a rack in a deep roasting pan just large enough to hold the bird.

Add:
- **1 inch of water**

Bring to the boil on top of the stove and cover pan tightly.
Reduce heat and steam for 1 hour [30 minutes].
Check on the water level occasionally, adding more if it has boiled off.
Remove steamed bird from the roaster (let the goose cool 20 minutes).
Preheat oven to 325 degrees.
Pour the liquid out of the roaster. You will have several cups of fat which will rise to the surface when chilled. Save the fat (See Note).
Place a double sheet of foil over rack in roaster. Lay the bird, breast DOWN.
Add around the bird:
- **1 each carrot, onion and celery stalk, coarsely chopped**
- **2-3 [1 ½ c] red wine, white wine, chicken stock or water**

Cover tightly and braise 1 – 1 ½ [½] hour(s).
Check the goose occasionally and baste with accumulated juices.
The braising is done when the legs feel almost tender when pressed.
Remove rack with bird to a shallow roasting pan.
Turn the bird breast UP and baste with pan juices.
Roast the bird, uncovered, at 325 [375] degrees for 30 [30-40] minutes, to brown and crisp the skin. If the bird is browned before the time is up, cover with the pan lid set askew.
The goose is done when the legs feel quite tender when pressed; the duck when the legs feel reasonably tender.
Meanwhile, skim fat off cooking liquid. Simmer the liquid, mashing in the vegetables. Boil until almost syrupy. Strain, pressing the juices out of the vegetables. Serve the sauce with the bird.
Note: both goose and duck fat are worth saving. Chill the liquid from the steaming phase until the fat rises to the top and solidifies. Store in a tightly covered container

in the refrigerator. You can save the fat from the braising phase, but it will be flavored with whatever liquid and aromatic vegetables you have used. It will still be very good, but will have less uses than the fat from the steaming phase which is not flavored.

Quail – one of the sweetest and most tender of game birds. It is a small bird weighing between 4 and 8 ounces each with the breast making up the majority of the weight and edible portion. These can be roasted whole, or boned and broiled or sautéed.

Pheasant – one of the most popular of game birds. Its mild pinkish white meat does really resemble chicken. A 2-3-pound pheasant will serve two people. Pheasant can be cooked in any way as chicken, but pay close attention to temperature and timing as its lean structure cooks faster than chicken and is subject to becoming quickly dry and tough. The famous "pheasant under glass" was devised in order to keep the meat moist between oven and table. Otherwise, it is simply a roasted bird.

Braised Pheasant

This recipe is based on one of my favorite drinks—the Martinez: two parts sweet vermouth and one part gin served over ice with two lime slices. Easy to prepare in the slow cooker but can be made on the stovetop in which case cooking time will be 35-40 minutes.
Rinse and pat dry:
> **1 2-3-lb pheasant**

Season inside and out with:
> **Salt and pepper**

Tie the legs together.
Heat in a Dutch oven or large skillet until hot:
> **2 T lard or oil**

Add the pheasant and cook, turning as needed, until golden on all sides. Remove pheasant to slow cooker.
Add to fat in pan:
> **¼ c sliced green onions**
> **1 clove garlic, minced**

Add to the pheasant along with:
> **1 c chicken stock**
> **1 c gin**
> **½ c sweet vermouth or sherry**
> **½ t crushed juniper berries**
> **2 bay leaves**
> **2 epazote leaves, optional**

Cover and cook on high until liquid boils. Reduce to low and cook until pheasant is tender and juices from the thigh are clear when the skin is pierced.

Remove the pheasant to a platter and cover to keep warm
Strain the sauce, skim fat and place sauce in a saucepan. Bring to a boil and cook until reduced and slightly thickened, about 5 minutes. Remove from heat and add:
    3 T minced fresh parsley or chervil
    2 T butter
    Salt and pepper to taste
Carve pheasant and serve with sauce.

Squab and Pigeon – I don't understand why people think pigeons are nuisance birds. These type of doves are beautiful in their myriad colors and are a tasty alternative to the menu. Although pigeon is not sold commercially, you can find squab at the grocer and through on-line sources. Squabs sold today are farm-raised young pigeons that have not yet learned to fly with dark, rich, succulent flesh. I remember Aunt Geraldine, in her advanced years, telling how she would climb to the heights of the barn to get squab for a meal. If overcooked, squab takes on a "livery" flavor. It adapts to several cooking methods and can be roasted or braised whole, or split and then broiled, grilled or sautéed. Always begin cooking breast-down so the thin layer of fat can baste the meat as it finishes cooking.

Fish
Cooking fish, like meat dishes, is simple and uses basic cooking methods. Fish, like vegetables, usually had a season in which certain varieties were available. However, most fish (shellfish and fin fish) today is raised on a farm (think shrimp and catfish) and some like bay scallops and tilapia are exported from China (which I always avoid) among other countries. However, there is hope because you can still find wild-caught fish in some grocers and fishmongers, where available. Be wary, however, of fish wild-caught in the United States, but processed in another country. We were fortunate to have several ponds on the family farm which supplied bass, crappie and catfish as well as bullfrogs. We knew our source and processed our catch with utmost care and expediency. Today most consumers have access only to fish available through their grocers or via on-line resources. Therefore I dispense with catching, cleaning and cutting these creatures.
It is well to cook fish as soon as possible after purchasing. If you must store your fish, fill a refrigerator crisper with ice and bury your fish in it. Fish freezes well when tightly wrapped. Thaw frozen fish in the refrigerator (after removing from packaging) or in cold water to cover.
Grocers or fishmongers should store fish on ice or in refrigerated cases at 33 degrees to maintain maximum freshness. When purchasing fish, chose specimens which have firm, unmarked flesh and smell of fresh seawater. The surface should be bright, clear and almost translucent. Pink spots indicate bruises; brown spots spoilage. If buying a whole fish, the gills should be red, the skin bright and reflective, the flesh firm and the scales undamaged—essentially they should look alive as if they just jumped from the sea into your shopping basket. If buying frozen fish, look for signs of freezer

burn—dry-looking meat and chalky white spots. Freezer burn dramatically affects the taste and texture of fish.

Cooking Methods - a commonly used rule of thumb is to cook fish for 10 minutes per inch of thickness. Begin testing at 7 – 8 minutes so that you don't overcook the fish. For sure results, use a meat thermometer. All fish is cooked through at 137 degrees.

Frying - we fried our fish and frog legs. Fish responds well to frying whether you coat the fish in flour or cornmeal or a combination of both. Boneless fillets are excellent coated with Bound Breading and deep fried or sautéed. You can buy any variety of prepared and flavored fish coatings.

Broiling – the most basic of fish cookery. Preheat the broiler for 15 minutes before cooking. Place oven rack so the fish will be 2 inches from the heat source. Line a shallow baking sheet with foil. Lightly oil the foil. Place on the fish fillets which have been rinsed and patted dry. Brush with olive oil or melted butter, and sprinkle with salt and pepper. Broil undisturbed for 4 minutes. The fish will be done as soon as the exterior turns opaque. Half-inch fillets should be done in 4-5 minutes; 1-inch fillets may take 6-8 minutes. If cooking for the longer periods, baste again with more olive oil or butter. If broiling thicker fillets (1 ½ inches or more), turn and baste and cook another 5-6 minutes.

Roasting – this is a very easy cooking method that works well with all types of fish. Preheat oven to 500 degrees. Line a shallow baking sheet with foil. Lightly oil the foil. Place 1 ½ - 2 pounds fish fillets on the foil. Baste with olive oil or melted butter, and sprinkle with salt and pepper. Roast, undisturbed, until done according to a meat thermometer inserted into the thickest part. (Note: to avoid overcooking, I remove the fish from the oven at 132-135 degrees or when the last traces of translucence disappears; tent with foil and let rest 5-10 minutes before serving. The residual heat will finish the cooking to perfection.)

Baking – baked fish follows the same procedure as roasting, but heat the oven to 350 degrees. You can season the fish with any number of rubs or coatings when baking. The Chili Rub is especially good with catfish. The same method used in Oven-fried Chicken also works well with fish fillets. I like the following coating on salmon, cod or whitefish: combine 1 T each grated lemon, lime and orange zest; combine with 1 T sesame seeds, 1 t kosher salt and ½ t pepper.

Poaching – fillets, steaks or whole fish can be poached. Place fish in a large pot. Cover with cold water. Add 1 T salt, and the following wrapped in cheesecloth: 1 small onion, sliced; 1 lemon, sliced; 1 bay leaf, and ½ t black peppercorns. Cover pot and bring the water to boiling over high heat. Immediately remove the pot from the heat and let stand 10 minutes. Remove the fish from the liquid and serve immediately, or let cool and refrigerate if serving cold.

Frog Legs

The American bullfrog, a member of the family of "true frogs," has more uses than as a dissecting specimen in biology class. American bullfrogs are harvested for food in North America and several other countries where it has been introduced. We hunted bullfrogs at our ponds when growing up. These large, olive-green-colored frogs can weigh 1-2 pounds. The legs are the only part of the frog used for food. Two large frog legs are sufficient for one serving; serve six per person if the legs are small. You can buy skinned frog legs at some markets, usually imported from another country. If you are fortunate to harvest your own, cut off the legs close to the body. Separate and wash in cold water. Begin at the top and strip off the skin like a glove (unless you want to witness the same event Galvani did when he discovered the electric current that bears his name, chill the legs before skinning). The often desultory phrase, "Tastes like chicken," does in fact apply to frog legs which resemble chicken in flavor and texture. Frog legs are good braised, deep-fried, or simmered until tender and served with mushroom sauce.

Braised Frog Legs

Have ready:
>**6 large frog legs**

Season with:
>**Salt and Pepper**

Roll in:
>**Flour**

Melt in a skillet:
>**6 T butter**
>**2 T oil**

Add:
>**½ c chopped onions**

Fry the frog legs until nicely browned.
Reduce heat and add:
>**¾ c boiling chicken stock, dry white wine, white vermouth or gin**

Cover skillet and cook until the legs are tender, about 10 minutes.
Melt:
>**6 T butter**

Sauté in the butter:
>**1 ¼ c bread crumbs**
>**¾ c finely chopped hazelnuts**

Add:
>**1 t lemon juice**

Roll the cooked frog legs in the bread crumbs and serve sprinkled with:

Parsley, minced

Deep-fried Frog Legs
Prepare:
> **Frog legs**

Coat them in:
> **Bound Breading**

Let dry on a rack for 1 hour.
Fry in deep fat, heated to 375 degrees until golden. Drain
Serve with:
> **Tartar Sauce**

Frog Legs in Mushroom Sauce
Prepare:
> **6 large frog legs**

Cut the meat off the bones into 3 or 4 pieces.
Place meat in a saucepan. Add to cover:
> **Chicken stock**

Add:
> **2 lemon slices**
> **¼ t pepper**
> **¼ c each diced carrot, onion and celery**

Simmer, covered, until tender. Drain well.
Make:
> **1 ½ c Medium White Sauce**

Using the strained cooking liquid and adding:
> **1 c Sautéed Mushrooms, sliced**

Season to taste with salt and pepper.
Beat well:
> **3 egg yolks**
> **3 T heavy cream**

Add to the sauce, along with the cooked meat. Let mixture thicken off heat for about 10 minutes.
Serve at once with:
> **Rice**, if desired.

7 AN ODE TO MEXICO

The recipes for Mexican inspired dishes are a nod to Aunts Marcelline's and Aunt Geraldine's favor of Mexican food and Juan's heritage. They frequented a Mexican restaurant in Atchison. The recipes here are my own, but are faithful to the original cuisine.

Tamale Pie

Tamale Pie which gained popularity in the 1950s and of which there are as many variations as there have been years since. Vary the heat by changing the amount or type of chili powder used. I also like to add a 4-oz can of chopped green chilies. Preheat oven to 350 degrees. Have ready a greased 2 ½-quart casserole.
Bring to boiling in a heavy saucepan over high heat:
- **4 c water**
- **1 t salt**

Whisk in:
- **1 ½ c cornmeal**

Cook, stirring constantly until thick and smooth.
Beat in:
- **2 T butter or lard**

Spoon three-fourths of mixture into prepared casserole. Using a spoon or spatula, spread mixture evenly over bottom and up sides of casserole. Set aside.
Keep remaining mixture covered while preparing the filling.
Heat until hot in a large heavy skillet:
- **2 T fat**

Add:
- **1 onion, peeled and chopped**
- **1 sweet green pepper, cored, seeded and chopped**
- **1 clove garlic, peeled and minced**

Cook until vegetables begin to soften, about 5 minutes.
Add:
- **1 ½ pounds hamburger**
- **1 T chili powder**
- **1 t ground cumin**

Cook until meat is no longer pink, crumbling into small pieces.
Add:
- **1 can crushed tomatoes**
- **½ c beef broth**
- **½ t salt (or to taste)**

Cook and stir 5 minutes.
Spoon meat mixture into casserole.
Cover with remaining cornmeal mixture. I find it easiest to place the remaining mixture between two sheets of waxed paper and roll into shape slightly smaller than casserole dish. Remove top paper. Invert rolled crust onto top of casserole and

remove paper.

Bake, uncovered, until filling is bubbling and crust is browned about 30-35 minutes. Let sit 5 minutes before serving.

Variation on a Theme: Use 4 c chicken, cooked and shredded, 1 c shredded Monterrey Jack cheese, 1 c shredded Cheddar cheese and 1 recipe Red Chili Sauce along with the cooked onion, green pepper and garlic to make the filling.

Red Chili Sauce

A good all-purpose sauce to serve with tamales, enchiladas, etc.
In saucepan, melt:
- **2 T lard**

Stir in:
- **2 T flour**
- **¼ c chili powder**

Stir to completely moisten.
Gradually stir in:
- **1 c water**

Stir until chili powder is dissolved, making sure no lumps form.
Stir in:
- **1 8-oz can tomato sauce**
- **1 – 2 T vinegar**
- **½ t garlic salt**
- **½ t salt**

Cover; simmer 15 minutes.

Refried Beans

You can make refried beans with canned beans, but I think the results are superior with freshly cooked dried beans. I cook one pound of beans in the slow cooker by covering with water and adding two or three cloves of garlic. I add salt half-way through cooking. Also, if you cook the beans ahead, heat until warm before proceeding with this recipe. They will be easier to mash or puree in the food processor. Epazote is a traditional Mexican herb with a fresh, grassy flavor and purported to reduce the flatulence beans may cause. You can buy it online, at some grocery stores and at Mexican markets. It is also very easy to grow. Get some if you can and add a few leaves to the beans when cooking. Remove after cooking and before proceeding with the recipe. Alternately, add it, ground, when seasoning the beans.

Have ready, using the directions listed in the recipe header:
- **1 lb cooked pinto beans**

Drain the beans and reserve the cooking liquid.
If the beans have been cooked ahead, reheat beans in liquid until warm. Drain well, reserving liquid.
Mash beans with a potato masher to desired consistency (smooth or coarse), adding

reserved liquid to make a very soft and light mixture which holds its shape when spooned.

Alternately, puree beans in a food processor, in batches if necessary, adding liquid to achieve desired consistency.

Heat in a large skillet:
- **1/3 c lard**

When hot, add:
- **3 cloves garlic, minced**
- **1 medium onion, grated**

Cook over medium heat just until beginning to brown.

Add beans and cook until heated through and about the consistency of stiff Mashed Potatoes.

Season to taste with:
- **Salt**
- **Pepper**
- **Cumin, if desired**

Black Beans and Rice

Cook until just tender in a slow cooker with water to cover:
- **1 lb black beans**

Add halfway through cooking:
- **2 t salt**
- **3-4 garlic cloves, peeled**
- **3-4 epazote leaves**

When done, drain beans; discard epazote; reserve garlic.

Heat in a large skillet or stock pot:
- **3 T lard**

Add:
- **1 onion, finely diced or grated**
- **The reserved garlic**

Cook until onions are tender, about 5 minutes.

Add:
- **Beans**
- **2 c Rice**

Cook until heated through.

Huevos Rancheros

"Ranchers Eggs" are poached eggs served with a hot (as in hot peppers) tomato sauce. Some poach the eggs separately and top with salsa when serving. I prefer to poach the eggs in the salsa. If you prefer a smoother sauce, use the Red Chili Sauce or the ancho pepper sauce in Enchiladas. Best served with sunny-side-up eggs as the runny yolk will combine with the salsa to make a very rich sauce. Serve with corn tortillas and Refried Beans.

Heat, in a skillet, with a cover, large enough to hold the eggs:
   1 qt. Salsa or another chili sauce
Bring to boiling, then reduce the heat so salsa simmers.
Make four shallow indentations in the salsa and add:
   4 eggs
Placing one in each indention.
Cover and simmer until eggs are cooked to desired doneness. About 4 minutes for sunny-side-up.

Pozole

My own recipe of a classical Mexican stew of pork and hominy. Best prepared at least one day ahead and reheated. Note the Ancho pepper sauce can be used to make enchiladas, burritos, etc.
Place into a crock pot:
   2 lb meaty pork bones or pork shoulder roast
   1 onion, quartered
   2 carrots, scrubbed and halved
   4 stalks celery, washed and halved
   1 T salt
   ½ T peppercorns
   2 bay leaves
Add:
   Water to cover ingredients.
Cover and cook on high 6-8 hours or until meat is falling from the bone.
Pour contents into a colander set in a large kettle.
Let drain and cool until you can easily handle the meat.
Refrigerate broth until fat solidifies. Remove fat.
Discard vegetables and spices.
Remove meat from bones, and fat from meat.
Place in a large microwave-safe container or saucepan:
   6 large Ancho chili peppers (these are dried Poblano chili peppers)
Pour in the reserved broth to cover the peppers. Bring to boiling. Remove from heat. Weight down with 1-cup glass measuring cup filled with water. Let sit 15-20 minutes to soften.
Remove chili peppers, reserving liquid. Remove stems and seeds from chili peppers. Transfer peppers to blender. Strain and add reserved soaking liquid to cover.
Add:
   ½ c lemon juice
   2 T vinegar
   2 t salt
   1 t pepper
   1 t ground cumin
   1 t ground coriander

2 t dried oregano leaves

Blend at high speed until liquefied, adding additional reserved soaking liquid, if needed. Taste and adjust seasonings.

Put through a sieve into the slow cooker; discard solids.

Add to the sauce in the slow cooker:

The deboned and defatted meat
1 16-oz can hominy, undrained

Cover and cook on high 4-5 hours.

Serve with chopped cabbage, sliced radishes and Sour Cream.

Chorizo

Mexican chorizo is a fresh sausage unlike Spanish chorizo which is more like salami. It is easy to make and your own will be so much better than what you can buy at the grocer—unless you buy freshly made chorizo from a Mexican market. You can coarsely grind your own meat. If you do, use 2 pounds of boneless pork shoulder. I find it has enough fat throughout you don't need to add additional fat in the form of collected fat from roasts or chops or fatty bacon or salt pork. Chorizo freezes well in plastic freezer bags or containers.

Place in a large mixing bowl:

2 lb fresh ground pork

Remove stems and seeds from:

6 oz (about 12 medium) dried Ancho chilies

Tear chilies into flat pieces and toast them on a hot griddle or heavy skillet, over medium heat, until aromatic, about 10 seconds per side. Press them flat with a metal spatula while toasting.

Place toasted chilies in a large bowl and cover with:

Hot water

Place a plate on top to keep chilies submerged in the water and let rehydrate about 20 minutes or until very soft.

Drain, reserving liquid, and transfer to a blender.

Add:

2 bay leaves, pulverized
1 ½ t ground cinnamon
1/8 t ground cloves
1 t each dried oregano, thyme and marjoram leaves
    or 1 T each fresh
1 ½ t salt
¼ c vinegar (white or cider)
2 T soaking liquid

Process until smooth, adding a little more soaking liquid, if necessary, to keep everything moving.

Press the mixture through a medium-mesh sieve over the ground meat in the mixing bowl.

Mix gently, but thoroughly.
Cover and refrigerate overnight to let the flavors meld.
Fry a little portion and taste for salt, adjust as necessary.

Chili Rellenos Casserole
Authentic Chili Rellenos are my favorite Mexican dish. It takes a pro to make a quality chili relleno—of which I am not one. However, when I am in the mood for these, but not able to go to a Mexican restaurant or store, I make this casserole. I tried several recipes for this, but the end result was quite often like a quiche. The recipes included a substantial quantity of milk. I wanted something similar to the authentic recipe without having to fry individual peppers. For that, I needed to be able to replicate the egg coating and the frying in a casserole. The result follows.
Preheat oven to 375 degrees. Have ready a greased 7x11-inch casserole or baking dish.
Prepare:
> **6 roasted, peeled, seeded and stemmed Poblano peppers (See *Roasted Peppers*)**

Place into each pepper:
> **8 oz Monterrey Jack cheese, cut into 6 slices**

Enfold cheese in peppers, covering completely. Set aside.
Melt:
> **¼ c butter**

Set aside and let cool.
Separate:
> **5 eggs**

Placing egg whites in a large mixing bowl and yolks in a small bowl.
Beat egg whites just until peaks form, do not overbeat.
Remove egg whites to a large mixing bowl.
Add yolks to mixing bowl which had the whites.
Beat yolks until thick and pale-lemon-colored and yolks leave a slowly dissolving ribbon when the beaters are lifted from the bowl, about 7 minutes.
Sift together:
> **2 T flour**
> **½ t baking powder**
> **½ t salt**
> **¼ t pepper**

Fold beaten egg yolks, flour mixture and melted and cooled butter into whites.
Place half of egg mixture into casserole.
Place peppers in casserole.
Top with remaining egg mixture, spreading evenly.
Bake 20 minutes or until egg mixture puffs and is golden brown and a knife inserted in center comes out clean.
Serve hot or at room temperature.

Tortillas

Tortillas are the best known flat-bread of Mexico just like the crepe of France, the naan of India, the focaccia of Italy and the pita of Greece. Once you master making your own, you will not want the commercially made varieties. I borrowed this method for making the best tortillas from Juan. He perfected his top-secret recipe and technique through multiple trials. Practice does make perfectly round tortillas. Cutting with a small biscuit cutter starts the tortillas off in a round shape. Like any bread dough, these benefit from the rests prescribed to relax the gluten which makes it easy to roll the dough and contributes to the characteristic "puff factor." Also important is what I call the "Juan steam," a period of rest covered in a clean towel before packaging. His tortillas have been a best-seller for several years at the Atchison Farmers Market.

Combine in a large bowl of an electric mixer:
- **2 c flour**
- **1 t baking powder**
- **1 t salt**
- **¼ c lard**
- **¾ c hot (130-150 degrees) water**

Mix on low speed until dough comes together. Knead by hand or with dough hook on medium speed 4-6 minutes or until smooth.

Turn dough out onto floured surface. Knead gently and form into a ball. Cover with a clean, odor-free towel and let rest 1 hour.

Roll dough ½-inch thick. Use a 2-inch biscuit cutter, dipped in flour, to cut as many pieces as possible. Set on lightly floured baking sheet. Cover with a clean, odor-free towel and let rest 20 minutes.

Place a piece of dough between two sheets of heavy plastic (a plastic freezer bag with top removed and sides split open works well). Press in a tortilla press, or use an 8-inch flat plate, pie plate or skillet and press as flat as possible.

Remove tortilla from plastic to a floured surface. Roll each piece into a 6 – 8-inch round, 1/8 inch thick. Stack rolled tortillas between sheets of waxed or parchment paper while rolling remaining tortillas.

Heat a cast-iron skillet or flat griddle over medium heat until very hot.

Place a tortilla on the hot skillet and cook until the bottom is darkly browned and the tortilla dramatically puffs. Turn to other side and cook until darkly browned in spots. Remove tortilla to a wide, deep bowl or pan lined with a clean, odor-free cloth or towel, preferably terry cloth.

Continue cooking and stacking tortillas until all are cooked.

Cover cooked tortillas with ends of towel or another clean, odor-free towel.

Let sit about 45 minutes or until barely warm.

Remove tortillas and restack in the bowl or pan, cover with the towel and let sit until completely cool before storing in a plastic bag or airtight container in the refrigerator. Reheat in a hot skillet until warmed through.

Tamales

Making tamal can sometimes be challenging, but as with all other cooking methods (steaming in this case) and preparation (a basic dough/batter), practice is key. It is best, I have found, to start small when venturing into new recipes. You can easily cut this recipe in half or into quarters to get started. The key to a good tamal is to beat it crazy. You want to incorporate as much air into the dough as possible so a small amount (a teaspoon-sized ball) will float in a glass of water. If it doesn't float, continue beating. Some recipes include baking powder, but I find that unnecessary with sufficient beating. Tamal can be made with either corn flour (masa harina) or with fresh-ground masa. The fresh-ground masa provides the best results. You can buy prepared masa (masa preparado) which already has lard (or shortening), salt, etc. already mixed. While convenient, I find it is not nearly as good as a tamal made with fresh masa, your own rendered lard and homemade stock.

The day before:

Prepare a pork roast or whole chicken using the Cooking in Liquid method. Drain meat; let cool until easy to handle, then remove bones and fat. Shred meat and moisten with:

Red Chili Sauce

Refrigerate meat.

Chill broth until fat solidifies. Remove fat.

Place in a large bowl or pan:

Dried corn husks

Cover with:

Boiling water

Weight down the corn husks so they are submerged under the water. Let soak at least 1 hour to soften. Then place upright in colander to drain.

In a large mixing bowl, combine:

1 lb lard, softened, but not at all runny

1 T salt

Beat until light and fluffy.

Add, in tablespoon-size pieces:

2 ½ lb fresh ground masa for tamales

Continue beating until mixture is light and fluffy.

Add:

¾ - 1 c reserved broth, room temperature

Continue beating until mixture is light, fluffy and the consistency of smooth Peanut Butter. Test by placing a teaspoon of batter in a small glass of warm water. If it floats, it is ready to use. If it does not float, add a little more lard and beat for several minutes.

Place a corn husk on plate or carving board with the wide end facing you. Starting at the middle of the husk, spread 2 T of the batter into a rectangle or oval shape downward toward the wide end. Leave about a 2-inch border on both sides and the bottom.

Place 1 ½ T meat filling down the center of the batter. Fold both sides into the center. Fold down the pointed end. Secure by tying with a thin strip of corn husk. Place each tamal as it is formed upright in a steamer basket.

Use a deep pot or a tamale steamer to steam the tamales. Fill with water so that the water does not enter the steamer basket. Place the filled steamer basket into the pot. Cover the tamales with extra corn husks.

Cover the pot tightly and bring to a boil over high heat. Reduce heat so the water simmers. Cook 2 ½ - 3 hours. Keep lid on tightly. Refill with boiling water as needed so the pot does not boil dry.

Test for doneness by removing a tamal to a plate and removing the husk. If the husk comes off without sticking to the tamal, it is done.

Pan Dulce (Sweet Rolls)

These are easy to make, with an interesting topping. The name is a bit misleading: the rolls are not too sweet. Similar rolls can be found in Mexican bakeries and markets. These are delicious with coffee or hot chocolate.

Measure into a bowl:
- **4 c flour**

Combine in an electric mixer bowl:
- **1 pkg. active dry yeast**
- **2 c of the measured flour**

In saucepan, heat until warm, stirring constantly:
- **1 c milk**
- **¼ c sugar**
- **1 t salt**
- **¼ c lard**

Add to flour-yeast mixture along with:
- **2 eggs, room temperature**

Beat at low speed for 30 seconds, scraping bowl. Beat 4 minutes at high speed. By hand, stir in enough remaining flour (1 ½ - 2 cups) to make a moderately stiff dough. Knead dough on lightly floured surface 8-10 minutes or till smooth. Place in greased bowl, turning once to grease surface. Cover; let rise until doubled. Punch down. Divide into 16 equal pieces; shape each into a smooth ball. Roll or pat each into 3-inch circle. Place 2 inches apart on greased baking sheet.

Combine in a small bowl:
- **2/3 c flour**
- **½ c sugar**

Cut in to make fine, even crumbs:
- **¼ c lard or butter**

With a fork, stir in:
- **2 beaten egg yolks**
- **¼ t vanilla**

Mix until well blended.

Divide into 16 portions. With rolling pin roll each into a 3-inch circle on lightly floured surface. Brush tops of rolls with water. With spatula, transfer each to a circle of dough on baking sheet. Slash top into squares, circles or shell forms.

Cover and let rise about 30 minutes or till doubled. Topping will separate where slashed.

Meanwhile, preheat oven to 375 degrees.

Bake for 15-18 minutes. Remove to wire rack to cool.

Polvorones (Mexican Sugar Cookies)

These colorful cookies are great treats for Trick-or-Treaters, stocking stuffers and Valentine's Day. I like to make them for many special occasions, dyeing them for each occasion: orange for Halloween; pink for Valentine's Day; red for July 4, etc. They are easy to make, freeze well and are sturdy enough to ship to family and friends the world over.

Preheat oven to 350 degrees. Have ready a large cookie sheet, preferably lined with a silicone baking mat.

In a large bowl, whisk together:

4 1/3 c flour
2 t baking soda
1 t baking powder
¾ t kosher or sea salt

Set aside.

Place in the bowl of an electric mixer:

1 ¾ c lard
1 ½ c sugar

Beat at medium speed until light and fluffy and the sugar has dissolved.

Beat in:

1 ½ t vanilla

Add, one at a time:

2 eggs, room temperature

Continue to beat until mixture is light, fluffy and well mixed, about 2 minutes.

Turn mixer speed to low, and add to flour mixture until fully combined.

Dye the dough to the desired color with:

Gel or powdered food coloring

After mixing, cover the dough and refrigerate for 1 hour.

While dough is resting, preheat oven to 350 degrees. Line several baking sheets with parchment paper or a silicone baking mat.

Scoop dough out into ¼ c sized balls

Roll balls in:

Sugar

Place balls on baking sheet (6 per sheet). Flatten balls using a wide spatula or glass to about ½-inch thick.

Sprinkle more sugar on top of cookies.

Bake 12-15 minutes or until cookies have spread out and cracked, but haven't browned.
Let cookies cool on baking sheets 5 minutes then remove to wire racks to cool completely.
Store in an airtight container.
For long-term storage: place in plastic freezer bags and freeze.

8 THE SLOW COOKER

The slow cooker is your friend! I know some who do not like to use a slow cooker. I do not understand why, especially now with models that have a removable insert which makes cleaning so much easier than before, not to mention the cooking bags and other things which have improved the process and the experience.

You will find if you do any research some sources which approve cooking frozen meat in a slow cooker. That is not a practice I follow. I now use the slow cooker, the majority of the time, to cook roasts, whole chickens and other large cuts of meat, dry beans of all types, and the dishes which follow.

Ribs

This is the only way I cook ribs now. The technique is my own. I like to serve ribs on the patriotic holidays: Memorial Day; Flag Day, Independence Day; Veterans Day and Labor Day. Accompany with baked potatoes or Onion Rings (or both) and coleslaw.

Cook in slow cooker on high about 3 hours once the liquid begins to boil.

- **1 slab of ribs, cut to fit slow cooker**
- **2 t salt**
- **½ t black peppercorns**
- **2 bay leaves**
- **1 onion**
- **1 carrot**
- **2 stalks celery**
- **Water to cover**

The meat should be just fork-tender and not falling off the bone.

Preheat oven to 250 degrees. Remove ribs to a shallow pan, lined with aluminum foil, just large enough to hold all ribs.

Pour over the ribs in the pan:

- **One of the Barbeque Sauces or Everyday All-purpose Sauce**

Turn ribs to coat on all sides. Sprinkle over:

- **1 onion, thinly sliced**

Bake for approximately 3 hours until meat falls from the bones, sauce is thickened and caramelized, and onions are browned.

Potato Casserole

In a large bowl, combine:

- **2 c Sour Cream**
- **1 10 ¾-oz can cream of mushroom soup**
- **½ t ground black pepper**
- **2 c processed cheese, cubed**
- **½ c finely chopped onion, or green onions**
- **¾ t salt**

Gently fold in:

2 lb frozen hash brown potatoes, thawed

Spoon into slow cooker that has been sprayed with non-stick cooking spray. Cover and cook on high setting 1 ½ - 2 hours; turn to low setting and cook 2 hours longer or until potatoes are cooked, cheese is melted, and casserole is bubbly throughout.

Lasagna

Cook until done:
>**2 lb hamburger**

In:
>**2 T fat**

Drain.
Return hamburger to pan and add
>**4 c Spaghetti Sauce**

Use about 1 c water to rinse all sauce out of jars.
Heat to boiling; set aside.
Combine:
>**1 24-oz carton small-curd cottage cheese**
>**1 1/2 c shredded mozzarella cheese**
>**1 c grated Parmesan cheese or three-cheese Italian blend**
>**2 eggs**
>**½ t ground black pepper**
>**1 t mixed dried herbs (Italian seasoning or other blend)**

Open:
>**1 pkg. lasagna noodles**

Coat bottom of slow cooker with some sauce.
Place single layer of noodles in slow cooker, breaking some to fit.
Continue layering as follows: meat sauce, noodles, cheese mixture, noodles, meat sauce.
Cover and cook on high 1 hour. Change to low setting and cook 3 ½ - 4 hours longer or until noodles are tender and cooked through, and casserole is bubbling. Turn off slow cooker and let sit, covered, 15 minutes before serving.

Variations on a Theme:

Cook 1 lb mushroom slices in 3 T olive oil until tender. Add to spaghetti sauce in place of hamburger.

Add 1 10-oz package frozen spinach, thawed, drained well and chopped, to cheese mixture.

You can also replace all or some of the noodles with Baked Eggplant Slices or Fried Eggplant Slices or Fried Zucchini Slices.

Enchiladas
This substantial casserole tastes even better made the day before and reheated. It also freezes well in individual portions.
Soak in boiling water to cover until soft:
>**5 large dried Ancho chilies**

Drain chilies, reserving liquid, and remove seeds and stems.
Place in blender container:
>**Ancho chilies**
>**2 cans diced tomatoes with juice**
>**2 T lemon juice**
>**1 – 2 T vinegar**
>**1 t ground cumin**
>**½ t salt**
>**½ t pepper**
>**½ t dried ground coriander**

Liquefy, adding reserved soaking liquid, to make a smooth sauce with a texture similar to tomato sauce.
Taste and correct seasonings, if needed.
Press through a sieve or strainer. Reserve sauce. Discard solids.
Cook:
>**1 medium onion, chopped**

In:
>**3 T oil**

Add:
>**1 c vegetables, see *Variations***
>**3 c meat, see *Variations***
>**1 10 ¾ oz can cream of mushroom soup**
>**1 c milk**

Bring to boiling. Remove from heat.
Cover bottom of slow cooker insert with a layer:
>**Ancho Sauce**

Layer, in the following order:
>**2 6-inch tortillas or 1 10-inch tortillas (corn, flour or wheat)**, plus more cut to fit into the slow cooker
>**Meat-vegetable mixture**
>**2 6-inch tortillas or 1 10-inch tortillas (corn, flour or wheat)**, plus more cut to fit into the slow cooker
>**Ancho Sauce**
>**2 6-inch tortillas or 1 10-inch tortillas (corn, flour or wheat)**, plus more cut to fit into the slow cooker
>**1 lb sliced cheese, see *Variations***
>**2 6-inch tortillas or 1 10-inch tortillas (corn, flour or wheat)**, plus more cut to fit into the slow cooker

Spread remaining Ancho Sauce over top layer of tortillas.
Cover and cook on high 3-4 hours or until heated through and mixture is bubbling.
Uncover and let stand 10 minutes before serving.

Variations on a Theme:
Shredded roast beef, sautéed green and red peppers, Monterrey Jack cheese.
Shredded chicken, cauliflower florets (boiled or steamed), Provolone cheese.
Shredded pork roast, pepperoncini peppers (mild or hot, drained), Cheddar cheese.
Chorizo, diced potatoes, Asadero, Cotija or other Mexican cheese. Use Red Chili Sauce, if desired. Omit soup and milk from chorizo-potato mixture.

Creamed Corn

Place in slow cooker:
>   3 (15.25-ounces) cans whole kernel corn, drained

Stir in:
>   1 cup milk
>   ½ c heavy cream
>   1 tablespoon sugar
>   1/4 teaspoon pepper

Without stirring, top with
>   8 oz cream cheese, cubed
>   ½ c unsalted butter, cut into thin slices

Cover and cook on high heat for 2-3 hours. Uncover and stir until butter and cream cheese are well combined. Cover and cook on high heat for an additional 15 minutes. Serve immediately.

Variations on a Theme:
Creamed Peas – substitute 2 lb frozen peas, thawed, for the corn.

Creamed Spinach

More substantial than the other Creamed Spinach recipes, this makes a hearty side dish. Have ready your slow cooker with the pot greased.

Combine in a large mixing bowl:
>   2 10-oz pkgs. frozen spinach, thawed and drained well
>   2 c cottage cheese
>   4 T butter, cut into small pieces
>   1 ½ c cubed processed American cheese or cream cheese
>   3 eggs, beaten
>   ¼ c flour
>   1 t salt
>   ½ t pepper
>   1/8 t nutmeg

Stir well to blend.
Turn mixture into the crock pot. Cover and cook on low 4-5 hours.
Variation on a Theme: Add 2 c cubed ham to make a complete meal.

9 FOR THE BOYS

The original boys were Rafa and Javier. Rafa was a pure-bred Black Lab. Javier is probably a Yellow Lab or a mix. Juan and I got Rafa in 2008 while living in Indiana. I got Javier in 2009 from a co-worker to be a companion to Rafa. They got along well. Unfortunately, Rafa was killed in a hit-and-run on March 17, 2014.

Rafa was incredibly intelligent. I would ask him to find his "blue ball" or "red bone," and he would go and immediately find any item where he had it last. I could write another book about all the things he could do and did during his short life. I miss him so.

Both loved to take rides in my PT Cruiser. Every Sunday after Mass and brunch, when they heard the dish water draining in the sink, they would sit by the door to the garage and wait for me to let them in the car to go for an afternoon drive. I also took them on rides before I went to work in the morning whenever the weather was not good for taking a walk.

Rafa loved trash trucks. The trash pickup was on Wednesday and Thursday. I would walk the boys in the morning before going to work. Whenever Rafa saw a trash truck, he would immediately stop walking, sit down and watch the truck until it turned the corner or disappeared from his sight. Then, we would resume walking. He also liked to watch planes flying overhead, especially the planes that performed flyovers and turn-arounds at the annual air show in Greenfield. One year, we were walking mid-morning, and he saw hot-air balloons flying over our neighborhood. He stopped and watched until all those passed over.

I got Malia, an American Fox Hound (some say she was a Beagle, but I disagree) in 2012. She was with us a couple of days before she jumped the fence. She was gone a week, but she came back (thank you, St. Francis!). It wasn't long before she became pregnant (by both Rafa and Javier). The result: five brothers—David, Israel, Joey, Raul and Tony. David is definitely Javier's son; and Israel is definitely Rafa's. The others? Could be either one's, but they resemble Malia more than their fathers. Unfortunately, Malia died from a hit-and-run on January 31, 2014. The boys however, live on. I love them so.

The first year we had Rafa, he became terribly ill from processed dog food. I decided I would cook for him and Javier. I got a $400 doctor bill, and they got home-cooked meals! At first, I pressure-cooked five whole chickens, skinned and deboned those, and added 12 cans of vegetables and several cups of cooked brown rice or oatmeal. I then branched out to other meals and treats. I present these recipes in this chapter.

Tuna Melt
Scramble in a non-stick skillet:
>**2 eggs**

Add:
>**1 can tuna in oil, undrained**
>**1 c whole wheat breadcrumbs**
>**1 t fresh minced parsley**

Mix well.
Top with:
>   ¼ c shredded cheese

Heat until cheese melts.
Cool and serve.

Meat Loaf

My boys absolutely love this. This recipe makes a 9x13x3-inch loaf, which today for six puppies (I still call them puppies even though they are now middle-aged) makes for treat-like portions, not a full meal. Note the pan size is 3 inches deep; mine was made by Wilton.

Preheat oven to 350 degrees. Have ready one greased 9x13x3-inch pan.
In a very large mixing bowl, combine:
>   **3 large carrots, shredded**
>   **4 large potatoes, peeled and shredded**

Mash before adding to the carrots and potatoes:
>   **1 lb navy beans, cooked**

Mix well, then add:
>   **4 lb hamburger**
>   **4 eggs**
>   **¼ c wheat germ**
>   **1 T low-sodium beef bouillon powder**

Combine with hands until evenly mixed.
Turn into prepared pan.
Bake approximately 1 ½ hours or until done.
Remove from oven and cool in pan on rack.
Slice into servings depending on size/breed of dog.
May be wrapped in foil, placed in freezer bags and frozen.

Stews

The following are proportions for one serving, again depending on size/breed.

Stew I

Bring to a boil and then simmer:
>   **2/3 c meat – turkey, liver or hamburger**
>   **½ c Rice, cooked**
>   **½ c peeled, diced potato**
>   **½ c diced carrot**
>   **1 c water, or chicken or beef broth**

Stew II

Cook until done:
>   **1 boneless, skinless chicken breast, cut into ½-inch pieces**
>   **½ c diced carrots**

In:
> **Water, or chicken broth to just cover**

Cool and add:
> **½ c cooked Rice**
> **½ c cottage cheese**

Cool and serve.

Pumpkin and Peanut Butter Treats

I usually buy several pumpkins in the Fall to decorate the front porch and the mantel, and then cook them. Cooked, mashed pumpkin freezes well for several months.
Preheat oven to 350 degrees. Have ready a large rimmed baking sheet lined with parchment, foil or a silicone baking mat.
Whisk together:
> **2 ½ c flour**
> **2 eggs**
> **½ c pumpkin puree**
> **2 T Peanut Butter**
> **½ t salt**
> **½ t cinnamon, optional**

Add a bit of water to make the dough workable. You want a stiff, dry dough.
Roll into a 1-inch thick roll. Cut into ½-inch slices. Place on baking sheet.
Bake about 40 minutes or until cooked through.
Remove to a wire rack to cool.

Treats Master Recipe

I created this recipe to have a base which can be flavored numerous ways by varying the additions.
Preheat oven to 350 degrees. Have ready several baking sheets either lightly greased or lined with a silicone baking mat.
Cook in large bowl in the microwave or a large saucepan about 5 minutes or until the oatmeal absorbs the liquid:
> **2 c old-fashioned oats**
> **3 c beef, pork, chicken or turkey stock**
> **¼ olive oil**

Let cool until tepid.
Add:
> **4 eggs**
> **Flavorful additions, see below**

Mix well.
Stir in:
> **Whole wheat flour**

The amount will depend on what type of treat you want to make.
To make balls: add enough flour to make a dough that is stiff enough to hold its

shape when scooped onto a baking sheet using a cookie scoop.

To make treats which you roll and cut into various shapes: add enough flour to make a dough stiff enough to knead. Turn dough out onto a well-floured, or cornmeal-covered, surface and knead until dough is smooth. Cover and let rest 10 minutes before rolling ½-inch thick and cutting.

Place both forms onto prepared baking sheets. Bake 1 – 1 ½ hours, depending on size, or until treats are cooked through and crisp, turning over half-way through cooking.

Remove to a wire rack to cool completely before storing in an airtight container.

Flavorful additions: add one or more of the following to flavor the treats:

1 c Peanut Butter (add to oatmeal before cooking)
½ honey (add to oatmeal before cooking)
1 c hulled sunflower seeds or chopped roasted, unsalted peanuts
1 c diced dried fruit (apples, pears, blueberries, cranberries or cherries)
1 c diced cooked ham or crumbled bacon
1 c shredded cheese
1 c pumpkin puree or mashed sweet potatoes
¼ c fresh (or 2 T dried) minced parsley, mint, rosemary or thyme or a combination; if using dried herbs, add to oatmeal before cooking

AFTERWORD

Aunt Mill would often say, "If you have your health, you have everything." She could not have been more correct.

This book is the final leg in the course I set out on circa 1993. It is the culmination of the journey to me.

I wrote in the Forward that this book is about "...a time and place I cherish." That is only partially true. I had to rediscover and re-learn most of what this book chronicles. In 1993, I was afflicted with a severe case of diabetic ketoacidosis (DKA). At that time, I had lived with Type 1 diabetes for 21 years. I had other episodes of diabetic coma through the years, but nothing like DKA. It happens when the blood sugar is very high and acidic substances called ketones build up to dangerous levels in the body coupled with a low level of insulin.

I talked to my then current and former doctors and learned about the affects diabetic comas, especially DKA, can have on a person. It can cause brain swelling which can lead to memory loss.

I lost almost all memory of life prior to the DKA episode. I still remembered most people by name, places and information that had become rote over time. It wasn't immediately apparent but was revealed over the course of several months when I was asked about certain past events, people, etc., and I could not associate any memories to those.

Renee, my first office mate when I worked in Kansas City, once told me that in any situation you have two courses of action: 1) what you can do; and 2) what you can do about it. I knew I couldn't regain the lost memory, but her counsel was the catalyst to turn to the future and to begin the journey to re-learn and rediscover through notes, journals, photo albums, scrapbooks, conversations and observations. Fortunately, I had documented many details about people, events, etc. through these media, and there were still people in my life I could interview (casually) to flesh out even more details. Mother knew the dates when everyone was born, married and died, and even the weather on those dates.

I realized the shocking extent of the damage when I decided to pursue a master's degree in accounting and a Certified Public Accountant (CPA) license. Not only did the DKA rob me of memories, it also robbed me of what I had learned but not often used, most notably accounting. I earned a bachelor's degree in accounting but had not used that learning much after I started working full-time for the Department of the Army— governmental accounting is vastly different from private-sector accounting. In short, I had to re-learn basic accounting and everything business-related to my bachelor's degree in order to complete my master's degree and sit for the CPA exam. I eventually earned my master's degree in 2001 from Rockhurst University by taking night classes. Three years later, after multiple attempts, I passed the CPA exam.

At the same time during those years, and in the years hence, —more than half my life now—I have been blessed with basically good health, a rewarding career with opportunities many do not experience, and friends and co-workers beyond compare. I sometimes hear people say they would like to relive a period in their lives. I don't want to relive any period in my life, but there are some things I would like to do again. I'd like to complete the Army and Air Force confidence courses again. I'd like to work in the Pentagon again. I'd like to play sand volleyball again, among other things. But, as a former mentor once told me, "You're right where you need to be. It doesn't mean you have to stay there forever, but for now it's where you're needed."

This journey, which I can best liken to the gradual renewal of a man, has helped me to grow confident and independent, and to make everyday count.

What you can do, and what you can do about it.

Jim Weishaar
Nortonville, KS
September 2020

INDEX

Abbreviations, 16
Apples
  about, 193
  Baked, 194
  Cake, 194
  Crab, 166
  Dumplings, 195
  Red Hot, 194
  Sauce, 193
Apricots
  about, 99
  Filling, 31
Asparagus
  about, 83
  Roasted, 83
Avocados
  about, 99
  Filling, 100
  Guacamole, 99
  Stuffed Tomatoes, 100
  Tart, 100
Banana
  Cream Pie, *305*
Barbeque
  Sauce I, 46
  Sauce II, 46
  Sauce III, 47
  Sauces, about, 46
Bars
  Breakfast, 74
  Rhubarb, 92
BBQ. *See* Barbeque
Beans
  Baked, 308
  Barbecued, 309
  Black, and Rice, 337
  Green, about, 101
  Green, Asian, **103**
  Green, I, 102
  Green, II, 102
  Refried, 336
  Sweet Barbecue, 309
  Sweet Barbecued, 309
  Wax, about, 101
Beef
  about, 316
Beets
  about, 101
  greens, 101
  Pickled, 165
Berries
  about, 103
Biscuits
  Angel, 211
  Cheddar, 37
  Drop, 37
  Everyday, 37
  Pizza Crust, 37
Bison. *See* Buffalo
Blanching
  Vegetables, 172
Blood Sausage, 265
Blueberries
  about, 103
  Compote, 104
  Filling, Topping or Compote, 103
  Lemon, Tart, 104
  Tart, 104
Boursin, 45
Brains
  about, 268
  Sautéed, 268
Breading
  Bound, 35
Breads
  about, 211
  Apple Cheese, 227
  Apricot Nut, I, 224
  Apricot Nut, II, 225
  baked, preserving, 20
  Banana, 226
  Basic Receipt, 213
  Batter, 218
  Caraway Cheese, 9
  Cherry Nut, 226
  Cinnamon Crisps, 218
  Cranberry Orange, 227
  Cream Cheese Fruit Rolls, 216
  English Muffin, 212
  Everyday, 38

358

Everyday, Cinnamon, 39
Everyday, Garlic, 39
Everyday, Raisin, 39
Long Johns, 215
Pan Dulce (Sweet Rolls), 343
Poppy Seed, 225
Potato Refrigerator Rolls, 79
Pumpkin Nut, 200
Quick, about, 223
Raisin, 213
Raspberry Rolls, 217
Rhubarb, I, 230
Rhubarb, II, 230
Sweet, 221
Whole Wheat, 221
Zucchini, I, 132
Zucchini, II, 134
Brining
   about, 269
Broccoli
   about, 104
   and Rice Casserole, 80
   Puff, 105
Brownies, 245
Brussels Sprouts
   about, 196
   Roasted, 197
Buffalo
   about, 323
Butchering
   about, 261
Butter
   homemade, 25
Buttercream
   Apricot, 292
   Chocolate, 292
   Coffee, 292
   Fruit (Raspberry, Strawberry, Lemon, Lime, Orange), 292
   Maple, 292
   Master Recipe, 291
   Mocha, 292
   Vanilla, 292
Buttermilk
   homemade, 23
Cabbage
   about, 105
   Leaves, Stuffed, 106
   with Sausage and Apples, 106
Cactus
   about, 84
   Nopales Pie, 85
   Nopales Salad, 84
Cakes
   Angel Food, 279
   Angel Food, Chocolate, 280
   Apple, 194
   Apple Upside-Down, 284
   Apricot Upside-Down, 285
   baked, preserving, 20
   Banana Upside-Down, 285
   Carrot, 293
   Cheesecake, Master Recipe, 286
   Chocolate Cream, 277
   Chocolate Lemon Roll, 277
   Chocolate Peanut Butter Roll, 277
   Chocolate Peppermint Roll, 277
   Chocolate Roll, 276
   Chocolate Sheet Cake, 280
   Chocolate Zucchini, 138
   Cocoanut Carrot, 288
   Coconut, 278
   Coconut Ice Cream, 276
   Coconut-Pecan Upside-Down, 285
   Cranberry Coffee, 282
   Cream Cheese Pound, 275
   Devil's Food, 295
   Everyday Chocolate, 39
   Ginger Lemon Pudding, 292
   Gingerbread I, 289
   Gingerbread II, 290
   Hot Fudge, 281
   Icing, 290
   Jelly Roll, 296
   Lemon, 278
   Peach Upside-Down, 285
   Pear Upside-Down, 284
   Plum Upside-Down, 285
   Pumpkin Roll, 297
   Rhubarb Upside-Down, 93, 285
   Rocky Mountain Slide, 281
   Rosemary, 10
   Upside-Down, 283
   White, 278

Yellow, 278
Yule Log, 208
Zucchini Pineapple, 137
Calzones, 215
Candies
  about, 257
  Aunt Viv's Caramel Corn, 259
  Fudge, 257
  Marshmallows, 257
  Peanut Butter Fudge, 259
Canning
  and Preserving, about, 157
Cantaloupe
  Jam, 116
Carrots
  about, 107
  Cookies, 249
  Glazed, 107
  Peas and, 89
Casseroles
  Broccoli and Rice, 80
  Broccoli Puff, 105
  Cabbage with Sausage and Apples, 106
  Chicken and Rice, 327
  Chili Rellenos, 340
  Eggplant, 113
  Eggs, 73
  Enchiladas, 349
  Hamburger, 320
  Lasagna, 348
  Macaroni, 310
  Potato, 347
  Potato, II, 61
  preserving, 20
  Reuben, 71
  Rice, 64
  Salmon and Noodle, 69
  Salmon Bake, 68
  Sausage Potato, 75
  Spicy Sweet Potato, 308
  Squash, I, 134
  Squash, II, 135
  Stuffed Cabbage Leaves, 106
  Sweet Potato, I, 202
  Sweet Potato, II, 203
  Sweet Potato, III, 203

Tuna and Noodles, 67
Turnip, I, 204
Turnip, II, 207
Zucchini, I, 135
Zucchini, II, 136
Zucchini, III, 137
Cauliflower
  about, 107
  Baked, 108
Celery
  about, 108
  Braised, 109
Chard. *See* Swiss Chard
Cheese Balls
  Boursin, 45
  Chocolate, 45
  The Cream Cheese Bar, 46
Cheesecakes
  Apricot Swirl, 287
  Blue, 288
  Blueberry, 287
  Cherry, 287
  Chocolate Chip, 287
  Chocolate, I, 287
  Chocolate, II, 287
  Cookies and Cream, 287
  Cranberry, 287
  Fiesta, 288
  Lemon, 287
  Lime, 287
  Orange, 287
  Peanut Butter, 287
  Pumpkin, 288
  Raspberry, 287
  Sour Cream Topped, 288
  Strawberry, 287
  Walnut-Caramel, 287
Cheeses
  about, 56
  Cottage, homemade, 23
  Head, or Brawn, or Souse, 264
  Pimento, homemade, 53
Cherries
  about, 109
Chicken
  and Rice Casserole, 327
  Breasts, baked, 327

Burgers, Everyday, 42
Fried, 325
Oven-fried, 328
Pecan Salad, 155
Pressed, 326
Tarragon, Loaf, 11
Chili
  Rub, 46
Chili Rellenos Casserole, 340
Chocolate
  Angel Food Cake, 280
  Apricot, Chip Cookies, 246
  Banana Oatmeal, Chip Cookies, 255
  Brownie Muffins, 237
  Cake Roll, 276
  Cake, Everyday, 39
  Cheese Ball, 45
  Chip Cookies, 253
  Cookies, 248
  Covered Cherry Cookies, 247
  Crackle Cookies, 250
  Cranberry, Chip Cookies, 254
  Cream Cake, 277
  Cream Cheese, Chip Cookies, 250
  Cream Pie, *305*
  Dessert, Cheryl's, 80
  Fudge, 257
  Ganache, 33
  Hot Fudge Cake, 281
  Lemon Roll, 277
  Muffins, Chip, 236
  Peanut Butter Roll, 277
  Peanut Butter, Chip Cookies, 250
  Peppermint Roll, 277
  Pineapple, Chip Cookies, 247
  Pudding, 272
  Pumpkin, Chip Cookies, 255
  Shortcake, 294
  Truffles, 33
  Zucchini Cake, 138
Chopped, 16
Chorizo, 339
Christmas Dinner, 207
Coarsely Chopped, 16
Coconut
  Cake, 278
  Cream Pie, *305*

  Toasted, 30
Coffee Cakes
  Cocoa, 228
  Coffee Cake, 298
  Cranberry, 282
  Jelly-filled, 220
  Prune, 283
Cookies
  about, 241
  Almond Bars, 244
  Apricot Bars, 244
  Apricot Chocolate Chip, 246
  baked, preserving, 20
  Banana Oatmeal Chocolate Chip, 255
  Bar, 241
  Bar Cookies, about, 241
  Brownies, 245
  Butterscotch, 254
  Carrot, 249
  Chocolate, 248
  Chocolate Chip, 253
  Chocolate Covered Cherry, 247
  Chocolate Espresso, 249
  Coconut Bars, 244
  Crackle, 250
  Cranberry Chocolate Chip, 254
  Cream Cheese Chocolate Chip, 250
  Cream Wafers, 252
  Date Oatmeal, 251
  Drop, about, 246
  Everything, 255
  Fruitcake Bars, 242
  Lemon Bars, 243
  Lime Bars, 243
  Mexican Hot Chocolate, 249
  Orange Bars, 243
  Peanut Butter Chocolate Chip, 250
  Pecan Pie Bars, 246
  Pineapple Chocolate Chip, 247
  Polvorones (Mexican Sugar Cookies), 344
  Pumpkin Chocolate Chip, 255
  Quick-mix, about, 253
  Quick-mix, Master Mixing Method, 253
  Ranger, 254
  Sour Cream Cranberry Bars, 242

Teatime, 252
unbaked, preserving, 20
Zucchini, 138
Cooking Methods
   Dry-heat, 314
   Moist-heat, 315
Corn
   about, 109
   Aunt Viv's Caramel, 259
   Bread Pudding, 110
   Creamed, 110
   Creamed, slow cooker, 350
   To freeze, 172
Corn Breads
   about, 228
   Dressing, 208
   I, 229
   II, 229
   III, 229
   Muffins, 234
Corned Beef
   Dinner, 70
   homemade, 268
   Reuben Casserole, 71
Cornmeal
   Mush, Fried, 76
Cottage Cheese
   homemade, 23
Cranberries
   about, 197
   Chocolate Chip Cookies, 254
   Coffee Cake, 282
   Dessert Quiche, 190
   Muffins, 237
   Salad, 191
   Sauce, 192
Cream
   Whipped, 32
Crème Fraiche
   homemade, 23
Crumb Topping, 188
Cucumbers
   about, 111
   I, 111
   II, 112
   Relish, 170
   Sauteed, 112

Cupcakes
   Cherry-Vanilla, 285
   Everyday Chocolate, 39
   Key Lime, 286
Curd
   Lemon, 31
   Lime, 31
   Orange, 31
Dandelions
   about, 85
   Wine, 86
Desserts
   about, 271
   Baked Pumpkin Pudding, 293
   Fruit Sherbet, 177
   Lemon Sherbet, 177
   Meringue Shells, 271
   Pistachio Dessert, 271
   Puddings, 272
Diced, 16
Dips
   Crab, 50
   Reuben, 51
   Rose's, 49
   Shrimp, 50
Dog Foods
   Meat Loaf, 352
   Pumpkin and Peanut Butter Treats, 353
   Stews, 352
   Treats Master Recipe, 353
   Tuna Melt, 351
Doughs
   unbaked, preserving, 20
Dressing, 187
   Cornbread, 208
   Cranberry, 197
Duck
   about and to cook, 328
Dumplings, 223
   Apple, 195
Eggnog, 55
Eggplant
   about, 112
   Casserole, 113
   Fried, 113
   Spicy, 114

Stuffed Slices, 113
Eggs
  Eggs (breakfast casserole), 73
  Hard-boiled, 29
  Huevos Rancheros, 337
  Noodles, 189
  preserving, 19
  Scrambled, 73
  Soft-Fried, 74
Elderberry
  Wine, Blossom, 55
Enchiladas, 349
Equipment, 16
Fats
  Rendering, 261
Finely Diced, 16
Fish
  about, 331
  Cooking Methods, 332
Freezing
  Fruits and Vegetables, 171
French Toast, 77
Fritters
  Blossom, 301
  Fruit, 301
  Master Recipe, 300
  Meat, 301
  Vegetable, 301
Frog Legs
  about, 333
  Braised, 333
  Deep-fried, 334
  in Mushroom Sauce, 334
Frosting
  Buttercream, 291
  Cake Icing, 290
  Cream Cheese, 288
Frostings
  Mocha, 296
  Peppermint Stick, 296
  Seafoam, 296
  Seven-Minute, 296
Fruitcakes
  about, 181
  Dorothy's, 184
  White, I, 181
  White, II, 182
  White, III, 183
Fruits
  dried, preserving, 21
Fudge
  Chocolate, 257
  Peanut Butter, 259
Garlic
  Roasted, 29
Goose
  about and to cook, 328
Gooseberries
  about, 114
  Fool, 115
  Poached, 115
Gravy
  about, 28
  Pan, 28
  Stock, 28
Guacamole, 99
Hash, 59
Head Cheese, 264
Herbs
  about, 8
  Blends, 13
  Butters, 12
  Drying, 12
  Freezing, 12
  Jellies, 12
  Storing, 12
  Teas, 13
  Vinegars, 12
Horseradish
  about, 164
Hush Puppies, 223
Ice Creams
  about, 175
  Butter Pecan, 176
  Cherry Nut, 176
  Chocolate, 176
  Chocolate Chip, 176
  Coffee, 176
  French Vanilla, *176*
  Fruit, 177
  Lemon, Lime or Orange, *176*
  master recipe, *175*
  Mint Chocolate Chip, 176
  Peanut Butter, 176

Pistachio, 176
Jams
  about, 33
  Cantaloupe, 116
  Gingered Rhubarb, 92
Jellies
  about, 33
  Herb, 12
Jicama
  about, 115
Ketchup, 159
Kohlrabi
  about, 198
Lamb
  about, 322
  Roasted on a Vegetable Rack, 322
Lard
  about, 261
Lasagna, 348
Lemon
  Cake, 278
  Curd, 31
  Pudding and Pie Filling, 273
  Sherbet, 177
Lettuce
  about, 86
  Peas and, I, 88
  Peas and, II, 88
Lime
  Curd, 31
Liver
  about, 266
  and Onions, 267
  I, 266
  II, 267
Macaroni
  and Cheese Master Recipe, 307
  and Cheese with Ham and
    Cauliflower, 307
  and Cheese, Easy, 307
  and Cheese, Quick, 307
  Casserole, 310
Marshmallows, 257
  Chocolate, I, 258
  Chocolate, II, 258
  Peppermint, 258
Master Mixing Methods

Muffins, 233
Quick-mix Cookies, 253
Master Recipes
  Buttercream, 291
  Cheesecake, 286
  Chocolate Roll, 276
  Dog Treats, 353
  Ice Cream, 175
  Macaroni and Cheese, 307
  Marshmallows, 257
  Pudding, 272
  Rice, 35
  Seven-Minute Frosting, 296
  Spaghetti Sauce, 160
  Stuffed Mushrooms, 119
  Upside-Down Cake, 283
  Zucchini Bread, 132
Mayonnaise
  homemade, 34
Measures, 15
Measuring, 15
Meat Loaf
  Everyday, 40
  Ring, 319
Meatballs
  and Gravy, 320
  Hot Barbequed, 54
Meats
  about cooking, 313
  Dry-aging, 313
  Oven Baked, 75
Melons
  about, 116
  with Shrimp, 117
Meringue
  Shells, 271
  Successful, 302
Mincemeat, 263
Muffins
  about, 233
  Bacon Cornbread, 234
  Banana, 235
  Blueberry Cornbread, 234
  Blueberry Poppy Seed, 238
  Brownie, 237
  Caraway Rye, 234
  Chocolate Chip, 236

Corn, 234
Cranberry, 237
Jalapeno Cheese Cornbread, 234
Master Mixing Method, 233
Nutmeg, 235
Nutty Rhubarb, 91
Pumpkin, 236
Raisin Bran, 235
Raisin Cornbread, 234
Sweet Potato, 236
Toppings for, 239
White Velvet, 238
Mushrooms
 about, 118
 Creamed, 119
 Deep-fried, 118
 Sauteed, 118
 Steaks, 317
 Stuffed, 119
Nectarines
 about, 120
Noodles
 Egg, 189
Nuts
 Glazed, 30
 preserving, 21
 Toasted, 30
Onions
 about, 120
 Baked, 121
 Creamed, I, 122
 Creamed, II, 122
 Glazed, 122
 Liver and, 267
 Pie, 85
 Rings, 120
 Stuffed with Sauerkraut, 123
Orange
 Curd, 31
Oxtails
 about, 264
Pancakes, 77
 Meat and Vegetable, (Patties), 128
 Potato, 128
 Vegetable, 128
Parsnips
 about, 198

Pasta
 Plan Overs, about, 62
 Salad, 63
 Spaghetti Pie, 62
Pastry
 baked, preserving, 20
 unbaked, preserving, 20
Peaches
 about, 123
Peanut
 Sauce, Spicy, 52
Peanut Butter
 Chocolate, Roll, 277
 Fudge, 259
 homemade, 51
 Pudding, 273
Pears
 about, 199
 Poached, 199
Peas
 about, 86
 and Carrots, 89
 and Lettuce I, 88
 and Lettuce II, 88
 Creamed, 87
 Creamed, slow cooker, 350
 in Cream, 87
Peel
 fruits and vegetables, 30
Peppers
 about, 124
 Pickled, 168
 Rings, Stuffed, 126
 Roasted, 30
 Stuffed, I, 124
 Stuffed, II, 125
Pesto, 8
Pheasant
 about, 330
 Braised, 330
Pickles
 Bread and Butter, 171
 Dill, 165
 Dill, Sweet, 168
 Dilly Green Beans, 165
 Sweet, 166
 Sweet, Modern, 167

Watermelon Rind, 145
Pickling Spice, 169
Pies
  About, 299
  baked, preserving, 21
  Banana Cream, *305*
  Blueberry Tart, 104
  Butterscotch Pecan, *305*
  Chiffon, 301
  Chocolate Cream, *305*
  Coconut Cream, *305*
  Cranberry-Raisin (Mock Cherry), 304
  Cream, 305
  Crema Fruit, 305
  Crumb, 304
  Crust, 299
  Fresh Strawberry, 96
  Fruit, 303
  Fruit Crisps, 302
  Green Tomato, 142
  Lemon Filling, 273
  Lemon Meringue, 303
  Lemon-Blueberry Tart, 104
  Nopales (cactus), 85
  Onion, 85
  Peanut Butter, 305
  Pecan, 300
  Potato, 85
  Pumpkin, 188
  Spaghetti, *62*
  Sweet Potato, 188
  Tamale, 335
  unbaked, preserving, 21
  Watermelon Chiffon, 144
Pigeon
  about, 331
Pistachio
  Dessert, 271
  Pudding, 273
Pizza
  Crust, 214
  Roll, 215
  Stuffed, 215
Plan Overs
  about, 59
Pork
  about, 321

Loin with Fruit, 321
Pot Pie, 59
Potatoes
  about, 126
  Baked. Everyday, 41
  Casserole, 61, 347
  Casserole II, 61
  Fried, 128
  Mashed, 127
  Oven French Fries, 129
  Pancakes, 128
  Patties, 61
  Pie, 85
  Plan Overs, 60
  Rolls, Refrigerator, 79
  Salad I, 60
  Salad II, 61
  Sausage, Casserole, 75
  Scalloped, 129
  Scalloped, Easy, 130
  Scalloped, Loaded, 130
  Scalloped, Quick, 130
  Scalloped, with Cream and Wine, 130
Poultry
  about, 325
Pozole, 338
Preserves
  Strawberry, 95
Puddings
  Butterscotch, 273
  Chocolate, 272
  Coffee, 272
  Corn Bread, 110
  Lemon, 273
  Master Recipe, 272
  Peanut Butter, 273
  Pistachio, 273
Pumpkins
  about, 200
  Bars, 201
  Chocolate Chip Cookies, 255
  Muffins, 236
  Nut Bread, 200
Punch
  Sherbet, 56
Puree
  Raspberry, 32

Strawberry, 32
Purslane
  about, 89
  Salad I, 89
  Salad II, 90
Quail
  about, 330
Quiche
  Cranberry Dessert, 190
  Everyday, 42
Rabbit
  about, 323
  Slow Cooker, 324
  Smothered, 323
Radishes
  about, 90
  cooked, 90
Raspberries
  Puree, 32
Recipe
  Action Verbs, 15
Relishes
  Cucumber, 170
  Sweet Meat, 170
  Zucchini, 169
Rhubarb
  about, 90
  Bars, 92
  Jam, gingered, 92
  Muffins, nutty, 91
  Sauce, 92
  Upside-Down Cake, 93
Ribs, 347
Rice
  Black Beans and, 337
  Braised, 309
  Casserole, 64
  Casserole, Broccoli and, 80
  Croustades, 63
  Master Recipe, 35
  Pilaf, 309
  Plan Overs, 63
  Wild, salad, 64
Rolls
  Cream Cheese Fruit, 216
  Everyday, Almond-Poppy Seed, 39
  Everyday, Cinnamon, 39

Everyday, Pecan, 39
Everyday, White Chocolate
    Cinnamon, 39
Long Johns, 215
Pan Dulce (Sweet Rolls), 343
Potato Refrigerator, 79
Salad Dressings
  Basic, I, 47
  Basic, II, 48
  Creamy Oriental, 48
  Everyday, 41
  French, 48
  Green Goddess, 155
  Ranch, 49
  Thousand Island, 52
Salads
  Apricot, 152
  Bacon and Egg, 154
  Basic Gelatin for Fruit, 150
  Cabbage, 149
  Cabbage, Molded, 150
  Carrot, I, 148
  Carrot, II, 149
  Cherry Pineapple, 152
  Cherry, Frozen, 148
  Chicken Pecan, 155
  Coconut, 152
  Coconut Cherry, 153
  Crab, 154
  Cranberry, 191
  Fiesta, 310
  Lemon Walnut, 153
  Meat, Everyday, 43
  Nopales (cactus), 84
  Orange, 151
  Orange-Pineapple, 151
  Pasta, *63*
  Pistachio, 151
  Potato, 1, 60
  Potato, II, 61
  Purslane, I, 89
  Purslane, II, 90
  Shrimp, 154
  Spinach, Chicken and Orange, 149
  Three-Bean, 147
  Three-Bean, Hot, 148
  Tomato and Onion, 147

Waldorf, 191
Wild Rice, 64
Salisbury Steak, 318
Salmon
  Bake, 68
  Loaf I, 69
  Loaf II, 69
  Noodle Casserole, 69
  Patties, 67
Salsas
  about, 161
  Arbol, 162
  Tomatillo, 140
  Tomato, 161
Sandwiches
  Bacon and Egg, Filling, 154
  Crab, Filling, 154
  Fillings, Everyday, 43
  Shrimp, Filling, 154
Sardines, 70
Sauces
  Apple, 193
  Barbeque, I, 46
  Barbeque, II, 46
  Barbeque, III, 47
  Cocktail, 54
  Cranberry, 192
  Everyday All-purpose, 41
  Horseradish, 164
  Mole, 52
  Red Chili, 336
  Rhubarb, 92
  Spaghetti, 160
  Spicy Peanut, 52
  Taco, Larry's, 163
  Tartar, 53
Sauerkraut
  homemade, 163
  Onions Stuffed with, 123
Sausage
  Blood, 265
  Chorizo, 339
  Potato Casserole, 75
  Summer, 263
Scrapple, 262
Sherbet
  Fruit, 177

  Lemon, 177
  Punch, 56
Shortcake, 95
  Chocolate, 294
Shrimp
  Melon with, 117
Soups
  Cream, 28
  preserving, 19
  Tomato, 158
Sour Cream
  homemade, 24
Sources, 13
Spaghetti
  Pie, *62*
Spinach
  about, 94
  Creamed, about, 94
  Creamed, I, 94
  Creamed, II, 94
  Creamed, slow cooker, 350
Squab
  about, 331
Squash
  and Zucchini, about, 130
  Casserole I, 134
  Casserole II, 135
  Stuffed Acorn, 139
Steak
  Oven Swiss, 317
  Salisbury, 318
Stock
  Meat and Poultry, 316
Strawberries
  about, 94
  Pie, fresh, 96
  Preserves, 95
  Puree, 32
Streusel, 189
Substitutions, 16
Summer Sausage, 263
Sweet Potatoes
  about, 201
  Casserole I, 202
  Casserole II, 203
  Casserole III, 203
  Mashed, 202

Muffins, 236
Pie, 188
Spicy, Casserole, 308
Swiss Chard
  about, 140
Tamale
  Pie, 335
Tamales
  homemade, 342
Thanksgiving Dinner, 187
Tomatillos
  about, 140
  Salsa, 140
Tomatoes
  about, 141
  Baked, I, 143
  Baked, II, 144
  Canned, about, 160
  Crushed, canned, 161
  Diced, canned, 161
  Dill, 165
  Fried Green, 143
  Green, Pie, 142
  Juice, canned, 162
  Ketchup, homemade, 159
  Paste, homemade, 158
  Soup, homemade, 158
  Spaghetti Sauce, homemade, 160
  Stewed, canned, 161
  Whole, canned, 161
Tongue, 264
Toppings
  Crumb, 188
  Streusel, 189
Tortillas
  homemade, 341
Turnips
  about, 203
  Casserole I, 204
  Casserole II, 207
Vegetables
  preserving, breaded, 19
  Scalloped, 28
Venison
  about, 324
Waffles, 76
Watermelon
  about, 144
  Chiffon PIe, 144
  Rind Pickles, 145
Whipped Cream, 32
  Chocolate, 33
  Fruit, 33
  Fruit Curd, 33
  Mocha, 33
White Sauce, 27
Wines
  Dandelion, 86
  Elderberry Blossom, 55
Zucchini
  Bread I, 132
  Bread II, 134
  Casserole I, 135
  Casserole II, 136
  Casserole III, 137
  Chocolate Cake, 138
  Cookies, 138
  Fried, 132
  Pineapple Cake, 137
  Relish, 169
  Rounds, 137
  Squash and, about, 130
  Stewed, 132
  Stuffed, 131

ABOUT THE AUTHOR

Jim Weishaar grew up on the family farm in Nortonville, KS. He earned a Bachelor's degree from Emporia State University and a Master's degree from Rockhurst University. During his career, he has lived in Kansas, Missouri, Washington, D.C. and Indianapolis, IN. He has served as a federal civil service career employee for more than 33 years in the Department of Defense and the Department of Veterans Affairs. He returned to Nortonville in 2013 and currently resides just around the corner from the family farm. He shares his current home and hobby farm with his six boys, David, Israel, Javier, Joey, Raul and Tony (all of the canine variety), and his best, platonic friend for more than 20 years, and business partner, Juan.

Made in the USA
Middletown, DE
07 December 2020